Saving Puget Sound
A Conservation Strategy for the 21st Century

Environmentalism is still widely viewed, especially in the United States, as a special-interest lobby. Its proponents, in this blinkered view, flutter their hands over pollution and threatened species, exaggerate their case, and press for industrial restraint and the protection of wild places, even at the cost of economic development and jobs.

Environmentalism is something more central and vastly more important. Its essence has been defined by science in the following way. Earth, unlike the other solar planets, is not in physical equilibrium. It depends on its living shell to create the special conditions on which life is sustainable. The soil, water, and atmosphere of its surface have evolved over hundreds of millions of years to their present condition by the activity of the biosphere, a stupendously complex layer of living creatures whose activities are locked together in precise but tenuous global cycles of energy and transformed organic matter. The biosphere creates our special world anew every day, every minute, and it holds it in a unique, shimmering physical disequilibrium. On that disequilibrium the human species is in total thrall. When we alter the biosphere in any direction, we move the environment away from the delicate dance of biology. When we destroy ecosystems and extinguish species, we degrade the greatest heritage this planet has to offer and thereby degrade our own existence.

Humanity did not descend as angelic beings into this world. Nor are we aliens who colonized Earth. We evolved here, one among many species, across millions of years, and exist as one organic material linked to others. The natural environment we treat with such unnecessary ignorance and recklessness was our cradle and nursery, our school, and remains our one and only home. To its special conditions we are intimately adapted in every one of the bodily fibers and biochemical transactions that gives us life.

That is the essence of environmentalism.

—Edward O. Wilson, *The Future of Life*, Alfred A. Knopf, New York, 2002, pages 39–40

Saving Puget Sound
A Conservation Strategy for the 21st Century

John Lombard

American Fisheries Society
Bethesda, Maryland, USA

in association with

University of Washington Press
Seattle and London

A suggested citation format follows:

Lombard, J. 2006. Saving Puget Sound: a conservation strategy for the 21st century. American Fisheries Society, Bethesda, Maryland.

Front cover photographs: spotted owl photo courtesy of Tom Kogut, U.S. Forest Service; salmon photo courtesy of Thomas Quinn, University of Washington; girls with starfish photo courtesy of Ellen Banner for The Nature Conservancy; orca photo courtesy of www.killerwhaletales.org; and snow geese photo courtesy of Terri Smith.

Printed in the United States of America on acid-free paper.

Library of Congress Control Number 2006933383

American Fisheries Society
5410 Grosvenor Lane, Suite 110
Bethesda, Maryland 20814
www.fisheries.org
ISBN 1-888569-83-2

University of Washington Press
Post Office Box 50096
Seattle, Washington 98145
www.washington.edu/uwpress
ISBN-13 978-0-295-98674-3
ISBN-10 0-295-98674-3

To Jenny, who made this book possible,
and to Forrest and Summer,
who will inherit the world this book hopes to influence

Contents

Foreword

In May 2003, a full page op-ed in *The Seattle Times* advocated a "total effort" to recover salmon in the Puget Sound region. Noting that Seattle's creeks "were once choked with salmon," the headline asked, "Do we have the courage to bring them back?" (Simmons 2003). Unfortunately, this is the wrong question—dangerously wrong if our goal is to save not only salmon but also the larger natural heritage of our region.

The danger lies in the false assumption that we can make up for all the ways a large human population alters nearby fish and wildlife habitat, if only we have the courage to take difficult but necessary actions. The op-ed was a far from isolated example of this belief. In various forms, it underlies many of our most important environmental laws. The Clean Water Act's objective is "to restore and maintain the physical, biological and chemical integrity of the Nation's waters"; the Endangered Species Act prohibits all "take" of endangered species; and Washington's Growth Management Act and Shoreline Management Act have been interpreted as requiring "no net loss" of the functions and values of fish and wildlife habitat as surrounding lands develop. Whether this belief is born out of naiveté, hubris, or simply hope overtaking realism, the myth that we can protect fish and wildlife from the impacts of hundreds, thousands, or millions of us is dangerous because it keeps us from asking the right questions. Of course, we should take care to limit our impacts, but in a rapidly growing region we must answer the following questions if we are to conserve our natural heritage:

- *Where* are we going to allow significant new harm to occur?
- *Where* are we going to do our best to avoid it?
- *Where* are we going to make up for past harm?
- *How* are we going to pay for all this?

I say this as someone who would love to see urban creeks "choked with salmon" again, if that were possible. I have devoted over a thousand hours to restoring habitat and protecting water quality in Thornton Creek, the largest stream system in Seattle. From 2003 to 2004, I was president of Thornton Creek Alliance, Washington's largest creek conservation group, and I remain an active member of its Executive Committee. My family and I live along Victory Creek, which flows into Thornton Creek less than 100 feet from our house. The year we moved in, I filled more than 50 yard waste bags with ivy and invasive blackberries that I tore by hand from our streambank, replanting the bank with native species. Professionally, from 1996 to 2000, I oversaw salmon recovery planning for local governments throughout the 700-square-mile Lake Washington watershed, which encompasses the most urbanized part of the Puget Sound region, including the Thornton Creek basin.

To use the harshest terms of some opponents, I admit that I am advocating we "write off" urban streams—for some purposes, including regional salmon recovery. There are other reasons to invest in protection and restoration of urban natural areas.

Victory Creek is at the base of a steep bank, making the stream invisible from most of our property, yet when we bought the house in early 2002, the sales flyer advertised it as "waterfront property." This was real estate hyperbole, to be sure, but it reflects an important reality in today's market: home buyers prefer, and will pay a premium for, properties that come with their own natural areas. The premium is even higher if that natural area includes running water, especially a stream that supports at least a few returning salmon each year (which Victory Creek does not, in part because of a blockage downstream). Neighbors appreciate the additional birds and wildlife attracted by the stream and riparian areas, the aesthetic value of mature trees in protected buffers, and the ecological benefits that private natural areas can provide to public open spaces nearby or downstream. Protecting and improving the habitat and water quality of urban streams, and addressing flooding and erosion problems, are therefore important to thousands of people, primarily because the improvements make their neighborhoods more enjoyable places to live. Urban natural areas offer a much-needed respite from intensely developed surroundings. They also serve educational purposes, introducing residents (most importantly children) to native ecosystems found in a much less disturbed state elsewhere in the region. Occasionally, they provide important benefits to ecologically more valuable areas to which they are connected. Otherwise, they have minimal importance for conserving salmon or the natural heritage of the Puget Sound region.

Over the next 50 to 100 years, what happens in areas that are now rural will largely settle the fate of our natural heritage. Growth management directs the majority of new development to designated urban areas, but the population in rural areas continues to increase, often at a faster rate than in urban areas, simply by starting from a lower base. We could accommodate a large population increase in the region (perhaps double or more current levels) and *improve* conditions for most of our fish and wildlife if we use our land and water with the latter goal in mind. Making that happen is the supreme practical challenge. It can't be done by regulation alone. Rural residents and their elected officials won't support that, and, after a certain point, neither will the courts. Nor will simple economics, since reducing the economic viability of forest and farm lands will increase pressures to develop them. But, consistent with the region's recent experience trying to protect "critical areas" under the Growth Management Act, conservation in rural areas does require more regulation than residents there have been used to. The ultimate answer must involve a mix of regulations, incentives for landowners, investments in habitat acquisition and restoration on a scale greater than our impacts, and a commitment to reduce those impacts by changing how we, individually and collectively, use land and water.

Any realistic solution will not be cheap. However, the total price is probably less than subsidies the region already provides for environmental degradation. All of us pay taxes that go toward roads, schools, and other infrastructure that are needed only because of new development, though growth ultimately drives the incremental loss of our natural heritage. General tax revenues supplement taxes on fuel and vehicles to cover costs of the road system, which fragments habitat and degrades water quality. We withdraw water for free (paying only for storage, treatment and conveyance to our pipes), though drawing 250 billion gallons each year from the region's streams and aquifers has profound ecological costs. Permits that allow discharge of pollutants have no fees related to the harm they cause. Correcting these and other misdirected subsidies could pay for an ambitious regional conservation program while *reducing* general taxes substantially.

However, while money is crucial to a solution, it is far from sufficient. We should take heart, though, in knowing that most of what needs to be done is within the control of the people who live in the Puget Sound region. The most important issues concern how we use land and water. These issues are largely matters of state and local law, and of individual choice. In fact, the most important role the federal government may ultimately play regarding our region's natural heritage remains obscure to most people living here. Over the next decade, federal courts will decide whether the region's Indian tribes have a treaty right to protection of the habitat needed to produce harvestable runs of salmon and, if so, how that right should be defined. These decisions could have a profound effect on the region's future, potentially more important than federal statutes, programs, or money.

Legal liability, however, is an uninspiring and, by itself, probably an ineffective means of bringing about major changes in the way we live. Congress can abrogate treaties; where habitat cannot be adequately protected or restored, liabilities can be settled with money; and, as a practical matter, an abstract legal right to habitat protection may be unable to stop ongoing losses driven by population and economic growth and how we use land and water.

If we in the region are to undertake the changes needed to conserve our natural heritage, we must therefore do so largely voluntarily, albeit with some pushes and restrictions from federal law and, potentially, tribal treaty rights. The issues involved are fundamental: population growth, land and water consumption, property rights, taxes, economic subsidies, and environmental laws. Change in any one of these issues is difficult; coordinated change across most or all of them, required for long-term success, may seem impossible. If there is any chance of success, advocates of change must have a good response to the question, "Why?"

As a matter of policy, if not the heart, it is useful to begin by noting that the economic argument for doing what we must to conserve our natural heritage is strong. Benefits include

- Maintaining and improving our ability to attract an educated labor force, which is crucial to the region's global competitiveness. Knowledge industries like software, aerospace, and biotechnology and other health sciences attract workers who can live more or less wherever they choose. This is essentially what more than 100 economists had in mind when they sent a letter to President Bush and the governors of 11 western states in December 2003. "The West's natural environment is, arguably, its greatest, long-run economic strength," they wrote. "The natural landscapes of the western states…underlie a quality of life that contributes to robust economic growth by attracting productive families, firms, and investments" (Whitelaw 2003).[1] Some of the Puget Sound region's economic advantages lie in mountain scenery that has permanent protection, but what we do with our rivers, shorelines, foothill forests and other special places can either add immeasurably to that advantage for our global competitiveness or subtract from it forever.

- Increasing property values, largely for the same reasons of quality of life and the high demand to live here.
- Increasing tourism and recreational spending, which would result if major parts of the region (e.g., the Skagit River, Hood Canal) became even more attractive places to experience nature.
- Increasing production of natural resources that depend on land and ecosystem conservation, which include salmon and other fish, shellfish, agriculture, and timber harvest.
- Improving goods and services that nature currently provides us for free, including clean water and air, trapping of greenhouse gases, flood protection, pollination, soil development, and pest and noxious weed control. The economic value of these goods and services has not been calculated, but it is undeniably large and a compelling argument for conservation on its own.

The economic argument is even stronger if we pay for conservation by addressing misplaced subsidies. Ultimately, however, I find the economic argument even less motivating than the legal one. While the region would come out ahead by comparing our collective wealth and income with and without the proposal, the economic benefit to me or any other individual who might devote years of effort to the cause would generally be slight compared to the cost in personal time and energy. Moreover, the drive to reduce public policy proposals to strictly dollars and cents is generally misguided. Just as we would be repelled by an individual who cared for nothing besides money (if psychopathology truly that extreme is even possible), so we should be repelled by a mindset that would evaluate all policies or a vision for a society that way. A proposed policy must make economic sense, but if it touches many other aspects of our lives it must be valuable in non-economic ways, too.

Personally, I am motivated to work for conservation above all by the knowledge that my children and future generations will inherit the region as we leave it for them. We don't have full control over this, of course. A terrorist attack, for example, or some other calamity could destroy much that we value in both our human and natural environments. Nevertheless, it is largely up to us to determine how good things can be. When the time comes for me to leave this world, I want my children, grandchildren, and future generations to have the opportunity to enjoy a Puget Sound region at least as wild and natural as the one I've known. In my opinion, that is far

[1] The same point was made specifically for Seattle in an Associated Press study of the percentage of citizens with a college degree in 70 of the largest cities in the country (Ohlemacher 2006). Seattle had the highest percentage, which was largely attributed to its quality of life. In turn, the highly educated population was found to be a major attraction for high technology companies to locate here.

more important for the quality of their lives than whether their inflation-adjusted incomes are greater than mine.

A friend and old colleague at the King County Department of Natural Resources has backpacked all over Washington and much of Alaska, British Columbia, and northwestern Canada. About the time I was completing the first draft of this book, he delivered a brown bag talk for the department with photographs from his trips over more than 20 years, which I was fortunate enough to attend. At one point, he commented that his hikes in the North Cascades were as beautiful as any he had ever made, but when he thought of what they lacked in comparison to the others, the answer was simple: wildlife. In the North Cascades you might see the occasional bear (the U.S. Fish and Wildlife Service estimates that there are 5 to 20 grizzly bears in the entire range), or possibly a lynx (the Washington Department of Fish and Wildlife estimates that there are fewer than 100 in the state) or, if you are very lucky, hear a wolf (the Washington Department of Fish and Wildlife believes a small population might have entered the area from Canada, after wolves were extirpated in the 1930s). On his trips farther north, my friend saw countless bears and moose, heard wolves night after night, encountered cougars from a (grateful) distance, and watched a huge variety of birds in their native habitats.

As well-protected and remote as much of the North Cascades Mountain Range is, their lack of wildlife is partly an inevitable result of their proximity to so many people, roads, and other intrusions. Some of the lack is due to historic killings, from which wildlife populations have yet to fully recover. But much is due to changes we have made outside of formally protected areas that we can at least partly reverse such as the huge reductions in runs of salmon that formerly helped feed bears and entire ecosystems with animal protein and nutrients brought back from the ocean.

Can we return to conditions before Euro-Americans arrived? No, of course not. Even today's Native Americans would not want all the changes required for that. But can we restore some salmon runs, and the river ecosystems that support them, to a far greater extent than we have ever attempted so far? Can we protect and restore Puget Sound shorelines and estuaries so that they provide better habitat for the entire web of life that depends on them? Can we protect our state and private forests, so that they support both a timber industry as well as forest ecosystems that are anchored by old growth in national forests and parks? Can we combine productive, thriving local farm economies with restoration of the ecologically vital floodplains where farms are typically located? Can we protect and restore unique, smaller-scale ecosystems, such as the prairies of south Puget Sound, which provide both ecological diversity and variety for our own enjoyment of the landscape? Yes, certainly.

The purpose of this protection and restoration goes beyond improving the experience of hikers, fishermen, hunters, birders, kayakers, and others who love the outdoors in our region, though if we add up all of those groups we might already have a solid majority of voters. The purpose also goes beyond economics or our legacy to future generations. It is more fundamental than that. The purpose explains *why* conserving and restoring native ecosystems improves our experience of the outdoors, enhances the quality of life that supports our economy, and keeps faith with our children and future generations. It relates to why my young son is fascinated by our cat and loves trips to the zoo and the aquarium, and why children's toys and clothing are dominated by animal themes. Animals help us to know ourselves, to place ourselves in the universe. They played that role for Native Americans, whose art in the Northwest celebrates that relationship as well as any in the world. And animals play that role for us today, a role needed all the more given the prominence of technology in our lives. We need relationships with things that we did not create, but which nevertheless share a common bond of life with us. Fish and wildlife native to our region teach us what it means to call this place home. If they can no longer live here, we ignore that message at our peril. The message is not just that resources we mutually depend on are being degraded or lost. Something fundamental to our humanity is being lost as well.

References

Ohlemacher, S. 2006. Grad tidings for Seattle and other big cities: We're tops for educated citizens, but homes pricey. Seattle Post-Intelligencer (April 11):A1 and A7.

Simmons, B. 2003. Seattle's creeks were once choked with salmon. Do we have the courage to bring them back? The Seattle Times (May 11):D1.

Whitelaw, E. 2003. A letter to President Bush and the governors of eleven western states regarding the economic importance of the West's natural environment. Available: http://www.salmonandeconomy.org/pdf/120303letter.pdf (October 2005).

Author's Note and Acknowledgments

The two-part structure of this book is unusual. It was not my plan until late in the process of writing, and I'd like to offer a little explanation.

I wrote Part II first, along with a more extended version of Chapter 2. With apologies to Henry Adams, I might title them together as "The Education of John Lombard." For a decade, I worked in high-level natural resource policy jobs, but my research for this book taught me crucial things about conservation biology, the Endangered Species Act, the Clean Water Act, water law, the Growth Management Act, and tribal treaty rights that my work had never exposed me to. I found this liberating. Like nearly all conservation professionals, my jobs have forced me to focus on relatively small parts of the whole, even as I've come to believe that real solutions for these parts cannot be separated from the overall challenges for conservation in our region.

I organized what I learned on different topics into separate chapters. When I finished my research, I wrote a conclusion and an introduction and considered my manuscript *done*. The core of my argument was complete and has not, in fact, changed for over two years. But when I began delivering talks to different audiences, it quickly became obvious that parts of my book (especially my recommendations) needed more detail, while other parts were background references—important to document my reasoning, but not of central interest to most readers. Reviewers of the manuscript were impressed by my research, but quickly skipped ahead to the conclusion. They did not want to be taken painstakingly through my education before hearing what I had to *say*. They also repeated advice I had heard before, albeit in a more concise, memorable phrase: "No one cares how much you know until they know how much you care."

So, I pushed the research into a new Part II and created a Part I, which could stand on its own. Part I incorporates all of my essential arguments, but in a more accessible style, related better to my personal experience, and with more detail on my recommendations. Many professionals, academics, and students may be interested in Part II, but most general readers may consider it a tough slog to read straight through. They may find the concluding chapter and the summaries at the beginning of other chapters valuable, but otherwise may refer to Part II only when they are intrigued by a certain argument or want more detail on some specific point. That is fine. My hopes to influence the debate over our region's future rest mainly on Part I.

Acknowledgments

I'd like to begin my acknowledgements by thanking University of Oregon Professor Dave Hulse, who co-led the single most valuable scientific study I used in this book (on the Willamette River basin, but with many transferable lessons for the Puget Sound region). He has always been generous with his time and advice since I first met him four years ago. I also would like to thank University of Washington Professor Dave Montgomery and his colleagues Brian Collins and Amir Sheikh for their brilliant work reconstructing the pre-Euro-American floodplains of the Puget Sound area and for their thoughts on how that knowledge should guide aspects of river restoration today. I owe an additional debt to Kurt Beardslee, Bill Blake, Ned Currence, Kathy Fletcher, John Floberg, Andy Haas, Kollin Higgins, Steve Hinton, Roger Hoesterey, Michael Purser, Charlie Raines, Pat Stevenson, and David Troutt for helping me identify many of the most important places in the Puget Sound region to protect and restore. I particularly thank Gino Lucchetti and Bob Fuerstenberg, two of my favorite former colleagues from King County government, who taught me most of what I know about salmon ecology—though any errors on that and other subjects in this book are, of course, my own.

Many lawyers helped me with my legal research, particularly University of Indiana Law Professor Rob Fischman and National Wildlife Federation (now EarthJustice) attorney Jan Hasselman, as well as Karen Allston, Bob Anderson, Nina Bell, Michael Blumm, Kaleen Cottingham, Mason Morisset, Charlie Roe, Dick Settle, Richard Smith, and Roger Wynne.

Many friends and colleagues reviewed chapters or key sections of chapters. Some of the most valuable suggestions (and support!) came from Pati An, Bruce Bennett, Bob Lackey, Gary Minton, Ed O'Brien, Derek Poon, Steve Ralph, Anne Steinemann, Joe and Patrice Tovar, and Dave White.

Others who helped me understand key issues include Hedia Adelsman, Jim Armstrong, Dave Atcheson, Susan Braley, Allison Butcher, Kelly Cassidy, Dave Catterson, Dave Clark, Geoff Clayton, Michelle Connor, Alan Copsey, Curt Crawford, Pam Davidson, James Doyle, John Ehrenreich, John Gamon, Patti Goldman, Christian Grue, Chris Hansen-Murray, David Hartley, Mark Hicks, Tom Holz, Bob Johns, Peggy Kain, Kirk Lakey, John Lehmkuhl, Deb Lester, Chris Maynard, Ron McBride, Cindy Mitchell, Jan Newton, Reed Noss, Bill Painter, Chris Parsons, Rocky Piro, Candy Pittman, Rob Plotnikoff, Richard Rice, Klaus Richter, Clare Ryan, Janet Sears, Peter Singleton, Charles Stark, Don Stuart, Don Taylor, Ted Thomas, Tim Trohimovich, Ramon Vanden Brulle, Doug Zimmer, and many others I apologize for not naming.

In my efforts to get this book published, the following offered advice and moral support when both were needed most: Mary Braun, Barbara Dean, Alice Acheson, Jonathan Kirsch, Ayesha Pande, and Kate Rogers. Michael Duckworth and Beth Fuget of the University of Washington Press have been wonderful to work with. Aaron Lerner, Director of Publications for the American Fisheries Society, not only made the key decision to publish, but also has been extraordinarily responsive and helpful from beginning to end. I could not have asked for a better editor. Leslie Wall was a great copyeditor, Debby Lehman was immensely helpful with a variety of editing and production details, and Alisa Coffin did tremendous work from a continent away with the maps.

My friend Terry Lavender has been my most faithful reader, reviewing every chapter and offering advice and encouragement throughout. I don't know that I could have completed this project without her support. I deeply admire the passion and commitment she has brought to conserving salmon in the greater Seattle area and particularly the Bear Creek basin, where she has lived for as long as I have known her. I will always be grateful for her belief in me.

Cleve Steward has offered me not only steady encouragement, but also a part-time and flexible work schedule since 2002 that has made writing this book possible. I could not have asked for a better employer and am proud and happy to consider him a close friend as well. Janne Kaje and Michael Maher, two of my colleagues at Steward and Associates, also were of great help with the book's Web site and Figure 3-2, respectively.

Last, but certainly not least, I thank my wife, Jenny Haykin, for her love and support from the time I first began considering ideas for this book through all its evolutions, the emotional ups and downs, and the extra years it actually took to turn my ideas into reality. In between, we got married, bought a house, and started a family; her faith and trust in me has never wavered. She is my best friend, now and forever. I am extraordinarily lucky to share my life with her.

Part I: A Practical Long-Term Proposal

Chapter 1. The Challenge

> Solving shared problems together on behalf of a shared place is the essence of democracy. [Kemmis 2001]

At the base of my property, next to Victory Creek, there is a hollowed-out cedar stump, which still bears the notches loggers cut about 100 years ago for their springboards, where they stood while cutting the tree down. Back then, my neighborhood in north Seattle was covered in old-growth forest. Not the massive old growth found in the rain-drenched foothills of the mountains; this cedar was 12 feet around where the loggers stood—sizable but not enormous, meaning that the tree was probably less than 200 years old at the time it was cut. The absence of much larger stumps in our neighborhood indicates that a big fire or windstorm probably swept through north Seattle before this tree was born, clearing much of the forest.

The loggers harvested all of the timber worth cutting. After World War II, the majority of the trees they spared or that grew up later in our neighborhood were cut to prepare for our subdivision. However, the builders left a good number of trees standing, especially along Victory and Thornton creeks. The presence of many large conifers was part of what attracted my wife and me to the neighborhood. We love the views to the west and south of our house, which are mostly of trees. The surrounding Douglas-firs *Pseudotsuga menziesii*, cedars, hemlocks, alders, maples, and cottonwoods are home to a wide variety of birds, including Pileated woodpeckers *Dryocopus pileatus* and Downy woodpeckers *Picoides pubescens*, Anna's hummingbirds *Calypte anna*, an occasional passing eagle or heron (once even a Peregrine falcon *Falco peregrinus*!), and the usual assortment of songbirds, sparrows, finches, and, of course, crows and starlings. I love the 30-foot-tall hemlock whose roots snake down the side of the cedar stump, the red huckleberry *Vaccinium parvifolium* growing out of the stump's side, and the Indian plum *Oemleria cerasiformis*, salmonberry *Rubus spectabilis*, Oregon grape *Mahonia aquifolium*, trailing blackberry *R. ursinus*, and other native plants that survived the onslaught of ivy and Himalayan blackberry *R. armeniacus*, before I began to restore the backyard.

I use the word "restore" in a loose sense: the native plants I have put in are suited to the site and were probably found in the general vicinity before it was first logged. I am not restoring the site to its "historic" condition. Even if I could be certain of what that condition was (and there can never be one "historic" condition—it would have been radically different before and after a big fire, for example), truly restoring the site is not possible because it does not exist in isolation. My neighborhood has undergone almost a complete transformation during the last 100 years. Roads, buildings, and landscaped yards now cover the majority of the land. Interstate 5 is half a mile away, and thousands of people live nearby, part of a metropolitan area of approximately 3 million people. Today, there are few fish in Thornton Creek, which is dominated by cutthroat trout *Oncorhynchus clarkii*, a species that was probably difficult to find here 100 years ago. The bird and animal populations of the area have changed dramatically as well, favoring species best adapted to urban environments. My "restoration" will benefit some of the native species holding on, but it will be used by these invaders as well. I hope my children will grow up exploring Victory and Thornton creeks, appreciating the birds and wildlife of our backyard (my son already is fascinated by the non-native Eastern gray squirrels *Sciurus carolinensis*). But there is almost nowhere they could go to explore what our neighborhood was like more than 100 years ago. The few patches of old-growth forest in lowland Puget Sound are just that: patches. Without strong connections to the wider ecosystems of which they were once part, these patches have been transformed, too, though from certain vantages they may not look so different from their old selves.

Everything is connected ecologically. We cannot transform part of a landscape without affecting the rest of it in some way. The natural features we value in parts of our region depend on how we use the rest of the landscape. Even the snow and ice on our highest mountains are affected by the greenhouse gases we emit (which also affect every other ecosystem on the planet). We cannot conserve an old-growth *ecosystem* without conserving much more than a few patches of old growth here and there. Similarly, we cannot conserve orcas *Orcinus orca* in Puget Sound without conserving the salmon they eat, or conserve salmon without protecting the different habitats they need across their life cycles, or conserve river and stream habitats without restoring key aspects of the surrounding landscape, and so on.

People live in the Puget Sound region, too, of course, in large numbers that are only going to increase in coming decades. If everything is connected and our growing population needs land, water, and other resources, some new damage to our environment is unavoidable. But it can be more than made up for, if that is our goal. All parts of the landscape are not of equal value, for either us or the ecosystems in which we live. Past carelessness toward the natural world does, at least, provide us an opportunity to make amends today in places that still have—or could be restored to have—high ecological value. Some of these places were exploited decades ago for their economically valuable resources; some inherently have little economic use; some would require a conscious choice between development and conservation. One of the purposes of this book is to identify these high-value places as the foundation for a regional conservation strategy.

More Population Is Inevitable; More Net Ecological Losses Are Not

The state of Washington projects that the Puget Sound region's population will increase by 1.4 million in the first quarter of this century (see Figure 1-1 [1]), a little below the 1.6 million increase of the previous 25 years. If this projection proves accurate, it would mark the first sustained period of slower absolute growth in the

[1] Clallam, Island, Jefferson, King, Kitsap, Pierce, Mason, San Juan, Skagit, Snohomish, Thurston, and Whatcom counties are included in this projection. Part of Clallam, Jefferson, and Mason counties drains directly to the Pacific Ocean and so is technically outside of the area that drains to Puget Sound or the Strait of Juan de Fuca. This other area is mostly in the Olympic National Park or the Olympic National Forest and has negligible population in comparison to the totals shown for the ecoregion.

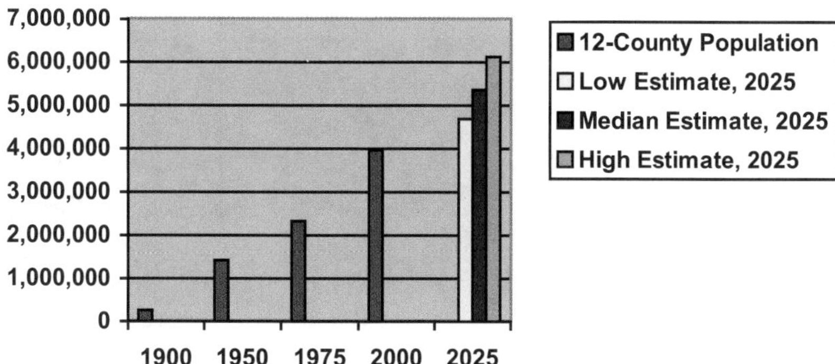

FIGURE 1-1. Puget Sound population growth, 1900–2025. Numbers include Clallam, Island, Jefferson, King, Kitsap, Pierce, Mason, San Juan, Skagit, Snohomish, Thurston, and Whatcom counties. Small parts of Jefferson and Mason counties drain directly to the Pacific Ocean and so are outside of the Puget Sound ecoregion, as I define the area in the next chapter. These parts of the two counties are mostly in Olympic National Park or Olympic National Forest and have negligible population in comparison to the total for the ecoregion. In contrast, small parts of Kittitas and Lewis counties are in the ecoregion, but are not included in these totals. These areas also have small populations. Source: Washington Office of Financial Management.

region's population since the beginning of Euro-American settlement. This is good news for the environment. But it is still enough growth to expect that someday the region's total population will at least double the 4 million here today—if not in 50 years, then probably in 100. Moreover, the rate of growth tends to be highest in the less developed areas that are most important to the region's ecosystems (see Figure 1-2). Between 2000 and 2025, just under half the increase is projected to come from natural growth of the existing population—the number of births minus the number of deaths. About 53% is projected to come from net migration—the number of people who move to the area minus the number who move away. A fundamental challenge for protecting our natural heritage is that if we succeed, we will almost certainly ensure that net migration to the region remains positive, thereby continuing the pressures that are currently driving our trend of incremental ecological decline.

The real significance of historical decline is easily lost across generations. When my children are older, they will be able to compare the restoration in our backyard to neighboring properties dominated by ivy and blackberries. But, like me, they will not know what our neighborhood looked like before development, as one remaining first-time buyer does. That elderly neighbor, however, never knew Thornton Creek when it was thick with coho salmon *O. kisutch*, before the area was logged and headwater wetlands were ditched and drained for farms and peat extraction. His parents, long dead now, might vaguely have recalled Lake Washington before it was lowered 9 feet with a new outlet through the Ship Canal, but they could not have visualized the Puget Sound shoreline before it was logged, or the floodplains and estuaries of

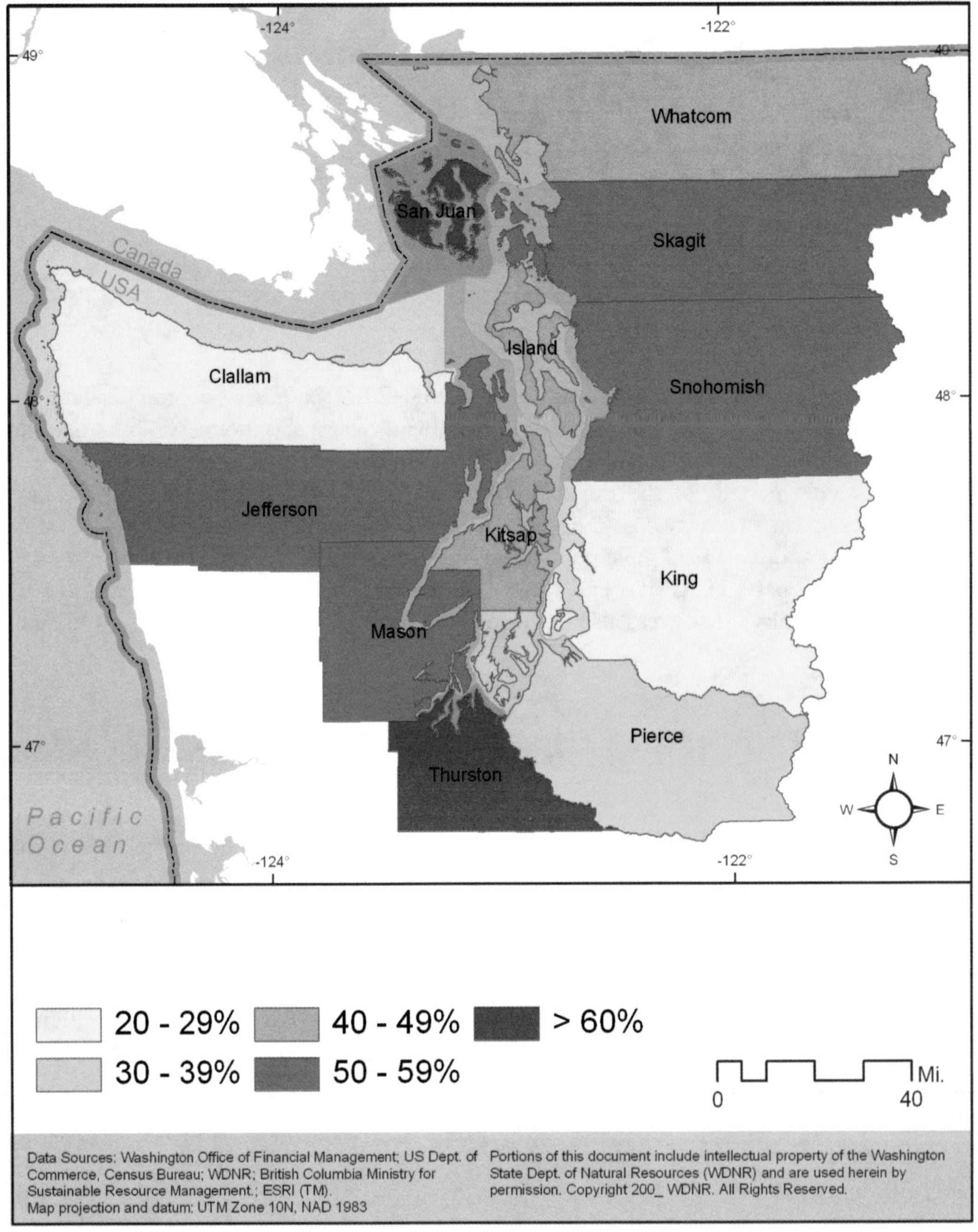

FIGURE 1-2. Projected Puget Sound population growth by county, 2000–2025. Projections reflect median estimates from Washington Office of Financial Management.

the region's major rivers before they were cleared, diked, drained, and turned into farmland in the late 19th century.

This is a common problem for judging ecological losses. Baselines shift as each generation recalls the environment of its youth. A recent study in Mexico's Gulf of California found that while older fishermen remembered better environmental conditions than younger ones recalled, few older fishermen commented on the once valuable fishery for pearl oysters *Pinctada maxima*, which collapsed just before their careers began, after centuries of legendary production (S'aenz-Arroyo et al. 2005). "Along the seacoast of the interior region, over a distance of one hundred leagues all that one sees are heaps of pearl oysters," Spanish explorers wrote. In the early 20th century, naturalists described the reef ecosystem as dominated by the Gulf grouper *Mycteroperca jordani*, a huge predator fish, "in unimaginable numbers" (Bancroft 1932, cited in S'aenz-Arroyo et al. 2005). Sport fishermen found it "virtually impossible to catch anything else." Today, most fishermen under 30 have never caught a Gulf grouper. In a survey for the study, 85% of fishermen over 55 years considered the species "depleted," while only 10% of the younger fishermen agreed. They had never known any different.

Losses like these are not inevitable. My children need not lose the opportunities I have had to see orcas on a regular basis in Haro Strait off of San Juan Island in the summer, to encounter tens of thousands of wintering snow geese in the Skagit Valley, to float past hundreds of eagles feeding on thousands of salmon farther up the Skagit River, to see a once common but now rare streaked horned lark *Eremophila alpestris strigata* in the south Puget Sound prairies, to kayak among river otters *Lutra canadensis* along the Puget Sound shoreline. With a different approach toward accommodating growth, there is reason to believe my children and future generations could enjoy a natural heritage richer than I have known in the Puget Sound region, even with a doubling of our current population. But this requires a very different approach than we have been taking. With millions more people living here, some localized impacts would be unavoidable. We would need to make up for these losses in other places, where our goal must be a net gain. Otherwise, our incremental decline will continue.

Five Fundamental Flaws in Our Current Approach

The challenge of population growth, and the increased consumption of land and water that comes with it, is very serious. Over the past few decades, as a nation and as a region we have passed myriad laws and announced myriad programs to protect and restore the environment, but they have fallen far short of meeting this challenge. They are, in fact, fundamentally flawed in the following five ways.

1. We focus too much at the wrong level of government

The primary issues for ecosystem conservation concern land and water use. Except for land owned by the federal government or under the jurisdiction of Indian tribes, land use is generally regulated by local governments within larger legal frameworks established by states, such as Washington's growth management laws. State governments also regulate water withdrawals, most of which in the Puget Sound region are made by local public utilities. States implement most aspects of the Clean Water Act, under authority delegated by the federal government. Local governments administer programs to manage stormwater (typically the largest source of water pollution) under permits issued by the state. Therefore, the state primarily determines the long-term fate of conservation, with local governments playing key roles. Yet the attention of conservationists has historically focused on the federal government. That focus was not misplaced during the initial environmental fights of the 1960s and 1970s, but today it neglects the most important opportunities for conservation wherever the federal government is not the dominant landowner or does not otherwise control the most important issues (e.g., federal dams).

Certainly, conservationists in the Puget Sound region should not ignore the federal government, which *does* have large landholdings here and which has many other important responsibilities for any regional-scale conservation strategy. But we must spread our attention around, wherever it is most needed. The defining characteristic of our federal system of government is the dispersal of power across different jurisdictions. Power sharing reduces opportunities for abuse and pushes decision making closer to the level of those citizens most affected, but it also results in the fragmentation of authority over key issues for ecosystems (encompassing land, water, and wildlife management).

One consequence of fragmented authority is that no existing governmental institution approaches ecological issues holistically. Actions by any one government agency generally address only parts of what is needed, and not necessarily the most important parts. This can seem an attractive reason to take no action at all. Watershed committees, which bring together interested stakeholders to conserve the resources of individual creeks or rivers, have become a popular means of addressing issues of fragmented authority. But focusing on watersheds ignores the needs of ecosystems at larger scales, such as the Puget Sound region as a whole, even though the most important decisions to conserve our natural heritage over the long term need to be made at the larger geographic scale. Watershed committees also pay little attention to terrestrial ecosystems. Perhaps most fundamentally, they almost always function on a strictly voluntary basis, which protects vested interests better than our natural heritage, even at the watershed level. The Shared Strategy for Puget Sound Salmon, in many ways an admirable attempt to expand the collaborative work of watershed committees to a larger geographic scale, exemplifies many of these weaknesses, as discussed in Chapter 3.

In focusing attention at the state level, we must consider basic issues of how we govern activities that affect ecosystems across multiple jurisdictions. Governance is not a sexy issue, but it is ultimately a crucial one for conservation. We do not necessarily need to create a regional level of government, smaller than the state but larger than local governments. But we must find new ways of working together, providing sufficient authority over the right issues at the right scales, as I discuss further in Chapter 4.

2. Our environmental laws are in denial

Congress passed the Endangered Species Act (ESA) almost unanimously in 1973, with only four members of the House of Representatives voting against it. Proponents at the time argued that most endangered species were at risk "for reasons that can be described most charitably as trivial" (Quote from Congresswoman Leonor Sullivan [D-MO], chair of the House committee assigned the legislation, Congressional Research Service for the Committee on Environment and Public Works, U.S. Senate 1982). The years since have proven that this view was naïve at best, but it had consequences for how the law was written. The ESA sweepingly prohibits all "take" of endangered species, including degradation of their habitat. However, Congress did not seriously consider the most important form of habitat degradation for salmon and many other listed species: the cumulative effect of many minor individual actions, including development and water withdrawals that may be many miles away from the listed species. This form of "take" is nearly impossible to enforce, as discussed in Chapter 7.

Similarly, the stated objective of the Clean Water Act is "to restore and maintain the physical, biological and chemical integrity of the Nation's waters." The act was very effective at stopping the gross abuse of our rivers, lakes, and harbors that was common when it was passed in 1972. But now that factories, sewage treatment plants, and other "point" sources of water pollution have become dramatically cleaner than they once were, we are faced with the more difficult job of reducing "non-point" pollution, which comes from multiple, small sources such as leaky cars, fertilized lawns, and developed land. The law requires that states develop clean-up plans whenever water quality standards are violated. But it provides little money for implementation and no mechanism for enforcing the plans against non-point sources. So, after an initial period of improvement, the integrity of the nation's waters is declining again.

These federal laws were passed when the environmental movement was young. Many of today's challenges were unknown or poorly understood at the time. State laws passed more recently, however, have similar failings. In 1995, the Washington legislature amended the Growth Management Act to require that local governments "protect the functions and values of critical areas" (which include streams, wetlands, shorelines, and other fish and wildlife habitat) using "best available science." State hearings boards for the act interpreted this requirement as setting a standard of "no net loss" of ecological functions, even as surrounding areas develop. In 2003, the Washington Department of Ecology took a similar approach with new guidelines for implementing the state's Shoreline Management Act, calling for "no net loss…of ecological functions" while still promoting water-dependent and water-related uses and enhancing public access to the shoreline. Yet ironically, the best available science is clear that developing areas cannot meet a no net loss standard. Some functions of critical areas depend on a larger protected landscape, including the entire area that drains into streams or wetlands. Many species require more undeveloped land than any regulatory buffer can provide. No net loss may be possible where ecological functions are already degraded, but in areas that still perform their natural functions relatively well, a no net loss standard is impossible, given continued growth as we know it.

Our environmental laws must allow for some net losses at local scales from human uses of land and water. To conserve ecosystems at the scale of Puget Sound or major river watersheds, using best available science, these impacts must be mitigated elsewhere.

3. *We provide enormous economic subsidies for environmental degradation*

According to any Economics 101 textbook, the efficiency of a free market depends on prices accounting for all relevant costs. When prices do not take important costs into account, the free market will misallocate resources, as buyers take advantage of the subsidy. Environmental costs are perhaps the most egregious example. To quote Øystein Dahle, retired Vice President of Esso for Norway and the North Sea,

> Socialism collapsed because it did not allow the market to tell the economic truth. Capitalism may collapse because it does not allow the market to tell the ecological truth. [Brown 2001:23]

I am not persuaded that this is an inherent fault of capitalism. Conceptually, it is often easy to identify a tax or fee on an economic transaction that could take these costs into account—perhaps not perfectly, but the pursuit of perfection in public policy can stand in the way of valuable and practical reform. We pay no fee to withdraw water from our streams and aquifers, for example, though clearly there are profound ecological costs when we withdraw 250 billion gallons each year from the Puget Sound region. We could easily set a per gallon fee on these withdrawals, which might be higher in summer and early fall (when ecological costs are greater) or higher for larger withdrawals (to encourage conservation). Must the fee exactly equal the ecological cost of the withdrawals? No. This would depend in any case on how much economic value we attribute to the ecological losses. Instead, the fee could depend on how much a given rate would likely reduce water consumption, how much is politically feasible, whether and how certain uses might be exempt, and so on. In addition to the fee's effect on economic choices, it would likely lead to substantial conservation simply as a powerful form of education regarding the effects of water use.

Our transportation system offers additional examples of subsidies for environmental degradation that could be corrected with taxes or fees. Roads dramatically alter the landscape, fragmenting habitat and profoundly changing the hydrology of streams and wetlands. Our vehicles are the primary source of many of the most harmful pollutants to our water and air, including the greenhouse gases causing global climate change. Yet drivers do not pay these environmental costs, nor do they even pay the full cost of constructing and maintaining our road system (especially at the local level, where general taxes pay roughly half this cost).

These and other subsidies lead to over use of resources (higher water withdrawals, more roads, more driving, less fuel-efficient cars, etc.), which causes immense damage to our natural heritage in the Puget Sound region. Chapter 4 discusses ways we could eliminate (or at least reduce) these subsidies in our region. This could not only change destructive economic behaviors, it could also easily pay for an ambitious conservation program, with enough funds to spare to allow for generous reductions in property, sales, or other taxes.

4. Our expenditures for the environment largely go for the wrong things

In addition to indirect subsidies for environmental degradation, we misdirect much of what we do spend "for the environment." Editorialists sometimes argue that we have "spent billions" on salmon conservation with little to show for it. On one level this is true, but before we resign ourselves to failure we should ask ourselves what exactly we have spent the money on, and whether it even qualifies as conservation. In the Columbia River system (where the large majority of funds and attention have gone toward salmon conservation in the Northwest, though Puget Sound has always produced more salmon than the Columbia), we have spent more than $10 billion since the 1970s on fish and wildlife programs, much of it to improve flows for salmon.[2] This accounting, however, assumes that the purpose of the river is to provide hydroelectric power; dams, reservoirs, and flows are therefore managed to maximize power revenues. Any deviation from this standard to benefit salmon is reflected as a cost. Should it be surprising that this system has not led to salmon recovery?

Most of the remaining funds spent "for salmon conservation" in the Columbia and the Northwest have gone toward operating hatcheries. Because hatcheries can provide a better chance at survival than natural conditions for salmon eggs and juveniles, advocates have argued for years that hatcheries could make up for huge losses in habitat or high harvest rates. Scientists now generally agree, however, that hatcheries have been a primary *cause* of the decline of salmon. In addition to encouraging continued habitat losses and high harvest rates, hatchery salmon degrade the genetic fitness of wild salmon through cross-breeding, compete with them for limited food and habitat, and concentrate and compound diseases found in the artificial hatchery environment, as discussed further in Chapter 8. Advocates for hatchery reforms have finally begun to have some success, but very few hatcheries today can seriously be described as operating primarily for the benefit of wild fish. The great majority are intended to produce fish for harvest. Precautions to protect wild fish—whose genetic legacy is important to ensure the continuation of harvestable runs, wild or hatchery—are only gradually being phased in, partly in response to lawsuits seeking reforms under the Endangered Species Act.

State expenditures for wildlife other than salmon are skewed toward game species, in part because a large portion of the funding for the Washington Department of Fish and Wildlife depends on hunting and fishing licenses. Only a few expenditures on the environment are allocated to actions that have a high likelihood of conserving our natural heritage if pursued on a grand enough scale, such as protecting and restoring habitat, removing dams, or purchasing water rights to restore stream flows.

---

[2] According to Northwest Power Planning Council 2002, the Bonneville Power Administration spent a total of $6.01 billion on its fish and wildlife program from 1978 to 2001, including power purchases to meet load requirements, and foregone revenues to maintain river flows for fish. This amount does not include other federal, state, local, or tribal expenditures on salmon recovery in the Columbia basin (including the extensive hatchery system) or any expenses since 2001.

5. The way we mitigate for growth is doomed to failure

Individual developments are required to mitigate for their environmental impacts project by project, as part of their permit conditions. Across the landscape, however, this can only fail, for the following reasons:

- *There will always be developments with inadequate mitigation.* Many developments are too small to trigger requirements; the drive to minimize costs will always place pressure on regulators to reduce those requirements; some developments will not comply; and some mitigation will not function as intended.
- *Project-scale mitigation ignores cumulative effects.* The most profound ecological losses do not occur from individual developments but from their accumulation, as forests are lost, habitat is fragmented, and developed land surfaces (such as roads, parking lots, and rooftops) are increased. Some regulations require individual projects to mitigate for their contributions to these cumulative effects, but under current law this is not practical to enforce widely.
- *Some impacts are best mitigated elsewhere.* Regulations typically have a strong bias toward locating mitigation as close to impacts as possible. This makes sense for site-scale effects that can, in fact, be mitigated. But for cumulative effects and for sites that would be only marginally improved even after extensive mitigation, it makes sense to target mitigation at a larger scale, where it could do the most good.

The alternative approach I advocate, in which impact fees would help pay for mitigation in the highest priority places, could simultaneously ease regulatory burdens for development and better conserve the environment.

The Good News

None of these five fundamental reasons for the continued loss of our natural heritage is beyond our ability to correct. They are all choices, which we can change.

There is more good news. Although the Growth Management Act needs amending to realize its promise for long-term ecosystem conservation, it provides arguably the best state framework for land-use laws anywhere in the country. The Northwest Forest Plan provides an outstanding foundation for conserving the most important features of our forest ecosystems. Washington has the most protective private timber regulations in the country. The Washington Department of Natural Resources is generally doing a good job managing state forest and aquatic lands. Planning processes for salmon conservation in Washington have succeeded at getting the right parties talking to one another and identifying the highest priority places to protect and restore listed salmon species. Non-profits in the region—the Cascade Land Conservancy, The Nature Conservancy, Trust for Public Land, and many others—have done outstanding work conserving our landscape and natural heritage. Experts at these non-profits, the University of Washington, state and federal agencies, Indian tribes, and other organizations have helped identify many of the crucial actions left to be taken.

In a parallel effort to the south, a 6-year, $10 million study of the Willamette

River basin (nearly the same size as the Puget Sound basin, with similar ecosystems and facing similar pressures from population growth) found that most indicators of ecological health could be improved *even after doubling the human population over the next 50 years* (Hulse et al. 2002). The formula to accomplish this, which underlies much of what I have written above, was fairly simple:

- Minimize new ecological losses by directing growth to where it will do the least harm;
- Strengthen existing protections for places with the greatest ecological importance; and
- Mitigate for the remaining losses by restoring ecologically important places degraded by past land uses, especially river floodplains and riparian areas.

Ian McHarg popularized much the same general strategy nearly 40 years ago in his classic work *Design with Nature* (McHarg 1992). The Willamette study shared McHarg's guiding principle: let natural features of the landscape determine where human land uses are concentrated and where natural processes are allowed to operate with little human intervention. Figure 1-3 is a map that applies this same principle to the Puget Sound region. If we think of the region as an ecosystem, much of what needs to be done to conserve it is relatively straightforward.

Chapter 2 discusses this map in detail, relating it to other priorities for a regional conservation strategy. Chapter 3 summarizes a comprehensive set of legal and programmatic actions to realize the vision based on this map, recommendations developed by regional experts, and an analysis of key environmental laws and institutions discussed in Part II (which serves as a reference for Part I). Chapter 4 examines how to address the biggest practical challenges for a regional conservation strategy, including funding, governance, and the urban/rural political divide. Chapter 5 concludes Part I by reviewing why we should waste no time getting started, while acknowledging that we must be patient advocating for such fundamental change.

There was no federal mandate for growth management in Washington State. Nor was there a federal mandate for the Seattle area to clean up Lake Washington 50 years ago (the first major commitment to fight pollution by any metropolitan area in the United States [Chasan 1981]). We undertook those initiatives out of concern for our own shared future. Faced with a clear understanding that our natural heritage continues to decline in the face of growth, there is reason to believe we will do so again. The threat is more subtle this time, however, because the most important losses are occurring incrementally over decades and farther away from the region's main population centers (see Figure 1-4). There are no easy ways to protect the natural heritage of a growing region with 4 million people, who mostly live in wood houses on separate lots, drive thousands of miles a year, enjoy eating salmon, and receive their water from local streams and aquifers. We can begin with our own yards and neighborhoods, as I have along Victory Creek. But if our children and grandchildren are to have a similar or better environmental baseline for appreciating the Puget Sound region as an ecosystem, we must also work collectively at larger scales.

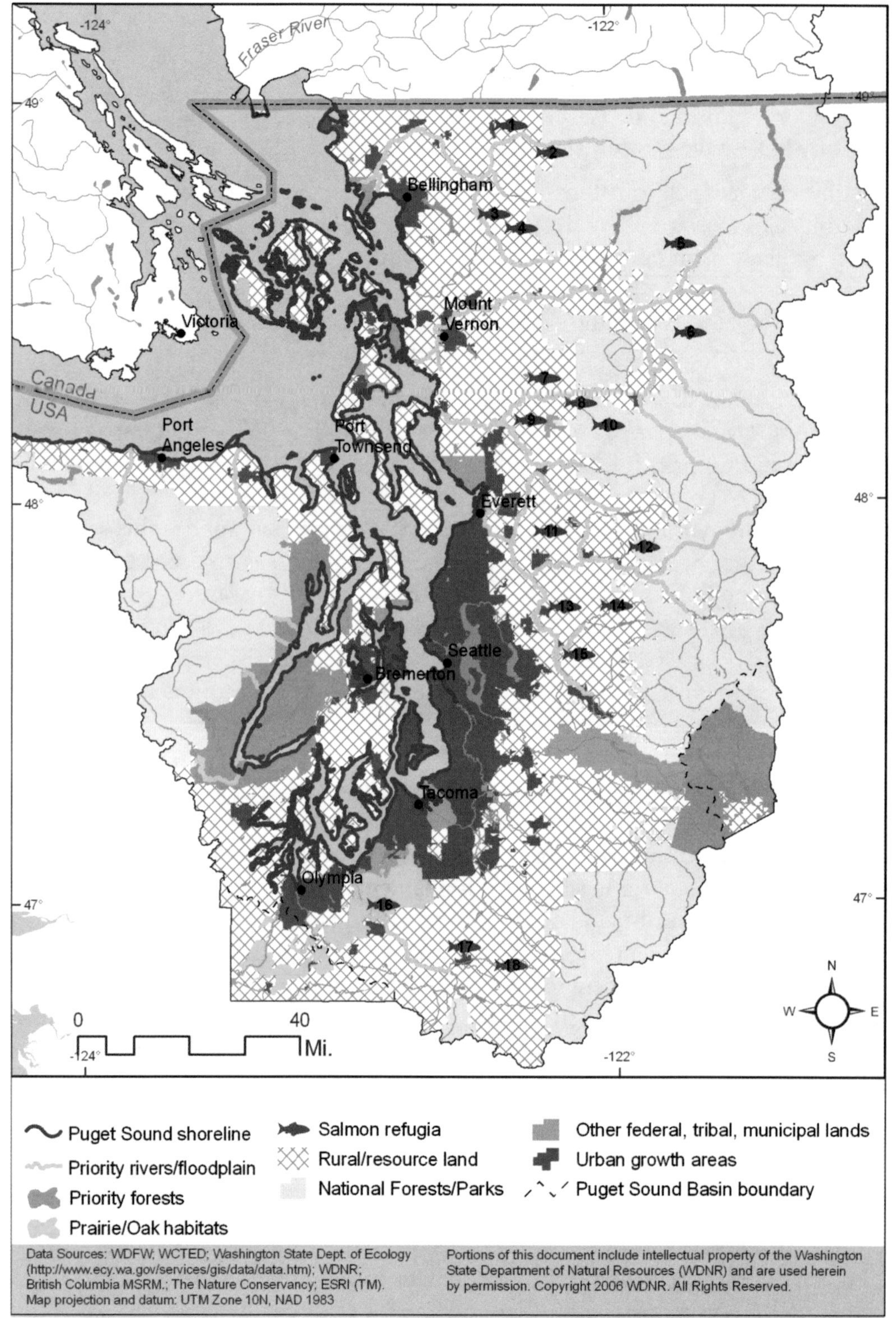

FIGURE 1-3. Habitat conservation priorities in the Puget Sound region. See notes, next page.

Notes, Figure 1-3

This map represents my synthesis of many studies, including Cassidy et al (1997), Floberg et al (2004), Frissell et al (2000), and Shared Strategy Development Committee (2005). It also reflects consultations with many local and regional experts, though responsibility for the final map is mine alone.

The map identifies general priority conservation areas. Final selection of sites for acquisition, restoration or special protections would require further scientific review and discussion with local landowners and stakeholders. Key considerations include

- *Puget Sound shoreline:* This is the most productive and sensitive part of the marine ecosystem, with the strongest ecological ties to the rest of the ecoregion. Not all of the shoreline is of equal value or would have the same conservation strategy, but all is shown here as an ecoregional priority. Further study is needed to identify and prioritize recommended actions across this area, though Floberg et al. (2004) includes an excellent initial prioritization of areas to conserve biodiversity.
- *Priority rivers/floodplains:* These are the most diverse habitats in terrestrial and freshwater areas, supporting the greatest number of species. All river floodplains should be at least local conservation priorities, but not all are shown as ecoregional priorities because some have been heavily affected by development, water withdrawals, and other alterations and are likely to be further impacted by future growth.
- *Priority forests:* All forests provide important habitat and ecological functions, but the forests around Hood Canal are particularly important for water quality and habitat for birds and amphibians, while the Snoqualmie Pass area is a crucial wildlife corridor between the North and South Cascades, threatened by historic land ownership patterns.
- *Prairie/oak habitats:* This rare habitat type supports a unique set of threatened species.
- *Salmon refugia:* Because smaller streams are very sensitive to clearing and development, salmon recovery depends on extra protections being provided to refugia streams distributed across multiple watersheds. Potential choices are identified more specifically below.
- *Rural/resource lands:* The sprawl in these areas that would be allowed under current land use laws is the most significant long-term threat to terrestrial and freshwater ecosystems in the region. Transfer of development rights and other compensation to landowners, as well as changes to the Growth Management Act, should be used to protect forest cover in these areas and to cluster new development away from sensitive areas.

See Chapter 2 for more details on these conservation strategies. Chapter 9, particularly Figure 9-1, provides more detail on the conservation status of forest lands.

Not all priority areas for protection and restoration are identified on this map. Some (such as most riparian areas) are too small to show at this scale. Others may be priorities at local levels but are not among the highest priorities at an ecoregional level. Local priorities could potentially be eligible for assistance from an ecoregional conservation plan, perhaps with larger local cost-shares and other stricter conditions than projects that are higher regional priorities.

Salmon refugia basins

1. Maple Creek	6. Illabot Creek	11. West Fork Woods Creek	16. Muck Creek
2. Thompson Creek	7. Deer Creek	12. Upper Wallace River	17. Ohop Creek
3. Hutchinson Creek	8. Lower Boulder River	13. Cherry Creek	18. Lower Mashell River
4. Skookum Creek	9. Jim Creek	14. North Fork Tolt River	
5. Bacon Creek	10. Squire Creek	15. Griffin Creek	

FIGURE 1-4. When Seattle area voters approved creating the Metro sewer system to clean up Lake Washington and parts of the Puget Sound shoreline in the 1950s, the consequences of failure were easy to see. Long-term, incremental losses in the region's ecosystems are more difficult to recognize and address. Courtesy of King County.

References

Bancroft, G. 1932. Lower California: a cruise. The flight of the least petrel. GP Putnam and Sons, New York.

Brown, L. R. 2001. Eco-economy. W.W. Norton & Company, New York.

Cassidy, K. M., M. R. Smith, C. E. Grue, K. M. Dvornich, J. E. Cassady, K. R. McAllister, and R. E. Johnson. 1997. Gap analysis of Washington State: an evaluation of the protection of biodiversity. Volume 5. Washington Cooperative Fish and Wildlife Research Unit, Seattle.

Chasan, D. J. 1981. The water link: a history of Puget Sound as a resource. University of Washington Press, Seattle.

Congressional Research Service for the Committee on Environment and Public Works, U.S. Senate. 1982. A legislative history of the Endangered Species Act of 1973 as amended in 1976, 1977, 1978, 1979 and 1980. U.S. Government Printing Office, Serial No. 97-6, Washington D.C.

Floberg, J., M. Goering, G. Wilhere, C. MacDonald, C. Chappell, C. Rumsey, Z. Ferdana, A. Holt, P. Skidmore, T. Horsman, E. Alverson, C. Tanner, M. Bryer, P. Iachetti, A. Harcombe, B.

McDonald, T. Cook, M. Summers, and D. Rolph. 2004. Willamette Valley-Puget Trough-Georgia basin ecoregional assessment, volume one: report. Prepared by The Nature Conservancy, Seattle, Washington, with support from the Nature Conservancy of Canada, Toronto, the Washington Department of Fish and Wildlife, Olympia, the Washington Department of Natural Resources (Natural Heritage and Nearshore Habitat programs), Olympia, the Oregon State Natural Heritage Information Center, Portland, and the British Columbia Conservation Data Centre, Victoria, British Columbia.

Frissell, C., P. Morrison, J. Kramer, and M. Mentor. 2000. Conservation priorities: an assessment of fresh water habitat for Puget Sound salmon. Trust for Public Land, Seattle.

Hulse, D., S. Gregory, and J. Baker. 2002. Willamette River basin planning atlas: trajectories of environmental and ecological change. Oregon State University Press, Corvallis.

Kemmis, D. 2001. This sovereign land: a new vision for governing the West. Island Press, Washington, D.C.

McHarg, I. L. 1992. Design with nature. John Wiley and Sons, Inc., New York

Northwest Power Planning Council. 2002. Second annual report to the northwest governors on expenditures of the Bonneville Power Administration to implement the Columbia River Fish and Wildlife Program of the Northwest Power Planning Council. Northwest Power Planning Council, Council Document 2002-13, issued September 12, 2002. Available: http://www.nwcouncil.org/library/2002/2002-13/Default.htm (March 2006).

S'aenz-Arroyo, A., C. M. Roberts, J. Torre, M. Carino-Olvera, and R. R. Enriquez-Andrade. 2005. Rapidly shifting environmental baselines among fishers of the Gulf of California. Proceedings of the Royal Society B 272:1957–1962 Available: http://www.cobi.org.mx/esp/publicaciones/cobi05_shifting_baseline_gulf_california.pdf (December 2005).

Shared Strategy Development Committee. 2005. Draft Puget Sound Salmon Recovery Plan. Shared Strategy for Puget Sound, Seattle.

Chapter 2. A Conservation Vision for the Region

The land speaks first. [*Bremerton v. Kitsap County* 1995]

In conservation, as in life, it is best to consider where we want to go before planning how to get there. In coming decades the Puget Sound region will have more people in its urban and rural areas, and the boundaries of our urban areas will be pushed outward. All realistic visions for the region's future should anticipate this expansion. But that does not mean all realistic futures look the same.

The science is generally clear and consistent regarding conservation priorities across the Puget Sound landscape, summarized on the map in Figure 1-3. It is impossible to predict how much of our natural heritage we *can* conserve if we follow those priorities, especially given the uncertainties of climate change. But there are reasons to be optimistic that we can achieve net gains in large parts of our region. We can be certain that if we do not follow these priorities, our losses from both climate change and future growth will be greater. The scale of the map is too coarse to show exactly where restoration projects should take place. The map also does not identify projects outside of priority areas that, cumulatively, would still be important across the region. But the map does show, broadly, where we should seek to improve conditions if we are to conserve as much of our natural heritage as possible over the next century. Although future studies will correct details, the map is supported by overlapping recommendations from over a decade of regional research, not to mention basic principles of ecology and conservation biology.

In one possible future for our region, the ecosystems of our major rivers will grow substantially healthier over time, as a consequence of protection and restoration in the map's priority areas. With this improvement, more salmon will support targeted harvests, as well as a stable or increasing population of orcas *Orcinus orca* in Puget Sound. The carcasses of spawning salmon will also bring more nutrients from the ocean to sustain local watersheds, in one of the most fundamental natural cycles of our region. Some marginal farmland in floodplains will be restored for its natural values, but despite a substantial rise in the total amount of developed land across the region, the amount of active farmland will remain stable, as farmers take advantage of strengthened ties to local markets and compensation for ecological services. Maturing forests best suited to complement old-growth reserves will be conserved for their ecological value, while timber harvest elsewhere will become a global model, again supported by compensation for ecological services. The small population growth in rural areas will be clustered away from the most sensitive habitats, while the total amount of native vegetation in rural areas will rise, also supported by compensation to property owners. The length of shoreline along Puget Sound with native vegetation and without bulkheads will increase. Water quality will improve across the Sound, including in Hood Canal. The number and diversity of birds, mammals, fish, and amphibians in priority conservation areas will expand, as will opportunities for people to enjoy them. All this will occur even as the region's population doubles.

In a different possible future, a similar population expansion will spread into our most ecologically valuable areas, displacing farmland in the floodplains, fragmenting rural and forested habitats, and degrading salmon streams across the landscape, even after the region spends hundreds of millions of dollars on restoration projects. Agricultural communities will decline below the minimum size necessary to sustain them, encouraging further encroachment from suburban development and the conversion of farmland to rural estates. Similar conversions of forest land will isolate old-growth reserves and will decrease timber production. The resident orca population will slide inexorably toward extinction, in part because of further decline in their salmon food supply. The entire marine ecosystem will undergo radical change as more of the Puget Sound shoreline is developed, compounding stresses on salmon from loss of freshwater habitat and climate change. Across the landscape, indicator species for all major ecosystems will decline; only those species best adapted to human environments, such as crows and raccoons, will thrive.

Which future do we want? This chapter focuses on what is needed to bring about the first future. The next two chapters provide more details regarding the laws, programs, and funding necessary to make that happen.

Defining the Puget Sound Ecoregion

In developing a regional conservation strategy, the first step is to decide what the "region" is. This is more difficult than some people might expect, because ecosystems rarely have precise boundaries. Where a conservation strategy defines the borders depends in part on which species it focuses on, as well as more practical considerations, such as who will carry it out.

The Nature Conservancy, the World Wildlife Fund, the U.S. Environmental Protection Agency, and others divide the terrestrial portions of the Puget Sound area into at least three separate "ecoregions": the Puget Sound lowlands (often extended from the Georgia Basin to the Willamette Valley), the Cascade Mountains (frequently separated into north and south ecoregions at Snoqualmie Pass), and the Olympic Mountains (sometimes grouped with other coastal areas). By definition, an ecoregion shares a common climate, vegetation, geology, and general physical form, but the interpretation of these characteristics depends on the intended scale. In a different study, for example, the World Wildlife Fund includes the entire Puget Sound area in a larger "Northeast Pacific Coast" ecoregion, extending from the mouth of the Columbia River to south-central Alaska.

Fishery managers tend to group salmon from Puget Sound and the Strait of Juan de Fuca as a management unit distinct from salmon from coastal streams or the Columbia River system. This is because, while most salmon faithfully return to the river systems where they were born, some stray into other areas, over time establishing genetic relationships with salmon from nearby watersheds. Salmon from adjacent watersheds also often mingle in the marine nearshore and open ocean as rearing juveniles and maturing adults, further linking them through adaptations to common environments.

Puget Sound mixes with the Strait of Juan de Fuca and the Strait of Georgia, making any exact designation of where one begins and the others end arbitrary. They are all part of one system, but they have important ecological and practical management differences—not least that two countries are responsible for different parts of the whole.

Taking into account ecosystem types, priority species, and practical considerations, the best ecoregional approach includes the entire Puget Sound drainage basin through the Strait of Juan de Fuca, the central Cascades immediately east of Snoqualmie Pass, and the remainder of Thurston County. The last two additions include, respectively, the narrowest part of the wildlife corridor between the north and south Cascades and most of the south Sound's distinctive woodland/prairie habitats. This 16,000 square mile area, which I call the "Puget Sound Ecoregion," excludes wetter coastal areas and most of the drier eastern Cascades, where vegetation cover is different and rivers do not flow into Puget Sound. This region also excludes most of the southern Cascades and southern portions of the "Puget Trough" or the "Puget Lowlands," which extends under some definitions into Oregon's Willamette Valley. The northern boundary, the U.S.–Canada border, while ecologically arbitrary, at least has an obvious practical rationale. The rationale for the southern boundary is also partly practical: most people in Thurston County think of themselves as living in the Puget Sound area, while the majority in Lewis County (let alone points further south) do not.

Putting the Puget Sound Ecoregion in Global Context

At a global level, the World Wildlife Fund includes the whole Northeast Pacific Coast as one of its 200 priority ecoregions for protecting biodiversity worldwide (Ricketts et al. 1999). The region makes the list not because it supports a particularly high number of native species but because it supports two "globally outstanding" ecological phenomena—the world's largest remaining temperate rain forest and some of the world's largest runs of anadromous fish (which spawn in freshwater but spend part of their lives in marine waters, in this case salmon). In this vast ecoregion, the Puget Sound area is distinctive for three reasons. First, its low- to mid-elevation forests are among the most productive on the coast. Second, it is at the southern end of the zone that supports the greatest diversity of salmon species. Third, the marine life of Puget Sound, the nation's second largest estuary (behind Chesapeake Bay), is distinctly different from that of the ocean.

In their classic study, *Natural Vegetation of Oregon and Washington*, Jerry Franklin and Ted Dyrness pile on superlatives when discussing the forests of western Washington and northwestern Oregon:

> These forests represent the maximal development of temperate coniferous forests in the world in terms of extent and size....Every single coniferous genus represented finds its largest (and often longest lived) [species] here—and sometimes its second and third largest as well....[T]he coniferous forests in this region continue to grow substantially in height and accumulated biomass for decades or even cen-

turies after others have essentially reached a state of equilibrium. [Franklin and Dyrness 1988:53–54; J. Franklin, University of Washington, personal communication].

Historically, these forests were particularly impressive in lowland Puget Sound. Douglas-fir *Pseudotsuga menziesii*, the largest and longest-lived of the trees, was more common in the Puget lowlands than elsewhere, because it is more tolerant of the area's glacial soils and the rain shadow from the Olympic Mountains (Franklin and Dyrness 1988). The milder climate and rainfall of the lowlands also historically made for a more productive growing environment than mountainous areas.

The Puget Sound area is also notable with respect to the other globally outstanding phenomenon of the northeast Pacific: salmon. As shown in Table 2-1, Puget Sound currently produces an estimated 5 to 10 times as many wild salmon as the entire Columbia River basin. Given the legendary status of Columbia salmon runs, it is even more impressive that Puget Sound outproduced the Columbia historically as well, at least in numbers (the tonnage of salmon returning to the Columbia was greater than in Puget Sound because Chinook salmon *Oncorhynchus tshawytscha*, the largest salmon species, were more common in the Columbia). In the table, Puget Sound's production may appear dwarfed by Alaska and British Columbia, but the latter areas are approximately 45 and 28 times the size of the Puget Sound basin, respectively. When adjusted for this size difference, Puget Sound historically out-produced Alaska and British Columbia and to a certain degree can still compete with them today.

Puget Sound lies within the zone on the Pacific Coast that supports the most diverse collection of salmon species (Nehlson 1996). North of this zone, extreme variations in temperature and less stable river channels favor species that spend less time in freshwater, such as pink salmon *O. gorbuscha* and chum salmon *O. keta*. (Sockeye salmon *O. nerka* also do well in northern latitudes because they rear in lakes and are therefore less vulnerable to temperature extremes and unstable channels.) South of Washington, higher stream productivity favors species that spend longer periods in freshwater, such

TABLE 2-1. Estimated historical (late 1800s) and current (late 1900s) run sizes of wild salmon in western North America. (All numbers are in millions of wild salmon and are rounded.)

Area size	Historical run size	Current run size	Percent of historical run
Alaska	150–200	115–259	106.7
British Columbia (non Columbia River)	44–93	24.8	36.2
Puget Sound	13–27	1.6	8.0
Washington coast	2–6	0.07	1.8
Columbia basin	11–15	0.11–0.33	1.7
Oregon Coast	2–4	0.10–0.032	7.0
California	5–6	0.28	5.1
California, Oregon, Washington, Idaho	33–58	2.16–2.60	5.2

Source: Gresh et al. (2000)

as Chinook salmon and coho salmon *O. kisutch*. In the intermediate zone, all five Pacific salmon species thrive, along with steelhead *O. mykiss* and a variety of sea-run and resident trout and char (which are also salmonids).

There has never been a systematic survey of the animal and plant life of Puget Sound, but temperate estuaries are generally among the biologically richest marine areas in the world (Kruckeberg 1991). The complex geography of Puget Sound makes it particularly so. The 2,469-mile long shoreline creates an abundance of nearshore habitat, where different biological communities live above, below and within the zone washed by the tides (PSWQAT 2002). Puget Sound's long pathway from the ocean causes its tidal zone to be unusually large for its latitude, resulting in world-class conditions for shellfish. (The difference between high and low tide averages 8 feet at Port Townsend, 11 feet near Seattle, and 15 feet near Olympia [Kruckeberg 1991]). Underwater, the geography of Puget Sound is also complex. Shallow "sills" at Admiralty Inlet, the Tacoma Narrows, the entrance to Hood Canal, and other locations inhibit the flushing of water to the ocean, providing a relatively stable environment for freshwater to mix with nutrient-rich ocean water. This creates excellent conditions for the growth of phytoplankton, the base of the marine food chain, particularly in the Main basin of Puget Sound, between Admiralty Inlet (to the west of Whidbey Island) and the Tacoma Narrows (Strickland 1983). Eelgrass, which forms critical underwater habitat for salmon and marine organisms along sandy shorelines, is also unusually productive and diverse in Puget Sound.

The Center for Biological Diversity recently identified 7,013 species across the 16,000 square mile Puget Sound basin, including 1,318 animals, 1,501 plants, 851 fungi, and 392 algae (Center for Biological Diversity 2005). There are almost certainly additional species that have not yet been identified, but the total from the center's search is already greater than the total species of flora and fauna found in 31 individual states. This richness is due to the unusual diversity of habitats, including the marine and nearshore habitats just discussed, the wide range of land elevations (from sea level to 14,411 feet at Mt. Rainier), the large number of separate river systems, and distinct, smaller-scale habitats such as the prairies found in south Puget Sound and in the rainshadow of the Olympic Mountains. The center calls the Puget Sound region "a significant hotspot for biological diversity" nationwide.

The center identified 957 species as imperiled in the region (14% of the total), using lists from federal and state agencies, scientific organizations, and the Audubon Society. This may overstate the problem, because even one listing as a "species of concern" or a "vulnerable" species placed it on the "imperiled" list. There were, however, 285 species on the center's "critically imperiled" list, which has stricter criteria. And, of course, even species that are not "imperiled" can be losing population.

Lessons from the Willamette River Basin

There is no one comprehensive, in-depth conservation study that covers the entire Puget Sound Ecoregion, but multiple studies together cover the most important issues:

- The Nature Conservancy and the Washington Department of Fish and Wildlife have developed biodiversity strategies for the Puget Sound lowlands, the Cascades, and Olympics (Floberg et al. 2004).
- Watershed groups have developed detailed plans to protect and restore salmon habitat across the entire Puget Sound basin (Shared Strategy Development Committee 2005).
- In the mid- to late-1990s, a University of Washington research team identified the most important habitats across the state for birds, mammals, amphibians, and reptiles (and also compared their biological importance to their level of protection under current ownership and management; Cassidy et al. 1997).
- Every 2 years, the Washington Department of Natural Resources updates its Natural Heritage Plan, which evaluates habitats and species across the state for their rarity and risk of loss.
- Every 2 years, the Puget Sound Action Team (in the Governor's Office) updates its management plan for the marine waters and nearshore habitats of the Sound.

Where these studies overlap, they tend to agree concerning the places that are most important to conserve. They also tend to agree with the Willamette River basin study mentioned in Chapter 1 (Hulse et al. 2002), with respect to an overall strategy for the landscape. Because the Willamette study is both comprehensive and in-depth, I will start with it before coming back to results from the Puget Sound studies. There is much we can learn from the Willamette "Alternative Futures Project."

Funded by the Environmental Protection Agency and led by two professors from the University of Oregon and Oregon State University, the Alternative Futures Project worked with a diverse group of stakeholders from throughout the basin as well as a team of technical experts. The Willamette River basin is about 11,500 square miles, slightly smaller than the 13,100 square miles of land in the Puget Sound basin (the 16,000-square-mile figure for the ecoregion includes about 3,000 square miles of marine waters). The Willamette basin is experiencing similar population growth, with current trends indicating a possible doubling of its population from 2 million to 4 million in the next 50 years. The two areas also share many common ecological characteristics, as demonstrated by the common grouping of the Willamette Valley with the Puget Sound lowlands as one ecoregion. The Olympic Mountains are similarly often grouped with the Oregon Coast range, as are the Cascade Mountains in both states.

The Willamette stakeholders developed three alternative futures for comparison. As a matter of fairness and to recognize that many of the forces influencing the region's growth are outside of the region's control, each alternative future had to accommodate the same number of people, doubling the current population. Plan Trend 2050 did not change existing laws, policies, and practices; Development 2050 relaxed restrictions on many land and water uses, projecting the results of decisions based more on market forces; and Conservation 2050 followed the prescription discussed in Chapter 1: let the natural features of the landscape be the primary determinant of where growth and conservation efforts are targeted.

Some of the key findings are listed below.

- In general, habitat conditions in the Willamette basin have changed so profoundly since 1850 that no plausible future for 2050 could equal the change that has already occurred.
- Conservation 2050 could improve nearly all indicators for natural resources (such as the abundance of habitat for native terrestrial wildlife, or an index for the biological integrity of lowland streams), in some cases by more than half the estimated decline from 1850 to 1990, even with a doubling of the human population of the basin (see chart, Figure 2-1).
- In contrast, despite Oregon's having some of the strongest growth management laws in the country, all natural resource indicators were projected to decline under Plan Trend 2050, because of cumulative losses like those discussed in Chapter 1.

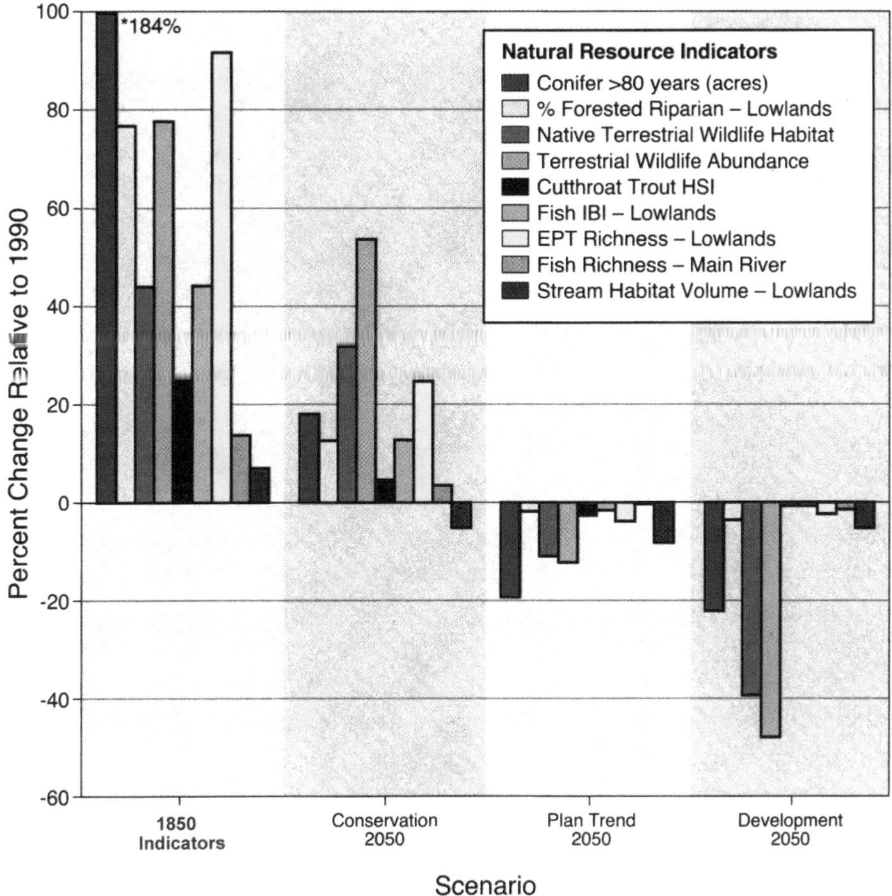

FIGURE 2-1. Natural resource indicators for 1850 and the Willamette basin's alternative futures, compared to 1990. Notice decreases in natural resource indicators under the Plan Trend and Development scenarios. For detail on indicators identified in the legend, see Hulse et al. (2002). Courtesy of Oregon State University Press.

- Not surprisingly, the projected decline was even greater under Development 2050, though some species that are better adapted to human environments and disturbed habitats might thrive.
- While urban growth areas provide the worst overall habitat for most native fish and wildlife, they make up a relatively small portion of the Willamette basin's land area—6% in 1990, growing to 7.8% by 2050 under the Development 2050 scenario.
- At the scale of the entire basin, the most important land-use issues that distinguish Conservation 2050 are
  - ⇒ *Rural sprawl.* Conservation 2050 would minimize loss of native vegetation in rural areas and cluster impacts away from high-quality habitats.
  - ⇒ *River floodplains.* Where feasible, Conservation 2050 would return rivers to more natural flow patterns (through changes in dam operations and water withdrawals), remove levees and other hardened banks (to allow natural interactions between rivers and their floodplains), and purchase flood-prone properties—particularly farmlands—for restoration of floodplain vegetation and complex channel features.
  - ⇒ *Riparian vegetation.* Conservation 2050 would restore gaps in the first 100 feet of stream riparian areas, using native vegetation.
  - ⇒ *Mature, coniferous forests.* In areas that could complement old-growth reserves, Conservation 2050 would allow 40- to 80-year-old forests to mature with at most selective harvest (Summary of conclusions drawn from Hulse et al. 2002 and D. Hulse, University of Oregon, personal communication).

The Willamette study made three important simplifying assumptions: it did not attempt to account for climate change; it ignored possible worsening threats from non-native species; and it assumed that native fish and wildlife would recover proportionate to the recovery of their habitats, which is unlikely. Correcting each of these assumptions makes it less certain that net gains across the region are possible even under Conservation 2050. But correcting these assumptions would reduce the predicted natural resource indicators more—potentially much more—under the Plan Trend or Development scenarios than under Conservation 2050. As will be discussed later in this chapter, experts on climate change believe that conserving and restoring ecosystems are the best ways to enhance the resilience of native species to the most likely climate changes in the Northwest (and the world) over the next century. Non-native, invasive species tend to do best in disturbed habitats, so conserving natural ecosystems is also crucial to protecting native species from this threat. Lastly, because plants and animals are generally distributed in "subpopulations" (which boosts genetic diversity and helps maximize use of available habitats), the best way to ensure that they can take advantage of conserved habitats is to maintain as many subpopulations as possible and protect their connections to one another. The Plan Trend and Development scenarios would conserve fewer subpopulations and would disconnect these populations from each other.

The Willamette results are not completely transferable to the Puget Sound

Ecoregion. Most obviously, the Willamette has no marine waters, which are at the heart of our region. We also have a much larger human population—about twice that of the Willamette basin, though growth rates in the two areas are comparable. However, in considering the ecological sensitivity of each region to its population level, Puget Sound's marine waters may actually be an equalizer, since they separate individual river basins and thus limit the environmental impacts of highly urbanized areas on other parts of the region. Our marine waters also flush some regional wastes to the ocean. Studies from the Puget Sound Ecoregion tend to highlight the same issues and recommendations as the Willamette basin. Where our region differs, this generally adds recommendations to those from the Willamette, but does not change them. The Willamette study's technical breadth and depth give us reason to be optimistic that an alternative future for the Puget Sound Ecoregion could conserve much of our natural heritage even with population growth, climate change, and other threats.

Conservation Priorities for Our Ecoregion

Drawing from all of the Puget Sound studies identified above together with the Willamette study, the most important issues for a conservation strategy in the Puget Sound ecoregion are the following:

- *Minimize rural sprawl, conserve riparian vegetation, and restore mature forests*, as in the Willamette's Conservation 2050 scenario. I will discuss rural sprawl in more detail below. In general, the value of mature forests is widely recognized, but I discuss it in some detail in Chapter 9. Riparian corridors are generally "the most diverse, dynamic and complex biophysical habitats on the terrestrial portion of the Earth" (Pollock 1998). The Washington Department of Fish and Wildlife estimates that 85% of the state's terrestrial vertebrate species use riparian habitat "for essential life activities" (Knutson and Naef 1997).
- *Protect and restore the floodplains and estuaries of the Skagit, Nooksack, Stillaguamish, Snohomish, Nisqually, Dungeness, and Elwha river systems*, again following the Willamette's Conservation 2050 recommendations (increase natural interactions between the rivers and their floodplains and return flow patterns closer to their natural variability). Unconstrained, low-gradient floodplains contain the greatest diversity of riparian and instream habitats, including backwater eddies and sloughs, side channels, riparian wetlands, and other off-channel habitats (see Figure 2-2).
- *Protect and restore the Puget Sound shoreline*, the most productive and sensitive part of our marine ecosystem.
- *Provide extra protection for select stream basins*, where land clearing and development would be minimized. Land use within the entire area that drains to small and medium-sized streams has an enormous effect on their ability to support robust salmon runs and a diversity of aquatic life.
- *Conserve the forests along Hood Canal*, which are particularly important for multiple reasons: they help protect Hood Canal's water quality (which currently threatens

FIGURE 2-2. The lower dam on the Elwha River, which is scheduled for removal beginning in 2007. While removal of this and the Glines Canyon dam on the river will restore access to more than 100 miles of pristine mainstem and tributary habitat in Olympic National Park, the downstream movement of sediment behind the dams creates challenges and uncertainties for the project. Ultimately, the floodplain of the lower river should be restored to the greatest extent possible to take full advantage of the newly accessible habitat upstream. Courtesy of the National Park Service.

the future of its marine ecosystem); they support important amphibian populations on the Olympic Peninsula, especially through connections to the mature forests of the Olympic National Park; and they provide important habitat for a wide diversity of birds on the Kitsap Peninsula (see Figure 2-3).

- *Restore the wildlife corridor near Snoqualmie Pass*, which is just outside the area draining to Puget Sound, but which is the narrow "choke point" connecting the north and south Cascades. Restoration would include better wildlife crossings over and under Interstate 90 and correcting the "checkerboard" pattern of alternating square-mile sections of federal and private timber ownership (see Figure 2-4), which is the legacy of an 1864 federal land grant to the Northern Pacific Railroad, now held by the Plum Creek Timber Co. (J. Armstrong, Cascades Conservation Partnership, personal communication).
- *Restore at least part of the South Sound prairies*, which still support a unique set of

FIGURE 2-3. Shellfish gathering at the mouth of Eagle Creek, which empties into southern Hood Canal. The entire marine ecosystem of Hood Canal, including its rich shellfish beds, is at risk from poor water quality, largely due to surrounding land uses. Courtesy of Toni Weyman Droscher, Puget Sound Action Team.

threatened species, including butterflies, pocket gophers, birds, and flowers (see Figure 2-5). Outside of a large remaining patch at Fort Lewis, most of the prairies have been lost to development or encroaching forest.

- *Conserve other, smaller-scale habitats*, such as important wetlands and Garry oak *Quercus garryana* stands, which are too small to appear on a map of the entire ecoregion but which provide valuable habitat even when not directly connected to larger conservation areas.

Of all these issues, rural sprawl is the widest-ranging and perhaps the most poorly understood. Growth management in Washington has focused on the ills of urban sprawl—deservedly so for many issues, including some aspects of environmental protection. Without question, urban areas generally provide the worst habitat for native species. Much can be done to improve urban habitats, but this will mostly benefit species with a relatively high tolerance for proximity to humans and habitat alterations. From an ecological perspective, establishing limits to urban growth is an excellent first step for conserving the landscape, but it is not enough. Across the ecoregion, substantially more land is rural, or used for agricultural or forest production, than is urban or suburban. With higher resource values and greater land area, what happens in

FIGURE 2-4. Part of the fragmented forest straddling the watersheds of the upper Green and White rivers, within the "checkerboard" area of ownership in the Snoqualmie Wildlife Corridor. Not all of the "checkerboard" area contrasts as dramatically as this between sections that are federally or privately owned, but wherever the ownership pattern remains, so does the long-term threat of extreme habitat fragmentation. Courtesy of The Wilderness Society.

these areas is crucial to the region's ecological future. Unfortunately, the science indicates that dividing up the rural area in 5-acre lots, as currently allowed under growth management, would drive the continued loss of our natural heritage over the next 50 years (especially if most rural landowners are allowed to permanently clear all or most of their land). The resulting fragmentation of terrestrial habitats and degradation of aquatic habitats would be devastating.

Let me be clear that the solution I advocate, discussed further in the next two chapters, is not to impose draconian regulations on rural property owners. People who live in rural areas typically do so in large part because of their appreciation for the natural features of the land. Their property values have already been cut by the introduction of five-acre zoning, which greatly decreased the number of buildable rural lots. After talking with many rural property owners, I believe a majority could support the actions I propose. We must empower rural residents to help shape the conservation actions we take in the region—not to the exclusion of urban residents, but with a genuine recognition of the crucial and unique role rural residents play on the landscape. Their role is illustrated by how scientific thinking has changed regarding reserves.

FIGURE 2-5. Part of the Mima Mounds Conservation Area, a distinctive landscape within the south Puget Sound prairies managed by the Washington Department of Natural Resources. The cause of the topographic pattern in this area is uncertain, but may be due to how water and sediment flowed out of the retreating glacier that carved Puget Sound 12,000 years ago. Courtesy of Washington Division of Geology and Earth Resources.

Isolated Reserves Will Not Work

Historically, scientists and land managers have sought to protect species through reserves, such as national parks or wildlife refuge areas, where the goal was to maintain habitat with as little human disturbance as possible. Over time, experts grew interested in corridors between reserves, to meet the needs of species that migrate over larger areas. Increasingly, however, these experts have broadened their perspective to incorporate the landscape that surrounds and includes reserves and corridors, for these five reasons:

1. *There will never be enough reserves, particularly of sufficient size and in the right locations.* Scientists widely agree that large reserves are best, because they typically include more diverse habitats (which therefore support more species), best serve the needs of wide-ranging species, are the least vulnerable to "edge effects" (such as the intrusion of non-native species from outside the reserve), and support larger

populations of individual species. But large reserves are the most difficult to create, for the obvious reason that they face greater competition from alternative uses of the same land. That competition is typically greatest for the most productive land, such as the lowlands of Puget Sound.

2. *The integrity of reserves depends on the integrity of the surrounding landscape.* Edge effects are numerous (including not only intrusion of non-native species, but also changes in the mix of native species, susceptibility to fire and disease, changes in temperature and other weather conditions, etc.). The intensity of these effects typically depends on whether the surrounding landscape is hostile or complementary to the reserve. An old-growth forest that is surrounded by mature second-growth, for example, can be much smaller and still provide historic habitat conditions in its interior than if it is surrounded by clearcuts (Franklin 1993).
3. *Landscape conditions control key processes, such as stream flows, which in turn create and sustain habitat in reserves.* The historic focus on reserves reflected a belief that ecosystems tend toward equilibrium, where they remain in a steady state if unaffected by humans. Over time, though, scientists have increasingly recognized that ecosystems are naturally dynamic; disturbances, such as floods or fires, regularly create and destroy habitats. Scientists now emphasize maintaining natural habitat-forming processes, including the frequency and severity of disturbances (Botkin 1990), rather than maintaining particular habitat features without change. These processes generally depend on the larger landscape around reserves.
4. *Many terrestrial species, probably most, do not disperse along corridors.* Other than riparian corridors along streams and rivers, linear corridors are generally not an effective means to connect different populations of species, or to connect areas with surplus population to areas of marginal but still useable habitat (Franklin 1993). The condition of the entire landscape between reserves is at least as important for connecting isolated populations as the existence of protected corridors (with the exception of stream and riparian corridors).
5. *Habitats for different species vary in scale.* As the forest ecologist Jerry Franklin has noted, "Many species do not require reserves in the traditional sense; their habitat requirements are at the scale of individual structures, such as dead trees, logs, hedgerows, gravel beds, large soil aggregates, etc." (Franklin 1993). These habitat requirements can be met on lands with sizable human populations, if the lands are managed with these requirements in mind.

Reserves are still important. Protected areas with minimal human alteration will always be crucial to sustaining native species, especially as refuges and sources for population expansion. But reserves are not enough. What happens on the surrounding landscape is also crucial.

The Challenge of Restoration

Conservation is not just protection. Because we can expect some ecological losses from additional demands on land and water due to population growth, a conservation strategy for the region must include a major component of restoration as well. Those working on conservation in the region typically describe any project designed to improve the quality or quantity of habitat as "restoration." The root meaning of the word, however, requires that habitat be returned to a pre-defined condition (commonly set just before Euro-American settlement). This can be an impossibly strict definition (not least because of the difficulty in establishing exactly what that condition was), but the casual use of the word can be given greater rigor by limiting it to cases where the past is used as a general reference, so "restoration" means moving habitat closer to what we believe was its historic condition. Fully restoring that condition may not be possible—or desirable, given today's competing needs and values. Nevertheless, the past remains a useful general reference ecologically, for two fundamental reasons. First, native species adapted to historic conditions in ways that are still reflected in their genetic makeup (and in the community of species found in an area). Second, restored conditions should require less maintenance, because the on-going ecological processes (erosion, plant succession, etc.) that established the historic conditions should sustain the restoration. In fact, restoring ecological processes (e.g., the natural interactions between rivers and their floodplains) is typically the most reliable way to restore habitat sustainably. That does not make it easy to do.

River floodplains and estuaries are probably both the biggest challenge for restoration and also the biggest potential payoff. Most of the historic habitat of lowland rivers in Puget Sound has been lost, as river channels were cleaned of downed trees and locked in place by levees, riparian forests were harvested, and floodplains were drained, diked, and developed. Nevertheless, using archival materials, including 19th century maps and field notes from the General Land Office, the U.S. Coast and Geodetic Survey, and the Corps of Engineers, University of Washington researchers have determined in detail what the historic rivers and floodplains were like (see Figure 2-6). These sources were compared to historic aerial photographs (which often show remnants of old river channels and wetlands), current topography and soils, and a few remaining reference sites, including a 10-kilometer reach of the Nisqually River within the Fort Lewis Military Reservation, which has seen little human alteration in the past 150 years (Collins et al. 2003). This historical recreation is not perfect: even the General Land Office materials begin after 1850 and so cannot account for habitat changes caused by the previous widespread trapping of beaver, which almost certainly decreased the extent of off-channel ponds and wetlands, preferred habitats for juvenile coho salmon and many other species (D. Montgomery, University of Washington, personal communication). But this historical approach yields insights that cannot be determined any other way.

The University of Washington (UW) researchers determined that geology forced most Puget Sound rivers to follow one of two distinctive patterns. Rivers that cut through wide, low-gradient valleys formed by subglacial runoff (such as the Snoqualmie, the Snohomish, and the lower Nooksack rivers) deposited their own sediment in a stable belt higher than the rest of the valley. The main channel meandered through this belt and stayed roughly in place for centuries. Large floods overtopped the banks and

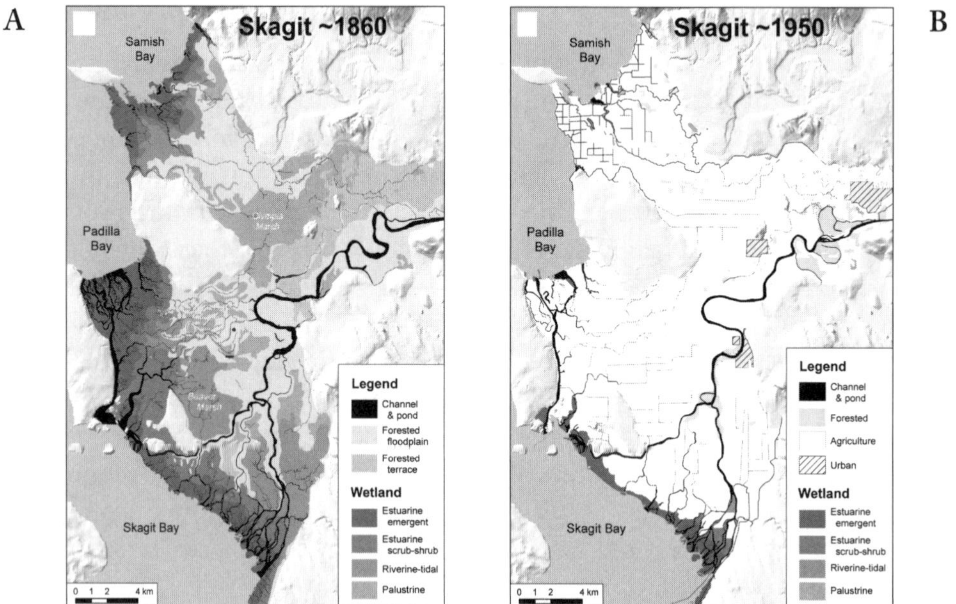

FIGURE 2-6. Based on archival materials, (A) University of Washington researchers have mapped conditions of the Skagit River delta in 1860. (B) By the middle of the next century, most of the vast wetlands of the delta had been diked and drained, and many sloughs closed off. Maps from Collins et al (2003).

fed enormous valley wetlands, which were joined near the river mouths by extensive estuarine and tidal wetlands. In contrast, rivers that cut through steeper valleys (such as the Stillaguamish, Skykomish, and Nisqually rivers) developed multiple, branching channels, through which they frequently changed course. Log jams were critical to river dynamics, forming where channels split and sometimes stabilizing parts of the pattern for centuries (Collins et al. 2003). Distinct from both these types, the Skagit-Samish delta was unique in the region, both for its large size and its origin from Glacier Peak lahars (mud flows caused by volcanic warming of glaciers) some 5,000 years ago. The combination resulted in a wetland system that dwarfed other estuaries (Collins et al. 2003).

Not surprisingly for a region with the world's greatest temperate coniferous forests, Puget Sound's historic river valleys were filled with enormous trees. Western red cedar *Thuja plicata* was the largest and most common conifer, averaging 61 centimeters (2 feet) in diameter at breast height but documented as large as 381 centimeters (13 feet). In areas that frequently flooded, deciduous trees were common and also grew very large—black cottonwood *Populus trichocarpa* were found up to 203 centimeters (nearly 7 feet) in diameter, while some big leaf maples *Acer macrophyllum* had diameters up to 183 centimeters (6 feet; Collins et al. 2003). Trees were more than a terrestrial fixture of the valleys, they were also integral to the shape and character of the rivers themselves at every scale, determining the location of channels, eddies, sloughs, wetlands, and other complex habitats. Log jams could be a square kilometer or more, storing vast amounts of sediment and spawning gravels (see Figure 2-7). At a smaller scale, logs altered river flow to scour deep pools that were used by many species, including salmon (Collins et al. 2003). Dead trees "were so abundant and well-lodged in riverbeds that logging and upstream settlement was stymied until settlers and the [U.S.] Army [Corps of] Engineers could pull, blast, and cut wood from rivers in the 1870s–1890s" (Collins et al. 2003). After more than 25 years of such work, and the simultaneous logging of the lowland riparian forests that were the source of much of the wood, a report of the Corps still found dead trees to have an almost overwhelming presence in Puget Sound rivers in 1907:

> ...channels are strewn with immense trunks, often two hundred feet long, with roots, tops, and all...[forming] jams, which frequently block channels altogether. ...[T]he supply is practically unlimited, and the quantity carried by a great flood is such that very little can be done [to limit the damage]...[Quoted in Collins et al. 2003]

Given the extent of development that now occupies major river valleys, recreating conditions that Puget Sound residents and the Corps of Engineers went to such pains to eliminate a century ago is out of the question. But history can teach us where different types of restoration actions are likely to be the most effective today. In rivers run-

FIGURE 2-7. A logjam on the Queets River today. With its floodplain protected by Olympic National Park, the Queets is a contemporary reference for how old-growth forests helped shape western Washington rivers. Photo from Montgomery (2003).

ning through glacial valleys, for example, *hydrologic* connection of the river with historic oxbows and floodplain wetlands should be the primary aim of restoration. In the narrower valleys of rivers that historically had multiple, shifting channels, the central tasks should be the restoration of valley-bottom forests and river migration, where feasible (Collins et al. 2003). Since large trees are critical to these migration patterns, initial riparian plantings should include faster-growing but less durable deciduous trees, which could restore river dynamics sooner (Collins et al. 2003).

The Challenge of Climate Change

"There are two major drivers of the future environmental quality in this region: the specific effects of global warming combined with the size and scale of the human footprint," wrote the co-director of the University of Washington's Climate Impacts Group in a report to the Governor's Puget Sound Action Team (Miles 2005). How the two drivers interact will determine the fate of our natural heritage. Global warming will probably have at least these four fundamental effects on the ecoregion:

- *Continued rises in temperature.* Although an obvious effect of global warming, this may be deadly all on its own, especially for some aquatic organisms. Ecologically, the most harmful effect may be on phytoplankton and other plants at the base of the marine food web. Forests will also be stressed by longer periods of summer drought, especially at lower elevations, exacerbating fire and insect damage. In the mountains, higher temperatures will change the distribution of plant species (trees will encroach on alpine meadows, for example).
- *Continued alteration of river and stream flows.* With decreased snowpack and earlier snowmelt, normal summer low flows in Washington streams will get lower (stressing human water supplies as well as river ecosystems), while high spring flows (which many juvenile salmon depend on to reach the Sound) will come earlier.
- *More flooding.* With more winter precipitation falling as rain instead of snow, flooding will increase. Native species have adapted to periodic flooding, but bigger and more frequent floods could overwhelm some populations, especially if they are already in decline due to other causes.
- *Accelerated rates of sea-level rise.* This may threaten nearshore habitats around the region, particularly in the south Sound, where land has been sinking at a rate of approximately eight inches per century.

The extent of these effects cannot be predicted precisely. How much and how fast global climate will change and how this translates to the region's climate is too uncertain. But the changes listed above will happen; the question is to what degree. As the UW report to the Governor states, "Given the residence times of greenhouse gases in the atmosphere (several decades) and the long time it takes for the ocean to fully communicate with the atmosphere (several centuries), even if we stopped emitting CO_2 today, warming would continue for many decades" (Snover et al. 2005).

So what do we do? By and large, experts recommend the same fundamental strategy as this book has so far: conserve the natural functioning of ecosystems to the greatest extent possible. With respect to climate change, the two primary goals for this strategy are to enhance the resiliency of ecosystems and to protect the diversity of species, which have developed different ways of adapting to changes in their environment. Concerns about climate change strengthen the importance of focusing on the whole landscape, not just reserves, because reserves will be incapable of conserving diversity as climate change alters fundamental ecological processes (such as the hydrologic cycle and the frequency and severity of fires) and the distribution of species. As two University of Washington climate experts wrote concerning salmon recovery, "If we are interested in purchasing long-term climate insurance for wild salmon...we will likely get the best return on investments aimed at restoring the health and integrity of our beleaguered watersheds" (Mantua and Francis 2004). The same holds true for ecosystems generally.

One last point is worth noting. Currently, Pacific Northwest forests "are a net source of carbon emissions to the atmosphere" (Keeton et al., in press) despite their enormous capacity to sequester carbon (and thereby decrease greenhouse gases in the atmosphere). The majority of timber harvested in the region goes into products with short life spans, such as paper, cardboard, and wood pallets, or becomes waste, some of which is used as fuel. Even with these ultimate uses of our wood, relatively modest improvements in harvest practices could result in the storage of an additional one billion metric tons of carbon over the next 50 to 75 years in the forests of western Washington and Oregon alone. This is almost half of the total greenhouse gas emissions projected from all human activities in the Puget Sound area over that same period. The harvest practices recommended for carbon storage would also further other conservation goals: protect mature forests, extend harvest rotations (ideally up to 100 years or more, instead of the current 40 to 60 years), and preserve some live trees, snags, and downed woody debris during harvest (Keeton et al., in press).

Monitoring Progress

Given that climate change will continue, experts warn that, for conservation planners, "the past may not be a dependable guide to the future" (Snover et al. 2005). Stormwater planning should anticipate more intense flooding, for example, while rising sea levels mean conservation of coastal wetlands should use adjustable easements that can expand inland.

A regional conservation strategy must expect surprises and be flexible to changing conditions, given the complexity of ecosystems. This would be true under any circumstances; the uncertainties of climate change only make it more important. A regional conservation strategy should therefore make a commitment to long-term monitoring of certain key indicators, which can teach us how well or poorly the strategy is performing and whether and how it should be changed. We rarely do this sort of monitoring now, as demonstrated by a recent review of projects to restore juvenile salmon habitat in 30 Pacific Northwest streams. The study found that a majority of the projects did not show statistically significant improvements in the abundance of salmon—not necessarily because the projects actually did little good, but because salmon populations naturally fluctuate so much that short-term monitoring means little, and projects on only six of the streams were monitored for more than 5 years (Roni et al. 2003). "Indicator species," chosen because their status tends to reflect the health of a whole community of species, could simplify the demands of monitoring and put recognizable (and popular) faces on the abstract notion of our natural heritage. These species would be tracked for trends in abundance, distribution, and other features (e.g., average size, genetic diversity). Orcas, coho salmon, tree frogs, river otters *Lutra canadensis*, pileated woodpeckers *Dryocopus pileatus*, and chipping sparrows *Spizella passerina* could all be good candidates, telling us about the fates of their distinct habitats.

More and better monitoring, however, means little without a commitment to act on the results, especially when they conflict with expectations. Monitoring today is rarely designed as a well-planned set of scientific experiments to test fundamental assumptions underlying negotiated compromises and to teach us whether we should change our approach (Ralph and Poole 2003). For example, what would be the actual effects on wild salmon in different rivers from closing some hatcheries and operating others differently? What would be the actual effects of different land-use choices on otherwise comparable stream systems? Our reluctance to monitor is partly because at least one party could "lose" depending on the results. But avoiding such tests completes a vicious circle, because monitoring over long time periods is then considered an expense with little tangible benefit. We therefore do not learn important lessons. We continue to spend conservation funds on the wrong things and we continue to mitigate the impacts of growth ineffectively. Meanwhile, the environmental baseline for future generations continues to decline, without our even really knowing what we have lost.

Our choices are between alternative futures. Population growth and climate change will create losses in our natural heritage. But it is within our power to minimize those losses and make up for them, or to allow them to accumulate, intensifying each other and transforming our region into a lesser place forever. Creating the first future would not be easy, but we cannot say that we do not know what needs to be done. Study after study confirms the same recommendations. Exactly how to accomplish them may not always be clear, but the best way to learn is to try, conscientiously attempting to get better as we go along.

References

Botkin, D. 1990. Discordant harmonies: a new ecology for the twenty-first century. Oxford University Press, New York.

Bremerton v. Kitsap County, CPSGMHB No. 95-3-0039c, Final Decision and Order (1995).

Cassidy, K. M., M. R. Smith, C. E. Grue, K. M. Dvornich, J. E. Cassady, K. R. McAllister, and R. E. Johnson. 1997. Gap analysis of Washington State: an evaluation of the protection of biodiversity. Volume 5. Washington Cooperative Fish and Wildlife Research Unit, Seattle.

Center for Biological Diversity. 2005. The Puget Sound basin: a biodiversity assessment. Available: http://www.biologicaldiversity.org/swcbd/ecosystems/pugetsound/report.pdf (January 2006).

Collins, B. D., D. R. Montgomery, and A. J. Sheikh. 2003. Reconstructing the historic riverine landscape of the Puget Lowland. Pages 79–128 *in* D. R. Montgomery, S. B. Bolton, D. B. Booth, and L. Wall, editors. Restoration of Puget Sound rivers. University of Washington Press, Seattle.

Floberg, J., M. Goering, G. Wilhere, C. MacDonald, C. Chappell, C. Rumsey, Z. Ferdana, A. Holt, P. Skidmore, T. Horsman, E. Alverson, C. Tanner, M. Bryer, P. Iachetti, A. Harcombe, B. McDonald, T. Cook, M. Summers, and D. Rolph. 2004. Willamette Valley-Puget Trough-Georgia basin ecoregional assessment, volume one: report. Prepared by The Nature Conservancy, Seattle, Washington, with support from the Nature Conservancy of Canada, Toronto, the Washington Department of Fish and Wildlife, Olympia, the Washington Department of Natural Resources (Natural Heritage and Nearshore Habitat programs), Olympia, the Oregon State Natural Heritage Information Center, Portland, and the British Columbia Conservation Data Centre, Victoria, British Columbia.

Franklin, J. F. 1993. Preserving biodiversity: species, ecosystems, or landscapes? Ecological Applications 3(2):202–205.

Franklin, J. E., and C. T. Dyrness. 1988. Natural vegetation of Oregon and Washington. 2nd edition. Oregon State University Press, Corvallis.

Hulse, D., S. Gregory, and J. Baker, editors. 2002. Williamette River basin planning atlas: trajectories of environmental and ecological change. Oregon State University Press, Corvallis.

Keeton, W. S., J. F. Franklin, and P. W. Mote. In press. Climate variability, climate change, and forest ecosystems in the Pacific Northeast. In E. L. Miles, A. K. Snover, and the Climate Impacts Group. Rhythms of change: climate impacts on the Pacific Northwest. MIT Press, Cambridge, Massachusetts.

Knutson, K. L., and V. L. Naef. 1997. Management recommendations for Washington's priority habitats: riparian. Washington Department of Fish and Wildlife, Olympia. Available: http://www.wdfw.wa.gov/hab/ripxsum.htm (March 2006).

Kruckeberg, A. R. 1991. The natural history of Puget Sound country. University of Washington Press, Seattle.

Mantua, N., and R. C. Francis. 2004. Natural climate insurance for Pacific Northwest salmon and salmon fisheries: finding our way through the entangled bank. Pages 127–140 in E. E. Knudsen, D. D. MacDonald, and Y. K. Muirhead, editors. Sustainable management of North American fisheries. American Fisheries Society, Symposium 43, Bethesda, Maryland.

Miles, E. 2005. Foreword. Pages 4–5 *in* A. K. Snover, P. W. Mote, L. Whitely Binder, A. F. Hamlet, and N. J. Mantua. 2005. Uncertain future: climate change and its effects on Puget Sound. A report for the Puget Sound Action Team by the Climate Impacts Group. University of Washington, Joint Institute for the Study of the Atmosphere and Oceans, Center for Science in the Earth System, Seattle.

Nehlson, W. 1996. Pacific Salmon status and trends—a coastwide erspective. Pages 41–50 *in* D. J. Stouder, P. A. Bisson, and R. J. Naiman, editors. Pacific salmon and their ecosystems: status and future options. Chapman and Hall, New York.

Pollock, M. M. 1998. Biodiversity. Pages 430–452 *in* R. J. Naiman, R. E. Bilby, and S. Kantor, editors. River ecology and management: lessons from the Pacific coastal ecoregion. Springer, New York, Springer.

PSWQAT (Puget Sound Water Quality Action Team). 2002. 2002 Puget Sound update: report of the Puget Sound Ambient Monitoring Program. Puget Sound Water Quality Action Team, Olympia, Washington.

Ralph, S. C., and G. C. Poole. 2003. Putting monitoring first: designing accountable ecosystem restoration and management plans. Pages 226–245 *in* D. R. Montgomery, S. B. Bolton, D. B. Booth, and L. Wall, editors. Restoration of Puget Sound rivers. University of Washington Press, Seattle.

Ricketts, T. H., E. Dinerstein, D. M. Olson, C. J. Loucks, W. Eichbaum, K. Kavanagh, P. Hedao, P. Hurley, K. M. Carney, R. Abell, and S. Walters. 1999. Terrestrial ecoregions of North America: a conservation assessment. Island Press, Washington, D.C.

Roni, P., M. Liermann, and A. Steel. 2003. Monitoring and evaluating fish response to instream restoration. Pages 318–339 *in* D. R. Montgomery, S. B. Bolton, D. B. Booth, and L. Wall, editors. Restoration of Puget Sound rivers. University of Washington Press, Seattle.

Shared Strategy Development Committee. 2005. Draft Puget Sound Salmon Recovery Plan. Shared Strategy for Puget Sound, Seattle.

Snover, A. K., P. W. Mote, L. C. Whitely Binder, A. F. Hamlet, and N. J. Mantua. 2005. Uncertain future: climate change and its effects on Puget Sound. A report for the Puget Sound Action Team by the Climate Impacts Group. University of Washington, Joint Institute for the Study of the Atmosphere and Oceans, Center for Science in the Earth System, Seattle.

Strickland, R. M. 1983. The fertile fjord: plankton in Puget Sound. University of Washington Press, Seattle.

Chapter 3. A Regional Strategy

> The significant problems we face cannot be solved at the same level of thinking we had when we created them. [Albert Einstein]

So what should we do? If the places and issues highlighted in the last chapter are the keys to conserving our natural heritage, how should we respond? Human institutions are complex—perhaps not as complex as ecosystems, but complex enough to daunt serious efforts at reform. I would argue, however, that just as it is possible to identify decisive issues out of the vast complexity of regional ecosystems, it is possible to do so with the human institutions that affect them.

This chapter focuses on specific changes to laws and programs to realize the vision for conservation discussed in the last chapter. The next chapter addresses necessary changes in funding, governance, and political support. In most cases, my recommendations have real world examples where a version of them is being implemented. Not all examples are as ambitious as they need to be, and no place in the world is yet implementing all of them, but there is no reason we could not be the first. We have led the way before. In fact, two of the most ambitious examples I cite are from our area: the Shared Strategy for Puget Sound Salmon and the Cascade Agenda. Still, while I admire both of these initiatives and hope my proposal can build on their good work, I conclude this chapter with a discussion of their limitations and those of past efforts to protect Puget Sound.

The Foundation: An Ambitious Land Conservation and Restoration Program

The most essential component of our conservation strategy must be an ambitious program to protect and restore the ecologically most important places in our region. These places would generally become reserves—not the entire floodplain of the Skagit River, for example, but the parts of it most important to protect and restore. Many of these sites have already been identified through watershed plans or the various studies discussed in Chapter 2. Final selection would depend on willing landowners, further discussion with affected communities, and scientific criteria developed to guide the overall conservation strategy. Not all properties must be purchased outright, but at a minimum conservation easements would be needed from current owners. These easements would restrict the economic uses allowed on the land and would provide long-term protection for restoration taken on by the public.

This would not be cheap. The Cascade Agenda, developed by the Cascade Land Conservancy with similar goals in mind for Snohomish, King, Pierce, and Kittitas counties, is estimated to cost $7 billion (see Figure 3-1). San Diego County, which is about one-third the size of the entire Puget Sound ecoregion, has developed a long-term, multispecies conservation plan with land conservation as its main component, estimated to cost $1.4 billion in 2003 dollars (not counting contributions from the federal and state governments and private mitigation; M. Cox, San Diego Association of Governments, and J. Onaka, Onaka Planning and Economics, personal communications). The Cascade

Land Conservancy argues that the majority of its proposal could be funded through transfers of development rights from the areas we want to conserve to the areas where we would target growth. Buyers would pay for the right to develop their land more densely, using development rights given up in the conserved area. Although I believe it is unrealistic to expect that the majority of conservation costs can be paid this way, it could lessen the overall cost of the most expensive part of my proposal.

Compensate Property Owners for Restrictions Beyond a Regulatory Baseline

As discussed in the last chapter, reserves are not enough. Conservation must extend farther across the landscape to succeed. To this end, local governments across western Washington have recently updated their regulations to protect critical areas, which include wetlands, floodplains, and other fish and wildlife habitat conservation areas, as required by the Growth Management Act (GMA). Some of these updates, such as King County's, were extremely controversial, while others were not, including some that adopted similar requirements as King County. However, the GMA overpromises what these ordinances can do, as discussed in more detail in Chapter 10. It is not possible to protect all "functions and values" of critical areas when surrounding areas develop, even with the largest buffers recommended by state agencies. In the latest updates, local governments generally improved their environmental protections but did not strictly follow even the state recommendations, as they balanced protection of the environment with other growth management goals (such as accommodating growth in urban areas, promoting affordable housing and economic development, and protecting private property rights).

FIGURE 3-1. The Snoqualmie Tree Farm, looking north, with Mount Si to the right. In September 2004, King County purchased the development rights on this 90,000-acre working forest from the Hancock Timber Resource Group for $22 million. Courtesy of Cascade Land Conservancy.

Some regulatory baseline is needed for environmental protection, to set reasonable expectations for what property owners owe each other and the ecosystems in which they live. Property rights have never allowed absolute freedom for owners to do whatever they wish regardless of consequences to the public welfare, as discussed in greater detail in Chapter 6. Whether recently adopted regulations to protect critical areas should be the regional baseline is a question the voters must ultimately decide. But those regulations are clearly not enough to protect ecological functions as the region grows. Merely protecting those functions—let alone achieving a net gain in places—almost certainly goes beyond what can be achieved through regulations alone. If, for example, rural landowners must cluster their housing away from sensitive areas, forego the right to clear their land for pasture, and collaborate in the restoration of native land cover, some form of compensation is necessary. They and their elected officials will revolt otherwise. I would, too. Moreover, state courts would probably overturn a strictly regulatory attempt to accomplish all of these goals, on the grounds that it would place an "undue burden" on rural property owners (see Chapter 6 for more detail).

There are a few existing mechanisms in Washington that can provide compensation like this, including the Public Benefit Rating System (PBRS) and Current Use Taxation. PBRS provides tax breaks for property owners who provide public benefits—such as extra environmental protection or public access—that go beyond regulatory requirements. It is, however, a complicated and cumbersome process to qualify for PBRS, and the tax reductions allowed are not sufficient to attract widespread interest. Current use taxation allows some properties to be taxed for their current use—such as for agriculture or forestry—rather than the market-driven "highest and best use" normally used for property assessments. Both of these mechanisms could potentially be modified to provide the compensation I propose, but ultimately a different mechanism outside the property tax system might be necessary, too.

The forestry industry offers a clear example of this issue. When the Washington Forest Practices Board adopted the current regulations governing timber harvest on private lands, it had a cost-benefit analysis performed on the alternatives. The analysis, by a UW professor of forestry and discussed in more detail in Chapter 9, found that the new regulations would decrease the value of timber assets by about $2.7 billion (11% of their total value of $24.8 billion) compared to the regulations in place, and would also lead to $2.4 billion to $3.4 billion of lost wages over 20 years (discounting dollars from future years to create a single "net present value" figure [Perez-Garcia 2001[1]; J. Ehrenreich, Washington Forest Practices Association, personal communication]). An alternative proposed by environmental groups and some Indian tribes, which was stricter on many issues (particularly buffers for seasonal streams without fish), would have decreased tim-

---

[1] The report might have overstated costs by using conservative assumptions regarding the percentage of forest streams that were fish-bearing or perennial. It assumed that 57% of forest stream miles in western Washington were fish-bearing, 14% were perennial and non-fish bearing, and only 29% were non-fish bearing and seasonal. The Washington Forest Practices Association estimated considerably higher percentages for both types of non-fish bearing streams—see Chapter 9, footnote 22.

ber asset values by an additional $5.7 billion (for a total reduction of 34% of their existing value). The study did not calculate the cost of this alternative in lost wages, though it suggested that the amount could be proportionate to the lost timber value (Perez-Garcia 2001). The Forest Practices Board chose the first alternative, in part because one of its goals was to keep the timber industry economically viable in the state. I would stress that this is not just an economic issue. From an ecological standpoint, if land is not going to be set aside wholly for conservation, forestry is the preferred use for vast parts of the Puget Sound Ecoregion and Washington State. When timber harvest loses its economic return, the pressure to convert to development can be unstoppable. The alternative proposed by the environmental groups and Indian tribes contains many goals that should be sought in a regional conservation strategy over the long term. But it would be counterproductive to require that forest landowners pay its full cost.

Agricultural lands pose an even greater challenge, because they tend to be in some of the region's most ecologically important areas (frequently floodplains) and tend to have even more intense economic pressures to convert them to development. At a national level, farming is heavily subsidized, but in the Puget Sound area most farms pay more in taxes (particularly at the local level) than they receive back in services. I review a comprehensive proposal for Puget Sound agriculture at the end of Chapter 4.

Amend the Growth Management Act to Address Ecological Priorities at the Right Scale

For environmental protection and many other purposes, Washington's GMA provides probably the best overall framework for land-use laws of any state in the country. But it was not written with ecosystems in mind, and it shows.

As discussed in more detail in Chapter 10, the GMA divides the landscape into categories of urban, rural, farming, forestry, and mining areas. It refers to ecosystems only once, in its definition of "critical areas," which it generally treats at the small scale of wetlands, shellfish beds, stream reaches, and the like. Other than creating open space and controlling water pollution, the GMA does not mention any ecological goal for how county and city comprehensive plans must address land use. It mandates regulation of development to protect the ecological functions of critical areas using best available science, but it also mandates the accommodation of growth, without acknowledging that the best available science is clear that these mandates cannot be accomplished together—at least if protecting functions and values is interpreted to mean "no net loss," as state agencies have articulated the standard. Furthermore, the GMA does not require that planning connect land-use activities to the water needed to support them.

All of these problems must be corrected for the GMA to serve as the fundamental basis for ecological conservation in the Puget Sound area. Only the GMA can play this role. It is Washington's basic framework for land-use laws, which are the most fundamental environmental laws of all. The GMA must include a new category for places where ecological conservation is the primary goal, distinct from natural resource lands (which are designated for agricultural, timber, or mineral production). This new category would not exclude human activities, but would require that they are compatible with ecological priorities for these lands. Conservation lands must be identified at the Puget Sound regional level because their ecological importance goes well beyond the jurisdictional lines of counties and cities. Details of exactly which properties are placed in this new category could still be decided by local governments in their comprehensive plans, consistent with regional criteria. Just as compensation should be paid to landowners asked to accept restrictions beyond a given standard, local governments whose tax base may be limited by restrictions from conservation lands should be eligible for some assistance, too.

Local governments need clearer guidance for land-use regulations, recognizing that no net loss of ecological functions is an impossible standard if jurisdictions also must meet other growth management goals. The GMA could authorize a range of standards for acceptable environmental protections, which could relate to environmental impact fees on new development. These fees, discussed in more detail in the next chapter, would be one source of revenue for a regional conservation program. Impact fees could be higher where local governments implemented protections at the low end of the acceptable range (100-foot buffers for salmon streams, for example, are at the low end of what the science supports). This would both reflect the greater harm of development with less environmental protection and serve as an incentive for more protective regulations.

An amended GMA should also require that land-use plans are coordinated and consistent with watershed plans. As discussed in more detail in Chapters 11 and 12, watershed plans are the product of collaborative processes that the state has required or encouraged for every major watershed across Washington (e.g., the entire Nooksack River basin). The plans are intended to guide state and local actions for water withdrawals, salmon conservation, water quality, and targets for instream flows. But the plans are weakened by being strictly voluntary. There is no mechanism to require that local land-use plans be consistent with watershed plans, despite the fact that land use drives most issues related to water. Attempts to coordinate local land-use plans across jurisdictions were similarly hamstrung before the GMA required the plans to be consistent and established county-wide and regional processes to accomplish that.

Amend State Vesting Laws

"Vesting" laws determine the point during the development process after which land-use regulations applied to a proposed development cannot be changed—it is "vested." Developers need certainty, but Washington vests development (freezing new land-use laws) earlier in the process than any other state in the country, as discussed in more detail in Chapter 10. This creates major challenges just to meet the current goals of growth management (see Figure 3-2). If these laws are left unchanged, it could doom a regional conservation strategy, which must adapt to unpredictable ecological outcomes and new scientific understanding over time. Most states in the country vest developments when permits are issued or when developers begin actual construction. California and Texas are the only states similar to Washington, but even they do not go

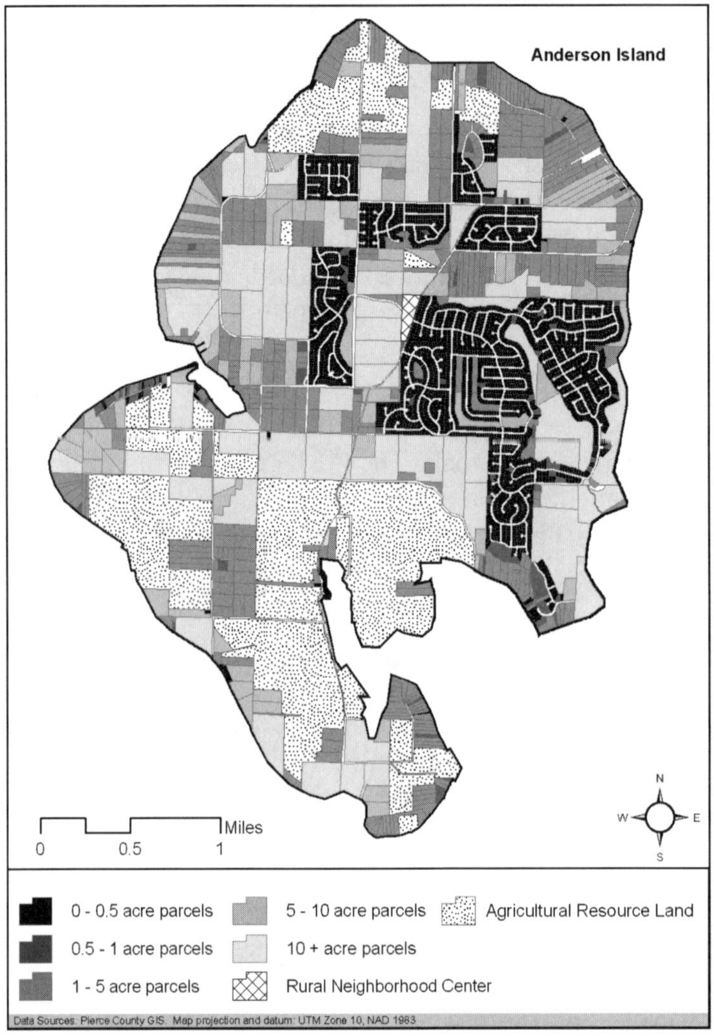

FIGURE 3-2. Subdivided land parcels on Anderson Island, Pierce County. While growth management policies have generally called for rural lots to be at least 5 acres, in many parts of the region rural properties are vested at much higher densities because of previous land subdivisions. Anderson Island, located in Puget Sound about midway between Tacoma and Olympia, is a representative if somewhat extreme example. While most of the island is zoned for rural, 10-acre lots, about 65% of this zone is composed of parcels that are smaller, in many cases far smaller. Courtesy of Steward and Associates.

so far in granting property owners the right to develop under laws in effect when owners *apply* for initial permits to subdivide land. For many small developments of four units or less (especially common in rural areas), Washington permanently forbids the application of new regulations, even if the property owner or future owners allow decades to pass before actually proposing a development. This "virtually invites subversion of the public interest," states the leading textbook on Washington land-use law

(Settle et al. 1983). Vesting later in the development process, like most other states in the country, would vastly improve the prospects for a successful regional conservation strategy.

Expand Water Conservation Programs across the Region

There are no easy answers to meet the Puget Sound region's needs for water, given the combination of an expanding human population, the widespread ecological problems already caused by existing water withdrawals, and decreased snowpack in the mountains because of climate change. Essentially, there are only four possible solutions: dramatically expand water conservation; transfer water between different parts of the region; enlarge storage behind higher dams in the mountains; and reuse wastewater or stormwater, at least for non-drinking purposes. In different locations, some combination of these strategies may make sense. As a fundamental, region-wide strategy, however, expanding water conservation is the obviously preferred choice.

Transferring water simply transfers problems. In the water business, it is said that "water flows toward money." The most likely transfers would be from less developed, ecologically more valuable areas to highly developed, ecologically less valuable areas. There is no such thing as "surplus" water—a concept in vogue 25 years ago but rejected by ecologists today. Some withdrawals do less damage than others, but all have some ecological cost. On a limited or emergency basis, transfers between basins and between different water systems can be justified, but large, ongoing transfers would be a sign of regional water planning failure. Large transfers of water also would risk litigation under the Endangered Species Act, tribal treaties, or both (see Chapters 7 and 13).

Storing water behind dams amounts to a different type of transfer, across time instead of space. This type of transfer robs spring flows to provide water in summer and early fall, when human demands are highest and rainfall in our region is lowest. This is what every dam in the Northwest does now. As a result, there is already less water to help juvenile salmon migrate to Puget Sound. Expanding this practice, especially when climate change will also decrease spring flows and melt snowpack earlier in the year, could be devastating to many species. It also would probably invite litigation under the Endangered Species Act, tribal treaties, or both.

Reusing wastewater or stormwater is expensive, much more so than expanding water conservation. Reused wastewater must be treated extensively. It is typically used for irrigation or industrial processes and requires a separate set of pipes for delivery. Stormwater must be stored until it is needed, but it is very difficult to provide adequate storage facilities to keep water until the dry season. On a small scale, this problem is exemplified by the rain barrel in my yard, which my downspout quickly fills during storms but which sits dry for most of the summer. Some people have proposed storing stormwater in aquifers, but this poses serious risk of polluting groundwater supplies, which rely on the natural filtration process of the soils above them—a process that would be overwhelmed by the quantity of stormwater washing off of streets and roofs.

Water conservation remains the cheapest, easiest, readiest, and most environmentally friendly choice. The City of Seattle already has one of the best conservation programs of any water utility in the West, but its example has not been followed widely in the region. Seattle's program, developed partly in response to a citizen initiative, has focused on subsidizing customers' purchase of water-efficient equipment, from toilets that meet the latest plumbing code to new commercial irrigation systems.[2] Seattle has not yet included an aggressive program to fix leaks in the city's aging infrastructure. In 2001, a consortium of utilities and county governments in Central Puget Sound estimated that applying Seattle's existing program across Snohomish, King, and Pierce counties would save 149 million gallons a day in the summer and 111 million gallons a day year-round. The second amount approximately equals the water use of Seattle, Bellevue, Redmond, and Issaquah combined (Central Puget Sound Water Suppliers' Forum 2001; estimate of water use for cities, B. Bennett, King County Department of Natural Resources and Parks, personal communication). King County estimates that applying Seattle's program across the region would cost the average customer an extra $5 a month (Bennett, personal communication). Simply changing rate structures to charge more for above-average use of water might get similar results at little cost to most customers.[3]

Begin Settling All Legal Rights to Water

In our region, water law is the supreme "Lord of Yesterday," a phrase coined by Colorado Law Professor Charles Wilkinson for laws governing mining, grazing, and other resource extraction industries in the West (Wilkinson 1992). These laws may have made sense when they were written, but they are radically unsuited to the West now, even as they shape our future. In water law, the most fundamental principle across the West is "first in time, first in right." Water rights granted earlier always have priority over rights granted later. Although fish and wildlife were obviously here before us, they are not first in right because legally we did not begin to recognize their needs for stream flow until 20–30 years ago. Even then, these rights were allocated for only a few selected rivers, where they remain junior to all other rights granted before them. Elsewhere, there is no legally recognized right to a minimum stream flow at all.

The right to withdraw and use water is a property right—it cannot be taken without compensation. This ensures that straightening out our mess will take a substantial amount of money and time. First, we have to determine who has a valid water right. The legislature has provided multiple opportunities over the years to file water claims, which ostensibly pre-date 1917 (when the current system of water rights was estab-

[2] For details on Seattle's program, see http://www.seattle.gov/util/Directory/Conservation_Index/index.asp.

[3] For examples of reductions due to changes to rate structures and a good discussion of how demand for water changes with price, see Nieswiadomy and Fox 1996; for an example from Texas of how rates decreased consumption by 15%, see Chesnutt et al. 1997

lished; the claims would therefore be senior to all rights granted under the system). In much of the state—and nearly all of western Washington—the state has made virtually no effort to systematically evaluate these claims, which now total about 169,000. "Short of litigation," the Attorney General's Office notes, "it is impossible to assess how many of these claims represent vested water rights. Many claims may be invalid, overstated, overlapping, abandoned, reduced, or modified in their scope" (Pharris and McDonald 2000). Without a formal court review of water rights and claims, we cannot know how much water can legally be withdrawn in any given area.

Oregon, Idaho, Montana, and other states are addressing similar problems. Their experience shows that adjudicating water claims and rights is best done through a special court system, which can develop and apply the necessary expertise without tying up the already overburdened regular court system. The work can be a dull and lengthy process. A systematic evaluation of all water rights and claims in the Yakima River basin began in 1977 and is still underway. But lessons and court decisions from the Yakima basin should speed up other efforts. It is a daunting, not terribly inspiring, but necessary task, if we are to move our management of water into the 21st century.

The greatest unknown factor in this process is the right of Indian tribes to flows necessary to support their fishing. In contrast to a tribal right to habitat protection, the tribal right to water for fish is well-recognized in the federal courts, though the precise flows involved must still be quantified in any particular case. Tribal rights date at least to the 1850s, when their treaties were signed, if not from "time immemorial." Either way, their rights would have seniority and therefore priority over all rights granted since. Tribal rights are so fundamental to any final decisions about water allocations, and potentially so consequential for all of society, that the state may need to negotiate these on a separate but parallel track to the general process of evaluating other water claims.

Reform Stormwater Requirements

In the Puget Sound region, stormwater from developed or cleared areas is the main source of water pollution. Stormwater also affects water quantity, dramatically increasing peak flows and the "flashiness" of streams (meaning they quickly rise and fall in response to storms) and decreasing base flows during dry periods. (Thornton Creek, which has a year-round average flow of about 11 cubic feet per second near its mouth, shot up to over 1,000 cubic feet per second during one day of heavy rain about seven months into my term as President of Thornton Creek Alliance.) These hydrologic changes have profound effects on stream life, from bugs to salmon to riparian vegetation.

Management of stormwater is therefore a crucial issue for conservation as the region continues to grow and develop. It is also costly. New standards in the latest Washington Department of Ecology stormwater manual add $10,000 or more to the cost of the average new house, and much more to new commercial development. Combining private developments and public capital projects, the region probably spends more than $1 billion each year to meet stormwater requirements. Investing even 1% of that amount in studies that could modify the "one-size-fits-all" standards issued by the Department of Ecology to the actual conditions of specific stream basins could dramatically improve conditions in our streams, potentially at lower overall costs. But there have been few such studies so far in the region.

Even more importantly, we must recognize that the same goals cannot apply to all streams. In intensely urbanized areas, trying to return streams to undeveloped conditions not only would fail at great cost, it would have the perverse effect of creating economic incentives to build in undeveloped areas, where the cost to meet the Department of Ecology's generic requirements is much less. I know, as an active leader in Thornton Creek Alliance, that it is not easy to advocate lowering goals for streams that people love and devote themselves to. But that does not mean writing them off. It means having realistic expectations for what even very substantial investments can accomplish, and honestly acknowledging the greater potential of other streams to contribute to regional ecosystems.

Finally, I cannot leave the subject of stormwater without mentioning what has come to be called "low-impact development." Many different techniques fall under this heading—designing a building site so that natural vegetation, soils and topography help manage stormwater to the greatest extent possible, applying new technology such as green roofs and permeable pavement, narrowing roads, and making other modifications to traditional building practices that decrease the amount of stormwater and pollutants discharged from a developed site. The Puget Sound area has become one of the most active places in the nation experimenting with this approach to development, but almost entirely in public projects so far. This is understandable. Governments can afford the extra cost to gain additional public benefits when building roads, libraries, office buildings, and the like. Governments need not borrow from lenders that are more comfortable financing projects similar to those they have financed previously. Governments can also more easily modify rules for road widths, pavement, and parking requirements for their own projects than they can for others But in the long run low-impact development must become the rule, rather than the exception, wherever we hold out hopes for maintaining the health of our streams in the face of growth.

Expand Reforms of Salmon Harvest and Hatcheries

In the Northwest, salmon are not just a species close to our hearts. They are also a "keystone" species crucial to the entire ecoregion, a source of food for 138 other animals (not including ourselves), and a source of marine nutrients for plants and animals at the base of the food web. Below passage barriers, salmon are almost omnipresent in the region's streams, since various species have evolved to use every accessible aquatic habitat at different times of the year. The actions listed above should conserve sufficient habitat to maintain and increase salmon runs in the region's most important river systems. But wild salmon suffer from two other major causes of decline in the Puget

Sound region: overharvest and poor management of hatcheries, as discussed in more detail in Chapter 8 (see Figure 3-3).

Within Puget Sound and the Strait of Juan de Fuca, salmon harvests have dropped dramatically from 10 years ago, largely because of the Endangered Species Act. Fisheries now target marked hatchery salmon; unmarked wild salmon are supposed to be released back into the water, though listed salmon are still caught in the tens of thousands. The most important reform remaining must restrict and ultimately end "mixed stock" fisheries, where healthy and endangered salmon from different rivers cannot be distinguished from each other and are caught together. Most harvest of Puget Sound salmon occurs off of British Columbia, particularly off the west coast of Vancouver Island. However, Canadian fishermen cannot solely be blamed for this since a large portion of Canadian salmon are caught in Alaskan waters. Puget Sound fishermen are not blameless, either. They also engage in "mixed stock" fisheries before the salmon separate for their final journeys home.

The solution, as discussed in more detail in Chapter 8, is "terminal" fisheries— harvesting salmon near their rivers of origin, where healthy populations can be caught without harming weak populations, as Indian tribes have always done. For the health of our salmon, terminal fisheries are most important off of Vancouver Island and the coasts of Alaska and mainland British Columbia, but we would undoubtedly have to lead by example to make this change possible. In Puget Sound, this would mostly affect recreational fisheries. Along the coasts of Alaska and British Columbia, the change must come from commercial fisheries governed by the Pacific Salmon Treaty. We can encourage this reform if consumers demand salmon not caught in the open ocean (see Chapter 8 for details about "eco-fish" certification programs).

FIGURE 3-3. Hatchery proponents cite large increases in survival during egg incubation as a major benefit of artificial production. However, subverting the natural selection process allows weakened genetic traits to enter the wild population when hatchery fish mate with wild fish. Major reforms of hatchery operations in the Puget Sound region have been proposed, as discussed in Chapter 9. Photo courtesy of Kurt Beardslee, Washington Trout.

Hatcheries in the Puget Sound area have begun reforms guided by recommendations from the Hatchery Scientific Review Group (HSRG), a federally funded independent body established in 2000 (See HSRG 2003). Reforms have also resulted from a lawsuit brought by Washington Trout and the Native Fish Society, which has prompted the development of a first-ever Environmental Impact Statement for Puget Sound hatchery programs. Ongoing legal pressure will probably force continued improvements in hatchery operations, especially if monitoring recommended by the HSRG and other scientists provides evidence of "take" under the Endangered Species Act (and it almost assuredly will). But pressures from fishing interests to maintain hatchery production remain strong. Many scientists believe hatcheries harm wild salmon no matter how well they are managed, except in the rare case when small-scale hatchery production can prevent a wild run from going extinct while its habitat is restored. In most other cases, hatcheries can provide harvest opportunities, but at the cost of ongoing losses to wild salmon that harm the genetic integrity—and therefore the long-term viability—of both wild and hatchery runs. Scientists have long lamented the lack of rigorous monitoring and experimentation to test the actual effects of hatcheries on salmon. We need that information to get beyond the faith- and interest-based arguments that still dominate this debate.

Limitations of Other Initiatives

Washington Governor Christine Gregoire's Puget Sound Initiative is still under development as I write. From all indications, it holds promise for the future of conservation in the region, as does the Alliance for Puget Sound Shorelines recently announced by People for Puget Sound, Trust for Public Land, and The Nature Conservancy. Other major initiatives that parallel at least parts of my proposal are the Shared Strategy for Puget Sound Salmon and the Cascade Agenda. In my view, though, none of these initiatives, whether alone or in combination, will prove sufficient to conserve our region's natural heritage in the face of continued population growth and climate change. They are ambitious, but not ambitious enough.

Although most details are not yet available on the governor's Puget Sound Initiative, it should be evaluated in light of similar initiatives in the past, most notably the creation of the Puget Sound Water Quality Authority in 1983. The Puget Sound Water Quality Authority began as an advisory commission, which then became a citizen-led council responsible for developing a comprehensive plan to clean up and protect the sound and for coordinating the plan's implementation. The plan achieved some progress, but it was never adequately funded. Opponents gathered strength, and in 1996 the Puget Sound Water Quality Authority was restructured as the Puget Sound Action Team, which continues today as a state agency responsible for coordinating work affecting the sound across different state departments. The Puget Sound Action Team also provides outreach and technical assistance to local governments and the public. Both the Puget Sound Water Quality Authority and the Puget Sound Action Team have done valuable work, most notably in helping focus attention and resources on cleaning up contaminated sites. But they have had little clout, funding, or regulatory authority. They also have focused most on water and sediment pollution—important issues, to be sure, but not as important as the continued loss of shoreline habitat around the sound.

The Alliance for Puget Sound Shorelines has been organized in large part to address that issue. It has a goal of raising $80 million in public and private funds over the next 3 years, which would go to shoreline restoration and the creation of ten new parks and protected natural areas around the sound. The alliance will develop a long-term plan for conserving the sound, which may merge with aspects of the governor's Initiative. The alliance has received an initial grant of $3 million from The Russell Family Foundation but, as of Spring 2006, few details are known regarding where it will focus its restoration and protection efforts or where it will find the additional funds it is seeking.

In north Puget Sound, the Alliance for Puget Sound Shorelines would be well-advised to work cooperatively with the Northwest Straits Marine Conservation Initiative, which has identified conservation priorities along the marine shorelines of Clallam, Island, Jefferson, San Juan, Skagit, Snohomish, and Whatcom counties. Citizen-based Marine Resources Committees in each county have worked with local, state, federal, and tribal scientists to identify these priorities and take early actions. The initiative and these committees have led efforts to remove derelict fishing gear, such as abandoned fishing nets that continue to entangle and kill sea life, throughout north Puget Sound and the Strait of Juan de Fuca. But their total annual budget for all activities has been barely more than $1 million, which is radically insufficient.

The Shared Strategy was organized to develop a recovery plan for Puget Sound salmon listed under the Endangered Species Act. The plan attempts to integrate actions addressing harvest, hatcheries and habitat across the sound. Through a very collaborative process, the Shared Strategy has brought together top representatives of the National Marine Fisheries Service, the U.S. Fish and Wildlife Service, the Washington Department of Fish and Wildlife, Indian tribes, local governments, businesses, and environmental groups.[4] It has gotten the right leaders talking to one another, not just for salmon recovery but for many of the key long-term issues to conserve our natural heritage, and it has begun broadening that conversation to the wider public. It also has done a good job identifying specific priorities for habitat protection and restoration across the Puget Sound area, at least as they relate to listed salmon, and has encouraged and facilitated early actions to address all causes of salmon decline.

But the Shared Strategy has three fundamental limitations, which I believe will ensure its failure if not addressed:

- First, especially when it comes to habitat, the Shared Strategy has generated almost no commitments to implementation. Essentially all of its habitat recommendations are from voluntary watershed planning processes, which have committed

[4] See http://www.sharedsalmonstrategy.org/who-we-are.htm for members of the Shared Strategy's board and committees.

no new money and have rarely even discussed funding options besides asking for more money from the state and federal governments. Watershed plans lack the authority to require specific regulations and have almost never dared to recommend them. Shared Strategy leaders may argue that their plan is a first step, but without commitments to implementation, the plan is a relatively small step, given all of the time and effort that has gone into it. By far the hardest work remains.

- Second, the Shared Strategy's narrow focus on listed salmon misses the region's broader natural heritage. Shared Strategy leaders often argue that their plan is really about our quality of life, but most habitat elements in the plan specifically ignore the needs of salmon species not listed under the ESA, let alone other species or ecosystems. The plan also ignores other actions we could take on the landscape to benefit our quality of life (to improve recreation opportunities, say, or for urban projects that might make our cities more enjoyable places to live).
- Third, and perhaps most important, almost all habitat actions in the Shared Strategy focus on *projects*—acquire this parcel, restore that reach, and so on. This provides useful specificity, but it ignores the key lesson of history: ultimately, it is transformation of the landscape that drives salmon extinct. This was true in Europe and on the East Coast of North America, and it has been true on the Pacific Coast as well. Transformation of the landscape will overwhelm individual projects if urban areas expand, rural sprawl continues, and farm and forest land is converted to housing or is managed poorly.

The Cascade Agenda was developed by the Cascade Land Conservancy, working with civic leaders in the Central Puget Sound area and thousands of citizens who participated in the Cascade Dialogues. The agenda directly addresses my last criticism of the Shared Strategy: it focuses on actions we can take in the next few decades to conserve the most important features of the landscape of Snohomish, King, Pierce, and Kittitas counties over the next century, given projected regional growth. I applaud this focus and the agenda's long-term vision, which seeks to emulate the 100-year vision that shaped the Seattle parks system.

Nevertheless, I identify three limitations for the agenda as well. These are not meant to criticize how the agenda is doing its important work or the choices its leaders have made in defining that work. Agenda leaders are doing what they do best, in the parts of the region where they are generally the best at it. But there is still much more to do:

- First and most important, the geographic focus of the agenda excludes the overwhelming majority of the most important places for our ecoregion's natural heritage. If our goal is conservation, we need to think in terms of ecosystems, not political boundaries. The four counties where the agenda is focused are where the Cascade Land Conservancy has traditionally operated, but this should not set the limits for a regional conservation strategy.
- Second, the agenda relies heavily on transfer of development rights to fund its conservation vision. Identifying where development rights are to be transferred

from, as the agenda generally does, is the easy part. The agenda has generally not yet identified where the rights are to be transferred *to*, which is the politically difficult task. Agenda leaders are well aware of this challenge, but I do not share their optimism that transfer of development rights could raise the equivalent of nearly $5 billion for conservation. The more money that can be raised this way the better, but over reliance on it could keep us from other creative ways to raise necessary revenues for conservation, such as those discussed in the next chapter.

- Third, although land conservation is the foundation of a regional conservation strategy, it is far from sufficient. As this chapter has argued, a successful strategy must take a broader approach, including changes to the Growth Management Act and other land-use laws, water management reform, widespread adoption of low-impact development techniques, and continued reforms in salmon harvest and hatchery management. Even in the four counties where it is focused, the scope of the agenda is too limited to conserve our natural heritage.

Leaders of these other initiatives may argue that my proposal, in comparison, is unrealistic. I certainly recognize that it faces many serious practical challenges, which are addressed in the next chapter. Realism, however, is not the same as pragmatism. We must be realistic about what our natural heritage actually needs to survive, not just what we are willing to do about it.

References

Central Puget Sound Water Suppliers' Forum. 2001. 2001 Central Puget Sound regional water supply outlook. Central Puget Sound Water Suppliers' Forum, Seattle.

Chesnutt, T. W., J. Beecher, P. C. Mann, D. M. Clark, W. M. Hanemann, G. A. Raftelis, C. N. McSpadden, D. M. Pekelney, J. Christienson, and R. Krop. 1997. Designing, evaluating, and implementing conservation rate structures. California Urban Water Conservation Council, Sacramento.

HSRG (Hatchery Scientific Review Group). 2003. Hatchery reform recommendations for the Puget Sound and Coastal Washington Hatchery Reform Project. Long Live the Kings, Seattle.

Nieswiadomy, M., and T. Fox. 1996. Calculating water savings using a spreadsheet program. Pages 105–110 *in Proceedings of Conserv96: Responsible Water Stewardship*. American Water Works Association, Denver.

Perez-Garcia, J. 2001. Cost benefit analysis for new proposed forest practices rules implementing the forests and fish report. Final report. University of Washington College of Forest Resources, Seattle.

Pharris, J. K., and T. McDonald. 2000. An introduction to Washington water law. Washington State Office of Attorney General, Olympia.

Settle, R. L., P. L. Buck, and J. E. Haggard. 1983. Washington land use and environmental law and practice. Butterworth Legal Publishers, Seattle.

Wilkinson, C. F. 1992. Crossing the next meridian: land, water, and the future of the West. Island Press, Washington, D.C.

Chapter 4. How We Get There

> The idea of rebuilding the salmon runs of an industrialized ecosystem is heroically optimistic—a hope that might not have occurred to anyone except those who had rehabilitated the Willamette River Basin in Oregon or Lake Washington near Seattle. [NRCC 1996:7]

My proposal faces three major practical challenges:

- *Funding*. Over the first 20 years, I estimate that my proposal would cost about $10 billion to implement, primarily for land conservation and compensation to property owners. As discussed in this chapter, I believe these funds can be raised in a way that could *lower* general taxes.
- *Governance*. Some form of regional governing body, intermediate between local governments and the state, would be needed to set land-use policies across the ecoregion and to raise and allocate billions of new dollars. In this chapter, I discuss how this could be accomplished with a minimum of new bureaucracy.
- *The urban/rural political divide*. A successful conservation strategy for the region requires long-term cooperation between urban and rural areas, based on widespread consensus on goals and actions that crosses the political parties. Over time and across the region, both Republicans and Democrats will control conservation decisions that must stay consistent for decades if they are to succeed. This is asking a lot, but there is evidence for hope. More than 15 years after the Growth Management Act was originally adopted (with bipartisan support), both parties still generally share its goals, particularly in the Puget Sound area. Leaders from both parties participate in the Shared Strategy and the Cascade Agenda. We live in one of the world's most beautiful metropolitan areas—an enormous asset, since political support for conservation ultimately depends on shared love of place. We must build on that love and on good will wherever we find it. How governance is addressed can also help heal political divisions, especially between urban and rural areas.

I will take up these challenges in order.

Funding

We must seek alternatives to existing taxes to fund a regional conservation program for two fundamental reasons. First, there are already too many competing demands for existing revenues. Since November 1993, a series of citizen initiatives have lowered state and local taxes and restricted the raising of new general revenues. Funding for natural resource agencies at the state level, never especially high, has dropped steadily under these conditions as a proportion of the overall budget (Figure 4-1). Voters clearly want lower taxes. Just as clearly, the legislature believes existing natural resource programs are a lower priority than other state responsibilities, such as public schools,

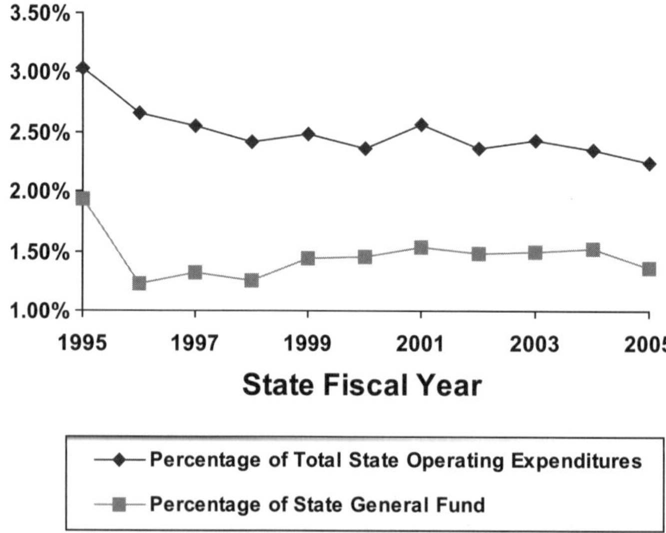

FIGURE 4-1. Natural resource spending as a percentage of state spending.
Source: Washington Office of Financial Management.
Note: Natural Resource agencies include Departments of Fish and Wildlife, Natural Resources, Ecology, and Agriculture; State Parks and Recreation Commission; Interagency Committee for Outdoor Recreation; State Conservation Commission; Environmental Hearings Office; Pollution Liability Insurance Program; Columbia River Gorge Commission.

Medicaid, and corrections (all of which have grown in their share of the state budget). Given these facts, it is very unlikely that a regional conservation strategy could be adequately funded by increases in sales, property, and business taxes, the primary existing sources of state and local revenues.

The second reason to seek alternative funding is arguably more profound: we must incorporate ecological costs into market decisions so those parties that create the costs pay for them (for a more complete discussion of these issues, see Durning and Bauman 1998). This would correct a structural problem in our economy that currently leads us to indirectly provide enormous subsidies for environmental degradation. Even a partial correction of this problem could raise far more money than the cost of my conservation program, and thus could provide for a significant reduction in general taxes.

A prime example, affecting all of us, is the lack of charges for water withdrawals, despite their enormous ecological cost. We withdraw about 250 billion gallons per year in Puget Sound (Lane 2004; R.C. Lane, U.S. Geological Survey, personal communication). This profoundly alters the natural cycles to which native species adapted in our rivers, creeks, wetlands, and even Puget Sound itself. A tax averaging one tenth of a cent per gallon (which could be higher in summer, when ecological costs are greater, or higher for larger withdrawals, to encourage conservation) could raise $200 million or more a year across the region (the total would not simply be current withdrawals times the tax rate because the tax almost certainly would reduce withdrawals—which, of course, would be a good thing). An average household uses about 150 gallons a day, so this tax rate would equal about 15 cents a day, or less than $5 a month.

A tax rate that rose with larger withdrawals would be more progressive. Agriculture, which makes disproportionately large withdrawals, might be exempted if it implemented water conservation practices, including water-efficient equipment that the larger fund could help pay for. (Such an exemption would recognize some of the ecological benefits of agriculture, as discussed later in this chapter. The exemption would lower revenues by about 15%, or $40 million.) Where water withdrawals are not metered, the tax could apply to the related water right. This would make the tax easier to administer and create an incentive to meter withdrawals and give up unused water rights, both of which are important public policy goals in their own right.

FIGURE 4-2. The Evergreen Floating Bridge over Lake Washington at rush hour. Highways and arterials are currently subsidized by general taxes. However, based on the ecological damage that roads and vehicles cause, the gas tax and other vehicle charges should pay much *more* than the full cost of constructing and maintaining our roads, not less.

A second example, affecting all of us, is a change to the tax on gasoline. Our vehicles and road system have profound environmental effects. Roads and parking areas account for about two-thirds of all impervious surface on the landscape (see Figure 4-2). These surfaces dramatically alter aquatic habitat, eradicating or drastically reducing many native species by changing flood patterns, decreasing flows, and discharging toxic metals, hydrocarbons, and other pollutants. Roads also fragment terrestrial and riparian habitat across the landscape, blocking or degrading the natural dispersal patterns and interactions of a huge number of species. Our vehicles are the major source of our region's most harmful air pollutants, including particulates and ozone that are responsible for public health problems (and probably many ecological problems, though this has received little study). The majority of greenhouse gases produced in the Puget Sound area are from vehicle emissions, thus contributing to climate change that may devastate ecosystems worldwide in coming decades. Lighting for streets is another subtle but important way we alter the natural environment, which affects a huge number of species that rely on darkness for important life functions.

Instead of incorporating these ecological costs into the cost of driving, by taxing gas for more than the direct cost of road construction and maintenance, we subsidize road construction and maintenance with general tax revenues at the federal, state, and local levels.[1] Road construction projects are required to mitigate site-level effects on the environment, but they generally do not mitigate the cumulative effects on ecosystem processes or their indirect effects on development patterns and vehicle miles driven.

Currently, the state constitution (Article II, Section 40) requires that all revenues from the state gas tax be dedicated to transportation projects, under an amendment passed in 1944 (which sought to ensure the availability of funds for highway projects expected after World War II; for a history of this clause, see Utter 2002). This same amendment expressly allows for applying the general sales tax or a special sales tax to gas for non-highway purposes, though currently gasoline is one of the few consumer expenditures exempt from our sales tax. Each penny of the state gas tax raises about $33 million each year, with approximately two-thirds coming from the Puget Sound region (E. Meale, Washington State Department of Transportation, personal communication). Assuming an average price of $3.00/gallon, extending the state sales tax (currently 6.5%) to gas in the Puget Sound area could raise more than $440 million a year for regional environmental protection and restoration. Local sales taxes could also be extended to gas, which could raise another $100 million for local environmental programs. This would not come close to accounting for the true ecological cost of our transportation system. (A 2002 study of gasoline taxes in Great Britain and the United States estimated that the tax should be 40 cents a gallon to address the costs of air pollution alone [Parry and Small 2004][2]) It would, however, be an initial step, which would not only raise valuable revenues for conservation but would also raise awareness of the environmental effects of our driving habits.

Other impervious surfaces besides roads could also be charged for their ecological costs. Local stormwater management programs are already funded by charges on impervious surfaces, with single-family residences paying a flat fee and commercial and multifamily developments paying variable rates based on their acreage of impervious area. If the legislature enacted a similar fee across the Puget Sound region, an annual rate equivalent to $25 per single-family home would raise approximately $50 million a year for ecosystem restoration (R. Rice, King County Water and Land Resources Division, personal communication). Such a fee could include lower per-unit rates for denser residential developments, credits for low-impact design elements (such as forest cover retention), and other adjustments to recognize ecologically preferred land uses.

A further source of new revenues would not directly affect most of us, but would address the single most important long-term threat to our natural heritage, namely the cumulative effects of development and land clearing as our population and economy

[1] Local jurisdictions, in particular, pay the majority of expenses for roads with non-transportation-related funds. For a discussion of federal highway financing, see http://www.fhwa.dot.gov/policy/1999cpr/ch_06/cpm06_4.htm; for a discussion of state and local financing of roads and highways, see Transportation Pricing Task Force 1999

[2] Interestingly, the study concluded that the tax was too high in Great Britain, at least for the costs considered in its study (which focused on air pollution, accidents, and congestion). British officials responded that the alternative was to raise taxes on income or other economic goods. They preferred a tax that discouraged an activity that causes so much damage.

grow (see Figure 4-3). The state currently authorizes local governments to charge "impact fees" to help pay for the new schools, road improvements, parks, and other infrastructure needed to serve new development. The environmental effects of development are similar to these other impacts—just as new development adds students to local schools and traffic to local roads, new development cumulatively alters the environment in ways that individual developments do not pay for. A one-time environmental impact fee of $5,000 for each new house—probably a low estimate of the incremental effect from new development—would raise more than $100 million a year. This fee could limit the developer's responsibility for mitigating off-site environmental impacts. That would lower some costs and add some predictability for developers, potentially leading to support from the business community.

Moreover, most local governments in Washington currently charge much less in impact fees than they could, meaning that, through general taxes, all of us pay the huge majority of costs for infrastructure that would be unnecessary if not for new development. This is not a political or economic necessity. Local governments in California charge the full cost of infrastructure to new development, typically $20,000 to $30,000 for each new house, though the charge can be much higher for large, expensive homes.

FIGURE 4-3. The Cottage Lake area east of Woodinville, (A) in 1936 and (B) 1996. Mitigating for growth project by project is doomed to fail. An environmental impact fee could take into account the cumulative impacts of development and help mitigate them where restoration would do the most good.

As discussed in detail in Chapter 10, the Washington legislature could require, rather than authorize, local governments to charge impact fees for all (rather than some) of the cost of new development. The legislature could also mandate that the new revenues be balanced with reductions in existing sales, property, or business taxes. This would help limit the effect of higher impact fees on affordable housing (which is generally not new construction) and the cost of doing business in the state.

State voters and the legislature have already recognized another obvious target for an environmental tax: pollution. In 1988, voters passed Initiative 97, Washington State's superfund law, which includes a 0.7% tax on the wholesale value of hazardous substances (Washington State Department of Revenue 2002; Dodge 2004). This currently raises about $50 million a year, which is used by the Department of Ecology and local governments to manage hazardous wastes. In 1991, the legislature adopted a tax on crude oil and other petroleum products delivered to marine terminals, which raises about $6 million a year for oil spill prevention and clean-up programs. Going back further, in 1971 the legislature passed a litter tax on sellers of goods that were deemed most likely to contribute to state litter problems, which currently raises about $6 million a year for litter clean-up and education programs. In 1987, the legislature also passed a $30 fee on the sale of wood stoves, which raises about $250,000 a year for education programs concerning the effects of wood stoves on air quality.

These existing pollution taxes suffer from a variety of inequities and administrative problems. Hazardous substances, for example, are defined based on the federal superfund list (under the Comprehensive Environmental Response, Compensation, and Liability Act) as of March 1, 1989, when Initiative 97 went into effect, regardless of changes in the federal list since then. The hazardous substance tax also does not apply to chemicals sold for home use, which includes the majority of pesticides sold in the Puget Sound region. Items covered in the litter tax similarly do not correspond with major sources of litter currently collected from state highways and public places, such as tires, automobile parts, and construction materials. Looking ahead, new pollution taxes could address many pollutants that do not fit into existing taxes. Some contaminants, such as water pollutants included in permits under the Clean Water Act, are easily quantified and attributable to specific sources, making them easy to tax. Collectively, new or reformed taxes on pollutants might generate another $100 million a year for environmental programs in the Puget Sound area.

All of these new revenue sources would require authorization by the state legislature. They probably would not require voter approval.[3] However, since a successful regional conservation strategy must have enduring popular support, key aspects of its funding should go before the voters to ensure that the support is there. If proposed taxes or fees would be collected and spent just within the Puget Sound area, a vote

[3] Initiative 601 limits taxes only for the state's general fund, as demonstrated by recent legislative increases in the gas tax without voter approval.

might be organized for just Puget Sound counties, though this would require reforms in governance like those discussed later in this chapter.

At the rates I have suggested, the sources of revenue in this section could raise about $1 billion a year in the Puget Sound region (Figure 4-4), about twice the estimated cost of my proposed conservation program. These new revenue sources could provide a reduction in general taxes of perhaps $500 million a year (roughly equivalent to $1.25 off property tax rates for every $1,000 assessed value across the region),[4] *after paying for a conservation program to preserve our natural heritage.* European countries have been shifting taxes in this way since the early 1990s, reducing taxes on income and wages while raising taxes on environmentally destructive activities such as air and water pollution, fossil fuel sales, water consumption, landfilling and water consumption (Brown 2001:237). The concept is easy to understand and potentially has widespread support, as was demonstrated by the national "Since Sliced Bread" contest, sponsored by the Service Employees International Union in 2005. Despite the fact that criteria for the contest emphasized social and economic issues,[5] the winning idea (chosen by popular Internet vote and submitted by Peter Skidmore, a Nature Conservancy scientist in Seattle) argued for environmental taxes similar in concept to my proposal (see www.sinceslicedbread.com).

Although an environmental impact fee on new development would legally need to be used to mitigate the effects from development, there is no reason why other new sources of revenue could not contribute to the state's general fund in addition to paying

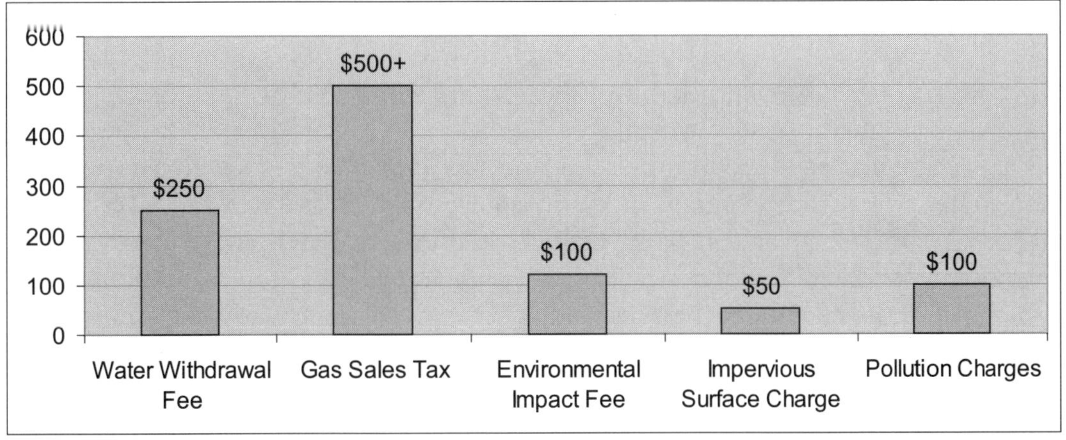

FIGURE 4-4. Potential annual revenue from ecological taxes in the Puget Sound region (in millions). Correcting current subsidies for environmental degradation could easily pay for an ambitious regional conservation program, with enough extra money to provide for substantial reductions in property or sales taxes.

---

[4] The total assessed value of the 12 Puget Sound counties was $370.5 billion in 2002, according to the Washington State Department of Revenue (Washington State Department of Revenue 2004).

[5] This is why I did not apply for the $100,000 prize. Sigh.

for an ambitious conservation program, just as "sin" taxes on cigarettes and alcohol can contribute to health programs and the general fund. (In fact, my proposal could be described as a set of "environmental sin taxes" akin to those on cigarettes and alcohol; both types of taxes are designed in part to discourage behaviors that create public costs.) The amount of the tax cut from my proposal would approximately double if we followed California's lead and started charging new development the full cost of the infrastructure needed to serve it, lowering general taxes an equivalent amount.[6]

The regional cost of the conservation strategy could potentially be lowered by attracting federal funds for implementation, as the Shared Strategy's leaders have hoped. Given the experience of other regional environmental initiatives elsewhere in the country, however, a large federal investment is unlikely. Even where the federal government has been a leading partner in developing large-scale restoration plans—such as for the Everglades, Chesapeake Bay, and the Sacramento River estuary—it has so far provided less funding than its projected share for implementation (Wiley and Canty 2003). Leaders for each of these three plans are now calling for larger federal investments (USACE and SFWMD 2005; CBWBRFP 2004; CB-DA 2005). The federal deficit and demands for funding from other programs have already led to large cuts in federal funding for a restoration study of the Puget Sound shoreline (Stiffler 2003). Even where federal agencies are directly responsible for major environmental initiatives, such as the Northwest Forest Plan, long-term funding is uncertain, as demonstrated by the plan's almost total reduction in funds budgeted for watershed restoration. I would not expect federal funding to pay for more than 10% of the cost of my proposal. The total cost to the region could also be lowered by expanding the use of transfers of development rights, as I discussed in my review of the Cascade Agenda.

Governance and the Urban–Rural Divide

As a practical matter, the most important issues for implementing a regional conservation strategy are setting geographic priorities for protection and restoration, establishing broad land-use plans consistent with those priorities, determining compensation and incentive policies for landowners, and raising and allocating funds for implementation. All of these issues are best decided at the regional level, across the entire Puget Sound area. Their geographic scope is beyond that of individual cities and counties, but it is much smaller than the entire state. A consistent state framework might be

[6] The state Office of Financial Management's median estimate for Puget Sound population growth from 2000 to 2025 is about 1.4 million, from 3.98 million to 5.36 million. If we assume 80% of this total population growth for 20 years and an average household size of two, this equates to about 550,000 homes. The low estimate for the cost of new roads, schools, and other infrastructure to serve growth is $23,000 per single-family home (see Chapter 7, page 46). Multiplying 550,000 by $23,000 equals $12 billion. However, some jurisdictions are charging impact fees already, average household size in the Puget Sound area is somewhat larger than two, and many new homes will be in multi-family buildings with smaller per-unit subsidies. This figure is high, but it also does not include any subsidies for commercial development and uses a low estimate for the cost to serve a single family home.

valuable if the rest of the state was ready to move forward with similar ecoregional plans, but how these issues are addressed in the Puget Sound region has little to do with most of eastern Washington, the Columbia River basin or the Washington coast. Because much of southwestern British Columbia is really part of the same ecoregion as the Puget Sound area, regional actions should be coordinated with Canada, but national boundaries make a fully unified program virtually impossible.

Puget Sound already has regional governing institutions for transportation and economic development. The Puget Sound Regional Council plans for transportation across King, Kitsap, Pierce, and Snohomish counties; it also coordinates with Thurston, Island, and Skagit counties (see Figure 4-5). The Council's plans guide federal and a large portion of state transportation funding. In the early 1990s, the Council also developed a strategic framework for economic development, which recommended thinking about the region's economy "as clusters of related enterprises, not as jurisdictional boundaries" (Puget Sound Regional Council 2001). The Regional Partnership, a public-private coalition that promotes economic development across King, Pierce, and Snohomish counties, argues that it is "a central reality" that "the three counties are a single economic region in competition with other regions

FIGURE 4-5. The 2005 annual meeting of the Puget Sound Regional Council. An ecoregional conservation strategy would require new regional governing institutions, reaching beyond the most urbanized counties where current institutions focus. Courtesy of Puget Sound Regional Council; William Wright, photographer.

throughout the world" (see www.regionalpartnership.org/faq.htm). Consistent with this view, in 2002 a leadership conference sponsored by the Greater Seattle Chamber of Commerce called for new regional institutions that cross jurisdictional boundaries, recognizing that "most of the regions of the world that we are competing with for economic development have organized themselves to pursue focused, long-term economic strategies" (Greater Seattle Chamber of Commerce 2002). Looking ahead, the conference report suggested, "There may be a Puget County in the future" (Greater Seattle Chamber of Commerce 2002).

Although the Puget Sound Regional Council and The Regional Partnership are not focused on environmental issues, transportation and economic development are obviously intertwined with land use, the most fundamental environmental issue. Moreover, despite the economic focus of the Chamber's leadership conference, the environment was central to its vision for the future, in which "our lakes, forests, clean air, pristine water, and fish are treasures that complement our neighborhoods and business centers." (Greater Seattle Chamber of Commerce 2002).

In 1989, *The Seattle Times* recruited Neal Peirce, a syndicated columnist and nationally recognized authority on urban affairs, to visit the metropolitan area and write a report on the key issues facing the region. For eight consecutive days, *The Seattle Times* featured his report on its front page (*The Seattle Times*, October 1–8, 1990). Peirce concluded that

> All of the top issues [for the Seattle metropolitan area] are indeed governance issues. There's not a ghost of a chance any of them can be dealt with until the region has some kind of a mechanism to drive the hard choices. That means a regional governmental authority empowered to decide the critical regional issues, the ones that in fact span city and town lines. [Pierce et al. 1993:97]

A governing body for a regional conservation strategy would have to reach beyond the most urbanized counties where current institutions focus to include the rest of the ecoregion, where most of the highest priorities for protection and restoration are located. It would probably be necessary that the governing body *not* be directly elected, at least by a region-wide vote, since voters from less developed areas would never accept being out-numbered on issues that will disproportionately affect them. As an alternative, elected officials from existing levels of government could be appointed or automatically assigned to the governing board of the new institution (e.g., it could comprise the 12 executive officers of the counties in the region).

The interests of rural residents, however, would still not truly be addressed by this, because even within their own counties they are outnumbered by urban residents (already a sore issue, since countywide elected bodies write the rules that apply in unincorporated areas; see Figure 4-6). I would suggest creating a rural council as part of the new governing institution. It could have directly elected representatives from the rural areas of each county (including farming, forestry, and "conservation" lands). It would have at least an advisory role with the governing body. For issues of greatest interest to rural residents, such as regional land-use plans and compensation for economic restrictions, the rural

PETITION FOR CREATION
OF
FREEDOM COUNTY

TO THE SECRETERY OF STATE: Please verify the below registered voters' signature who live in the area depicted below. We are declaring a new county under Article 11, Section 3 of the Washington State Constitution.

We desire to restore the American principles of freedoms and liberties upon ourselves, our senior citizens, our children, our farmers, our land owners and business owners and from this day forward declare our independance from Snohomish County.

(Legally described as T. 31 N., and T.32 N., R. 3 E. through R. 16 E. and that portion lying east of the center line of Hwy. 9 T. 30 N., R. 6 E. through R. 15 E. of Snohomish County, State of Washington.)

WARNING: Every person who signs this petition with any other than his or her name, or who knowingly signs more than one of the petitions, or who signs this petition when he or she is not a legal voter, or who makes herein any false statement, shall be punished [illegible] I have personally signed this petition. I am a legal voter in the State of Washington in the city (or town) and county written after my name, my residence address is correctly stated, and I have knowingly signed this petition only once.

RETURN THIS PETITION TO:
FREEDOM COUNTY

Call for pickup or more petitions

FIGURE 4-6. A petition to create Freedom County out of north and east Snohomish County. Following passage of the Growth Management Act and related local land-use regulations, rural unrest led to petitions and lawsuits to create new counties out of rural Snohomish and King counties. (The petition shown was an exhibit in a lawsuit.) While the courts ruled against these efforts, the sense of rural disenfranchisement is still widely shared. A successful regional conservation effort must provide political authority to rural areas that is proportionate to their contributions and responsibility.

council could have extra clout, perhaps requiring super-majorities from the governing body to override their recommendations. I believe rural residents deserve this sort of power because they have the greatest responsibility for the success of a regional conservation strategy, which depends so heavily on good stewardship of rural lands.

The governing body would also need an independent, interdisciplinary scientific advisory body, which could be appointed by the governor (perhaps from nominees proposed by universities and professional associations). This body might also be given extra clout on some issues, such as conservation priorities.

If taxes and fees for the conservation strategy are collected and spent just within the Puget Sound Ecoregion, popular votes would probably have to be organized across the 12 counties around the sound[7]. These counties approximately follow the ecoregion's boundaries, but not precisely. In particular, Clallam and Jefferson counties include parts of coastal Washington, while the wildlife corridor to the east of Snoqualmie Pass is in Kittitas County. An arrangement could potentially be made with the state for Puget Sound funds to pay for some coastal conservation, in return for the state paying for conservation in the wildlife corridor east of Snoqualmie Pass.

Under any scenario, the Seattle–Tacoma metropolitan area would contribute the majority of funding for the regional conservation strategy, yet see most of the funds spent elsewhere. If the executive officers of the 12 counties comprise the governing body, one way of protecting the financial interests of metropolitan area residents would be to require that actions by the governing body require both an absolute majority of county representatives and a majority weighted by population. I have seen this same formula work successfully to fund watershed planning across 27 jurisdictions in the Lake Washington watershed, where it protects the interests of Seattle, Beaux Arts Village and every jurisdiction in between them in size. The founding fathers of the United States solved a similar problem by requiring that legislation be approved by much the same two formulas, albeit in separately elected bodies, the House and Senate. But details of how the governing body should be structured are best decided through regional conversation, negotiations, and political compromise. People from across the ecoregion must feel they have contributed to the ultimate solution.

Reflecting on actual attempts to create regional institutions, authors in a 2000 report from the Brookings Institution counseled against "comprehensive solutions" except in rare cases:

> Reformers should focus on more modest initiatives that can succeed: creation of regional service districts, cost- and tax-sharing among municipalities and school districts, and area-wide land-use regulatory systems. [Yaro 2000:70]
>
> Metropolitan regionalism is best conceived as a political process that develops over time rather than something that is achieved in a single blow. [Weir 2000:149]

This is wise counsel. It argues for establishing a regional institution with no more authority than necessary to implement the conservation strategy. To the greatest extent possible, a new regional body should work through existing state agencies and local and tribal governments, though it will need some central staff, particularly for conservation science and administering grants. For better or worse, a Puget County that might address non-environmental issues would remain an idea for the future.

Creating a regional governing body would require action by the state legislature, which is the only institution with the requisite legal authority. Such a radical change probably could only happen in response to powerful political pressure. In the late 1980s and early 1990s, something like that led to the Growth Management Act. I believe it could happen again, if a broad enough coalition recognizes that we are bound to lose

---

[7] Clallam, Island, Jefferson, King, Kitsap, Mason, Pierce, San Juan, Skagit, Snohomish, Thurston, and Whatcom.

our natural heritage by staying on our current path, while an alternative that requires ecoregional coordination could succeed.

Denial: The Most Difficult Challenge of All?

Putting together a broad coalition and forcing political change faces one more enormous practical challenge: the human capacity for denial. In its way, this is the most fundamental challenge of all, grounded as it is in human nature, making every other challenge more difficult. The loss of our natural heritage, like the related issue of climate change, is a problem whose true extent is best measured over decades or longer. In both cases, the complexity and fluctuations of natural systems make it difficult to be confident of trends until they are well established. No one can doubt that our natural heritage has declined over the long term. However, because we have taken some steps to address this, it can be easy to argue that we have reversed the trend, or will reverse it if we just do a little more of what we have been doing. A more serious change, such as I have proposed, would be difficult and expensive; if it seems unnecessary, there will be many who will argue that we should wait and see. Those in power will be inclined to follow former Washington Governor Gary Locke's example, proclaiming that "extinction is not an option" while taking virtually no hard action in response to listings under the Endangered Species Act, even though the listings presume that extinction is likely without significant change.

In January 2006, I attended a conference in Portland called Salmon 2100, which addressed the threats salmon face in the Pacific Northwest over the next century. The day began with a sobering summary of the most important long-term policy drivers for the decline of salmon: regional population growth, increasing scarcity of water and other natural resources, global economic forces that drive cost-cutting behavior, and consumer preferences for lifestyles (bigger houses, cars, etc.) that conflict with the needs of salmon. I did not speak that day but contributed a chapter to a related book, where I largely summarized my arguments here. I believe they take these policy drivers seriously.

The conference was organized to give government leaders and policy makers the opportunity to respond to this analysis and to some of the policy proposals from the book presented that day. James Connaughton, Chairman of President Bush's Council on Environmental Quality, set the tone in the morning by praising the analysis of the challenge as the clearest and most concise he had ever heard, then completely ignoring it. He spoke only of harvest and hatchery issues, while the analysis mostly concerns habitat. William Ruckelshaus, the leader and spokesperson for the Shared Strategy, gave the keynote address over lunch. He never responded to the analysis, either, except to say that we should not give in to pessimism and that he was an optimist by nature. The rest of his remarks praised the Shared Strategy. The afternoon was filled with similar responses from leaders of salmon recovery efforts from Washington (represented by Jeff Koenings, director of the Department of Fish and Wildlife), Oregon, Idaho, Environmental Protection Agency, National Marine Fisheries Service, and the Bonneville Power Administration. No one seriously acknowledged the morning's analysis, although ostensibly it was the purpose of the conference to discuss the analysis and its implications.

The historic trend is clear. Despite the preference of our leaders for denial, there is no reason to expect the decline of our natural heritage to end without some profound changes in how we live—in particular, how we use land and water. Denial is made easier when the most serious losses take place incrementally, far away from where most of us live. These losses can be documented, but statistics and research are not the basis for a political movement. Ultimately, support for the kinds of changes I propose depends more on love of place and personal experience—on an intuitive understanding of the risks that our natural heritage faces—than on science. Ultimately, a successful movement will depend on our talking seriously with each other, and with ourselves, about the future of this place that we love, drawing from what we have seen with our own eyes and felt with our own hearts.

The Future of Agriculture: The Region's Most Important Land-Use Issue

I would like to conclude this chapter by discussing the future of agriculture in the Puget Sound region. I consider this our most important land-use issue as well as a valuable teaching tool regarding the practical challenges of conservation. Agriculture is the dominant land use in the ecologically vital floodplains of many of the region's most important rivers—the Skagit, Nooksack, Stillaguamish, Snohomish, Snoqualmie, Nisqually, and Dungeness—and in much of the south Puget Sound prairies. To those living in urban areas, agriculture can seem a minor activity in the region, but taken as a whole it is one of the region's larger business sectors, with nearly $1 billion in sales annually (USDA 1997) for all Puget Sound farms (about 20% of the state total of $5 billion). However, our farmland is being converted to rural estates (often of 10 acres or more) and suburban and urban developments at the rate of more than 8 square miles a year. In 1997, American Farmland Trust ranked Puget Sound (combined with the Willamette River valley) as having the fifth most threatened farmland in the country (Sorenson et al. 1997). The continuing loss of prime farmland is probably the worst land-use trend for the region's major ecosystems.

To be sure, farms are not necessarily an ecological boon. The most devastating ecological changes to the region's major floodplains came when they were first levied, diked, and drained for agriculture in the late 19th and early 20th centuries. Statewide, farmers use far more pesticides and withdraw far more water than any other user group (though in the Puget Sound area this is true only on a per capita basis, since they are so heavily outnumbered). Riparian buffers on farms are often small and degraded, providing little shade or filtration of pollutants and sediment. Clearing trees for farmland does not affect stream flows as radically as replacing forests with impervious surface, but the hydrologic change from forest to farm can be greater than the change from farm to developed land.

But farms grow and sell products that the rest of us need. Moreover, if the choice is between development and farms, especially farms with environmentally sensitive management practices, there is no question which is better for the region's ecosystems, particularly for birds and wildlife (see Figure 4-7). For example, the Skagit River Delta, even with its alterations, is home to the greatest number and variety of raptors in North America, including numerous peregrine falcons *falco peregrinus* and bald eagles *Haliaeetus leucocephalus* (Skagitonians to Preserve Farmland 2000). Every year, some 30,000 snow geese *Chen caerulescens* and 1,300 trumpeter swans *Cygnus buccinator* use farms in the Skagit valley for overwintering habitat (Skagitonians to Preserve Farmland 2003). In the region as a whole, about 70% of shorebirds and 90% of the migratory waterfowl use farm fields for food sources, such as residual grain, winter wheat, potatoes, and other crops (Skagitonians to Preserve Farmland 2003). Farmers are generally better stewards of the land than most residential or commercial property owners. When farms are converted to development, options for ecological restoration are lost forever. Puget Sound farms also provide not only fresh local produce but attractive open space for residents and visitors. Every year, between 300,000 and 500,000 people come to the Skagit valley to view tulips and daffodils (Andrews and Stuart 2003).

Nationally, agriculture is heavily subsidized, but in the Puget Sound region farmers generally subsidize the rest of us. Federal farm commodity payments are almost entirely directed to a small number of crops mostly grown elsewhere—corn, soybeans, barley,

FIGURE 4-7. Farms in the Skagit River delta provide overwintering habitat for 30,000 snow geese and other migrating birds every year. The future of existing farmland is the single most important land-use issue for a conservation strategy in the Puget Sound region. Courtesy of Terri Smith.

oats, cotton, rice, wheat, and oilseed crops (Boody 2002). Regional farmers do not receive the other largest federal subsidy to agriculture—low-cost water from federal hydro projects. Meanwhile, local governments and taxpayers make a profit from farms, which contribute more in local tax revenues than they require in services (American Farmland Trust 1999[8]). At the same time, the region's farms face major economic challenges from global competition. Labor, environmental, and land costs are lower in most developing countries. A few huge buyers dominate national and international food markets, shrinking the farmer's share of consumer food prices. The lower profit margins resulting from this squeeze pressure farmers to expand production, even as environmental regulations seek larger buffers and other costly improvements. Selling farmland for development often seems to make the most economic sense.

There are some bright spots in the picture. Federal and state farm programs are beginning to base more of their payments to farmers on conservation practices, which recognize the ecological services of farmland. Direct sales between local farmers and consumers have been increasing through roadside stands, farmers markets, and "community-supported agriculture" (where buyers sign up for regular deliveries of locally produced food). Direct sales reward farmers with a higher profit for their products; consumers get fresher, better-tasting food and more say in its production.[9] Direct sales could ultimately be the key to conserving farmland in the Puget Sound region. If the region's population purchased even 5% of its total food supply from local farmers, this might be sufficient to fully employ local farmland (Cascade Land Conservancy 2005).

Even so, I agree with the analysis of American Farmland Trust, which believes that existing programs supporting Puget Sound agriculture are too small and insufficiently coordinated to counter the trend of continued losses of farmland (D. Stuart, 2003 letter to P. Paquet, Northwest Power and Conservation Council). The Trust argues that agricultural assistance programs must be part of an interrelated package, for the following reasons:

- Investments in farm improvements, including conservation measures such as water-efficient irrigation or livestock fencing, only make financial sense if farmland is going to remain in agricultural use, thus providing sufficient time for a return on investments.
- Given the high price developers can pay for farmland in the Puget Sound area, keeping land in agricultural use frequently depends on purchases of development rights or agricultural conservation easements.

---

[8] The Cost of Community Services for Skagit County (American Farmland Trust 1999) study found that residential development cost Skagit County $1.25 for every $1 of tax revenue, while farms, forest, and open land cost $0.51 for every $1 of tax revenue, even with decreased taxes reflecting less than the "highest and best use" of the land. This result was consistent with studies by American Farmland Trust in 62 other communities across the country.

[9] All forms of direct sales have been increasing rapidly across western Washington over the past 10 years, particularly among vegetable growers, according to David Muehlerson, Washington State University Extension Program. Lecture in the Northwest Environmental Issues Course, The Mountaineers, March 22, 2004.

- In turn, agricultural easements can only succeed if farming the land remains profitable, which depends in part on enough farmers remaining in business to ensure that support companies, such as equipment dealers and feed stores, also remain profitable.

American Farmland Trust estimates that $60 million a year statewide for 10 years, split about equally between land easements, conservation improvements, and economic development assistance, could dramatically decrease continued losses in farmland and dramatically improve the ecological value of the farmland that remains (D. Stuart, American Farmland Trust, personal communication). A program targeting just the Puget Sound area might cost one-half to one-third of this amount. That is probably not far from the net tax contribution that Puget Sound farms are currently making to local governments (American Farmland Trust 1999). It would be a great regional investment, not just in conserving farmland and restoring habitat, but in healing the urban/rural divide.

References

American Farmland Trust. 1999. Cost of community services: Skagit County, Washington. American Farmland Trust, Northhampton, Massachusetts. Available: www.farmland.org/pnw/Skagit_County_COCS.pdf (March 2006).

Andrews, A., and D. Stuart. 2003. Economic impacts of agriculture in Skagit County, WA. American Farmland Trust, Puyallup, Washington.

Boody, G. M. 2002. Agriculture as a public good. Pages 261–275 *in* D. L. Jackson and L. L. Jackson, editors. The farm as natural habitat: reconnecting food systems with ecosystems. Island Press, Washington, D.C.

Brown, L. R. 2001. Eco-economy: building an economy for the earth. W. W. Norton & Company, New York.

Cascade Land Conservancy. 2005. The Cascade agenda: a 100-year vision for Pierce, King, Kittitas, and Snohomish counties. Cascade Land Conservancy, Seattle.

Dodge, J. 2004. Cascade pole site helped motivate initiative. The Olympian (March 14).

Durning, A. T., and Y. Bauman. 1998. Tax shift. Northwest Environment Watch Report No. 7, Seattle.

Greater Seattle Chamber of Commerce. 2002. From the 2002 Leadership Conference: a new style of leadership for a new era of economic strength. Greater Seattle Chamber of Commerce, Seattle.

Lane, R.C. 2004. Estimated domestic, irrigation, and industrial water use in Washington, 2000. U.S. Geological Survey, Scientific Investigations Report 2004-5015, Tacoma, Washington.

NRCC (National Research Council Committee on Protection and Management of Pacific Northwest Anadromous Salmonids). 1996. Upstream: salmon and society in the Pacific Northwest. National Academy Press, Washington D.C.

Parry, I. W. H., and K. A. Small. 2004. Does Britain or the United States have the right gasoline tax? Revised edition. Resources for the Future, Discussion Paper 02-12, Washington D.C.

Pierce, N. R., C. W. Johnson, and J. S. Hall. 1993. Citistates: how America can prosper in a competitive world. Seven Locks Press, Washington D.C.

Puget Sound Regional Council. 2001. Destination 2030: Metropolitan Transportation Plan for the Central Puget Sound Region. Puget Sound Regional Council, Seattle.

Skagitonians to Preserve Farmland. 2000. Strategic Plan 2000–2005. Mt. Vernon, Washington. Available: www.skagitonians.org/sp2005.cfm (June 2006).

Skagitonians to Preserve Farmland. 2003. Skagitonian. Director's notes. Mt. Vernon, Washington. Available: http://www.skagitonians.org/newsletters.cfm (June 2006).

Sorenson, A. A., R. P. Greene, and K. Ross. 1997. Farming on the edge. American Farmland Trust. Available: www.aftresearch.org/researchresource/foe2/report/foetab3.html (March 2006).

Stiffler, L. 2003. Puget Sound cleanup cash-starved: U.S. slashes money for the massive restoration project. Seattle Post-Intelligencer (November 20). Available: http://seattlepi.nwsource.com/local/149102_sound20.html (November 2003).

Transportation Pricing Task Force. 1999. The effects of the current transportation finance structure. Transportation Pricing Task Force, Puget Sound Regional Council. Available: http://www.psrc.org/datapubs/pubs/pricing2.pdf (March 2006).

USDA (U.S. Department of Agriculture). 1997. 1997 census of agriculture. U.S. Department of Agriculture. Available: http://www.nass.usda.gov/Census_of_Agriculture/1997/index.asp (March 2006).

Utter, R. F. 2002. The Washington State Constitution: a reference guide. Greenwood Press, Westport, Connecticut.

Washington State Department of Revenue. 2002. Alternative ways to pay for a clean environment. Washington State Department of Revenue report to the Washington State Tax Structure Study Commission, Olympia.

Washington State Department of Revenue. 2004. Assessed value of all taxable property by county. Available: http://dor.wa.gov/docs/reports/2002/Tax_Statistics_2002/Table27.pdf (December 2004).

Weir, M. 2000. Coalition building for regionalism. Pages 127–153 *in* B. Katz, editor. Reflections on regionalism. Brookings Institution Press, Washington, D.C.

Wiley, H., and D. Canty. 2003. Regional environmental initiatives in the United States: a report to the Puget Sound Shared Strategy. Evergreen Funding Consultants, Seattle.

Yaro, R. 2000. Growing and governing smart: a case study of the New York region. Pages 43–77 *in* B. Katz, editor. Reflections on regionalism. Brookings Institution Press, Washington, D.C.

Chapter 5. Be Patient, but Waste No Time

> When [the West] fully learns that cooperation, not rugged individualism, is the quality that most characterizes and preserves it, then it will have achieved itself and outlived its origins. Then it has a chance to create a society to match its scenery. [Stegner 1969:37–38]

I have always felt fortunate to have been born in the Puget Sound area. I went away for college and stayed away for seven more years, but reached a point when it was time to come home. In the St. Louis apartment where I lived at the time, I had hung a large watercolor painting over my bed of my favorite view from Seattle, looking out over the sound to the Olympic Mountains from Discovery Park. Friends who saw it asked incredulously, "That's in the *city*?" It was, in fact, about two miles from where I grew up.

I hope my children share my deep attachment to this area. Like all parents, I worry about the world they will inherit. Taking action to conserve our natural heritage will not protect them from every worry I have, but it is not irrelevant to others on my list. It can build relationships and institutions useful for addressing many other regional challenges. It can be a counter-example to the failures of our politics, and inspire us to address other needs. It is one of the best things we can do to strengthen our regional economy over the long term. Where it offers no direct help, it can still preserve, for our corner of the world, one of the most valuable and necessary sources of consolation we have.

We are as well-positioned to conserve our natural heritage as any region in the world. We are wealthy even by American standards, with an extraordinary concentration of philanthropic assets and a fundamentally strong economy based on knowledge-intensive industries such as software, aerospace, biotechnology, and health care. The natural beauty of our region inspires its own political support for protection. Even basic geography favors us, as Puget Sound dilutes and flushes out regional wastes and minimizes the environmental impacts of highly urbanized areas outside of their own individual river basins. Tribal treaty rights also give conservation in our region some unusual legal advantages (see Chapter 13), potentially providing crucial legal powers unavailable to most of the rest of the country.

The key issues of land and water management and natural resource tax policy are under our control. The federal government has important roles to play through the Endangered Species Act and Clean Water Act, funding, management of federal lands, interpretation of tribal treaty rights, immigration policy, and other issues, but I would argue that these are all ultimately peripheral to the central issues we have the power to decide. Most of the growth in our population is due to the migration of other Americans—not immigrants—to our region. There is no practical way for either us or the federal government to stop this. There is a limit to how much population growth our region can accommodate without ensuring the loss of our natural heritage, but we remain well below that limit now. We can choose between very different alternative futures.

Regional History Argues for Bold Action

The changes I have proposed are controversial and certain to incite opposition. A politician who would propose them today would fail. Elected officials cannot afford to get too far in front of their constituents, or they will not hold office for long. Opportunity for change must come from the bottom up. This must start with a widespread recognition that our current approaches, even if we throw more money at them, cannot solve our problem. It also must start with a recognition that we all want to solve this problem. No one commits his or her life to destroying our natural heritage. There are legitimate questions worth debating in any conservation proposal about private versus public interest, short- versus long-term gain, and environmental versus other values. I have proposed one potential solution, at least in summary form. The two crucial qualities for a successful proposal are that it must realistically address the relevant issues and that it must have widespread support across the region—urban and rural, Republican and Democrat, those who would accept the label "environmentalist" and those who consider themselves opposed to environmentalists. It will take time for any proposal to achieve those qualities. Advocates must be patient. But they also must talk with others inside and outside their normal circle about what they believe, why, and what it means for the natural heritage all of us share in this region.

Regional history can teach us some valuable lessons. In the 1950s and 1960s, civic leaders concerned about the Seattle area's explosive growth developed a series of far-sighted proposals to address the region's most important challenges. In 1958, on the second try, voters approved the creation of Metro to construct a regional sewer system to protect Lake Washington and the Puget Sound shoreline (see Figure 5-1). In the same elections, voters rejected a regional transit system and a regional planning agency. Ten years later, regional leaders came back to the voters with Forward Thrust, a set of tax proposals for major investments in community infrastructure, including rail rapid transit, parks, roads, and construction of the Kingdome. About half of the proposals passed, but rail rapid transit, which made up about half the cost of the total package, lost. Rail transit lost again in 1970, victimized in part by the Boeing Bust, the largest layoff in the company's history, which began that year.

Nevertheless, regional planning ultimately won out, through the Vision 2020 plan in the 1980s and the Growth Management Act that followed in 1990 and 1991. In 1996, rail transit won, too, when voters approved Sound Transit's proposal to build a 21-mile line from Seattle's University District to Seattle-Tacoma International Airport for $1.8 billion. In the years since then, the local share of the cost has increased to $2.7 billion for a 16-mile line from downtown to the airport (and for years threatenening to stop 2 miles short). The 1968 rail proposal was for 47 miles, which would have extended from Lake City and Ballard in north Seattle to Renton in the south and to Mercer Island and Bellevue in the east, at a projected regional cost of $385 million. In

METRO MEANS . . .

1. Seattle rule and domination.
2. Higher taxes.
3. Arbitrary property assessments, even if 100 per cent of property owners object.
4. Garbage collection, park purchasing and water installation can be added to sewers, planning and transportation without your vote.
5. Unlimited demands on the cities, towns and county for "supplemental income."
6. Tax-supported transportation system.
7. Granting unlimited authority to Seattle officials elected by and answerable only to Seattle.
8. Once Metro is voted in, there is no "getting out" or turning back. Seattle rules forevermore!
9. If Metro passes, the many constitutional and legal defects will result in years of expensive litigation, rather than any constructive action.
10. It is a grab for power by Seattle officials in the fields of transportation, planning, park purchasing, water and garbage collection in addition to sewers, clothed in the emotional appeal of "save Lake Washington now." Once this power is voted in the property owner is subject to unlimited taxes for any of the above purposes, at a time over which he has no further control or voice but solely at the pleasure of Arbitrary Seattle officials "who know what's best for their 'country cousins'." The second Lake bridge is a graphic example.

FIGURE 5-1. Anti-Metro propaganda from the 1950s. A conservation plan for the Puget Sound region in the early 21st century is likely to face worse opposition than Metro did, given that a serious plan must include new taxes or fees, new restrictions on many properties, an acceptance of localized losses where there is substantial new development, a general transfer of funds from urban to rural areas, and new governing institutions. Courtesy of University of Washington Press.

today's dollars, the regional per-mile cost for rail transit has more than tripled, from $48 million in 1968 to $169 million today. Besides saving money, a favorable vote for rail in 1968 would almost certainly have led to considerably less regional sprawl in the years since.

Similarly, in the mid-1960s, King County commissioned a study of how to best address flood control after voters passed bonds to build levees. The study noted that the Cedar River, which flows into south Lake Washington, "is the closest place in King County to the rapidly growing centers of population where wild lands, adjacent to clear, sparkling streams can be found" (Thomas 1964:26).

> Should King County acquire these lands and develop them into parks in such a manner as would permit high waters of the Cedar to do little damage, a general recreational benefit would accrue to the people of the county....As a matter of fact, the flood control funds disbursed on the Cedar River in recent years [about $3 million in the early 1960s (D. Clark, Water and Land Resources Division, personal communication)] would have covered acquisition costs of all lands along the river several times over (Thomas 1964:26).

King County did not follow this advice. Thirty years later, it produced a plan for the Cedar River with similar recommendations. By then, the estimated cost for just the highest priority acquisitions and restoration in the floodplain totaled $54.5 million (Watershed Management Committee 1998). This would have accomplished far less than the investment proposed in 1964, despite costing more than three times as much in inflation-adjusted dollars.[1]

Today, investments in protecting and restoring the Nooksack, Skagit, Stillaguamish, Snohomish, Nisqually, Dungeness, and Elwha rivers are rough parallels to investments in the Cedar River 40 years ago. The sooner they are made, the less they will cost and the more likely they will succeed. The same is true for investments to protect and restore Hood Canal, the Puget Sound shoreline, and the region's prairie habitats.

In 1853, more than 100 years before Metro and Forward Thrust were proposed and only 2 years after the first Euro-American pioneers settled in what became Seattle, a young adventurer from the East Coast visited the Puget Sound area. Awed by the region's wild grandeur and beauty, Theodore Winthrop believed that the human society destined to develop here would be inspired to greatness:

> Civilized mankind has never yet had a fresh chance of developing itself under grand and stirring influences so large as in the Northwest....No tameness of thought is possible here. [Winthrop 1913:210]

The realities of modern America have not always lived up to Winthrop's enthusiasm. Over the last century-and-a-half, our region has known both greatness and tameness. At times we have lived up to the promise of our surroundings. Today, the future of those very surroundings is at stake. No tameness of thought will save them.

---

[1] Based on the Consumer Price Index, $3 million in 1964 was equivalent to about $15.5 million in 1997, when the Cedar River Basin Plan was adopted.

References

Stegner, W. 1969. The sound of mountain water. Doubleday, New York.

Thomas, B. P. 1964. Comprehensive plan for flood control, King County, WA. Report prepared for the Board of King County Commissioners, Seattle.

Watershed Management Committee. 1998. Lower Cedar River basin and Nonpoint Pollution Action Plan. King County Department of Natural Resources, Seattle.

Winthrop, T. 1913. The canoe and the saddle. Franklin-Ward Company, Portland, Oregon.

Part II: The Relevant Laws

Chapter 6. Collaboration: Required by the Constitution

> [C]ooperation not only produces results on the ground; it also produces a unique satisfaction within its participants that they are then loath to let die....These feelings, these satisfactions, are fundamental to democracy as a human enterprise, and they are the core energy for any revitalization of "the Democracy." [Kemmis 2001:227]

Chapter Summary

As appreciation has grown for the need to protect biodiversity and ecosystems at a landscape scale, scientists and environmentalists have called for a federal "Endangered Ecosystems Act" to supplement the Endangered Species Act (NRC 1995; Noss 1999). Even if political conditions would support it, however, such an act would have to work within considerable limits set by the U.S. Constitution, including restrictions on what the federal government can regulate and how federal property must be managed. In the Puget Sound region, the state of Washington would have a somewhat freer hand with a similar state law, but the state would still have to work within limits set by the U.S. and state constitutions. Washington could not, for example, control the 40% of the ecoregion that is federal property. Checks on government power in the U.S. and state constitutions ensure that any attempt at ecosystem management across the region must be collaborative, encompassing all levels of government and the public and private sectors. Collaborative ecosystem management requires extensive compromise and patience (one book on the subject is humorously but accurately titled *Beyond the Hundredth Meeting* [Cestero 1999] playing off the title of Wallace Stegner's famous book on the American West, *Beyond the Hundredth Meridian* [Stegner 1992]). This is particularly true in Washington, where the state's constitution and laws disperse power widely, and deeply rooted political traditions limit the power of state government, deferring important decisions to local authorities.

Most major federal environmental laws were adopted in the 1960s and 1970s, after a period dating to the late 1930s when constitutional limits on federal regulatory powers were interpreted very broadly. Starting in the early 1990s, however, the U.S. Supreme Court began to reverse this approach. The Court did not directly address constitutional limits for environmental legislation, but two decisions that it issued regarding the Army Corps of Engineers' jurisdiction under the Clean Water Act were consistent with a narrower view than had held since the act was passed (*Rapanos v. United States*; *SWANCC v. Corps* 2001). In other decisions that the Court issued, it set further limits on the ability of the federal government to control the actions of state and local governments (*New York v. United States* 1992; *Seminole Tribe of Florida v. Florida* 1996; *Idaho v. Coeur D'Alene Tribe* 1997; *Printz v. United States* 1997; *Alden v. Maine* 1999).

Ironically, the federal government's ownership of land actually constrains its own ability to collaborate. Federal land management agencies must ultimately answer to federal officials, since all Americans own federal land. The agencies are generally prohibited from binding themselves to regional decision-making processes, which are often at the heart of efforts to protect large-scale ecosystems. It can be difficult for federal agencies even to participate in such processes, because of restrictions in the Federal Advisory Committee Act (FACA; U.S. Code, volume 2, section 9[b], appendix 2) and related regulations, which were originally designed to protect the public interest against special interests.

Providing the Puget Sound region some measure of direct control over how its federal lands are managed would require an explicit act of Congress or, arguably, a Presidential Executive Order. National environmental groups have generally opposed this type of power-sharing, out of fear that local interests would harm environmental values for short term economic gains. Their views may be changing, however, given how the second Bush administration has managed federal lands and the gradual rise in local support for environmental protection in some regions. Opposing power-sharing with local interests has arguably come at great political cost to environmentalism (and the Democratic Party) across much of the West, where the Republican Party now dominates in many rural areas (Kemmis 2001). The Puget Sound region could potentially be a national model for a new approach.

Property rights, protected by the U.S. and state constitutions, further reinforce the need for a collaborative approach toward ecosystem management. Throughout history, property laws have nearly always allowed owners to put their land to some use. Restrictions have focused on what uses are allowed and under what conditions. From an ecological perspective, however, ecosystems are already "using" land independent of human action. Successful ecosystem management across landscapes as large as the Puget Sound region would require prohibiting or severely restricting economic uses over substantial areas. The U.S. Supreme Court has ruled that the Fifth Amendment requires compensating property owners if regulations deny them all economic use of their property. Washington State's Supreme Court provides property owners even greater protections. Some compensation would undoubtedly be necessary for successful ecosystem management. However, success would also require the growth of a stewardship ethic among property owners across the region. Over time, this might lead to changes in the very nature of some property rights, which have evolved substantially over the centuries.

Constitutional checks on government power make it considerably easier to predict what a successful conservation program would look like on the ground in the Puget Sound area than how it might be implemented legally and institutionally. The latter can only be known well after the "hundredth meeting."

Federal Environmental Regulations and the Commerce Power

In the 1990s, the U.S. Supreme Court made a number of decisions to clarify—many would say reshape—the relationship of the federal government to the states. These decisions harken back to what Chief Justice William Rehnquist has called "first principles" (*United States v. Lopez* 1995:552), quoting James Madison from *The Federalist Papers*:

> The powers delegated by the proposed Constitution to the federal government are few and defined. Those which are to remain in the State governments are numerous and indefinite. [Rossiter 1961]

The authority to regulate interstate commerce is perhaps the least clearly defined of the federal government's "few and definite" powers. Until 1937, the Supreme Court took a narrow view of the commerce power out of concern that, were it to do otherwise, "there would be virtually no limit to the federal power and for all practical purposes we should have a completely centralized government" (*A.L.A. Schechter v. United States* 1935:548). As the American economy became increasingly national in scale in the early twentieth century, this approach frustrated numerous attempts to enforce federal laws governing working conditions and business practices. The Supreme Court finally reversed this approach in *NLRB v. Jones and Laughlin Steel Corp.* (1937). After that, the Court came to apply an expansive test of the Commerce Clause, asking only that Congress have a "rational basis" for determining that a class of activities it sought to regulate had a "significant effect" on interstate commerce.[1] The Court's recent decisions have primarily depended on whether a majority of the Court would grant that certain activities (such as possession of a gun in school [*United States v. Lopez* 1995] or gender-motivated crime [*United States v. Morrison* 2000]) met this test. In answering negatively, the majority has argued that doing otherwise "would require this Court to pile inference upon inference in a manner that would bid fair to convert congressional Commerce Clause authority to a general police power of the sort held only by the States" (*United States v. Lopez* 1995:567). ("Police power" describes a broad authority to make laws necessary for the health, morals or welfare of the public; it provides a legislative body wide discretion to define what these would require.[2])

In the field of environmental regulation, Congress rarely used its authority over interstate commerce until well into the 20th century. Before that, state governments were almost exclusively responsible for environmental issues. Courts had found that states were legally bound to manage fish and wildlife as a public trust, based on responsibilities they inherited from the British crown (*Martin v. Waddell* 1842:367). Important early congressional actions on the environment were mostly under its power to manage federal property, through the establishment of national parks, monuments, forest reserves, and wildlife refuges. As the 20th century began, President Theodore Roosevelt made unprecedented use of related executive powers to create 16 national monuments and dozens of forest reserves and wildlife refuges (Czech and Krausman 2001). Roosevelt led a shift in national policy from the prompt disposal of public lands into private ownership to the federal government's holding onto large tracts permanently, managing them for "multiple uses" (Fox 1981). This policy had an enormous effect on the West, preserving vast

---

[1] See *United States v. Lopez* (1995:557, 615). Justice Rehnquist's opinion notes that past decisions were not careful in distinguishing whether a regulated class of activities must have "an effect" or "a substantial effect" on interstate commerce. In his dissent, Justice Breyer uses the phrase "a significant effect" because "the word 'substantial' implies a somewhat narrower power than recent precedent suggests."

[2] See www.encyclopedia.com for a discussion of how the term has evolved in American law.

areas in a more natural state than would have been the case otherwise but entangling the federal government in land-use controversies it avoided elsewhere.

The first serious national criticism of state wildlife regulations grew out of the near-extinction of bison on the Great Plains. Congress passed a bill to limit the massacre in 1874, but President Ulysses Grant vetoed it, arguing that destruction of the bison was essential to pacifying the Indian tribes that relied on them. Further attempts at such a law, which could have provided an early test of the commerce power against state control, ended 2 years later with Custer's defeat at Little Big Horn (Isenberg 2000). The Lacey Act of 1900, the first major federal wildlife regulation, was a careful use of the commerce power. It asserted no direct federal authority, but prohibited the interstate transport of "any wild animals or birds" killed in violation of state laws (Lacey Act Amendments 1981; Bean and Rowland 1997). Dramatic losses of migratory birds—epitomized in 1914 by the death in captivity of the last known passenger pigeon, once the most numerous bird in North America—led to further federal action. An initial federal law to protect migratory birds using the commerce power was struck down by district courts based on the doctrine of state "ownership" of wildlife (Bean and Rowland 1997). This led the Department of Agriculture to urge the Department of State to complete negotiations for a treaty with Great Britain (on behalf of Canada), signed in 1916, to serve as a stronger legal basis for federal regulation. The treaty's implementing legislation, the Migratory Bird Treaty Act, was upheld in 1920 by the Supreme Court in *Missouri v. Holland* (1920). The decision, written by Justice Oliver Wendell Holmes, delivered "a stunning blow" to the state ownership doctrine and laid the foundation for much future federal action:

> The State...founds its claim of exclusive authority upon an assertion of title....No doubt it is true that as between a State and its inhabitants the State may regulate the killing and sale of such birds, but it does not follow that its authority is exclusive of paramount powers. To put the claim of the State upon title is to lean upon a slender reed. Wild birds are not in the possession of anyone; and possession is the beginning of ownership....But for the treaty and the statute there soon might be no birds for any powers to deal with. We see nothing in the Constitution that compels the Government to sit by while a food supply is cut off and the protectors of our forests and our crops are destroyed. It is not sufficient to rely upon the States. The reliance is vain. [*Missouri v. Holland* 1920:434–435]

After the *NLRB v. Jones and Laughlin Steel Corp.* decision in 1937, federal laws under the commerce power expanded dramatically on many issues, including the environment. In 1979, this expansion led the Supreme Court to note that it would have found the Migratory Bird Treaty Act equally valid under the commerce power, based on the migration of birds across state lines (*Andrus v. Allard* 1979: note 19). During this period of expansive interpretation of the commerce power, courts also found it an adequate basis for federal regulation of nonmigratory species, including those that do not cross state boundaries. This set an important principle for the Endangered Species Act, as articulated in this federal district court decision:

> [A] national program to protect and improve the natural habitats of endangered species preserves the possibilities of interstate commerce in these species and of interstate movement of persons, such as amateur students of nature or professional scientists, who come to a state to observe and study these species. [*Palila v. Hawaii Department of Land and Natural Resources* 1979:985]

Regulating Isolated Wetlands: The "Outer Limits" of Congress' Power

The Supreme Court's recent decisions have not directly addressed the commerce power's role as a foundation for environmental law. Nevertheless, they relate to a series of other recent court decisions that have narrowed the scope of the Clean Water Act (CWA). While these other decisions have focused on how the U.S. Army Corps of Engineers interprets its authority under the CWA, they also have raised concerns about the constitutional foundation of the CWA itself.

In 2001, the Supreme Court invalidated the Migratory Bird Rule, which the Corps of Engineers issued in 1986 to clarify the scope of the CWA. The rule stated that the corps' jurisdiction under the act extended to waters within single states,

(a) which are or would be used as habitat by birds protected by Migratory Bird Treaties or
(b) which are or would be used as habitat by other migratory birds which cross state lines or
(c) which are or would be used as habitat for endangered species or
(d) used to irrigate crops sold in interstate commerce [USOFR 1986].

The 5–4 opinion said this interpretation of the CWA "involves the outer limits of Congress' power" (*SWANCC v. Corps* 2001:172), which the majority found was not Congress's intent (overriding a united and passionate dissenting opinion). The majority emphasized that the CWA explicitly acknowledges Congress's intent to "recognize, preserve, and protect the primary responsibilities and rights of States...to plan the development and use...of land and water resources" (CWA, U.S. Code, volume 33, section 1251[b]). The majority also noted that the CWA continues Congress's historic use of the phrase "navigable waters" to define the act's scope, even though the dissenting judges noted the act redefines the phrase to mean "the waters of the United States, including the territorial seas" (CWA, section 1362[7]). Nevertheless, the 5–4 majority opinion found the Migratory Bird Rule exceeded the authority that Congress had intended to grant the corps.

Justice John Paul Stevens, writing for the four dissenting judges, noted that the final congressional report on the CWA stated that the phrase "waters of the United States" was to "be given the broadest possible constitutional interpretation" (*SWANCC v. Corps* 2001:181). He said that the act was "watershed" legislation that "endorsed fundamental changes in both the purpose and the scope of federal regulation of the Nation's waters....Strikingly absent from its declaration of 'goals and policy' is *any* reference to avoiding or removing obstructions to navigation [emphasis in original]." If the Court accepted that Congress intended to cover non-navigable waters used by migratory birds under the Clean Water Act, the four dissenting judges said they would find this constitutional:

> The destruction of aquatic migratory bird habitat, like so many other environmental problems, is an action in which the benefits (e.g., a new landfill) are disproportionately local, while many of the costs (e.g., fewer migratory birds) are widely dispersed and often borne by citizens living in other states. In such situations, described by economists as involving "externalities," federal regulation is both appropriate and necessary. [*SWANCC v. Corps* 2001:195]

Even Stevens, however, said that without a tie to migratory birds or some other element of interstate commerce, isolated wetlands, "which are themselves only marginally 'waters', are the most marginal category of 'waters of the United States' potentially covered by the statute" (*SWANCC v. Corps* 2001:197). Since the question was not before them, the dissenting judges did not say whether they believed Congress had the authority to regulate such wetlands.

In 1997, the Fourth Circuit Court of Appeals (responsible for mid-Atlantic states from Maryland to South Carolina) invalidated an even broader portion of the corps's authority under the CWA. The relevant regulation asserts the corps's jurisdiction over

> All...waters such as intrastate lakes, rivers, streams (including intermittent streams), mud flats, sand flats, wetlands, sloughs, prairie potholes, wet meadows, playa lakes, or natural ponds, the use, degradation or destruction of which *could affect* interstate or foreign commerce....[Code of Federal Regulations, volume 33, section 328.3{a}{3}; emphasis by the court in its opinion {*United States v. Wilson* 1997:257}]

The Migratory Bird Rule was just a subset of this regulation. Because the broader regulation does not require a *substantial* connection to interstate commerce nor "any sort of nexus with navigable, or even interstate, waters," the Fourth Circuit found that it "expands the statutory phrase 'waters of the United States' beyond its definitional limit" (*United States v. Wilson* 1997:257). The court noted that if the act itself had used the corps's definition, "at least at first blush, it would appear to exceed congressional authority under the Commerce Clause" (*United States v. Wilson* 1997:256). As with the 2001 Supreme Court decision, the court found that Congress did not intend such a broad definition. Throughout the states covered by the Fourth Circuit, the decision invalidated the corps's regulation of all isolated, intrastate non-navigable waters. In Washington State, which is part of the Ninth Circuit, the broader regulation still applies, minus the Migratory Bird Rule.[3]

Given the confusion ensuing from the decisions, in 2003 the corps and EPA issued an advance public notice that they intended to modify the regulations that define the

---

[3] The Ninth Circuit has ruled that the Clean Water Act applies to irrigation ditches and canals if they are connected to navigable waters (see *Headwaters v. Talent Irrigation District* 2001:3075). To settle a lawsuit threatened by the National Wildlife Federation, the Corps of Engineers has agreed to regulate wetlands adjacent to these tributaries under the Clean Water Act (see Wetlands protection expanded: critics warn northwest development at risk 2004).

CWA's jurisdiction over isolated, non-navigable waters within single states. They also sought public comment on whether the regulations should define "isolated waters" (USOFR 2003). These changes could have narrowed the CWA's regulations more explicitly than court decisions had done up to that time. After receiving a protest signed by 225 members of Congress from both parties, the Bush administration backed away from these plans (Pegg 2003).

In 2006, the Supreme Court returned to the CWA in a manner that mostly added to the confusion (*Rapanos v. United States* 2006). In what was widely characterized as a "4–1–4" decision, Justice Anthony Kennedy delivered the deciding vote, siding with the Court's four most conservative justices in a ruling that sent the case back to district court for reconsideration, but on grounds that had more in common with the four dissenting judges. Kennedy ruled that the corps's jurisdiction over a wetland must have a "significant nexus" with "navigable waters in the traditional sense," meaning they were "navigable in fact or susceptible of being made so" (*Rapanos v. United States* 2006: Kennedy opinion, 22, 21). Kennedy said this nexus could and generally should be based on ecological concerns, which he noted "may not align perfectly with the traditional extent of federal authority." He noted that this raises constitutional issues, but asserted without elaboration that these issues were not "sufficient to support a presumption against" his view (*Rapanos v. United States* 2006: Kennedy opinion, 25).

The other four judges in the majority called for a much more radical narrowing of the CWA. Their opinion would have limited the act to perennial streams, lakes, and marine waters, as well as to wetlands "with a continuous surface connection" to these water bodies (*Rapanos v. United States* 2006: Scalia opinion, 23). The four dissenting judges upheld the corps's traditional approach. The result, as Kennedy said, was that the corps, lower courts and regulated entities will have to determine which wetlands have a "significant nexus" to navigable waters on a case-by-case basis, until or unless the corps issues new regulations to clarify its authority.

I am not aware of any similarly serious recent attempt to use the commerce power to narrow the scope of the Endangered Species Act (ESA), the other most far-reaching national environmental law. But the ESA is potentially vulnerable to arguments over its constitutional reach for species that are found only within single states, have no direct commercial value, and are not protected by international treaties. Such a limitation would affect many listed species, including proposed listings in the Puget Sound ecoregion for multiple subspecies of Mazama gopher and a petitioned listing for the Island Marble butterfly[4] as well as hundreds of species in Hawaii and Puerto Rico. Lower courts have previously decided that the Commerce Clause provides authority for including these species under the Endangered Species Act (*Palila v. Hawai Department of Land and Natural Resources* 1979), but the issue may be raised again given the current Supreme Court's stricter approach to the Constitution. There is, however, reason to believe that past expansive decisions on the scope of the act would be upheld. In the leading recent Supreme Court decision limiting federal jurisdiction under the Commerce Clause, Jus-

[4] See Tables 8-1(b) and 8-1(c) in Chapter 8.

tice Kennedy (joined by Justice Sandra Day O'Connor) concurred with the majority but called the decision "limited" (*United States v. Lopez* 1995:568). In a separate opinion, they warned,

> the Court as an institution and the legal system as a whole have an immense stake in the stability of our Commerce Clause jurisprudence as it has evolved to this point. *Stare decisis* ["to stand by things decided," the general rule that courts should follow established precedent] operates with great force in counseling us not to call in question the essential principles now in place respecting the congressional power to regulate transactions of a commercial nature.

Fundamental Conflicts for a Federal Endangered Ecosystem Act

Given the economic values that depend on healthy ecosystems, a federal law to protect endangered ecosystems almost certainly could be consistent with federal authority under the Commerce Clause. For land owned by the federal government, it could provide valuable direction for land management agencies—the National Park Service, the U.S. Forest Service, the Fish and Wildlife Service, and the Bureau of Land Management (each agency began developing its own approach to ecosystem management in the 1990s, trying to integrate it with their other mandates to serve park visitors, support timber harvest, and so forth [Keiter 1998]). But a federal law mandating ecosystem management would face two fundamental conflicts: first, the federal government wholly controls very few of the country's ecoregions, which are mostly comprised of private land; and second, in ecosystems with multiple jurisdictions and ownership, federal land management agencies cannot bind themselves to collaborative regional decision-making processes, because they are answerable to federal officials.

Procedural requirements of the Federal Advisory Committee Act, originally designed to lessen the influence of special interests, can be particularly problematic for collaborative decision making (Cortner and Moote 1999). Congress amended the act in 1995 to ease collaboration with state and local governments, but the amendment did not address collaboration with nongovernmental agencies and private citizens (Keiter 1998; Cortner and Moote 1999). Moreover, the act still requires that

> Unless otherwise specifically provided by statute or Presidential directive, advisory committees shall be utilized solely for advisory functions. Determinations of action to be taken and policy to be expressed with respect to matters upon which an advisory committee reports or makes recommendations shall be made solely by the President or an officer of the Federal Government. [FACA, section 9{b}, appendix 2]

As commentator Daniel Kemmis writes (2001:129–130),

> At the bottom of this difficulty lies the fact that the collaboration movement represents a form and philosophy of decision making fundamentally different from the decision structure in which the [federal] land management agencies are embedded. One is an inherently decentralized, democratic form of governing; the other is inherently centralized and hierarchical.

Given the frequent opposition of local economic interests to federal environmental laws such as the Endangered Species Act and the National Forest Management Act, environmentalists have generally favored a centralized approach to conservation (Kemmis 2001). They have stressed that public lands belong to all American citizens, not just those who live near them. But the tactics of the second Bush administration have made it less clear that federal control is necessarily better for the environment. Moreover, environmentalists' opposition to local control on principle has probably turned away some potential allies. Kemmis (2001:168) comments,

> [P]eople who live and work, raise their families and build their communities, on a particular landscape cannot be and will never be persuaded by any amount of purely legal reasoning that people who have no such dependence on or knowledge of those landscapes should have an equal say in their governance. In the end, sovereignty [over public lands] cannot be a matter of raw legal jurisdiction. Unless the way people actually live in a given place—their living relationship with land and landscape—is made a part of the pattern of sovereignty, that pattern cannot be sustained over time.

As to private land, most regulations governing its use are set by local governments, often under some broader framework set by state law, such as Washington's Growth Management Act. A federal Endangered Ecosystems Act that directly regulates these lands would break both legal and political precedents. As the Supreme Court noted, even the Clean Water Act, which probably has affected state and local development regulations more than any other existing federal law, states that it is congressional policy "to recognize, preserve, and protect the primary responsibilities and rights of States ... to plan the development and use...of land and water resources" (CWA, section 1251[b]).

Other recent Supreme Court decisions on constitutional issues would further constrain a federal Endangered Ecosystems Act. The Tenth Amendment to the Constitution reads, "The powers not delegated to the United States by the Constitution, nor prohibited by it to the states, are reserved to the states respectively, or to the people." Interpreting this amendment in light of the original arguments for the Constitution, the Supreme Court has found that states have a "residuary and inviolable sovereignty" (*New York v. United States* 1992:190; quote from Rossiter 1961:245), which limits what the federal government can require of state governments (or local governments, which legally are considered subdivisions of the states):

> The Federal Government may neither issue directives requiring the States to address particular problems, nor command the States' officers, or those of their political subdivisions, to administer or enforce a federal regulatory program. It matters not whether policymaking is involved, and no case-by-case weighing of the burdens or benefits is necessary; such commands are fundamentally incompatible with our constitutional system of dual sovereignty. [*Printz v. United States* 1997:933]

The Court described the value of this dual sovereignty as follows:

> Just as the separation and independence of the coordinate branches of the Federal Government [executive, legislative, and judicial] serve to prevent the accumula-

> tion of excessive power in any one branch, a healthy balance of power between the States and the Federal Government will reduce the risk of tyranny and abuse from either front....In the tension between federal and state power lies the promise of liberty. [*New York v. United States* 1992:181]

An additional purpose the Court gave for limiting federal control over state governments is to help citizens hold the appropriate level of government accountable for its actions:

> [W]here the Federal Government directs the States to regulate, it may be state officials who will bear the brunt of public disapproval, while the federal officials who devised the regulatory program may remain insulated from the electoral ramifications of their decision. Accountability is thus diminished when, due to federal coercion, elected state officials cannot regulate in accordance with the views of the local electorate in matters not pre-empted by federal regulation. [*New York v. United States* 1992:168–169]

Under these rulings, not only is Congress prohibited from requiring that a state or local government administer federal regulations, but federal courts are also prohibited from directing that state or local governments "enact a particular regulatory regime that enforces and furthers a federal policy" (*Strahan v. Coxe* 1997:169[5]; an example in the Puget Sound area could be stream buffers of a particular size to protect listed salmon). A federal court can still strike down a state or local law if it violates federal law. The court must, however, allow the state or local government some freedom to decide how to come into compliance. Congress may also offer incentives to state or local governments "to adopt suggested regulatory schemes," including "the choice of regulating [an] activity according to federal standards or having state [or local] law pre-empted by federal regulation" (*New York v. United States* 1992:167, 190). In the case of the Clean Water Act, state governments have generally chosen to administer most aspects of the act, albeit with oversight from the Environmental Protection Agency. As discussed in Chapter 12, however, most states have chosen to let the U.S. Army Corps of Engineers administer the Clean Water Act's wetland regulations, in part because the act still gives them the authority to review and amend the corps' decisions to protect water quality.

Through a series of 5–4 decisions in the 1990s, the Supreme Court also found that the Constitution limits Congress's ability to authorize citizen lawsuits to enforce federal laws against states. Drawing on original arguments for the Eleventh Amendment, the Court majority has argued that states had "sovereign immunity" at the time the Constitution was adopted—meaning that a state government could not be sued by citizens on a given subject without its consent.[6] A large percentage of lawsuits to enforce federal envi-

[5] For a more complete discussion of this case, see Chapter 7, pages 124–125.

[6] The Eleventh Amendment states: "The judicial power of the United States shall not be construed to extend to any suit in law or equity, commenced or prosecuted against one of the United States by citizens of another state, or by citizens or subjects of any foreign state."

ronmental laws have been brought by citizens under clauses like the ESA's, which specifically authorizes such suits "to enjoin any person, including the United States and any other governmental instrumentality or agency (to the extent permitted by the eleventh amendment to the Constitution), who is alleged to be in violation of any provision of this Act or regulation issued under the authority thereof" (ESA, section 1540[g][1][A]). The Supreme Court decisions clarify which suits are constitutionally permissible. Though the decisions would probably block suits under the ESA against state governments unless a state has consented otherwise, they would not block suits against the federal or local government (*Alden v. Maine* 1999:757). It is unclear how this rule applies when local governments are implementing a state law, such as Washington's Growth Management Act or the Shoreline Management Act (Perkins Coie 1999).

Ultimately, however, these decisions should not have a large affect on the ability of citizens to enforce federal environmental laws against state actions. They bar citizen lawsuits against state *governments*, but they make the fine distinction of allowing them against state *officials* (even when the officials are administering enacted state laws), if the aim of the suit is to end "an ongoing violation of federal law."[7] A recent lawsuit against Washington State hatchery operations for violating the Endangered Species Act, for instance, proceeded against the director of the Washington Department of Fish and Wildlife but not against the department or the state directly. Such a suit cannot seek damages, but it can halt implementation of state regulations or programs found in violation of the ESA. The Supreme Court decisions could potentially block lawsuits by Indian tribes against the state (two of the three key decisions on these Eleventh Amendment issues involved tribal lawsuits against states).[8] However, in the Puget Sound area, lawsuits interpreting tribal treaty rights to salmon fall under *United States v. Washington*, filed in 1970. The federal court in that case has already established jurisdiction, which would likely be maintained against any challenge based on more recent Supreme Court decisions (R. Anderson, University of Washington, personal communication).

Property Rights: A Further Constraint on Federal, State, and Local Environmental Laws

The Fifth Amendment to the Constitution protects private property from being "taken for public use, without just compensation." The Supreme Court has established a two-part test for this restriction: compensation is required if a law regulating private property "does not substantially advance legitimate state interests or denies an owner economically viable use of his land."[9] In the 1980s, the court referred to this formulation in cases, but it never actually applied the second protection or explained it until 1992, in *Lucas v. SCCC.*

[7] This is known as the doctrine of Ex Parte Young; see *Seminole Tribe v. Florida* 1996:73–76 *or Idaho v. Coeur D'Alene Tribe* 1997:276–277.

[8] *Seminole Tribe v. Florida* 1996 and *Idaho v. Coeur D'Alene Tribe* 1997; the third case was *Alden v. Maine* 1999.

[9] Dicta in *Agins v. Tiburon* 1980:260; this formulation was quoted in *Hodel v. Virginia Surface Mining and Reclamation Association* 1981:295–196 and *Keystone Bituminous Coal Association v. DeBenedictis* 1987.

That decision, said Justice Antonin Scalia in the majority opinion, was based "on citizens' historic understandings regarding the content of, and the State's power over, the 'bundle of rights' that they acquire when they take title to property" (*Lucas v. SCCC* 1992:1027).[10] Scalia said that protecting property owners against the loss of all economic value from their land was required by "the historical compact recorded in the Takings Clause that has become part of our constitutional culture" (*Lucas v. SCCC* 1922:1028). In only one circumstance does the *Lucas v. SCCC* opinion allow a complete taking: when the loss is based on restrictions that come with the property's title, based on a state's common law regarding property or public nuisances. For example, in Washington State, tidelands and shorelands are considered to be in the public trust. Even if the state sells them, it retains authority to regulate them to protect "the paramount public right of navigation and fishery" (*Orion Corporation v. State* 1987:640). Some commentators have argued that *Lucas v. SCCC* could allow substantial protections for fish and wildlife, since common law continues to recognize them as a public trust (Bean and Rowland 1997). Scalia warned, however, against broad use of the common law or nuisance exception, stating that regulations "leaving the owner of land without economically beneficial or productive options for its use—typically, as [in the case of *Lucas v. SCCC*], by requiring land to be left substantially in its natural state—carry with them a heightened risk that private property is being pressed into some form of public service under the guise of mitigating serious public harm" (*Lucas v. SCCC* 1992).

The majority decision, however, like many others discussed in this chapter, was supported by only five of the nine justices. Justice Kennedy concurred in its judgment for the plaintiff but disagreed with its reasoning, noting that the plaintiff's beachfront lot arguably still had some economic value even if it could not be developed (*Lucas v. SCCC* 1992:1032–1036). The issue, Kennedy said, was whether restrictions against development are "contrary to reasonable, investment-backed expectations," which he said "must be understood in light of the whole of our legal tradition" (*Lucas v. SCCC* 1992:1034–1035). Valid restrictions, he argued, should not have to be based in historic common law or nuisances, but could be created by a legislature to address contemporary concerns, including ecological protection.

As Justices Harry Blackmun and John Paul Stevens noted in their dissenting opinions, despite Scalia's reference to a "historical compact," history does not necessarily support the majority in *Lucas v. SCCC*. Both dissenting justices' opinions cited numerous cases dating from before passage of the Bill of Rights through the 1992 decision that upheld regulations denying all economic uses of property.

The Historical Evolution of Property Rights

Because both sides in the *Lucas v. SCCC* decision based their claims on history, it is valuable to step back for a brief review of how property rights have evolved over time.

[10] The "bundle" commonly includes the ability to exclude others, to occupy the land and put it to use, and to convey title to others, including one's heirs (McElfish 1994).

Since government must ultimately enforce property rights, at least some of the framers of the U.S. Constitution thought government was free to set the rules:

> Government must be established and laws provided, before lands can be separately appropriated, and their owner protected in his possession. Till then, the property is in the body of the nation, and they, or their chief as trustee, must grant them to individuals, and determine the conditions of the grant.—Thomas Jefferson [Washington 1859, cited by Talmadge 2000:867]

> Private property therefore is a creature of society, and is subject to the calls of that society, whenever its necessities shall require it, even to its last farthing; its contributions therefore to the public exigencies are not to be considered as conferring a benefit on the publick [sic], entitling the contributors to the distinctions of honor and power, but as the return of an obligation previously received, or the payment of a just debt. [Benjamin Franklin; Smyth 1907, cited in McElfish 1994:10234]

> The right to use all property, must be subject to modification by municipal law. *Sic utere tuo ut alienum non loedas* [use your property so as not to harm another's] is a fundamental maxim. It belongs exclusively to the local State Legislatures, to determine how a man may use his own, without injuring his neighbor.—John Marshall, First Chief Justice of the United States Supreme Court [*Gibbons v. Ogden* 1824:53–54, cited in Talmadge 2000:868]

At the time the Constitution was debated, property law in the United States was still inherited from Great Britain. British law emphasized the right of property owners to "quiet enjoyment," which protected them from injuries caused by their neighbors' use of land, such as water or air pollution or blocked sunlight (Horwitz 1977, cited in McElfish 1994:10237). This right, central to the interests of the landed English gentry, was incorporated into early American laws controlling the locations for slaughterhouses, distilleries, and other land uses often unpopular with neighbors. Laws inherited from the British tended to limit property owners to "natural," typically agrarian, uses of their land, or to uses that did not interfere with previously established uses on surrounding lands. As the 19th century progressed, however, this approach was at odds with the needs of an industrializing economy. The evolving economy required a balancing of interests that could not regularly block new uses of land and that allowed for economic organization on an increasingly large scale. However, some limits on the uses of property to protect the public welfare were all the more important in an industrialized economy. These limits took the form of regulatory legislation, which was challenged in the courts but gradually became accepted in the late 19th and early 20th centuries. In a classic decision, after state courts issued conflicting opinions on local zoning laws, the U.S. Supreme Court upheld zoning laws in 1926, commenting as follows:

> Until recent years, urban life was comparatively simple; but with the great increase and concentration of population, problems have developed, and constantly are developing, which require...additional restrictions in respect of the use and occupation of private lands....Regulations, the wisdom, necessity and validity of which, as applied to existing conditions, are so apparent that they are now uni-

> formly sustained, a century ago, or even half a century ago, probably would have been rejected as arbitrary and oppressive. [*Euclid v. Ambler Co.* 1926:386–387]

Local zoning laws, the Court said, were constitutional unless they were "clearly arbitrary and unreasonable, having no substantive relation to the public health, safety, morals, or general welfare."

As to other regulatory restrictions on land uses, courts frequently quoted Justice Oliver Wendell Holmes' vague maxim from 1922 that, "while property may be regulated to a certain extent, if regulation goes too far it will be recognized as a taking" (*Pennsylvania Coal Co. v. Mahon* 1922:415). As Scalia said in *Lucas v. SCCC*, in the 70 years following that case the Supreme Court "generally eschewed any 'set formula' for determining how far is too far, preferring to engage in essentially ad hoc, factual inquiries" (*Goldblatt v. Hempstead* 1962:594, cited in *Lucas v. SCCC* 1992:1015), which weighed the economic impact of regulations on property owners against the public interest served by the regulations. In his dissent in *Lucas v. SCCC*, Justice Blackmun quoted a Supreme Court decision from 1978 that said the Court's prior decisions "uniformly reject the proposition that diminution in property value, standing alone, can establish a 'taking'" (*Penn Central Transportation Co. v. New York City* 1978:131). Blackmun commented:

> These cases rest on the principle that the State has full power to prohibit an owner's use of property if it is harmful to the public. "Since no individual has a right to use his property so as to create a nuisance or otherwise harm others, the State has not 'taken' anything when it asserts its power to enjoin the nuisance-like activity." [Quoting *Keystone Bituminous Coal Association v. DeBenedictis* 1987:491]

Lucas v. An Ecological Worldview

In a fascinating article on *Lucas v. SCCC*, University of California Law Professor Joseph Sax argued that the decision is best understood as the Court's response to the new challenges an ecological worldview presents to property rights (1993). Regulations have traditionally assumed that land will be put to human use; the focus has been on what uses are allowed and under what conditions. As Sax says, however, from an ecological perspective, "Land is already at work, performing important services in its unaltered state." It is possible—in fact, if the strategy for protecting the Puget Sound ecoregion described in Chapter 3 is followed, it is *necessary*—that for substantial parts of the landscape, *any* human use could be regarded as sufficiently harmful to ecological values that it should be prohibited. From an ecological perspective, Sax (1993:1445) says:

> the landowner's role is perforce custodial at the outset, before the owner ever transforms the land. Moreover, the object of the custody generally extends beyond the owner's legally defined dominion [e.g., it is part of a watershed]. The notion that land is solely the owner's property, to develop as the owner pleases, is unacceptable.

This directly challenges what Sax calls "the very heart of the *Lucas* opinion—the concept that property ownership confers positive developmental rights." Under *Lucas v. SCCC*, the right to put land to use, not the ecological role the land already plays, is fundamental. *Lucas v. SCCC* characterizes protecting the land's pre-existing ecological functions as "pressing it into service." Yet as Sax notes, the current law's emphasis on an owner's right to develop is "a product of a modern economy that...destroyed common rights in property because such rights were no longer functional in a capitalist society."

American courts could have responded differently to the ecological perspective on land, and at first some courts did. In a classic example from 1972, the Wisconsin Supreme Court heard a case that challenged a law requiring a special permit for any change to the natural character of land within 1,000 feet of a navigable lake or 300 feet of a navigable river. Prior to the law's adoption, the plaintiffs had purchased lakefront property, subdivided it, and sold five parcels. The Wisconsin Supreme Court ruled against the plaintiffs, arguing that

> [a]n owner of land has no absolute and unlimited right to change the essential natural character of his land so as to use it for a purpose for which it was unsuited in its natural state and which injures the rights of others. The exercise of the police power in zoning must be reasonable and we think it is not an unreasonable exercise of that power to prevent harm to public rights by limiting the use of private property to its natural uses. [*Just v. Marinette County* 1972, cited in Sax 1993]

Sax anticipates that courts will move toward this view and away from *Lucas* as they increasingly recognize the ecological services certain lands provide:

> A consensus concerning the range of acceptable burdens on landowners will doubtless emerge—just as during industrialization, society determined the extent to which land owners would have to tolerate the new burdens of modernity, such as noise, traffic, and pollution. [Sax 1993:1454]

Such a consensus might approve regulations that completely eliminate any economic use of a landowner's property in some cases, but still treat such losses as automatic triggers for heightened judicial scrutiny.

"Substantive Due Process": Washington Courts Provide Even More Protection to Property Owners

Prior to *Lucas v. SCCC*, Washington State's Supreme Court had taken a less restrictive view of what constituted a regulatory taking: a regulation was not a taking if it was reasonably related to safeguarding "the public interest in health, safety, the environment or the fiscal integrity of an area" and did not destroy "one or more of the fundamental attributes of ownership—the right to possess, to exclude others and to dispose of property" (*Presbytery of Seattle v. King County* 1990:329, 330; WAGO 1995). An environmental regulation could therefore eliminate economic uses of a property without compensation if the owner retained these three rights. This aspect of Washington's property law is now superseded by *Lucas v. SCCC*. In some cases, however, Washington provides more protection for property owners than federal law does. If a court finds that a regulation is not primarily intended to prevent harm to the public interest but to confer a positive benefit to other publicly owned property, or if the regulation destroys one of the rights of ownership, under Washington law a takings analysis is triggered (*Presbytery of Seattle v. King County* 1990:329). The state supreme court has noted that determining whether the predominant goal of a given regulation is to prevent public harm or to confer a public benefit "must be made according to the facts of the case" and "will not always be an easy decision." Commenting on the same issue in *Lucas v. SCCC*, Scalia said, "Whether one or the other of the competing characterizations will come to one's lips in a particular case depends primarily upon one's evaluation of the worth of competing uses of real estate" (*Lucas v. SCCC* 1992:1025).

A takings analysis, according to Washington's Supreme Court, first considers whether the regulation "substantially advances legitimate state interests" (*Presbytery of Seattle v. King County* 1990:335, 336). If the regulation does not advance state interests, then it is a taking. If the regulation does advance legitimate interests, the court has found that it may still be a taking, based on "(1) the economic impact of the regulation on the property; (2) the extent of the regulation's interference with investment-backed expectations; and (3) the character of the government action."[11] (See Figure 6-1.) If a regulation exacts a taking, even for a limited time, the government must compensate the property owner for the loss.

Beyond takings, Washington State Supreme Court rulings also protect property owners against regulations that would deprive them of their property "without due process of law," in violation of the state constitution and the Fourteenth Amendment to the U.S. Constitution.[12] The purpose of this protection, the court has said, "is to prevent excessive police power regulations that would require an individual 'to shoulder an economic burden, which in justice and fairness the public should rightfully bear'" (*Weden v. San Juan County* 1998:706, quoting *Orion Corp vs. State* 1987:648–649). If a regulation does not exact a taking but violates "substantive due process," the government owes no compensation but the regulation is invalidated (*Presbytery of Seattle v. King County* 1990:332). The court noted that this "avoids intimidating the legislative body," which might not risk adopting regulations that could lead to a costly judgment against the government. To determine a violation of substantive due process, the court applies "the classic three-prong due process test":

(1) Whether the regulation is aimed at achieving a legitimate public purpose,
(2) Whether it uses means that are reasonably necessary to achieve that purpose, and
(3) Whether it is unduly oppressive on the landowner.

---

[11] An example of a taking based on the character of a government action would be a right of public access to private property, unless it is necessary to mitigate a harm directly caused by the land use, such as an easement to inspect or maintain stormwater facilities.

[12] Washington State Constitution, Article I, Section 3: "No person shall be deprived of life, liberty, or property, without due process of law."

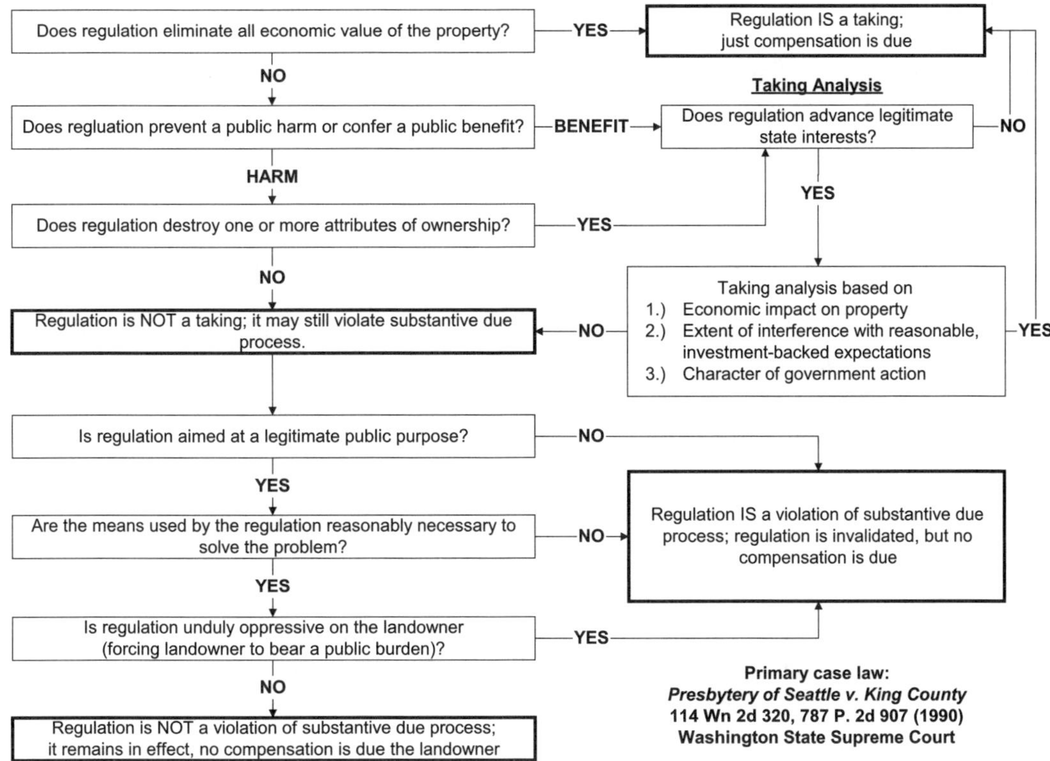

FIGURE 6-1. Washington legal tests for property "takings" or violations of substantive due process.

The third prong, the court has said, "will usually be the difficult and determinative one" (*Presbytery of Seattle v. King County* 1990:331). The court has suggested a number of different factors for evaluating the third prong, including "the nature of the harm sought to be avoided; the availability and effectiveness of less drastic protective measures; and the economic loss suffered by the property owner." Elaborating on how public and private interests should be balanced in considering possible violations of substantive due process, the court suggested the following factors, while acknowledging that others might also be relevant:

> On the public's side, the seriousness of the public problem, the extent to which the owner's land contributes to it, the degree to which the proposed regulation solves it and the feasibility of less oppressive solutions would all be relevant. On the owner's side, the amount and percentage of value loss; the extent of remaining uses, past, present and future uses, temporary or permanent nature of the regulation, the extent to which the owner should have anticipated such regulation and how feasible it is for the owner to alter present or planned uses. [*Presbytery of Seattle v. King County* 1990:331]

"How far is too far" remains a judgment call without any "set formula."

Additional Unique Conditions on Ecosystem Management in Washington

The state constitution, together with state laws that govern the management of key natural resource agencies, set additional unique conditions on ecosystem management in Washington. Amending the state constitution is a serious challenge, requiring a two-thirds vote of both houses of the legislature and support from a majority of voters statewide (Article XXIII, Section 1). Article XV, Section 1 of the constitution mandates that "harbors, estuaries, bays and inlets" within 1 mile of the "corporate limits of any city...shall be forever reserved for landings, wharves, streets, and other conveniences of navigation and commerce." This could potentially restrict ecological protection or restoration in these areas, unless these activities serve as mitigation for the effects of navigation and commerce. Article XVII, Section 1 asserts state ownership of "the beds and shores of all navigable waters in the state up to and including the line of ordinary high tide, in waters where the tide ebbs and flows, and up to and including the line of ordinary high water within the banks of all navigable rivers and lakes." This provision strengthens opportunities for ecological protection and restoration, but it does not bar the state from selling this land. Less than a year after the state constitution was adopted, the legislature authorized the sale of land between the high and low tides (WDNR 2000a). By 1971, when the legislature prohibited further such sales, only 40% of tidelands in the Puget Sound area remained in state ownership (Bish 1982), predominantly along the shores of the Strait of Juan de Fuca, the San Juan Islands, and Whidbey Island. Nearly all of the tidelands along Puget Sound's eastern shore and Hood Canal are now privately owned (see Figure 6-2). The state and local governments can still regulate how private tidelands are used, but state projects to restore ecological functions are restricted to the properties it owns (WDNR 2000b).

Washington gained statehood in 1889 and its constitution reflects the Progressive Era's heightened concern over the powers of government. It allows voters to pass their own laws, to reject laws passed by the legislature, and to recall elected officials. It also provides substantial autonomy to local governments by authorizing counties, cities, and towns to "make and enforce within [their] limits all such local police, sanitary and other regulations as are not in conflict with general laws" (Article XI, Section 11). In contrast to Oregon, which gained statehood thirty years earlier, Washington's Constitution disperses the executive power of the governor across nine separately elected officials, including the lieutenant governor, the attorney general, and the commissioner of public lands. State laws governing the Departments of Fish and Wildlife, Natural Resources, and Parks and Recreation further disperse policy-making power to appointed commissions:

- The Fish and Wildlife Commission must approve all state fish and wildlife regulations, budget proposals for the Department of Fish and Wildlife, and tribal, interstate, or international agreements that concern fish and wildlife (Revised Code of Washington [RCW] 77.04.055).
- The Board of Natural Resources must approve policies and regulations governing

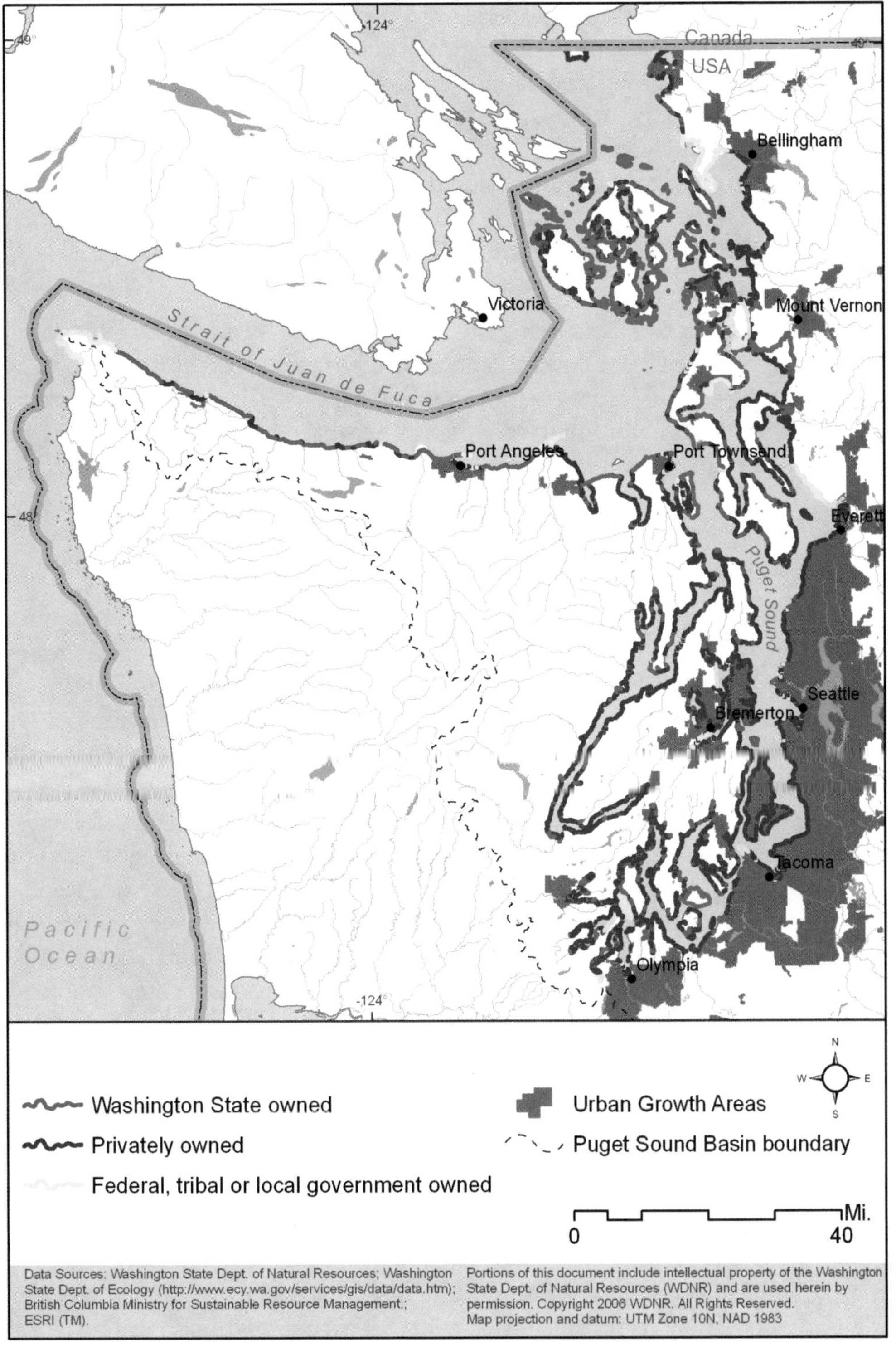

FIGURE 6-2. Ownership of Puget Sound tidelands. Notice that state ownership is concentrated in the north sound and along the Strait of Juan de Fuca.

"the acquisition, management, and disposition of all lands and resources" under the jurisdiction of the Department of Natural Resources (RCW 43.30.215; this covers 2.1 million acres of forest land and 2.6 million acres of aquatic lands).

- The Forest Practices Board must approve all regulations governing forest practices on state and private land (RCW 76.09.030).
- The Parks and Recreation Commission must approve state park policies and regulations as well as purchases for the state park system. It also oversees numerous administrative duties of the state Parks and Recreation Department (RCW 79A.05.030).

This dispersion of power is consistent with and reinforces Washington's long tradition of limiting the power of state government and deferring important decisions to local authorities. This tradition is discussed further in Chapter 10, comparing growth management laws in Washington and Oregon, and Chapter 11, regarding Washington's emphasis on watershed planning as the primary means to resolve conflicts over water use.

Broad Consensus: Essential to Successful Ecosystem Management in Puget Sound

Successful ecosystem management in the Puget Sound region, then, requires extensive collaboration between the federal, state, and local governments and the private and public sectors. The U.S. Constitution limits the roles that the federal government can play, and Washington State's Constitution, laws, and political traditions limit the roles that state government can play. In the face of continued population growth, successful ecosystem management in the region would decrease development potential and accompanying tax revenues in some areas (mostly rural), authorize greater housing densities and localized environmental losses in other areas (mostly urban), and raise taxes to pay for habitat purchases and restoration, which would generally transfer money from urban to rural areas. Implementing such large yet different sacrifices across the region would be an enormous political challenge. Success would require a broad consensus across urban and rural areas over a long-term vision for the regional landscape. This consensus would need to cross political party lines to provide a stable foundation for action over decades and to help develop and maintain consistent federal policies over the management of federal lands in the region.

Such a consensus would be impossible without widespread acceptance of a stewardship ethic by landowners in the region. A stewardship ethic is also necessary because there will never be enough public money to buy all of the property that must contribute to healthy ecosystems. If such an ethic would take hold, it might contribute to an evolution in how property rights are defined, as Sax suggests. It surely would affect how courts define "reasonable investment-backed expectations" of property owners. A stewardship ethic also would affect the extent to which a conservation strategy for the region might pay landowners for ecological services. Urban property owners have accepted extensive local regulations limiting what they can do with their land for approximately a century. Since ecological values are highest in rural areas, successful ecosystem management would generally require the most stringent restrictions there, in a part of the region especially resistant to restrictions on land use. Achieving regional consensus would almost certainly require some compensation to landowners hardest hit by the new regional vision. How much this compensation should be will depend in part on judgments of "how far is too far" to accomplish conservation through regulations.

Washington State's environmental laws and the way the Puget Sound region has responded to federal environmental laws provide one of the best starting points for regional ecosystem management in the country. The Growth Management Act, watershed planning for salmon recovery, and forest practices on public and private lands in the state are examples of progress toward successful ecosystem management that have few parallels elsewhere. Nevertheless, as later chapters on these subjects discuss, the region still has far to go if it is to match its political and legal institutions to the "time and space scales" of its major ecosystems (NRC 1996).

References

Agins v. Tiburon, 447 U.S. 255 (1980).

A.L.A. Schechter v. United States, 295 U.S. 495 (1935).

Alden v. Maine, 527 U.S. 706 (1999).

Andrus v. Allard, 444 U.S. 63 (1979).

Bean, M. J., and M. F. Rowland. 1997. The evolution of national wildlife law. Praeger Publishers, Westport, Connecticut.

Bish, R. L. 1982. Governing Puget Sound. University of Washington Press, Seattle.

Cestero, B. 1999. Beyond the hundredth meeting: a field guide to collaborative conservation of the West's public lands. Sonoran Institute, Tucson, Arizona.

Cortner, H. J., and M. A. Moote. 1999. The politics of ecosystem management. Island Press, Washington, D.C.

Czech, B., and P. R. Krausman. 2001. The Endangered Species Act: history, conservation biology and public policy. Johns Hopkins University Press, Baltimore, Maryland.

Euclid v. Ambler Co., 272 U.S. 365 (1926).

Fox, S. R. 1981. The American Conservation Movement: John Muir and his legacy. University of Wisconsin Press, Madison.

Gibbons v. Ogden, 22 U.S. 1, 53–54 (9 Wheat. 1824)

Goldblatt v. Hempstead, 369 U.S. 590 (1962).

Headwaters v. Talent Irrigation District, No.99-35373 (9th Cir. 2001).

Hodel v. Virginia Surface Mining and Reclamation Association, 452 U.S. 264 (1981).

Horwitz, M. J. 1977. The transformation of American law, 1780-1860. Harvard University Press, Cambridge, Massachusetts.

Idaho v. Coeur D'Alene Tribe, 521 U.S. 261 (1997).

Isenberg, A. C. 2000. The destruction of the bison. Cambridge University Press, New York.

Just v. Marinette County, 201 N.W. 2d 761 (Wis. 1972).

Keiter, R. B. 1998. Ecosystems and the law: toward an integrated approach. Ecological Applications 8(2):332–341.

Kemmis, D. 2001. This sovereign land: a new vision for governing the West. Island Press, Washington, D.C.

Keystone Bituminous Coal Association v. DeBenedictis, 480 U.S. 470 (1987).

Lacey Act Amendments. 1981. U.S. Code, volume 16, sections 3371–3378, volume 18, section 42.
Lucas v. SCCC (South Carolina Coastal Council), 505 U.S. 1003 (1992).
Martin v. Waddell, 41 U.S. 16 Pet. 367 (1842).
McElfish, J. M. 1994. Property rights, property roots: rediscovering the basis for legal protection of the environment. Environmental Law Review 24:10231–10249.
Missouri v. Holland, 252 U.S. 416 (1920).
NRC (National Research Council). 1995. Science and the Endangered Species Act. National Academy Press, Washington, D.C.
NRC (National Research Council). 1996. Upstream: salmon and society in the Pacific Northwest. National Academy Press, Washington, D.C.
New York v. United States, 505 U.S. 144 (1992).
NLRB (National Labor Relations Board) v. Jones and Laughlin Steel Corp., 301 U.S. 1 (1997).
Noss, R. 1999. A citizen's guide to ecosystem management. Wild Earth Special Paper #3. Biodiversity Legal Foundation, Boulder, Colorado.
Orion Corp. v. State, 109 Wn.2d 621 (1987).
Palila v. Hawaii Department of Land and Natural Resources, 471 F. Supp. 985 (D. Ha. 1979).
Pegg, J. R. 2003. Bush dumps controversial wetlands rule. Environmental News Service. Available: http://www.ens-newswire.com/ens/dec2003/2003-12-16-11.asp (December 2003).
Penn Central Transportation Co. v. New York City, 438 U.S. 104 (1978).
Pennsylvania Coal Co. v. Mahon, 260 U.S. 393 (1922).
Perkins Coie. 1999. A white paper: liability of state agencies and local governments under the Endangered Species Act. Perkins Coie LLP The Environment Group, Seattle. Available: http://www.perkinscoie.com/page.cfm?id=184 (March 2006).
Presbytery of Seattle v. King County, 114 Wn.2d 320 (1990).
Printz v. United States, 521 U.S. 898 (1997).
Rapanos v. United States, 547 U.S. ____ (2006). Slip opinion.
Rossiter, C., editor. 1961. The Federalist papers. New American Library, New York.
Sax, J. 1993. Property rights and the economy of nature: understanding Lucas v. SCCC Coastal Council. Stanford Law Review 45:1433–1455.
Seminole Tribe of Florida v. Florida, 517 U.S. 44 (1996).
Smyth, A., editor. 1907. Queries and remarks respecting alterations in the constitution of Pennsylvania. The writings of Benjamin Franklin. Macmillan Company, New York.
Stegner, W. 1992. Beyond the hundredth meridian: John Wesley Powell and the second opening of the West. Penguin Books, New York.
Strahan v. Coxe, 127 F.3d 155 (1st Cir. 1997).
SWANCC (Solid Waste Agency of Northern Cook County) v. Corps (U.S. Army Corps of Engineers), 531 U.S. 159 (2001).
Talmadge, P. A. 2000. The myth of property absolutism and modern government: the interaction of police power and property rights. Washington Law Review 75:857–911.
United States v. Lopez, 514 U.S. 549 (1995).
United States v. Morrison, 529 U.S. 598 (2000).
United States v. Wilson, 133 F.3d 251 (4th Cir. 1997).
USOFR (U.S. Office of the Federal Register). 1986. Migratory Bird Rule, Clean Water Act. Federal Register 51(13 November 1986):41217.
USOFR (U.S. Office of the Federal Register). 2003. Advance notice of proposed rulemaking on the Clean Water Act regulatory definition of 'Waters of the United States.' Appendix A, joint memorandum from Robert E. Fabricant, General Counsel, Environmental Protection Agency, and Steven J. Morello, General Counsel, Department of the Army. Federal Register 68:10(15 January 2003):1995–1998.
WAGO (Washington Attorney General's Office). 1995. State of Washington Attorney General's

recommended process and advisory memorandum for evaluation of proposed regulatory or administrative actions to avoid unconstitutional takings of private property. Washington Attorney General's Office, Olympia.

Washington, H. A. 1859. The proceedings of the government of the United States in maintaining the public right to the beach of the Mississippi, adjacent to New Orleans, against the intrusion of Edward Livingstone. The writings of Thomas Jefferson, volume 8. H. A. Washington, editor. Derby and Jackson, New York.

WDNR (Washington Department of Natural Resources). 2000a. Changing our water ways: trends in Washington's water systems. Washington Department of Natural Resources, Olympia.

WDNR (Washington Department of Natural Resources). 2000b. Aquatic resources policy implementation manual. March 2000. Available: http://www.dnr.wa.gov/htdocs/aqr/ (March 2006).

Weden v. San Juan County, 135 Wn.2d 678 (1998).

Wetlands protection expanded: critics warn northwest development at risk. 2004. The Seattle Post-Intel.

Chapter 7. The Endangered Species Act: The Most Successful Environmental Law?

> As it was finally passed, the Endangered Species Act of 1973 represented the most comprehensive legislation for the preservation of endangered species ever enacted by any nation. [Chief Justice Warren Burger, *TVA v. Hill* 1978:2294]

Chapter Summary

In 1993, then-Secretary of the Interior Bruce Babbitt called the Endangered Species Act (ESA, U.S. Code, volume 16, sections 1531–1543) "undeniably the most innovative, wide-reaching, and successful environmental law enacted within the past quarter century" (Babbitt 1994:355)—a period that included the National Environmental Policy Act, the Clean Air Act, and the Clean Water Act. For federal lands, such as the national forests where the northern spotted owl *Strix occidentalis* is found, Babbitt's assessment is probably true. Nonfederal lands, however, which are largely privately owned and regulated by state or local governments, provide all or a large percentage of the habitat for the majority of species listed under the act, including Puget Sound salmon.[1] The ecosystems of these species can only be conserved through the cooperation of these other governments, particularly local governments, since they typically have the greatest responsibility for regulating the development and use of private land.

Just how the ESA applies to state and local land-use regulations is currently an evolving issue in the courts. Clearly, a land use that causes the death of listed salmon is a "take." Less clearly, a state or local regulation that permitted the land use might be found a "take." If that regulation was designed to protect habitat, but arguably did so ineffectively, state or local liability is even less clear. In addition to these uncertainties, the relationship between most land uses and the death of salmon is complex and indirect. A new house near a stream may incrementally send more storm flows to the stream, which incrementally increases erosion of fine sediment, which incrementally lowers oxygen to some incubating salmon eggs, which incrementally decreases the number of eggs that develop into juvenile fish (though most eggs and juveniles do not survive anyway). It is certainly easier to predict such effects from the construction of hundreds of homes that would be permitted under one government's regulations, but whether regulations that are arguably substandard would take listed salmon is a difficult enough challenge to prove in court that not one lawsuit alleging it has been filed in the Puget Sound area. How such a suit would be decided has enormous consequences for Puget Sound salmon and other endangered species. The decision would clarify not just the regulatory responsibilities of state and local governments under the ESA. It would also clarify how the act applies to the most harmful type of take for Puget Sound salmon and many other endangered species, which is the cumulative result of many individually minor actions.

[1] In 1993, the General Accounting Office found that 90% of listed species had some or all of their habitat on nonfederal lands (GAO 1994).

The ESA has spurred extensive and unprecedented planning efforts to recover salmon in the Puget Sound area and elsewhere on the Pacific coast, as will be discussed in the next chapter. Throughout that large area, the act is clearly affecting how salmon are harvested and hatcheries are operated. The ESA has also had an enormous effect on the Pacific Northwest's forests, to protect salmon as well as the northern spotted owl and other old-growth species, as discussed in Chapter 9. So far, however, the ESA has had relatively little effect on regulation of the lowland areas that provide the most crucial habitat for salmon in Puget Sound. This chapter explores the legal reasons for that, examining the history of the ESA and how the courts have applied the law. In the end, salmon may prove to be one of the leading counter-arguments to Babbitt's assessment, if the ESA is evaluated against its first purpose (as stated by Congress in 1973): "to provide a means whereby the ecosystems upon which endangered species and threatened species depend may be conserved" (ESA, section 1531[b]).

Uncontroversial at the Time

The ESA was passed in 1973, at the height of the environmental movement. The Clean Air Act had been passed 3 years earlier, the Clean Water Act and the Marine Mammal Protection Act the year before. Though the ESA is now one of the most controversial of all environmental laws, it was not perceived so at the time. Passed almost unanimously by Congress, its adoption merited one sentence each in the *The New York Times* (President signs manpower bill 1973), *The Los Angeles Times* (President signs bill reshaping federal manpower programs 1973), and *The Washington Post* (Nixon signs bill to give states manpower funds 1973). *The Chicago Tribune* ignored the new law altogether. Congress and most observers originally saw it as an incremental improvement on existing laws for the protection of endangered species. Only when the ESA's actual language was applied and tested in court cases did the potentially radical meaning of its major clauses become widely apparent. Despite the powerful interests that have opposed the law since then, the ESA has shown remarkable resilience. But its weaknesses, which frequently highlight the contrast between how the law is applied now and what Congress thought it meant in 1973, have also grown more evident over time.

The first federal list of wildlife in danger of extinction was completed in 1964. Known as the Redbook, it included a total of 60 species: 35 birds, 16 mammals, 6 fish, and 3 reptiles. The committee of nine biologists that developed the list estimated that 35 to 40 species of North American animals had gone extinct within the span of American history (U.S. studying way to save wildlife, 1964). In succeeding years, recognition of the larger number of actual extinctions in the United States and across the world, and their implications, grew among scientists and the general public. The first federal law that attempted to respond to this problem was the Endangered Species Preservation Act of 1966 (ESPA; Public Law 89-669). The ESPA required that the Departments of Interior, Agriculture, and Defense "protect species of native fish and wildlife, including migratory birds, that are threatened with extinction, and, insofar as is practicable and consistent with the[ir] primary purposes,...preserve the habitats of such threatened species on lands under their jurisdiction" (ESPA, section 1[b]). It banned taking endangered species only in national wildlife refuges, where take could still be allowed with a permit. The Interior Department was directed to publish in the Federal Register the names of all native fish and wildlife species found to be threatened with extinction and to "encourage" all other federal agencies to protect these species "where practicable" (ESPA, section 2[d]). The department was authorized to acquire habitat for endangered species, using up to $15 million from the Land and Water Conservation Fund (ESPA, 2[b]–[c]).[2] Management goals for national wildlife refuges, formerly targeted primarily at waterfowl, were to include listed species as well. Finally, the secretary of interior was directed to "cooperate to the maximum extent practicable with the several States" in carrying out the act (ESPA, 3[a]; also see Bean and Rowland 1997).

In the following years, understanding of the extinction crisis grew, particularly regarding its international dimensions. This led to the Endangered Species Conservation Act of 1969 (ESCA; Public Law No. 91-135), which authorized the secretary of interior to add species "threatened with worldwide extinction" to the department's list and prohibited their import into the country except for certain limited purposes (ESCA, section 3[a]). It called for the secretary to convene "an international ministerial meeting" to develop "a binding international convention on the conservation of endangered species" (ESCA, section 5[b]). Four years later this resulted in the Convention on International Trade in Endangered Species of Wild Fauna and Flora (CITES). Domestically, the key change in the act clarified that the "fish and wildlife" to be listed by the Department of the Interior were to include "any wild mammal, fish, wild bird, amphibian, reptile, mollusk, or crustacean"; the department had previously listed only vertebrate animals (ESCA, section 12[a]; CRS 1982).

By the early 1970s, there was a widespread sense that the 1966 and 1969 acts did not do enough to protect endangered species. In particular, the protections they offered were seen as coming too late, after species were already near extinction. President Nixon reflected this view when he declared in his Environmental Message of February 8, 1972, that existing law "simply does not provide the kind of management tools needed to act early enough to save a vanishing species" (Nixon 1974a:183). The United States had led the negotiation and signing of CITES; members of Congress and the administration wanted to continue this international leadership by strengthening related American laws (CRS 1982).

However, the statement of congressional findings and purposes of the ESA of 1973 reflects a more profound approach to the extinction crisis than the earlier acts. Affirming that endangered wildlife and plants "are of esthetic, ecological, educational, historical, recreational, and scientific value to the Nation and its people," it declares that it is "the policy of Congress that all Federal departments and agencies shall seek to

[2] The act provided that no more than $5 million could be appropriated annually from the Land and Water Conservation Fund for such purposes and that no more than $750,000 could be spent for the acquisition of any one area.

conserve endangered species and threatened species and shall utilize their authorities in furtherance of the purposes of this Act" (ESA, section 1531[c]). It defines "conservation" to mean "the use of all methods and procedures which are necessary to bring any endangered species or threatened species to the point at which the measures provided pursuant to this Act are no longer necessary" (ESA, section 1532[3]) and extends protections to "any member" of both the animal and plant kingdoms (ESA, sections 1532[8] and 1532[13]).

Today, the most notable substantive features of the ESA are understood to be in Section 3 (which defines "take" of a species to include "harm," later defined by regulation to include harm to its habitat), Section 4 (which requires that species be listed based on "the best scientific and commercial data available"), Section 7 (which requires that "any action authorized, funded, or carried out" by federal agencies shall be found "not likely to jeopardize the continued existence" or degrade the "critical habitat" of any listed species), Section 9 (which prohibits take of any endangered animal species throughout the United States), and Section 11 (which authorizes citizen lawsuits to enforce the act; ESA, sections 1533[18], 1534[b], 1537[b], 1539[a], and 1541[g]). All of these features of the act received little discussion in Congress at the time (CRS 1982; U.S. House of Representatives 1982; U.S. Senate 1982).

Given what features drew Congress's attention, it is easy to see why the ESA was ignored by the national news media. The report from the House committee assigned the legislation listed the following "principal changes to be affected" by it:

1. It extends protection to animals which may become endangered, as well as to those which are now endangered.
2. It permits protection of animals that are in trouble in any significant portion of their range, rather than threatened with worldwide extinction.
3. It makes taking of such animals a Federal offense.
4. It eliminates existing dollar ceilings ($15 million, already consumed) on acquisition of critical habitat areas.
5. It gives management authority for marine species to the Department of Commerce.
6. It authorizes the use of counterpart funds, where proper.
7. It allows states to adopt more restrictive legislation than the Federal laws.
8. It clarifies and extends the authority of the Department of Agriculture to assist landowners to carry out the purposes of the act.
9. It directs a study of the problems involved in the domestic regulation of trade in endangered plants [CRS 1982].

The Senate's report, from the Committee on Commerce, was similar. It highlighted the first, third, and fourth changes above, while stressing that the ESA must "not pre-empt efficient programs" managed by states to benefit endangered species (CRS 1982). In both houses, this last issue was seen as key. Lawmakers believed they were creating the basis for a partnership, wherein the federal government set minimum standards for species protection, which would often be exceeded by state laws. Once states met minimum federal standards, they would receive federal funding for endangered species programs, which both houses believed the states were better equipped to implement (CRS 1982). The Senate Commerce Committee's report was characteristic of this sentiment:

> The Committee finds that the most efficient way to enforce the prohibitions of this bill and to develop the most appropriate and extensive programs is through utilization of the agencies already established for such purposes within the States and development of the potential for such State programs where they do not already exist or have less than sufficient authority to meet the need....Nationwide, State agencies employ approximately 6,000 enforcement agents. In contrast, the Federal Government, in fiscal year 1973, employed 158 enforcement agents, most of whom were located in ports of entry in order to enforce laws prohibiting the transport of endangered species in foreign commerce. [CRS 1982]

Senator Ted Stevens (R-Alaska), when giving his reasons for support of the bill, described its provisions for cooperation with states as "the major backbone of the act" (CRS 1982:362). Though Congress acknowledged that the loss of habitat was "the most significant" threat to endangered plants and animals, supporters of the legislation believed that it could be primarily addressed through acquisition of key areas. The report of the House Committee on Merchant Marine and Fisheries stated,

> Clearly it is beyond our capability to acquire all habitat which is important to those species of plants and animals which are endangered today, without at the same time dismantling our own civilization. On the other hand, there are certain areas which are critical which can and should be set aside. It is the intent and purpose of this legislation to see that our ability to do so, at least within this country, is maintained. [CRS 1982:144]

Removal of the ceiling on funds for habitat acquisition was understood to be the primary means necessary to address this issue (CRS 1982). To the extent that there was any recognition that the act might limit use of private property by prohibiting take of listed species, congressional leaders believed that this issue could be addressed through acquisition of critical habitat. Again, the Senate Commerce Committee's report was characteristic:

> Often, protection of habitat is the only means of protecting endangered animals which occur on non-public lands. With programs for protection underway, and worthy of continuation into the foreseeable future, an accelerated land acquisition program is essential. [CRS 1982:303]

Congress was far from alone in not appreciating the consequences of literally applying the ESA's terms. No major special interest group testified against the bill, while scientists and agency administrators, every major environmental organization, the National Rifle Association, and others urged its passage. The only testimony in opposition came from two groups representing state fish and game agencies (which helped prompt the above attention to their issues) and one spokesman for the fur industry (Petersen 2002). *The Washington Post* was the only major newspaper that covered debate on the act. It editorialized in June 1973, "With little opposition" to the ESA, there was no reason for inaction "except congressional inertia" (Protecting endangered species, 1973). On December 19, the Senate approved the final bill by a vote of 92 to 0. The next day the House passed the bill by a vote of 345 to 4, with 73 not voting, due to many members already having left for the Christmas holiday. On December 28, 1973, President Nixon signed the ESA into law, saying, "Nothing is more priceless and more worthy of preservation than the rich array of animal life with which our country has been blessed" (Nixon 1974b:1027–1028).

What the Words Mean: Initial Regulations and Court Cases

The U.S. Fish and Wildlife Service (FWS), the primary agency charged with implementing the new law, approached the ESA cautiously. Upon passage, 126 species in the Redbook were automatically listed. The next year, FWS developed regulations for the listing process and did not list any new species. One new detail with enormous long-term consequences was how or whether degradation of a listed species' habitat by a party other than a federal agency should be covered under the act. Unfortunately, the act did not directly address this issue. Noting that the stated purpose of the act was to conserve ecosystems, FWS chose to treat habitat degradation as a take, which it placed under its definition of harm. (The ESA defines "take" to mean "to harass, harm, pursue, hunt, shoot, wound, kill, trap, capture, or collect, or to attempt to engage in any such conduct" [ESA, section 1532], but it does not further define any of these terms.) Later revised under the Reagan administration, FWS's original definition of harm was

> an act or omission which actually injures or kills wildlife, including acts which annoy it to such an extent as to significantly disrupt essential behavioral patterns, which include, but are not limited to, breeding, feeding or sheltering; significant environmental modification or degradation which has such effects is included within the meaning of "harm." [USOFR 1975[3]]

Though FWS acknowledged in passing that the act absolutely prohibited such take, it did not treat this definition as momentous, instead issuing the definition along with a set of other regulatory actions for the ESA titled Reclassification of the American Alligator and Other Amendments (USOFR 1975). Meanwhile, FWS exercised its new powers under the ESA carefully. In one of the first noteworthy tests of its authority over other federal agencies under the act, FWS declined to veto a federal highway construction project that would have destroyed at least seven known nesting sites of the listed Mississippi sandhill crane *Grus canadensis*. Although FWS attempted to negotiate with the Department of Transportation, a citizen lawsuit stopped the project until the plan was modified sufficiently to protect the crane's habitat. On ap-

[3] Though some court decisions have determined that habitat degradation might also "harass" a listed species and thereby also be a "take" under that term, the original Federal Register notice is clear that "the concept of environmental degradation" applies only to the word "harm."

peal, the Fifth Circuit Court came to a potentially contradictory decision concerning FWS's authority in the case. It found that Section 7 of the ESA imposed a "mandatory duty" (*NWF v. Coleman* 1976) on federal agencies to ensure that their actions did not destroy or modify the critical habitat of endangered species or jeopardize their continued existence. (FWS defines the latter phrase to mean "to engage in an action that reasonably would be expected, directly or indirectly, to reduce appreciably the likelihood of both the survival and recovery of a listed species in the wild by reducing the reproduction, numbers, or distribution of that species" [Code of Federal Regulations, volume 50, chapter 4, section 402.02].) However, the court also found that

> once an agency has had meaningful consultation with the Secretary of the Interior concerning actions which may affect an endangered species, the final decision of whether or not to proceed with the action lies with the agency itself. Section 7 does not give the Department of Interior a veto over the actions of federal agencies, provided that the required consultation has occurred. [*NWF v. Coleman* 1976]

Since the court nevertheless halted the highway project, its decision raised doubts whether an agency could proceed with an action that the Department of Interior believed would jeopardize a listed species. In its first decision on the ESA, the Supreme Court answered this question definitively in *TVA v. Hill* (1978). The decision prohibited completion of Tellico Dam on the Little Tennessee River to protect the snail darter *Persina tanasi*, a 3-inch perch. This led to a painful awakening in Congress and across the country that protecting endangered species might require more than "trivial" sacrifices.

Construction of Tellico Dam began in 1967, six years before the ESA became law. Eleven years later, at the time of the Supreme Court decision, the dam was "virtually completed and essentially ready for operation" (*TVA v. Hill* 1978:158). The Department of Interior, however, determined that impounding water behind the dam "would result in total destruction of the snail darter's habitat" (*TVA v. Hill* 1978:162). Congress had been made aware that the dam carried this risk but continued to appropriate funds for the project after hearing that efforts were being made to transplant the darter. In 1976, it was unclear whether the transplants would be successful. Opponents of the dam, who previously had stopped the project on other grounds, filed suit in February to stop its completion pursuant to the ESA (*TVA v. Hill* 1978:158–166). The suit was first heard in district court, where it was decided against the dam opponents. The judge commented,

> At some point in time a federal project becomes so near completion and so incapable of modification that a court of equity should not apply a statute enacted long after inception of the project to produce an unreasonable result. Where there has been an irreversible and irretrievable commitment of resources by Congress to a project over a span of almost a decade, the Court should proceed with a great deal of circumspection. [*TVA v. Hill* 1976]

However, the Sixth Circuit Court of Appeals reversed this decision, finding that completion of the dam would violate Section 7 of the ESA. Courts, it said, were not in a position to balance the competing values of saving an endangered species and completing the dam:

> It is conceivable that the welfare of an endangered species may weigh more heavily upon the public conscience, as expressed by the final will of Congress, than the writeoff of those millions of dollars already expended for Tellico in excess of its present salvageable value. [*Hill v. TVA* 1977]

By a 6–3 decision, the Supreme Court agreed. Chief Justice Warren Burger wrote for the majority.

> One would be hard pressed to find a statutory provision whose terms were any plainer than those in Section 7 of the ESA. Its very words affirmatively command all federal agencies "to insure that actions authorized, funded, or carried out by them do not jeopardize the continued existence" of an endangered species...This language admits of no exception....[E]xamination of the language, history, and structure of the legislation under review here indicates beyond doubt that Congress intended endangered species to be afforded the highest of priorities. [*TVA v. Hill* 1978:173–174]

In reaching this conclusion, the Court noted frequent statements in congressional debate over the act that the value of a lost species was "incalculable" or "irreplaceable." The Court also noted the "pointed omission of the type of qualifying language previously included in endangered species legislation" (e.g., that federal agencies should protect endangered species "insofar as is practicable and consistent with the[ir] primary purposes"). This language was contained in initial versions of the ESA and remained in the bill first passed by the Senate. It was dropped in the final version of the act, which used the stricter language of the House bill (*TVA v. Hill* 1978:174–182). The Court's argument was weakened by the fact that there was no discussion of this change in the Senate, despite its immense significance (CRS 1982) to the case. However, the Court pointed to comments by the bill's floor leader in the House, Representative John Dingell, before the ESA came to a final vote:

> The purposes of the bill include the conservation of the species and of the ecosystems upon which they depend, and every agency of government is committed to see that those purposes are carried out...[They] can no longer plead that they can do nothing about it. They can, and they must. The law is clear. [CRS 1982:481]

Dingell gave two examples of how this obligation would work in practice. If bombing practice by the Air Force along the gulf coast of Texas threatened the whooping crane *Grus americana*, "perhaps the best known of our endangered species," the practice would have to be modified. In the second example, all relevant federal agencies would have to protect grizzly bears *Ursus arctos horribilis* in the continental states, to ensure that the species was "not driven to extinction."

In dissenting from the Supreme Court's decision, Justice Lewis Powell took the majority's argument to its logical extreme:

> The only precondition...to...destroying the usefulness of even the most impor-

> tant federal project in our country would be a finding by the Secretary of the Interior that a continuation of the project would threaten the survival or critical habitat of a newly discovered species of water spider or amoeba....If the relevant Committees that considered the Act, and the Members of Congress who voted on it, had been aware that the Act could be used to terminate major federal projects authorized years earlier and nearly completed, or to require the abandonment of essential and long-completed federal installations and edifices, we can be certain that there would have been hearings, testimony, and debate concerning consequences so wasteful, so inimical to purposes previously deemed important, and so likely to arouse public outrage....I have little doubt that Congress will amend the ESA to prevent the grave consequences made possible by today's decision. [*TVA v. Hill* 1978:202, 210]

Amendments to the ESA Begin to Acknowledge Its Complexity and Challenges

Powell was correct, but though Congress acted swiftly, it did so with notable restraint. Despite extraordinary pressure, Congress's first action was not to exempt Tellico Dam from requirements of the ESA, nor did it weaken the language in Section 7 obligating federal agencies to avoid jeopardizing listed species. Instead, Congress established a formal process for exempting projects that present an "irresolvable conflict" with that obligation, to be approved by a seven-member Endangered Species Committee. Dubbed the "God Squad" for its power to authorize species extinctions, the committee includes the secretaries of interior, agriculture, and the Army; the chair of the Council of Economic Advisors; the administrators of the Environmental Protection Agency, and the National Oceanic and Atmospheric Administration; and an individual nominated by the governor of the state in which the proposed federal action would take place. The committee may exempt an action only if at least five of its members determine "there are no reasonable and prudent alternatives" to the action, its benefits "clearly outweigh" the benefits of conserving the species, "the action is of regional or national significance," and the agency proposing the action did not make "irreversible or irretrievable" commitments to it after initiating consultation with the federal service responsible for the listed species (ESA, section 1536). Decisions by the committee are subject to judicial review. To address the crisis over Tellico Dam, Congress created an expedited process for the committee to consider an exemption immediately. In one of the many ironies of the Tellico case, the committee surprised Congress and voted against the dam as wasteful on economic and social grounds, without even needing to account for impacts on the snail darter (CRS 1982). The House reacted by attaching an exemption for Tellico to a larger bill for energy and water projects nationwide, which the Senate ultimately supported after a series of close and highly contested votes (CRS 1982). Amid much publicity, President Jimmy Carter reluctantly signed the bill into law, saying that he wanted to prevent a more substantive and comprehensive weakening of the ESA (Carter 1980). In a final irony, in 1980 additional healthy populations of the snail darter were found elsewhere; completion of Tellico Dam did not exterminate the species.

In addition to creating the God Squad, the same 1978 legislation changed how the act treats critical habitat for listed species. Section 7 prohibits federal agencies from jeopardizing the continued existence of listed species and from destroying or modifying habitat determined to be "critical" to recovery of the species. These are closely related obligations—close enough that the Fish and Wildlife Service treats them as nearly identical (USOFR 1999c), arguing that the loss or degradation of critical habitat would necessarily jeopardize a listed species. In its 1978 amendments, however, Congress saw the obligations as distinct, particularly in their treatment of habitat not currently occupied by the species, which might still be determined critical to its recovery. Congress mandated that, "to the maximum extent prudent and determinable," critical habitat be designated at the time a species is listed "after taking into consideration the economic impact, and any other relevant impact" of the designation. This was the first and only explicit introduction of economic considerations into the ESA. Congress also clarified that critical habitat "shall not include the entire geographical area which can be occupied" by a listed species, "[e]xcept in those circumstances determined by the Secretary" (EPA, sections 1536[a][3] and 1536[b][2]).

By limiting the extent of critical habitat, potentially on economic grounds, Congress attempted to reduce the sweeping effects of the ESA, consistent with its general reaction to *TVA v. Hill.* However, the amended bill used confusing language that has created problems for implementation. FWS has viewed the designation of critical habitat as adding no protections for listed species beyond those already provided by the jeopardy standard. Therefore, for years FWS policy was to delay "all critical habitat determinations for a species in order to comply with other statutory requirements that provide greater conservation benefit and furtherance of the purposes of the Act" (USOFR 1999d). Environmental groups, however, have seen at least two added benefits of designating critical habitat. First, important but unoccupied habitat might receive greater protection than it would otherwise. Second, parties whose actions might affect critical habitat would receive earlier and clearer notice of their obligations under the ESA (Feldman and Brennan 2001; *Sierra Club v. U.S. Fish and Wildlife Service* 2001). The courts have generally supported this interpretation, though they have acknowledged the possibility that designating critical habitat on private land could be "imprudent" if FWS could show that the practical effect would be to expand threats to the species. For example, to avoid the threat of future liability for takings landowners could destroy habitat that a species might later occupy (*Conservation Council for Hawaii v. Babbitt* 1988; *Natural Resources Defense Council v. U.S. Department of the Interior* 1997). Since Section 7 deals only with federal actions, this would be legal unless such destruction required a federal permit. However, courts have also agreed with potentially regulated parties that designating critical habitat requires an economic analysis and have overturned designations on that basis (*Middle Rio Grande Conservancy District v. Babbitt* 2000; *New Mexico Cattle Growers Association v. FWS* 2001, cited in Feldman and Brennan 2001). In the case of Puget Sound Chinook salmon *Oncorhynchus tshawytscha* and other listed salmon, a lawsuit filed by the National Home Builders Association led the National Marine Fisheries Service (NMFS) to withdraw its initial designation of critical habitat, as discussed in more detail in the next chapter. The administrative and legal confusion over critical habitat has led numerous parties to urge amendment of the ESA to clarify Congress's intent, but the language has not changed since 1978 (Bean and Rowland 1997; Feldman and Brennan 2001).[4]

The 1978 amendments also limited the scope of the ESA by allowing distinct population segments to be listed only for vertebrate animals. The original act followed the Marine Mammal Protection Act and CITES by defining "species" to include subspecies of animals or plants or "distinct population segments" of animals (the latter was never applied to plants).[5] This broad definition recognized that taxonomic distinctions between species and subspecies vary and that a population segment can represent an important and distinct part of the genetic heritage of a species, potentially with its own unique evolutionary future. (As discussed in the next chapter, this is the basis for the listing of Puget Sound Chinook salmon under the ESA, even though Chinook salmon populations are healthy elsewhere.) There is no scientific rationale for restricting the concept of distinct population segments to animals, let alone vertebrates (see discussion in NRC 1995). The policy rationale for both restrictions appears simply to have been to limit the scope of the ESA's regulations. The FWS and the National Marine Fisheries Service have noted this in their policy for listing distinct population segments, in which they state that Congress intended that they exercise this authority "sparingly" (USOFR 1996:4724).

One last amendment from 1978 deserves mention. Congress introduced the concept of recovery plans into the act, mandating that they be developed for all listed species. This requirement has frequently not been met, or has been met through inadequate plans whose implementation would still leave species at considerable risk of extinction (NRC 1995). Moreover, implementation of recovery plans is at the discretion of all parties, though federal agencies cannot arbitrarily ignore the plans, given their duty to "utilize their authorities in furtherance of the purposes" of the ESA (ESA, section 1536[a]; *Sierra Club v. Lujan* 1993; Bean and Rowland 1997). In Puget Sound, the recovery planning process for listed salmon (discussed in the next chapter) has tried to create a new national model for collaboration across federal, state, local, and tribal governments and the public and private sectors. Tribal treaty rights to harvestable runs of salmon, discussed in Chapter 13, could potentially give this plan greater legal weight by making at least some of its actions mandatory.

When Ronald Reagan became president and appointed James Watt as Secretary of the Interior, the nature of conflicts between Congress and the administration over the ESA changed. In 1981, the Reagan administration did not add one additional species to the list, while it downlisted some species from endangered to threatened and proposed

[4] When the National Academy of Sciences reviewed the ESA in 1995, it recommended creation of a new category of habitat, "survival habitat," which would be designated at the time of listing an endangered species. This habitat would be considered "necessary to support either current populations of a species or populations that are necessary to ensure short-term (25–50 years) survival, whichever is larger." It would be designated on an emergency basis without regard to economic consequences, to be superseded later by critical habitat, which would be identified within recovery plans. See NRC 1995. Congress never acted on this recommendation.

[5] See discussion in Bean and Rowland 1997.

that others be removed from the list altogether (And now the timber wolf 1982). In February of that year, President Reagan issued an executive order that required a cost-benefit analysis for all federal regulations, including each new ESA listing (USOFR 1981b). In June, the administration proposed to redefine "harm" in the ESA, eliminating any reference to environmental modification or disruption of essential behavior patterns (USOFR 1981a). After a storm of protest, the proposed definition was changed before being made final in November. The administration replied that it had never intended to exclude all forms of habitat degradation from the prohibition against take, just those that did not cause actual death or injury to a listed species. The final definition, which remains in effect today, was not substantively different than the 1975 version:

> "Harm" in the definition of "take" in the Act means an act which actually kills or injures wildlife. Such act may include significant habitat modification or degradation where it actually kills or injures wildlife by significantly impairing essential behavioral patterns, including breeding, feeding or sheltering. [USOFR 1981c][6]

The previous definition had specified that an act of omission could constitute harm. The administration said that removing this language did not change the meaning of the definition, stating, "the [Fish and Wildlife] Service feels that 'act' is inclusive of either commissions or omissions which would be prohibited" by the ESA.

These actions sparked a political battle over the ESA. The administration proposed a variety of amendments to weaken the act, which were opposed by environmentalists, scientists, and many in Congress, who proposed amendments to strengthen the ESA by focusing on the listing process. In the end, concerned by delays in listings, Congress amended the ESA to require that the status of species petitioned for listing be decided within 12 months, allowing a 6-month extension only if "there is substantial disagreement regarding the sufficiency or accuracy of the available data" (ESA, sections 1533[b][3][B] and 1533[b][6][B]). Both the House and Senate stressed that the act does not allow economic considerations in the listing process (U.S. House of Representatives 1982).

With little fanfare, the 1982 amendments also authorized take of listed species that is "incidental to, and not the purpose of,...an otherwise lawful activity" (ESA, section 1539[a][1][B]). This provision has come to have enormous significance. Prior to the provision, a literal reading of the ESA barred all non-federal parties from taking listed species except for scientific research or conservation purposes; in contrast, federal agencies were allowed to negotiate mitigation for take they might cause (USFWS and NMFS 1996). Even the Reagan administration did not see this as a serious problem,[7] presumably because to that point there had been no citizen suits or enforcement

---

[6] As discussed in the next chapter, NMFS did not issue its own definition of "harm" until 1999. The definition is the same as that of FWS, except that it defines "essential behavioral patterns" to include "breeding, spawning, rearing, migrating, feeding or sheltering."

[7] See letter from J. Watt, Secretary of the Interior, 1982 letter to Senator J. Breaux, saying that the administration did not seek amendment of the ESA except for changes to the Section 7 exemption process, in U.S. Senate 1982:37–39.

actions that raised major conflicts for private property owners (Bean and Rowland 1997). The 1982 amendment was modeled on an agreement between private developers, local governments, and environmentalists in the San Bruno Mountain area of San Mateo County, California. The agreement allowed the destruction of up to 13% of the habitat for two species of endangered butterflies in return for the preservation and restoration of their remaining habitat and commitments to its restoration and permanent protection (U.S. House of Representatives 1982). The amendment to Section 10 of the act authorized permits for incidental take through Habitat Conservation Plans (HCPs). An approved HCP must demonstrate that

(1) the taking will be incidental;
(2) the applicant will, to the maximum extent practicable, minimize and mitigate the impacts of such taking;
(3) the applicant will ensure that adequate funding for the plan will be provided;
(4) the taking will not appreciably reduce the likelihood of the survival and recovery of the species in the wild; and
(5) the federal agency responsible for the species determines that any other measures it deems necessary or appropriate will be implemented (ESA, section 1539[a][2][B]).

This amendment was included in a section of the bill that focused on what Congress perceived to be a more important issue—how take should be regulated for "experimental populations" of listed species introduced into habitats outside of their current range. In the first 10 years of the program through 1992, only 14 incidental take permits were issued. President Bill Clinton, who was elected that November, approached the program very differently. By August 1996, his administration had issued 179 incidental take permits and had encouraged approximately 200 additional HCPs under development (USFWS and NMFS 1996). In the Puget Sound area, HCPs have played an important role in protections for listed species and could become even more crucial in the future. To understand how HCPs have evolved from their modest beginnings, though, it is important to consider the long political and legal struggle over protection of the northern spotted owl.

The Spotted Owl: Reframing the ESA to Focus on Ecosystems

Legal efforts to protect the spotted owl began during the Reagan years but peaked during the first Bush administration. Initial lawsuits were based on the National Forest Management Act of 1976 (NFMA; U.S. code, volume 16, sections 1601–1614), later joined by the ESA. The NFMA, which was passed partly in reaction to a series of lawsuits over clear-cutting in national forests (see Bean and Rowland 1997), requires that plans be prepared for all units of the National Forest System to guide timber harvest and other land management activities. Among their goals, plans are "to provide for diversity of plant and animal communities based on the suitability and capability of the specific land area" (NFMA, section 1604[g][3][b]). Implementing regulations required that the Forest Service (FS) manage fish and wildlife habitat to

> maintain viable populations of existing native and desired non-native vertebrate species in the planning area. For planning purposes, a viable population shall be regarded as one which has the estimated numbers and distribution of reproductive individuals to insure its continued existence is well distributed in the planning area. [Code of Federal Regulations, volume 30, section 219.19]

The regulations (since removed by the Bush Administration; USOFR 2005) required that the Forest Service monitor the population trends of "management indicator species," to be selected "because their population changes are believed to indicate the effects of management activities" (Code of Federal Regulations, volume 36, section 219.19[a][1]). These species were to include

> [e]ndangered and threatened plant and animal species identified on State and Federal lists for the planning area; species with special habitat needs that may be influenced significantly by planned management programs; species commonly hunted, fished, or trapped; [and] non-game species of special interest. [Code of Federal Regulations, volume 30, section 219.19{a}{1}]

In 1985, FS determined that the northern spotted owl was an indicator species for old-growth forests in the Pacific Northwest (Gutierrez and Carey 1985). The next year, it issued a draft supplemental environmental impact statement for its Regional Guide for managing national forests in Oregon and Washington. The draft recommended setting aside as much as 2,200 acres of old-growth forest for each of 550 pairs of owls, thus prohibiting logging on up to 690,446 acres (U.S. Forest Service 1986). The proposal generated enormous controversy, drawing more public comments than all previous proposals in FS's history other than its nationwide recommendations on roadless areas (Bean and Rowland 1997). Environmentalists generally opposed any continued logging of old growth no matter where it was located. As part of this reaction, Green World, "a tiny environmental group operating out of a phone booth in Massachusetts," petitioned the Fish and Wildlife Service to list the spotted owl under the ESA in January 1987 (Yaffee 1994).[8] After taking the maximum 90 days allowed, the Regional Director of FWS found that the petition met the ESA's test of presenting "substantial scientific or commercial information indicating that the petitioned action may be warranted" (Yaffee 1994; ESA, section 1533[b][3][A]). That December, though, FWS disregarded the conclusion of its own scientists and determined that listing the owl was "not warranted." In April 1988, the Forest Service issued its final environmental impact statement for public comment, proposing to set aside only 347,700 acres of harvestable timber lands as owl habitat. The next month, the Sierra Club Legal Defense Fund filed suit on behalf of 25 environmental organizations to challenge FWS's decision not to list the spotted owl. That November, the U.S. District Court agreed, finding that the decision had been "arbitrary and capricious," and required that FWS

[8] Green World actually submitted its initial letter in October 1986, but the Fish and Wildlife Service did not accept it as a "petition" because it was not explicitly identified as such. This was corrected in the January 1987 resubmittal.

reconsider in light of available scientific information. The next month, the Forest Service proceeded with its recommended actions, with only minor amendments. On February 7 and 8, 1989, four lawsuits were filed against the Forest Service alleging violations of the National Forest Management Act, three by industry groups, which wanted more land for logging, and one by a set of environmental groups. In March, the district court hearing this last suit granted a temporary injunction against 139 planned timber sales—about half of those planned across Washington and Oregon (Yaffee 1994; Bean and Rowland 1997). From the perspective of the Forest Service, as commentator Steven Yaffee put it, "all hell had broken loose" (Yaffee 1994).

There were many reasons for this conflict. The Forest Service had traditionally viewed old-growth forests as less productive for wood products than plantations of fast-growing tree species. Congressional budgets required high timber harvests, even as Congress called for protecting fish and wildlife habitat. The Reagan and Bush administrations directed the Forest Service and the Fish and Wildlife Service to emphasize economic development over environmental values, even where this might conflict with legal requirements (Yaffee 1994). At its foundation, though, the conflict was over the country's nearly century-old approach to "multiple uses" on public land. Fish and wildlife had never been given priority on lands that were most productive for human uses. Even at the risk of extinction, fish and wildlife were consistently relegated to those areas with the least economic value. Any serious departure from this policy required politically difficult choices that were unforeseen by Congress when it passed the ESA. Environmental groups were therefore apprehensive when FWS announced in April 1989 that it would propose listing the owl as threatened, though this was precisely the action they had sued for. It was not clear whether they might "win the owl battle but lose the endangered species war," by seeing the ESA dramatically weakened by amendment (Yaffee 1994). In this atmosphere, most environmental leaders did not oppose a bill passed by Congress that October, which lifted the court injunction on timber sales and insulated other sales from most court actions for 1 year. The bill protected all habitat areas identified by the Forest Service for the spotted owl and provided time for the possibility of a longer-term compromise (Yaffee 1994). An Interagency Scientific Committee, which the bill created, was chartered in October 1989 to develop a plan that could meet legal requirements for the owl. In April 1990, the committee issued its report, which called for protection of larger blocks of habitat than those previously proposed for individual pairs of owls (Thomas et al. 1990). Two months later, FWS Director John Turner accepted the inevitable and listed the spotted owl under the ESA, saying, "Our intent now...is to find ways to protect the owl with the least possible disruption to the timber economy of the Northwest" (Northern spotted owl is threatened 1990).

For the next two years, "political instability continued to be the norm as environmental and timber interest groups lobbied for their interests," heading for what many saw as a "train wreck" designed by the Bush administration to change the political climate for amending the ESA (Yaffee 1994). Under court order and largely based on the interagency report, in May 1991 the Fish and Wildlife Service proposed designating 11.6 million acres as critical habitat for the spotted owl (almost 17 times the amount proposed in 1986), including 3 million acres of private land. Two weeks later, U.S. District Court Judge William Dwyer prohibited all Forest Service sales on owl habitat until it completed a new spotted owl management plan and environmental analysis. He concluded,

> [t]he argument that the mightiest economy on earth cannot afford to preserve old growth forests for a short time, while it reaches an overdue decision on how to manage them, is not convincing today. It would be even less so a year or a century from now. [*Seattle Audubon Society v. Evans* 1991:1096]

In September 1991, the Bush administration initiated the God Squad process to exempt 44 timber sales on land managed by the Bureau of Land Management from the ESA. That November, as Congress heard proposals to amend the ESA, a powerful bipartisan coalition led by House Speaker Thomas Foley, Oregon Senator Mark Hatfield, and Representative Gerry Studds, Chair of the House Subcommittee on Fisheries and Wildlife, requested a report from the National Academy of Sciences to address questions concerning the ESA. (The report was issued in 1995; this book notes its key findings and recommendations [NRC 1995] when discussing related issues.)[9]

It was becoming clear that any scientifically credible proposal to protect the spotted owl and old-growth forests would come at the expense of jobs in the timber industry. Senator Slade Gorton (R-WA) urged his colleagues to consider exceptions to the ESA and other environmental laws that would save jobs and still provide some protection for the owl (U.S. House of Representatives, Committee on Interior and Insular Affairs, Subcommittee on National Parks and Public Lands 1992). In May 1992, the God Squad voted in favor of exempting the BLM timber sales from the ESA (the decision was overturned the next year, on grounds that the committee had been improperly influenced by communications with the president and his staff [*Portland Audubon Society v. Endangered Species Committee* 1993:1550]). In announcing the committee's decision, Secretary of the Interior Manuel Lujan also proposed a plan from the Bush administration for the spotted owl, which he admitted was not consistent with the ESA and would require either amending the law or providing an exception for the spotted owl (Schaefer and Pryne 1992). The day before, Senator Max Baucus (D-MT) led off a special hearing on the spotted owl crisis by attributing much of the economic trauma faced by timber communities to larger economic changes, which he said had been resisted by the Reagan and Bush administrations (U.S. Senate, Committee on Environment and Public Works, Subcommittee on Environmental Protection 1992). This theme was taken up by Bill Clinton in his campaign for the presidency. In August 1992, Clinton pledged that, if elected, he would convene a multiparty working group to resolve the controversy within the first 100 days of his administration (Mapes 1992).

[9] The Congressmen asked the Academy to evaluate six issues: (1) How the ESA defines "species"; (2) The significance of potential conflicts between the conservation needs of different species; (3) How successfully the ESA treats habitat protection in the context of its other requirements; (4) How well recovery planning is integrated into the ESA's other requirements; (5) How evaluations of risk should relate to various provisions of the ESA; and (6) The schedule for various actions within the act.

Clinton was true to his word and held a summit in Portland on April 2, 1993. As commentator Steven Yaffee said,

> The conference...was notable for explicitly reframing the controversy as something bigger than the spotted owl issue. The problem was defined as: how to protect a broad range of environmental values within the old growth ecosystem while dealing humanely within a regional economy that was undergoing a normal process of transformation. [Yaffee 1994]

"I cannot repeal the laws of change," said Clinton (Kenworthy and Devroy 1993). He called for completion of a "balanced and comprehensive long-term" plan to end the stalemate within 60 days. Following the summit, a scientific team was established to review alternatives for management of federal land. It was directed to "take an ecosystem approach to forest management and...address maintenance and restoration of biological diversity, particularly that of the late-successional and old-growth forest ecosystems; maintenance of long-term site productivity of forest ecosystems; maintenance of sustainable levels of renewable natural resources, including timber, other forest products, and other facets of forest values; and maintenance of rural economies and communities" (Forest Conference Executive Committee, 1993 "Statement of Mission" memorandum to the Forest Conference Inter-Agency Working Groups). For his Northwest Forest Plan, Clinton ultimately built on Option 9 from the science team's report, adding an Aquatic Conservation Strategy to protect and restore habitat for 257 stocks of salmonids at risk of extinction (see Chapter 9 for details; U.S. Forest Service and U.S. Bureau of Land Management 1994). Though challenged in court by both timber and environmental interests, Clinton's plan was upheld by Judge Dwyer, who commented, "The question is not whether the court would write the same plan, but whether the agencies have acted within the bounds of the law" (*Seattle Audubon Society v. Lyons* 1994:1300). The Ninth Circuit Court of Appeals agreed that the plan complied with the ESA, the National Forest Management Act, and other applicable environmental laws.

Success in court, however, did not end the controversy. Even moderate Democrats proposed amendments to the act in 1993 and 1994, though no amendments were adopted. In the fall of 1994, Republicans were elected to majorities in both the House and the Senate for the first time since the 1950s. No state in the country felt the shift in power more strongly than Washington, where the spotted owl controversy resonated widely. The state's congressional delegation went from an eight-to-one majority of Democrats to a seven-to-two majority of Republicans. Though new House Speaker Newt Gingrich failed in his pledge to rewrite the ESA (Skrzycki 1995), Congress imposed a moratorium on new listings of species through September 1996 (House panel's bill spares parks, limits ESA 1995). It also passed a rider to an appropriations act, which required that timber sales across much of the Northwest proceed "notwithstanding any other provision of law," insulating them from challenge under environmental laws (Emergency Supplemental Appropriations and Rescissions Act of 1995, Public Law 104–119, section 2001). Congress has regularly debated amendments to the ESA since that time, but political divisions have been strong enough that none have been adopted. The ESA has not been amended since 1988, when relatively minor amendments were passed increasing protections for candidate species and clarifying requirements for recovery plans.

Innovation within the Terms of the Act: The Clinton Administration's Approach

It was in this political environment that the Clinton administration's approach to the ESA was honed. Though Secretary of Interior Bruce Babbitt counseled, "We have to begin to think of ourselves as inhabitants of ecosystems and begin to live, think, and act accordingly," he argued this could be done "within the terms of the ESA," which the Clinton administration fought to keep from being weakened. In the approach Babbitt articulated for the administration, federal lands should be used "as the core of the protection scheme," while the ESA should be applied in "imaginative and creative ways" to regulate the use of private land consistent with private property rights (Babbitt 1994). The administration saw HCPs as the leading vehicle for this approach. By 1996, the administration was calling the HCP process "one of our greatest successes in seeking ways to reduce the Act's regulatory burden on private landowners while addressing the habitat needs of listed species" (USFWS and NMFS 1996). The Clinton administration encouraged an expansion in not only the number of HCPs, but also their size:

> As of late 1995, most HCPs approved were for planning areas less than 1,000 acres in size. However, of the HCPs being developed as of early 1996, approximately 25 exceed 10,000 acres in size, 25 exceed 100,000 acres, and 18 exceed 500,000 acres....These large-scale, regional HCPs can significantly reduce the burden of the ESA on small landowners by providing efficient mechanisms for compliance, distributing the economic and logistic impacts of endangered species conservation among the community, and bringing a broad range of landowners activities under the HCPs' legal protection. [USFWS and NMFS 1996]

To encourage HCPs, in 1994 the administration announced a "No Surprises" policy, which assured holders of incidental take permits "that no additional land use restrictions or financial compensation will be required...with respect to species covered by the permit, even if unforeseen circumstances arise after the permit is issued indicating that additional mitigation is needed for a given species covered by a permit" (USOFR 1998). The federal government would be responsible for the additional mitigation. Given that incidental take permits often are for 50 years or longer, scientists and environmentalists challenged this policy because it locked in environmental protections that might be proved inadequate by new information. Nevertheless, the administration codified the policy as regulation in 1998, saying that the policy "has accomplished one of its primary objectives—to act as a catalyst for integrating endangered species conservation into day-to-day management operations on non-Federal lands" (USOFR 1998). In an attempt to address the issues raised by environmentalists, the regulation distinguished between "changed" and "unforeseen" circumstances:

> Many changes in circumstances during the course of an HCP can reasonably be anticipated and planned for in the conservation plan (e.g., the listing of new species, or a fire or other natural catastrophic event in areas prone to such events), and the plans should describe the modifications in the project or activity that will be implemented if these circumstances arise. "Unforeseen circumstances" are changes in circumstances affecting a species or geographic area covered by an HCP that could not reasonably have been anticipated by plan developers or the [federal government] at the time of the HCP's negotiation and development, and that result in a substantial and adverse change in the status of a covered species (e.g., the eruption of Mount St. Helens was not reasonably foreseeable). [USOFR 1998].

To address data gaps or foreseeable changes in circumstances, the Clinton administration called for "adaptive management," which it defined as "a method for examining alternative strategies for meeting measurable biological goals and objectives, and then, if necessary, adjusting future conservation management actions according to what is learned" (USOFR 2000c:35252). Adaptive management "is not negated by the No Surprises assurances" because it is "an integral component of the operating conservation program," approved as part of an HCP (USOFR 1998). Though not all HCPs require adaptive management, the Clinton administration termed it "essential for HCPs that would otherwise pose a significant risk to [listed] species" because of data gaps (USOFR 2000b). Scientists and environmentalists remained skeptical of this approach, even more so when administered under the new Bush administration. HCPs are initiated not by the federal government but instead by applicants for incidental take permits; the applicants then control much of the terms of development. Public comment on HCPs typically comes after major negotiations with federal agencies have taken place, which decreases opportunities for meaningful amendments (Anderson and Yaffee 1998). Though HCPs can be overturned in court if federal agencies are found "arbitrary and capricious" in applying the standards in Section 10 of the ESA (see *Sierra Club v. Babbitt* 1998 or *NWF v. Babbitt* 2000), courts generally defer to agency expertise. Moreover, HCPs must be evaluated within the timeline for decisions mandated by the ESA based on the best available data, though scientists would generally prefer more time when relatively little data is available (for a general scientific critique of HCPs, see Kareiva et al. 1998).

The Clinton administration initiated two other important programs to encourage non-federal parties to protect and enhance habitat for endangered species. Candidate Conservation Agreements are similar to HCPs but apply exclusively to species that are not currently listed under the ESA but which have the potential to be listed in the foreseeable future. (Candidate species in the Puget Sound area include the Oregon spotted frog *Rana pretiosa*, the streaked horned lark *Eremophila alpestris strigata*, and other species, as discussed further in the next chapter.) Candidate Conservation Agreements allow the federal government to assure property owners that conservation actions they undertake to benefit a species will be all that is required of them during the term of the agreement, even if the species becomes listed. Proposed actions are evaluated based on whether listing the species would be unnecessary if similar measures were also implemented on other properties necessary for the species' conservation (USOFR 1999a). By

June 2000, the Fish and Wildlife Service had entered into approximately 60 Candidate Conservation Agreements, of which it estimated "about 14" had "contributed to making listing the covered species...unnecessary"; the National Marine Fisheries Service had entered into three such agreements, all of which had made listing unnecessary (USOFR 2000a).

Safe Harbor Agreements, the other new initiative from the Clinton administration, are more limited in scope than HCPs or Candidate Conservation Agreements. They apply to voluntary actions undertaken by non-federal parties to improve habitat for listed species. The parties are assured that their conservation actions will not increase their liability for take under the ESA, by authorizing incidental take of listed species back to an agreed upon baseline prior to their improvements. In contrast to HCPs or Candidate Conservation Agreements, Safe Harbor Agreements "run with the enrolled lands and are valid for as long as the participating landowner is complying with the [agreement] and associated permit" (USOFR 1999a).

Defining Take Case by Case

In 1995, the Supreme Court addressed the ESA for the first time since the snail darter case, in a lawsuit backed by the timber industry that sought to exclude habitat degradation from regulation under the ESA. The Washington, D.C. Circuit Court of Appeals agreed with the industry, finding that the word "harm" in the definition of "take" should apply only to "the perpetrator's direct application of force" against a listed species (*Sweet Home Chapter of Communities for a Greater Oregon v. Babbitt* 1994:1465). The Clinton administration appealed and, in *Babbitt v. Sweet Home Chapter of Communities for a Greater Oregon* (1995), the Supreme Court reversed the lower court's ruling. Justice John Paul Stevens delivered the 6–3 opinion of the court:

> The proper interpretation of a term such as "harm" involves a complex policy choice. When Congress has entrusted the Secretary [of Interior] with broad discretion, we are especially reluctant to substitute our views of wise policy for his. In this case, that reluctance accords with our conclusion, based on the text, structure, and legislative history of the ESA, that the Secretary reasonably construed the intent of Congress when he defined "harm" to include "significant habitat modification or degradation that actually kills or injures wildlife." [*Babbitt v. Sweet Home Chapter of Communities for Greater Oregon* 1995:707]

Justice Sandra Day O'Connor concurred with the majority but issued a separate opinion, in which she concluded,

> In my view, then, the "harm" regulation applies where significant habitat modification, by impairing essential behaviors, proximately [foreseeably] causes actual death or injury to identifiable animals that are protected under the Endangered Species Act. [*Babbitt v. Sweet Home Chapter of Communities for Greater Oregon* 1995:711]

The Court's decision left many important questions unanswered, including

- What level of certainty must there be that one or more members of a listed species will die or be injured from an activity that degrades habitat for that activity to be prohibited?
- How much must "essential behavioral patterns" of a listed species be impaired for an activity causing injury but not death to be prohibited?

The majority opinion deliberately left questions like these open, stating

> In the elaboration and enforcement of the ESA, the Secretary and all persons who must comply with the law will confront difficult questions of proximity and degree; for, as all recognize, the Act encompasses a vast range of economic and social enterprises and endeavors. These questions must be addressed in the usual course of the law, through case-by-case resolution and adjudication. [*Babbitt v. Sweet Home Chapter of Communities for Greater Oregon* 1995:707]

A key issue for salmon is the degree to which O'Connor's standard of "actual death or injury to *identifiable* animals" must be met, since her opinion was not joined by the five others in the majority. Even in the case of Puget Sound Chinook salmon, a relatively well-studied species, it is difficult to say with reasonable certainty that a given action, such as a proposed development, will actually kill specific Chinook salmon downstream. Land-use regulations primarily affect juvenile salmon, which are hard to find, even harder to distinguish from one another, and can naturally vary in number annually by factors of 10 or more. Presumably for reasons such as these, the National Marine Fisheries Service has broadly defined the sorts of evidence it would accept to determine "harm":

> Injury may be shown through a variety of methods and types of evidence. These include, but are not limited to, field surveys and assessments, population studies, laboratory studies, model based procedures, information and data in the scientific literature, or expert witness testimony consisting of inferences or opinions drawn from facts pertaining to a given act(s) of habitat modification or degradation. [USOFR 1999b]

Some commentators might argue that NMFS's definition will not hold up in court. A 2001 law review article summarized a variety of potentially contrary court decisions (all of which involved the Fish and Wildlife Service, not NMFS) as follows:

> [I]t is evident from several recent cases that scientific postulation about the effects of land use activities on a species, standing alone, is legally insufficient to prove that a take has occurred, or will occur, even when such theories are advanced by highly qualified biologists. The post-*Sweet Home* cases are not being decided based upon the question of whether it is possible that habitat modifications could or will result in harm; these cases are instead being won or lost on whether it can be proven with compelling evidence...that death or actual injury was incurred by identifiable members of the species, and that the activity in question was the foreseeable and proximate cause of said death or actual injury. [Glen and Douglas 2001]

Using Regulations to Meet the Sweet Home Test

As discussed at the beginning of this chapter, one strategy to strengthen a take case would be to target a government regulation, which authorizes individual actions that cumulatively are certain to kill or injure members of a listed species, even if any one such action might not cause a take. This strategy has great potential importance for salmon. The only way the ecological processes that create and sustain salmon habitat can be protected systematically is through a partnership involving local governments, with their control over most land uses. Developments regulated by local governments have enormous cumulative impacts on salmon habitat, particularly through their effects on stormwater and riparian areas. If local governments are found liable for take that occurs through these developments, the ESA could affect land-use regulations across much of the Pacific Coast.

The principle of "vicarious" liability—for take caused by a regulated activity—was first applied to a federal agency in 1989. In *Defenders of Wildlife v. Environmental Protection Agency*, the Eighth Circuit Court of Appeals determined that EPA's registration of pesticides made it liable for illegal take of black-footed ferrets (*Mustela nigripes*) that resulted from use of approved pesticides (*Defenders of Wildlife v. Environmental Protection Agency* 1989). Two years later, in *Sierra Club v. Yeutter* (1991), the Fifth Circuit found that the Forest Service's approval of a timber management plan made it liable when private timber harvesting under the plan impaired habitat for the red-cockaded woodpecker (*Picoides borealis*; *Sierra Club v. Yeutter* 1991). The two most important cases that have applied the principle of vicarious liability to non-federal agencies are *Strahan v. Coxe* (1997) and *Loggerhead Turtle v. Volusia County* (1998[10]). The Supreme Court denied hearing either case on appeal,[11] which strengthens their relevance as precedents. However, they involve substantially different circumstances than land-use regulations affecting salmon habitat.

In *Strahan v. Coxe*, the First Circuit Court of Appeals found the Massachusetts Division of Marine Fisheries liable in 1997 for taking of right whales because it licensed the use of gill nets and lobster pots "in specifically the manner that is likely to result in a violation" (*Strahan v. Coxe* 1997:164) of the ESA. The court found this violated Section 9(g) of the ESA, which provides, "It is unlawful...to...cause [a take of a listed species] to be committed" (*Strahan v. Coxe* 1997:163). The First Circuit upheld an injunction by the district court that required the state to apply for an incidental take permit under the ESA and to work with the plaintiff and other interested parties to modify restrictions on fishing gear to minimize harm to right whales. The First Circuit reasoned that these requirements did not violate the Tenth Amendment because they did not direct the state "to enact a particular regulatory regime that enforces and furthers a federal policy" (*Strahan v. Coxe* 1997:169). Instead, the injunction sought to bring the state's regulations "into

[10] The initial district court case can be found at *Loggerhead Turtle v. Volusia County* 1995; the decision on remand from the circuit court can be found at *Loggerhead Turtle v. Volusia County* 2000.

[11] Certiorari denied in *Strahan v. Coxe* 1998 and again on a second appeal, *Coates v. Strahan* 1998; certiorari denied in *Loggerhead Turtle v. Volusia County* 1999.

compliance with federal law," since it was "not possible for a licensed commercial fishing operation to use its gillnets or lobster pots in the manner permitted by the Commonwealth without risk of violating the ESA by exacting a taking" (*Strahan v. Coxe* 1997:170, 164).

Since *Strahan v. Coxe* concerned regulation of activity on public waters managed by the state, rather than private property, it may have less bearing on regulation of private developments affecting salmon habitat than *Loggerhead Turtle v. Volusia County*, which concerned the regulation of beachfront lighting from homes and businesses. Young turtles are guided by moonlight to the sea; artificial light landward of their nests can disorient them at a critical stage of their lives, leading to their deaths.[12] The Eleventh Circuit Court of Appeals used *Strahan v. Coxe* as a precedent to find that the turtles and their human allies had legal standing to sue Volusia County for inadequate regulation of beachfront lighting, which allegedly took listed turtles in four cities within the county. The court found that Volusia County's charter granted it "the authority—and arguably the duty—to 'establish minimum standards...for the protection of the environment...by ordinance'" throughout the incorporated and unincorporated areas of the county (*Loggerhead Turtle v. Volusia County* 1998:1249). Just as it was impossible to comply with Massachusetts fishing regulations "without risk of violating the ESA," the court of appeals reasoned, "a genuine issue of fact exists in this case that the lighting activities of landowners along Volusia County's beaches—as authorized by local ordinance—violate the ESA."

The district court that first heard the case had been concerned it could not apply this test without violating the Tenth Amendment:

> Volusia County's lighting ordinance does not violate, in and of itself, the ESA. If it did, the Court could strike the ordinance down by authority of the Supremacy Clause. But by what authority may the Court compel the County to enforce a proposed item of local legislation? It may be that the ESA vests such power in a federal court. This Court, however, will not exercise such authority without guidance from the higher courts. [*Loggerhead Turtle v. Volusia County* 1995:1181]

On appeal, the Eleventh Circuit agreed that the district court did not have the authority to mandate a particular regulation for beachfront lighting, but that it could still order "a wide range of effective injunctive relief," such as *Strahan v. Coxe*'s order to work with plaintiffs and others to modify the relevant regulations (*Loggerhead Turtle v. Volusia County* 1998:1253–1255). By the time the district court decided the case on remand, however, Volusia County had already modified its lighting standards to "virtually...eliminate beach illumination which may be harmful" to the turtles, according to the district court. More fundamentally, the court stressed that the county did not issue permits for beachfront lighting; it regulated

> to prohibit, restrict and limit...lighting, not to authorize, entitle, or legitimize it....Although Plaintiffs deny that they want the Court to compel the County to adopt an even more "turtle-friendly" ordinance (because that would raise a separa-

[12] Perhaps the best summary of the turtle's needs was in the district court decision on remand (*Loggerhead Turtle v. Volusia County* 2000:1304).

tion of powers conundrum), whether they admit it or not, that is the only remedy that would satisfy their complaint. Plaintiffs wish to hold the County liable for takings because its beach residents are not turning off their lights in compliance with the ordinance….This Court is only empowered to enjoin violators of the Act from taking the sea turtles. The question presented here is whether Volusia County's ordinance, which is aimed at protecting the turtles, violates the Act by causing takings thereunder. The answer is no. The true violators, the persons responsible for illuminating the beaches, are not before this Court [*Loggerhead Turtle v. Volusia County* 2000:1307, 1308].

In the Puget Sound area, local development regulations to manage stormwater runoff and protect streams and wetlands are similarly intended to benefit salmon, though scientists have generally found they still allow the cumulative effects of regulated development to degrade salmon habitat (see Chapter 8 for details). In contrast to Volusia County's regulation of beach lighting, however, local governments in the Puget Sound area *do* issue permits for development, which authorize developers to proceed in ways that could be alleged to take listed salmon. Would they be found liable for take that did occur? Perkins Coie, a major Seattle law firm, argues that the answer is no. In a widely circulated white paper, the firm stresses that state and local development permits affirm that an approved project complies only with the laws of the government issuing the permit, not with all relevant federal laws (see http://www.perkinscoie.com/page.cfm?id=184). The paper notes that Section 7 of the ESA addresses permitting liability for federal agencies by requiring that actions the agencies authorize must not jeopardize a listed species or adversely modify its critical habitat; the ESA contains no similar language for state and local governments.[13] Perkins Coie states that it is "unaware of any enforcement action brought by the United States alleging that state or local regulatory actions or inactions caused unlawful take, even though there are more than 1,000 listed species." Nevertheless, the same cannot be said of enforcement actions brought by third parties in court, such as *Strahan v. Coxe* and *Loggerhead Turtle v. Volusia County*. In 1996, a federal court in Seattle applied the principle of vicarious liability to a non-federal agency, ruling in favor of a lawsuit brought by three environmental groups against the members of the Washington Fish and Wildlife Commission for allowing bait and hound hunting for black bears (*Ursus americanus*) in the North Cascades, which made it more likely that listed grizzly bears would accidentally be killed (*Greater Ecosystem Alliance v. Lydig* 1996). More recently, in 2002 a federal court in Oregon supported the principle of vicarious liability in a case involving Oregon's permitting of clear-cuts in landslide-prone areas adjacent to habitat used by listed coho salmon (see *Pacific Rivers Council v. Brown* 2002). This case was ultimately dismissed because of a change in the status of the listing (P. Goldman, EarthJustice, personal communication), but it further establishes precedent for the principle of vicarious liability in the Puget Sound area.

---

[13] Numerous commentators have argued that *Defenders of Wildlife v. Environmental Protection Agency* and *Sierra Club v. Yeutter* were improperly decided since they focused on Section 9 prohibitions against take rather than Section 7, which applies to the permitting functions of federal agencies.

A lawsuit may succeed on that principle, however, and still lose on the *Sweet Home Chapter of Communities for a Greater Oregon v. Babbitt* standard that a prohibited act must be the "proximate cause" of the actual death or injury of a listed species. The causal connection between land uses, changes to aquatic habitat, and take of salmon is more complex than between fishing gear and take of right whales or between beachfront lighting and take of sea turtles. Most salmon eggs and juvenile salmon die under natural circumstances. Higher stormflows caused by land clearing and development will incrementally scour gravels with salmon eggs more deeply and more frequently. Higher stormflows will also incrementally increase erosion, which may cause additional fine sediments to suffocate incubating eggs. The most egregious and certain damage is cumulative, as forests are cleared, soils are paved, and the hydrology and habitat quality of streams changes accordingly. Take of salmon from land-use actions can rarely be traced to a specific development, in contrast to a whale caught in a single set of fishing gear. Take of salmon from a group of developments under a single land-use regulation may seem "proximate" (foreseeable) to a trained biologist using the models and population studies acceptable to NMFS. However, cumulative actions may seem less proximate to an elected official who must vote on the regulation or a judge who must decide a case, especially if the take must be of "identifiable" members of the species. The fact that not one case alleging such a take has been filed in the Puget Sound area—or, to my knowledge, anywhere salmon have been listed on the Pacific coast—indicates how pessimistic environmental attorneys are that they would win.

Cooperative Federalism Fails to Address Habitat: Section 6 and the 4(d) Rule

Section 6 of the ESA was Congress's attempt to address federal and state roles under the act. It offers cooperative agreements with federal financial assistance for up to 75% of the cost of state endangered species programs, or up to 90% when an agreement extends to two or more states (ESA, section 1535[d][2]). However, when Congress debated this section, it was not thinking of takings that relate to habitat degradation. Like water and air pollution, habitat degradation can occur through dramatic, obvious abuses but more typically is the consequence of multiple, minor individual actions. The Clean Water Act and Clean Air Act describe in detail how states are to address such problems, avoiding conflicts with the Tenth Amendment by giving states the choice of whether to administer the acts themselves or have them administered by the federal government (ESA, section 1535[d][2]). The ESA provides no details at all regarding how state or local governments should address habitat degradation.

---

[14] The Marine Mammal Protection Act was enacted as Public Law 92-522, 86 Stat. 1027. For a discussion of the relationship of the Marine Mammal Protection Act and the ESA, see Bean and Rowland 1997. Also see CRS 1982, including remarks by Senator Ted Stevens (R-AK): "The Federal Government has preempted the States [with the MMPA] and has not provided enough money to manage the program. Thus there is not enforcement agency to protect ocean mammals. This is the reason that the ESA of 1973 provides for a larger role for States and why there has been less opposition to it. I strongly support this trend."

Reviewing the legislative history, Congress modeled Section 6 of the ESA on the Marine Mammal Protection Act (MMPA; U.S. Code, volume 16)—which does not include harm, or any other reference that incorporates habitat degradation, in its definition of take (see MMPA, section 1372[a][3] and [4]).[14] The Marine Mammal Act created a political backlash by pre-empting the management authority of state governments. Congress believed it corrected this for endangered species by expressly allowing state laws to provide greater protection than the ESA and by the cost-sharing arrangements in Section 6. These provisions make some sense when approaching take as a matter of setting and enforcing fish and game laws; the provisions do not address the complex issues of protecting habitat for listed species. (Most state laws protecting endangered species, including Washington's, do not protect habitat; see Revised Code of Washington 77.15.120.[15])

The National Marine Fisheries Service has attempted to address the role of state and local land-use laws through use of Section 4(d) of the ESA, which authorizes special regulations for threatened (but not endangered) species. The regulations may allow some take of the species, so long as the issuing federal agency deems the regulations as a whole "necessary and advisable to provide for the conservation" of the species (ESA, section 1533[d]). NMFS issued what it called a "ground-breaking" 4(d) rule for salmon, intended to create incentives for state and local governments to address the "wide mosaic of activities" affecting salmon habitat, including development (USOFR 2000b). The rule provides criteria for NMFS's approval of development regulations and other activities, which would protect state and local governments from liability for take. When the 4(d) rule was issued, some observers saw it as a possible national model for addressing habitat issues under the ESA through cooperative federalism, as modeled by the Clean Water Act and Clean Air Act (see Fischman and Hall-Rivera 2002). But, as discussed in more detail in the next two chapters, the 4(d) rule has failed to live up to these hopes. Not one state or local government has sought NMFS's approval of its development regulations. Though some environmental groups have argued that NMFS's criteria for approval are too lenient,[16] it is impossible to know how high a standard they actually set without a test case. Absent a serious threat of legal liability for take, there is little incentive for a state or local government to choose to be that test case.

Whether such a threat is serious ultimately depends on the success of two legal arguments: first, that the principle of vicarious liability applies to state and local development regulations affecting salmon habitat; and second, that substandard development regulations (which might, for example, require only minimal stream buff-

---

[15] For a report on state endangered species laws across the country, see Defenders of Wildlife and Center for Wildlife Law "Saving Biodiversity: A Status Report on State Laws, Policies and Programs" (1995), by the Defenders of Wildlife at http://www.defenders.org/pb-bst00.html.)

[16] See, for example, *Washington Environmental Council v. National Marine Fisheries Service* 2002. The lawsuit was dismissed as not ripe because NMFS had not yet applied its criteria to specific land-use regulations.

ers or stormwater treatment) are proximate to the death of listed species. If these arguments fail, the ESA will also fail as a means to conserve salmon habitat in Puget Sound. The fact that no lawsuits have attempted to make these arguments so far has not gone unnoticed by state and local officials, developers, and the business community. As the next chapter will discuss, the resulting lack of perceived legal liability for take has dramatically affected how the region has responded to the salmon listings.

References

And now the timber wolf. 1982. The Washington Post (January 20):A21.

Anderson, J., and S. Yaffee. 1998. Balancing public trust and private interest: public participation in habitat conservation planning. University of Michigan School of Natural Resources & Environment, Ann Arbor.

Babbitt, B. 1994. The Endangered Species Act and "takings": a call for innovation within the terms of the act. Environmental Law 24(2):355–367.

Babbitt v. Sweet Home Chapter of Communities for a Greater Oregon, 515 U.S. 687 (1995).

Bean, M. J., and M. J. Rowland. 1997. The evolution of national wildlife law, 3rd edition. Praeger Publishers, Westport, Connecticut.

Carter, J. 1980. Public papers of the presidents of the United States, 1979. Volume 2. U.S. Government Printing Office, Washington, D.C.

Coates v. Strahan, 119 S.Ct 437 (1998).

Conservation Council for Hawaii v. Babbitt, 2 F.Supp.2d 1280 (D. Hawaii 1988).

CRS (Congressional Research Service for the Committee on Environment and Public Works, U.S. Senate) 1982. A legislative history of the endangered species act of 1973, as amended in 1976, 1977, 1978, 1979, and 1980. U.S. Government Printing Office, Serial No. 97-6, Washington, D.C.

Defenders of Wildlife and Center for Wildlife Law. 1995. Saving biodiversity: a status report on state laws, policies and programs. Defenders of Wildlife, Washington, D.C. Available: http://www.defenders.org/pb-bst00.html (March 2006).

Defenders of Wildlife v. Environmental Protection Agency, 882 F.2d 1294 (8th Cir. 1989).

Federation v. Coleman, 529 F.2d 371 (1976).

Feldman, M., and M. Brennan. 2001. The growing importance of critical habitat for species conservation. Natural Resources and Environment 16:88.

Fischman, R. L., and J. Hall-Rivera. 2002. A lesson for conservation from pollution control law: cooperative federalism for recovery under the ESA. Columbia Journal of Environmental Law 27:94–109.

GAO (General Accounting Office). 1994. Endangered Species Act: information on species protection on nonfederal lands. General Accounting Office, GAO/RCED-95-16, Washington, D.C.

Glen, A. M., and C. M. Douglas. 2001. Taking species: difficult questions of proximity and degree. Natural Resources and the Environment 16:65–69, 132.

Greater Ecosystem Alliance v. Lydic, unpublished, No. C94-1536C (WD Wash 1996).

Gutierrez, R. J., and A. B. Carey, editors. 1985. Ecology and management of the spotted owl in the Pacific Northwest. U.S. Forest Service, General Technical Report PNW-185, Portland, Oregon.

Hill v. TVA (Tennessee Valley Authority), 549 F.2d 1074 (CA6 1977).

House panel's bill spares parks, limits ESA. 1995. The Washington Post (June 16):A11.

Kareiva, P., S. Andelman, D. Doak, B. Elderd, M. Groom, J. Hoekstra, L. Hood, F. James, J.

Lamoreux, G. LeBuhn, C. McCulloch, J. Regetz, L. Savage, M. Ruckelshaus, D. Skelly, H. Wilbur, K. Zamudio, and NCEAS HCP working group. 1998. Using science in habitat conservation plans. National Center for Ecological Analysis and Synthesis, Santa Barbara, California and American Institute of Biological Sciences, Washington, D.C.

Kenworthy, T., and A. Devroy. 1993. Clinton pledges 'balanced' solution to forest policy crisis in 2 months. The Washington Post (April 3).

Loggerhead Turtle v. Volusia County, 896 F.Supp. 1170 (M.D.Fla. 1995).

Loggerhead Turtle v. Volusia County, 148 F.3d 1231 (11th Cir. 1998).

Loggerhead Turtle v. Volusia County, 119 S.Ct 1488 (1999).

Loggerhead Turtle v. Volusia County, 92 F.Supp.2d 1296 (M.D.Fla. 2000).

Mapes, J. 1992. Clinton vows NW forest summit: Bush eyes changes in species act. The Portland Oregonian (August 27).

Middle Rio Grande Conservancy District v. Babbitt, No. CIV 99-870 (D.N.M. 2000).

Natural Resources Defense Council v. U.S. Department of the Interior, 113 F3d 1121 (95h Cir. 1997).

New Mexico Cattle Growers Association v. FWS (Fish and Wildlife Service), 248 F.3d 1277 (10th Cir. 2001).

Nixon, R. M. 1974a. Public papers of the presidents of the United States, 1972. U.S. Government Printing Office, Washington, D.C.

Nixon, R. M. 1974b. Public papers of the presidents of the United States, 1973. U.S. Government Printing Office, Washington, D.C.

Nixon signs bill to give states manpower funds. 1973. The Washington Post (December 29):A1.

Northern spotted owl is 'threatened.' 1990. The Washington Post (June 23):A1.

NRC (National Research Council) 1995. Science and the Endangered Species Act. National Academy Press, Washington, D.C.

NWF (National Wildlife Federation) v. Babbitt, 128 F. Supp.2d 1274 (E.D.Cal. 2000).

NWF (National Wildlife Federation) v. Coleman, 529 F.2d 371 (5th Cir. 1976).

Pacific Rivers Council v. Brown, Case No. CV 02-243-BR, Opinion and Order (D.Or 2002).

Petersen, S. C. 2002. Acting for endangered species: the statutory ark. University of Kansas Press, Lawrence.

Portland Audubon Society v. Endangered Species Committee, 984 F.2d 1534 (9th Cir. 1993).

President signs bill reshaping federal manpower programs. 1973. The Los Angeles Times (December 29):A1.

President signs manpower bill. 1973. The New York Times (December 29):A13.

Protecting endangered species. 1973. The Washington Post (June 26):A22.

Schaefer, D., and E. Pryne. 1992. Bush takes offensive on spotted-owl debate. Seattle Times (May 14):A1.

Seattle Audubon Society v. Evans, 771 F.Supp. 1081 (W.D. Wash. 1991).

Seattle Audubon Society v. Lyons, 871 F.Supp. 1291 (W.D. Wa 1994).

Sierra Club v. Babbitt, 15 F.Supp.2d 1274 (S.D. Ala. 1998).

Sierra Club v. Lujan, 36 Environmental Rep. Cas. (BNA) 1533 (W.D. Tex. Feb. 1, 1993), *appeal dismissed*, 995 F.2d 571 (5th Cir. 1993).

Sierra Club v. U.S. Fish and Wildlife Service, 245 F3d 434 (5th Cir. 2001).

Sierra Club v. Yeutter, 926 F.2d 429 (5th Cir. 1991).

Skrzycki, C. 1995. Hill republicans promise a regulatory revolution. The Washington Post (January 4):A1.

Strahan v. Coxe, 127 F.3d 155 (1st Cir. 1997).

Strahan v. Coxe, 119 SC 81 (1998).

Sweet Home Chapter of Communities for a Greater Oregon v. Babbitt, 17 F.3d 1463, (D.C. Cir. 1994).

Thomas, J. W., E. D. Forsman, J. B. Lint, E. C. Meslow, B. R. Noon, and J. Verner. 1990. A conservation strategy for the northern spotted owl. Interagency Scientific Committee, Portland, Oregon.

TVA (Tennessee Valley Authority) v. Hill, 419 F.Supp. 760 (ED Tenn. 1976).

TVA (Tennessee Valley Authority) v. Hill, 437 U.S. 153 (1978).

U.S. Forest Service. 1986. Draft supplement to the environmental impact statement for an amendment to the Pacific Northwest Regional Guide, volumes 1, 2. U.S. Forest Service, Pacific Northwest Region, Portland, Oregon.

U.S. Forest Service and U.S. Bureau of Land Management. 1994. Final supplemental environmental impact statement on management of habitat for late-successional and old-growth forest related species within the range of the northern spotted owl. U.S. Forest Service and U.S. Bureau of Land Management, Washington, D.C.

U.S. House of Representatives. 1982. Endangered Species Act amendments of 1982. House Conference Report 97-835. (9th Congress, 2nd session, September 17).

U.S. House of Representatives, Committee on Interior and Insular Affairs, Subcommittee on National Parks and Public Lands. 1992. Joint oversight hearing on the spotted owl crisis. (102nd Congress, 2nd session, March 24).

U.S. Senate. 1982. Endangered Species Act amendments of 1982. Senate Report 97-418. (97th Congress, 2nd Session, May 6).

U.S. Senate, Committee on Environment and Public Works, Subcommittee on Environmental Protection. 1992. Hearing on conservation of the northern spotted owl. (102nd Congress, 2nd Session, May 13).

U.S. studying way to save wildlife. 1964. The New York Times (July 7):A16.

USFWS (U.S. Fish and Wildlife Service) and NMFS (National Marine Fisheries Service). 1996. Habitat conservation planning and incidental take permit processing handbook. U.S. Department of the Interior, Washington, D.C.

USOFR (U.S. Office of the Federal Register). 1975. Endangered and threatened wildlife and plants; reclassification of the American alligator and other amendments, Federal Register 40:188(26 September 1975):44412–44423.

USOFR (U.S. Office of the Federal Register). 1981a. Endangered and threatened wildlife and plants: proposed redefinition of "harm," Federal Register 46(2 June 1981):29490–29491.

USOFR (U.S. Office of the Federal Register) 1981b. Executive Order 12291, Federal Register 46(7 December 1981):13192.

USOFR (U.S. Office of the Federal Register). 1981c. Final rule: endangered and threatened wildlife and plants; proposed redefinition of "harm," Federal Register 46(4 November 1981):54748, 54750.

USOFR (U.S. Office of the Federal Register). 1996. Policy regarding the recognition of distinct vertebrate population segments under the Endangered Species Act, Federal Register 61(7 February 1996):4721–4725.

USOFR (U.S. Office of the Federal Register). 1998. Habitat Conservation Plan Assurances ("No Surprises") Rule, Federal Register 63:35(23 February 1998):8859–8873.

USOFR (U.S. Office of the Federal Register). 1999a. Safe harbor agreements and candidate conservation agreements with assurances; announcement of final safe harbor policy; announcement of final policy for candidate conservation agreements with assurances; final rule and notices. Federal Register 64:116(17 June 1999):32717–32726.

USOFR (U.S. Office of the Federal Register). 1999b. Endangered and threatened wildlife and plants; definition of 'harm.' Federal Register 64:215(8 November 1999): 60727–60731.

USOFR (U.S. Office of the Federal Register). 1999c. Endangered and threatened wildlife and plants; notice of intent to clarify the role of habitat in endangered species conservation. Federal Register 64:113(14 June 1999):31871–31874.

USOFR (U.S. Office of the Federal Register). 1999d. Endangered and threatened wildlife and plants. Final listing priority guidance for fiscal year 2000. Federal Register 64:204(22 October 1999):57114–57119.

USOFR (U.S. Office of the Federal Register). 2000a. Announcement of draft policy for evaluation of conservation efforts when making listing decisions, Federal Register 65:114(13 June 2000):37102–37108.

USOFR (U.S. Office of the Federal Register). 2000b. Final rule governing take of 14 threatened salmon and steelhead ESUs, Federal Register 65:132(10 July 2000):42421–42481.

USOFR (U.S. Office of the Federal Register). 2000c. Notice of availability of a final addendum to the handbook for habitat conservation planning and incidental take permitting process, Federal Register 65:106(1 June 2000):35241–35257.

USOFR (U.S. Office of the Federal Register). 2005. National forest system land management planning, Federal Register 70:3(5 January 2005):1023–1061.

Washington Environmental Council v. National Marine Fisheries Service, Case C00-1574R (W.D. Wash. 2002).

Yaffee, S. 1994. The wisdom of the spotted owl: policy lessons for a new century. Island Press, Washington, D.C.

Chapter 8. Applying the ESA: Salmon, Orcas, and What's Not on the List

> It is possible, hypothetically, that the reduced or declining trends of each of the individual species [under review] could be considered as insufficient for affording any of [them] legal protection under the ESA. But taking no action, under such circumstances, might be a major mistake if this collective information is an indication that the Puget Sound area, as an ecosystem, is experiencing major change. [Gustafson et al. 2000]

Chapter Summary

Two complications for the Endangered Species Act (ESA) discussed in the last chapter are profoundly affecting the act's ability to protect Puget Sound's major ecosystems. The first complication concerns the disputed importance of designating critical habitat. Until very recently, the long-held position of the Fish and Wildlife Service (FWS) that this action is a low priority led FWS to ignore it for the great majority of listed species. After a federal appeals court agreed with environmental groups in 1997 that designating critical habitat was mandatory under the ESA (see *Natural Resources Defense Council v. U.S. Department of the Interior* 1997), dozens of lawsuits have required FWS to address this backlog. Other successful lawsuits from business and property rights groups have required that all designations include an analysis of economic impacts (*Middle Rio Grande Conservancy District v. Babbitt* 2000 and *New Mexico Cattle Growers Association v. USFWS* 2001), making this job considerably more onerous. Collectively, these court orders have diverted much of FWS's listing budget. As a result, in the Puget Sound region and nationwide, since 2000, FWS has generally reviewed the status of species proposed for listing and has listed new species only by court order, even when FWS believes that listing is clearly warranted (USOFR 2005a). Environmentalists blame the Bush administration and Congress for this, but at least part of the problem is fundamental to the way the act is written.

The second complication concerns the unequal ways the ESA applies to different activities that can take listed species. Differences between federal and non-federal actions and how "proximate" harmful actions are to the actual death of listed species not only explain many of the differences in the region's experience with spotted owls versus salmon; they also explain profound differences in how activities harming salmon have been affected. Salmon harvests are now far below what they were in the mid-1990s. If not for treaties with Canada and Indian tribes, they almost certainly would be even less, since they are so obviously a take. Hatchery reforms that have been advocated for decades are finally beginning, because hatcheries, too (especially under traditional management), are obvious sources of take. But most activities affecting salmon habitat have changed little since the listings, in part for reasons discussed at the end of the last chapter—without any clear legal threat, there has been little incentive to make difficult changes.

Instead, a group of regional leaders has been developing the Shared Strategy for Puget Sound Salmon, which is intended to integrate actions addressing harvest, hatcheries, and habitat into an overall salmon recovery strategy. The Shared Strategy generally brings together the right organizations for this effort, but it faces many challenges. Perhaps the most fundamental challenges relate to the lack of progress on most habitat issues, with only one major exception: forestry. The fight over the spotted owl *Strix occidentalis* left valuable legacies for salmon, not only on federal lands but also in an industry ready to negotiate considerable habitat reforms, as the next chapter will describe. To put these changes in the context of the larger needs of Puget Sound's major ecosystems, though, it is important to begin with the rest of the picture.

The Listing Process: Dominated by Court Orders

Evaluating the status of species petitioned for listing is fundamental to implementing the ESA, as Congress recognized in 1982 when it set deadlines for listing decisions. Until a species is proposed for listing, the ESA does not require federal agencies to take any action to protect them; until a listing is final, the ESA provides no protection from non-federal actions. But Congress's 1982 amendment allowed two exceptions to its deadlines. The FWS or the National Marine Fisheries Service (NMFS) must initiate a status review of species petitioned for listing only "to the maximum extent practicable." If they do not have the budget for the review, they may defer it. After a status review, even if the agencies find that a species should be listed, they can determine that actually doing so is "warranted but precluded" by higher priority actions, so long as they are making "expeditious progress" in their listing decisions as a whole (ESA, section 1533[b][3]; USOFR 2005a). These exceptions have dominated FWS's listing process since the mid-1990s, for two reasons. First, Congress temporarily suspended the listing program in 1995 and has underfunded it ever since. Second, the court orders on critical habitat mentioned above have led to a large backlog of "candidate" species, which FWS has determined warrant listing but which it has been unable to list (or even propose to list)—286 species at the latest count (USOFR 2005a), in comparison to 1,880 species that have been listed since the ESA was passed in 1973.[1] These factors also have prevented FWS from reviewing the status of hundreds of additional species petitioned for listing, some of which may now be extinct. (See Tables 8-1[a], 8-1[b], and 8-1[c] for all listed, candidate, and petitioned species in the Puget Sound area.) NMFS has not developed a similar backlog, in part because there are fewer marine and anadromous species for it to review compared to the terrestrial and freshwater species for which FWS is responsible.

In 2003, the second Bush administration called the ESA "broken" because court orders to designate critical habitat were keeping it from taking more important actions to list species and develop recovery plans (U.S. Department of the Interior 2003). The assistant secretary of the Interior for Fish and Wildlife and Parks compared the situa-

---

[1] See http://ecos.fws.gov/tess_public/Boxscore.do.

TABLE 8-1(a). Endangered Species in Puget Sound: A Scorecard

Common name	Scientific name	Comments
Endangered		
Humpback whales	*Megaptera novaeangliae*	Found throughout all oceans; depleted by past overharvesting; vulnerable to pollution, disturbance by boat traffic, and entanglement in fishing gear.
Leatherback sea turtle	*Dermochelys coriacea*	At severe risk of extinction due to incidental take from longline fishing.
Marsh sandwort	*Arenaria paludicola*	Probably extirpated from Washington; freshwater marsh habitat vulnerable to development.
Orca (killer whale), Southern resident	*Orcinus orca*	Range includes Puget Sound in spring, summer, and fall; at risk from persistent toxins, reduced food population (salmon, especially Chinook salmon), vessel traffic, and possible major oil spill.
Threatened		
Bald eagle	*Haliaeetus leucocephalus*	In process for de-listing as recovered.
Bull trout	*Salvelinus confluentus*	Puget Sound/coastal populations listed as "distinct population segment."
Chinook salmon	*Oncorhynchus tshawytscha*	Puget Sound evolutionarily significant unit includes all American waters west to Elwha River.
Chum salmon (Hood Canal, summer)	*Oncorhynchus keta*	Evolutionarily significant unit includes Discovery and Sequim bays.
Golden paintbrush	*Castilleja levisecta*	Found in prairie and outwash soils; now known in only 12 sites from the Gulf Islands, B.C. to south of Olympia, Washington.
Gray wolf	*Canis lupus*	Rare in contiguous U.S. due to being targeted for killing from the late 1800s to approximately 1950. Reliable sightings of individual wolves in North Cascades in the past 20 years, but no verified pack activity.
Grizzly bear, North Cascades population	*Ursus arctos horribilis*	FWS believes "endangered" status is warranted, but lack of resources precludes reclassification; North Cascades population may now be as low as five.
Marbled murrelet	*Brachyramphus marmoratus marmoratus*	FWS has determined that murrelets in Washington, Oregon, and California are not a distinct population segment. Listing status will not change until review of overall population is complete.

TABLE 8-1(a). Continued.

Nelson's checker-mallow	*Sidalcea nelsoniana*	Prairie plant endemic to Northwest; may be extirpated from Washington.
Northern spotted owl	*Strix occidentalis caurina*	Declining 7% annually in Washington for past decade; FWS confirmed threatened status in 2004, but did not change to endangered.
Steelhead*	*Oncorhynchus mykiss*	Proposed in Puget Sound across all American waters west to Elwha River.
Steller sea lion	*Eumetopias jubatus*	Pacific Coast population to southeast Alaska generally stable; vulnerable to reduced food availability.
Water howellia	*Howellia aquatilis*	Found in small vernal wetlands in Northwest; since listing in 1993, range has expanded to include more than 20 occurrences in western Washington.
Western snowy plover	*Charadrius alexandrinus nivosus*	Declining on Pacific Coast, rare in Washington, vulnerable to beach development. FWS confirmed threatened status in April 2006, in response to a petition to delist.

* Proposed for listing; final decision likely in 2007.

TABLE 8-1(b). Believed by U.S. Fish and Wildlife Service to warrant listing.

Common name	Scientific name	Status[a]	Comments
Dolly varden	*Salvelinus malma*	PT	Proposed as "threatened" based on similarity of appearance to bull trout.
Fisher (West Coast)	*Martes pennanti pacifica*	C* 6	Fisher appears to be extinct in Washington; the Washington Department of Fish and Wildlife is studying reintroducing them to the Olympic Peninsula.
Mardon skipper	*Polites mardon*	C* 5	Rare butterfly found in Puget Sound prairie habitats and South Cascades.
Mazama gopher	*Thomomys mazama*	C* 3	Eight subspecies in western Washington, several presumed extirpated, are all candidates.
Oregon spotted frog	*Rana pretiosa*	C* 2	Extirpated from up to 90% of range; vulnerable to habitat degradation, predation by nonnative fish and bullfrogs.
Streaked horned lark	*Eremophila aplestris strigata*	C* 6	Extirpated from north Puget Sound and San Juan islands;

TABLE 8-1(b). Continued.

			less than 100 pairs in south sound and Washington coast and Willamette Valley.
Whulge (Taylor's) checkerspot	*Euphydryas editha taylori*	C* 3	Associated with prairies in B.C., Washington, and Oregon; fewer butterfly than 15 populations left.

[a] C: Candidate
C*: Candidate based on petition; FWS has found listing is warranted but precluded by higher priority actions, including court orders
PT: Proposed threatened
Numbers refer to priority category among pending listing actions. Categories range nationally from 1 to 12, based on the immediacy and magnitude of the threat of extinction and taxonomic distinctiveness (in order: monotypic genera, full species and subspecies, or distinct population segments).

TABLE 8-1(c). Petitioned for listing, but Fish and Wildlife Service has been unable to review.

Common name	Scientific name	Comments
Island marble butterfly	*Euchloe ausonides insulanus*	Known only from San Juan and Lopez islands. FWS review of petition found substantial information that listing may be warranted. A status review is underway.
Issaquah Creek early run	*Oncorhynchus nerka*	Believed by petitioners to have gone extinct since kokanee petition for emergency listing in 2000.
Western gray squirrel	*Sciurus griseus*	Within Puget Sound, found in south sound prairies.
Wolverine	*Gulo gulo*	Petitioned for listing across northern United States.

TABLE 8-1(d). Listing found "not warranted" by NMFS.

Common name	Scientific name	Comments
Puget Sound salmonids		
Chum salmon	*Oncorhynchus keta*	Includes all Puget Sound populations except Hood Canal summer ESU; small summer, winter runs called "intrinsically at risk."
Coho salmon	*Oncorhynchus kisutch*	Subject to continuing review; wild populations in south Puget Sound at risk.

TABLE 8-1(d). Continued.

Cutthroat trout	*Oncorhynchus clarki clarki*	Little information available, because not species of commercial interest.
Pink salmon	*Oncorhynchus gorbuscha*	Puget Sound even year ESU limited to small Snohomish River population, currently healthy; odd year ESU abundance is up since 1970s.
Sockeye salmon	*Oncorhynchus nerka*	Baker Lake ESU depends on human intervention;Bear Creek is provisional ESU, at risk from urbanization.
Other Puget Sound species		
Pacific cod	*Gadus macrocephalus*	Risk of extinction in Puget Sound/Georgia basin, but populations not sufficiently distinct from others that are healthy in northeast Pacific Ocean.
Pacific hake	*Merluccius productus*	Subject to continuing review; Puget Sound populations have declined steeply, but genetically related to healthy Georgia basin populations.
Pacific herring	*Clupea pallasi*	Puget Sound populations have declined steeply, but not sufficiently distinct from others that are healthy in northeast Pacific Ocean. Populations naturally vary in large cycles.
Rockfish	*Sebastes* spp.	Thirteen species on Washington State's "candidate" list. NMFS review focused on three because little data available on others. More recent data indicate lower abundance for these three species than available at time of NMFS review.
Walleye pollock	*Theragra chalcogramma*	Puget Sound populations have declined steeply, but not sufficiently distinct from others that are healthy in northeast Pacific Ocean.

Sources: http://endangered.fws.gov/wildlife.html; http://www.nwr.noaa.gov (see status reviews for individual species); USOFR 2005a; T. Thomas, U.S. Fish and Wildlife Service, personal communication; natureserve.org.

tion to "an emergency room where lawsuits force the doctors to treat sprained ankles while patients with heart attacks expire in the waiting room" (U.S. Department of the Interior 2003). Both the Clinton and the second Bush administrations have believed that designating critical habitat should be a low priority, arguing that it provides little, if any, additional protections for species (see Chapter 7). The Bush administration has estimated that it costs about $400,000 to designate critical habitat for a typical species, about twice the cost of the average process to list a species. The higher cost is due to the development of detailed maps and the required economic analysis, as well as what can be a more extended public review process (see Questions and Answers—Critical Habitat Issue, attached to U.S. Department of the Interior 2003). At the request of the Clinton and Bush administrations, Congress capped funding for critical habitat designations to keep courts from ordering the transfer of funds from recovery planning and other programs. Listing actions, however, are also under the cap, since the ESA mandates that critical habitat be designated at the time a species is listed, "to the maximum extent prudent and determinable" (ESA, section 1533[a][3]). Despite almost doubling the budget for listing species and designating critical habitat from $6.2 million in 2000 to $12.3 million in 2004, all of these actions have been under court order during the Bush administration. In 2003, the administration estimated that completing court-ordered actions under current budget levels would take until 2008. Congress could, of course, speed that process by appropriating more funds for listing species and designating critical habitat. However, that would not address the "real question," the Bush administration argues, which is "whether the benefits of critical habitat warrant the large expenditures that would be required were it to be designated for all listed species" (see Questions and Answers—Critical Habitat Issue, attached to U.S. Department of the Interior 2003).

Without question, many more species are at risk of extinction in the Puget Sound area than those shown in Table 8-1(b). As discussed in Chapter 2, out of an estimated 7,013 species in the Puget Sound region, the Center for Biological Diversity identifies 957 as "imperiled" and 285 as "critically imperiled" (see page 23).

To List or Not to List: A Matter of Judgment

The decision whether or not to list a species under the ESA involves three steps:

1. *Identify the group to be evaluated.* In addition to full species, listing decisions apply to subspecies and, for vertebrates, to distinct population segments (DPSs). NMFS defines a DPS for salmon as an "evolutionarily significant unit," or ESU.[2] The ESA defines all of these groupings as a "species" for purposes of implementing the act. Determining whether or not a grouping of the species qualifies as a DPS or an ESU involves two decisions: whether the group is distinct from other representatives of the same species, typically based on genetics, habitat, and life history patterns (e.g., a summer versus a winter run of salmon); and, if the group is distinct, whether it plays an important role in the evolutionary heritage of the species. These are both matters of judgment, on which knowledgeable scientists disagree.
2. *Identify the group's risk of extinction.* Under the ESA, "endangered" means that the species, subspecies, DPS, or ESU is "in danger of extinction throughout all or a

[2] See Waples 1991. For a broader discussion of the ESA's definition of "species," see Chapter 3 of NRC 1995. In the latter report, the National Academy of Sciences supported the ESA's inclusion of subspecies and distinct population segments under the term "species." It recommended use of the concept "evolutionary unit," similar to "evolutionarily significant units" for salmon, "to help provide scientific objectivity in identifying" distinct population segments. It also argued that there was no scientific reason for limiting distinct population segments to vertebrates, for purposes of the ESA's protections.

significant portion of its range" (ESA, section 1532[6]); "threatened" means it is "likely to become...endangered...within the foreseeable future throughout all or a significant portion of its range" (ESA, section 1532[19]). In 1995, the National Academy of Sciences recommended that these terms be quantified based on the percent chance of extinction over 100 years, but neither the ESA nor its implementing regulations have been amended to this effect (see NRC 1995[3]). Even if they had been, available models to calculate the actual risk of extinction involve a great deal of uncertainty, especially when little is known about a species (NRC 1995). Evaluating the risk of extinction, then, is also a matter of judgment, on which knowledgeable scientists disagree.

3. *Evaluate whether existing conservation efforts adequately address the risk.* The ESA requires that the decision whether to list a species take into account efforts being made to conserve it (ESA, section 1529[b][1][A]). Under the ESA's implementing regulations, this evaluation considers both the certainty that conservation efforts will be implemented and the certainty that they will be effective (see USOFR 2003). These issues, of course, also involve judgments, both scientific and political, on which reasonable people can disagree.

Courts will generally defer to the judgments of FWS and NMFS on these questions unless they find that the agencies have been "arbitrary and capricious" in their decisions. A recent example of such a finding came in December 2003, when a court ruled that NMFS had not used the best available science in determining that Puget Sound's Southern Resident population of killer whales (orcas) was not a distinct population segment of the species. The court found that NMFS had not given "the benefit of the doubt to the species" because it assumed, among other things, that all orcas worldwide were one species with no distinct subspecies, and that transient orcas that visit Puget Sound could potentially replace the Southern Resident population should it go extinct (see Krahn et al. 2002). The court did not require that the Southern Resident population be listed; instead, it required that NMFS rework its decision by December 2004 (Environmental News Service 2003). In this case, NMFS did ultimately decide to list Puget Sound resident orcas as endangered, as discussed in more detail on pages 151–152.

Listed Salmon: Bringing the ESA to Urban and Suburban Areas

For the Puget Sound region's urban and suburban areas, the decision to list Puget Sound Chinook salmon was the most momentous of all listing decisions to date, including even the listing of orcas. Chinook salmon migrate through, rear, and sometimes spawn in urban and suburban areas. All other listed species in the region are primarily found far away from where most people live. There may well be additional species in urban areas that are near extinction across all or much of their ranges,

[3] The National Academy of Science recognized that selecting particular degrees of risk for particular periods of time to trigger ESA decisions involves both scientific knowledge and societal values.

including certain snails, freshwater mussels, amphibians, insects, and numerous plants. Many such species may already be extinct, but they have generally been studied little, if at all. Those few that have been studied have had no advocates prepared to petition for their listing. As is true nationally, species that are listed are often "charismatic" and of conservation interest to the general population—salmon, grizzly bears, wolves, and so forth—or are indicators of the health of major ecosystems, such as old-growth forests. Given the current state of the listing process, at least for the terrestrial and freshwater species for which FWS is responsible, it is unlikely that less charismatic species from the region will be added to the list anytime soon, even if they have strong advocates well-armed with scientific information.

Evolutionarily sgnificant units of salmon must be reproductively isolated from other groups of salmon and must represent "an important component in the evolutionary legacy of the species" (see Waples 1991). There are two listed ESUs within the Puget Sound ecoregion: Puget Sound Chinook salmon (covering all American waters of the sound west to the Elwha River), and Hood Canal summer chum salmon (including adjacent bays on the Olympic Peninsula). Both were listed in 1999 as threatened, rather than endangered. In March 2006, Puget Sound steelhead were also proposed for a threatened listing; a final decision is expected in 2007. The listings of Chinook salmon and Hood Canal summer chum salmon resulted from coast-wide reviews of the status of Pacific salmon species, which NMFS began in the early to mid-1990s after a variety of environmental and fishing groups petitioned to list different ESUs across Washington, Idaho, Oregon, and California. The petitions and status reviews were prompted in part by a 1991 report from the Endangered Species Committee of the American Fisheries Society, which identified over 100 Pacific salmon stocks that had recently gone extinct across Washington, Oregon, California, and Idaho and 214 stocks that were at risk of extinction (Nehlson et al. 1991). As of April 2006, NMFS has listed 26 ESUs across the Pacific Coast (see Table 8-2). In addition, in 1999 FWS listed bull trout (which are under its jurisdiction because they are generally a freshwater fish) as threatened across their entire range in the coterminous United States. FWS considers bull trout in the Puget Sound area and along the Washington coast to be a distinct population segment, unique because it includes the only known anadromous populations of bull trout in the coterminous states (see USOFR 1999c).

NMFS established biological review teams (BRTs) to review the status of each species of Pacific salmon, composed of staff from its Fisheries Science Centers on the west coast (supplemented in some cases by staff from the National Biological Survey). FWS took a parallel approach for its listing decisions. The agencies followed the recommendations of these teams with regard to defining ESUs or DPSs and generally followed their recommendations regarding extinction risks. On the recommendations of BRTs, in the Puget Sound area NMFS decided against listing pink and sockeye salmons, cutthroat trout (the last decision was reached jointly with FWS, since some populations never leave freshwater), and all chum salmon in the area besides the Hood Canal summer ESU; NMFS did not list Puget Sound coho salmon, but did identify it as a "species of concern," consistent with the BRT recom-

TABLE 8-2. Endangered Species Act status of West Coast salmon and steelhead.

Species/ESU			ESA listing status
Sockeye salmon	1	Snake River	Endangered
Oncorhynchus	2	Ozette Lake	Threatened
nerka	3	Baker River	Not warranted
	4	Okanogan River	Not warranted
	5	Lake Wenatchee	Not warranted
	6	Quinalt Lake	Not warranted
	7	Lake Pleasant	Not warranted
Chinook salmon	8	Sacramento River winter run	Endangered
O. tshawytscha	9	Upper Columbia River spring run	Endangered
	10	Snake River spring/summer run	Threatened
	11	Snake River fall run	Threatened
	12	Puget Sound	Threatened
	13	Lower Columbia River	Threatened
	14	Upper Willamette River	Threatened
	15	Central Valley spring run	Threatened
	16	California Coastal	Threatened
	17	Central Valley fall and late fall run	Species of concern
	18	Upper Klamath – Trinity River	Not warranted
	19	Oregon Coast	Not warranted
	20	Washington Coast	Not warranted
	21	Middle Columbia River spring run	Not warranted
	22	Upper Columbia River summer/fall run	Not warranted
	23	Southern Oregon and northern California coast	Not warranted
	24	Deschutes River summer/fall run	Not warranted
Coho salmon	25	Central California coast	Endangered
O. kisutch	26	Southern Oregon/Northern California	Threatened
	27	Lower Columbia River	Threatened
	28	Oregon Coast	Not warranted
	29	Southwest Washington	Not warranted
	30	Puget Sound/Strait of Georgia	Species of concern
	31	Olympic Peninsula	Not warranted
Chum salmon	32	Hood Canal summer run	Threatened
O. keta	33	Columbia River	Threatened
	34	Puget Sound/Strait of Georgia	Not warranted
	35	Pacific Coast	Not warranted
Steelhead	36	Southern California E	Endangered
O. mykiss	37	Upper Columbia River	Threatened
	38	Central California Coast	Threatened
	39	South central California Coast	Threatened
	40	Snake River basin	Threatened
	41	Lower Columbia River	Threatened
	42	California Central Valley	Threatened
	43	Upper Willamette River	Threatened
	44	Middle Columbia River	Threatened
	45	Northern California	Threatened
	46	Puget Sound	Proposed
threatened			
	47	Oregon Coast	Species of concern
	48	Southwest Washington	Not warranted
	49	Olympic Peninsula	Not warranted
	50	Klamath Mountains Province	Not warranted
Pink salmon	51	Even-year	Not warranted
O. gorbuscha	52	Odd-year	Not warranted

Source: http://www.nwr.noaa.gov/ESA-Salmon-Listings/Salmon-Populations/Index.cfm (May 2006). All shaded Esus are within or include the Puget Sound basin.

mendation. NMFS also decided against listing seven other marine fish petitioned for listing. Table 8-1(d) provides very brief explanations of these decisions.

Split Decisions on Coho Salmon

The decision against listing Puget Sound coho salmon is worth considering in more detail both to illustrate the decision-making process and because it was particularly important. Listing coho salmon would have had a greater impact on human land uses in the region than listing any other salmon species, for two reasons: coho salmon spawn in small streams, which are more vulnerable to changes from human land uses than large rivers, where Chinook salmon and most other salmon species generally spawn; and coho salmon rear in freshwater streams for more than a year before migrating to the ocean, extending the period of their vulnerability.

In announcing its decision on Puget Sound coho salmon, NMFS acknowledged that risk assessments "are based as much on professional judgment as on hard data" (USOFR 1995:38024). The BRT found that coho salmon from Puget Sound and the Strait of Georgia (up to but not including Queen Charlotte Strait at the north end of Vancouver Island) are "a coherent genetic cluster" and are therefore part of the same ESU. It also found the ESU to extend to the Olympic Peninsula east of Salt Creek and up the lower Fraser River to Hope, British Columbia (Weitkamp et al. 1996). In assessing extinction risk, the BRT noted coho salmon in the ESU were relatively abundant compared to other coho salmon along the Pacific coast, with roughly 1.5 million adults returning annually. As of the BRT's initial report in 1994, returns to Canada had declined sharply since the 1950s, while run sizes in Puget Sound were generally stable. Approximately 62% of the latter, however, were from hatcheries, making it "difficult to identify self-sustaining, native stocks within this region." The BRT was especially concerned by a "dramatic" decline in the average size of Puget Sound coho salmon caught in terminal fisheries, from about 4 kilograms (8.8 pounds) in 1972 to about 2 kilograms (4.4 pounds) in 1993, which it said "could seriously reduce the fecundity and fitness of naturally spawning fish." It also was concerned by "extremely high" harvest rates, which it estimated to have fluctuated in the range of 60% to 90% in recent years. The BRT's original conclusion stated, "if present trends continue, this ESU is likely to become endangered in the foreseeable future" (Weitkamp et al. 1996:15). However, the BRT revised this conclusion after receiving further information indicating that hatchery-produced coho salmon made up a smaller percentage of spawners than it originally believed in the Skagit River and possibly elsewhere. It then said that either of two options would be reasonable: listing Puget Sound coho salmon as threatened, based on "substantial concern for the health of the natural populations and the importance of taking a risk-averse approach to conservation"; or determining that available information did not warrant listing but committing NMFS "to a thorough reevaluation of the status of the ESU within the year" (M. Schiewe, 1995 memo to W. Stelle, Jr., National Marine Fisheries Service). The regional director for NMFS recommended the latter option, emphasizing that regional conservation efforts held promise for benefiting Puget Sound coho salmon (W. Stelle Jr., 1995 memo[4] to R. Schmitten, National Marine Fisheries Service).

[4] "Puget Sound Coho Salmon—Recommendation Not to Propose to list as threatened under the Endangered Species Act."

In announcing its official decision not to list Puget Sound coho salmon, NMFS stressed a variety of uncertainties:

> Although the magnitude of artificial propagation in the Puget Sound region ensures that there are ample opportunities for adverse effects on natural populations, few studies have been conducted to determine the extent to which such effects actually occur. Similarly, because virtually no information is available on size of naturally spawning coho salmon in Puget Sound, NMFS' evaluation of the decline in adult size is based on data from terminal, in-river fisheries, which primarily target hatchery fish. Although harvest rates on natural populations appear to be high, whether fishing mortality is too high for natural populations to sustain has not been formally evaluated. Finally, during the course of this status review, only limited life history and abundance information was gathered for the substantial portion of this ESU that occurs in British Columbia. Because of the general lack of definitive information on the identified risk factors, and because the number of naturally-reproducing fish within the ESU is fairly large and apparently stable, NMFS concludes that a listing is not warranted for the Puget Sound/Strait of Georgia ESU at this time. However, there is sufficient concern regarding the overall health of this ESU, and therefore, NMFS is adding the Puget Sound/Strait of Georgia ESU to the candidate list. [USOFR 1995:38024]

(At the time, "candidate" species for NMFS were subject to further review for potential listing. In 2004, NMFS matched its definition with that of FWS, so candidate species for both agencies mean the species warrants listing but the agency is precluded from doing so because of higher priorities within its limited budget. Under this definition, Puget Sound coho salmon are no longer a candidate species, but have been relabeled a "species of concern.")

The coho salmon BRT updated its status review in late 1996, concluding that the Puget Sound/Strait of Georgia ESU did not warrant listing, primarily based on the large natural production in north Puget Sound. A minority within the BRT believed that the ESU "could be considered to be at risk in a significant portion of its range"— south Puget Sound, where coho salmon populations are dominated by hatchery production (West Coast Coho Salmon Biological Review Team 1996). The BRT called for close monitoring of "several risk factors," including harvest rates (especially off the west coast of Vancouver Island, outside of direct U.S. control) and "continued urbanization," which it said would place "increasing pressure on natural populations in the future."

Decisions on Chinook Salmon, Hood Canal Summer Chum Salmon, Bull Trout, Steelhead, and Orcas

The BRT for Chinook salmon (a different group of scientists than the one for coho salmon) found that the Puget Sound ESU "corresponds closely to the Puget Sound Lowland Ecoregion," in a distinct genetic grouping that includes the Nooksack River to the north but does not include populations from Vancouver Island or southern British Columbia (Myers et al. 1998). A majority of the BRT included the Elwha

River in the ESU, finding that its Chinook salmon are genetically transitional between populations from Puget Sound and the Washington Coast (Myers et al. 1998). As to extinction risk, the BRT expressed numerous concerns:

> Overall abundance of chinook salmon in this ESU has declined substantially from historical levels, and many populations are small enough that genetic and demographic risks are likely to be relatively high. Contributing to these reduced abundances are widespread stream blockages, which reduce access to spawning habitat, especially in upper reaches. Both long- and short-term trends in abundance are predominantly downward, and several populations are exhibiting severe short-term declines. Spring-run chinook salmon populations throughout this ESU are all depressed.... The BRT was concerned that the preponderance of hatchery production throughout the ESU may mask trends in natural populations and makes it difficult to determine whether they are self-sustaining. This difficulty is compounded by the dearth of data pertaining to proportion of naturally spawning fish that are of hatchery origin. There has also been widespread use of a limited number of hatchery stocks, resulting in increased risk of loss of fitness and diversity among populations. Freshwater habitat throughout the range of the ESU has been blocked or degraded, with upper tributaries widely affected by poor forestry practices and lower tributaries and mainstem rivers affected by agriculture and urbanization. There also is concern that harvest rates of natural stocks in mixed-stock fisheries may be excessive, as evidenced by recent declines in most stocks managed for natural escapement despite curtailed terminal fisheries. Finally, a special concern was expressed regarding the status of spring- and summer-run populations. [Myers et al. 1998]

Although many of these same concerns—particularly the influence of hatchery fish, the effects of urbanization and agriculture, and obstacles to migration in upper reaches—are generally more significant for coho salmon, a majority of the Chinook salmon BRT concluded that the Puget Sound ESU was "not presently in danger of extinction, but...likely to become so in the foreseeable future." A minority of BRT members concluded the ESU was not presently at significant risk or were uncertain about its status. Factors in support of the minority opinion included recent reductions in harvest rates and relatively large overall population numbers, when both hatchery and naturally spawned fish were counted.[5] The BRT estimated that the "recent average potential run size" of all Puget Sound Chinook salmon (hatchery and naturally spawned) was 240,000, counting those caught in ocean and regional fisheries (USOFR 1999a). This was about 35% of the total run size it estimated for 1908, "when both ocean harvest and hatchery production were negligible" (Myers et al. 1998:5).[6] Citing the concerns named by the BRT, NMFS

[5] A more recent study also found that increases in pink salmon runs in the Puget Sound area during even-numbered years (pink salmon follow an extremely reliable 2-year life cycle and so can be separated into distinct even- and odd-numbered year populations) could potentially explain the decline in Puget Sound Chinook salmon. After 1984, Chinook salmon survival declined in Puget Sound only in years when they competed against large numbers of pink salmon for food resources (Ruggerone and Goetz 2004).

[6] Chinook salmon naturally spawn in smaller numbers than coho salmon.

followed the majority opinion, announcing on March 24, 1999, that it would list Puget Sound Chinook salmon as threatened.

The BRT for chum salmon concluded that there were two ESUs in Puget Sound: one for a summer run that returns to streams in Hood Canal and adjacent bays on the Strait of Juan de Fuca and a second that covers all other runs of chum salmon in Puget Sound and the Strait of Georgia. "Genetic data indicate that [the first ESU is] part of a much more ancient lineage than summer-run chum salmon in southern Puget Sound," the BRT concluded (USOFR 1998:11777). It determined that listing of the wider ESU was not warranted, because "current abundance is at or near historic levels," with most stocks having "stable or increasing population trends" (USOFR 1998:11778). It noted, however, that summer-run stocks and one winter-run stock had small, localized populations that are "intrinsically vulnerable to habitat degradation and demographic or environmental fluctuations." It found this posed some risk to the genetic diversity of the ESU, which is mostly comprised of fall runs (USOFR 1998). In contrast, most members of the chum salmon BRT thought that the Hood Canal summer ESU deserved to be listed as endangered because it had steadily declined over 30 years and was completely absent in about half of the streams where it was historically found (USOFR 1998). In March 1999, NMFS decided instead to list the ESU as threatened because of a recent rebound in numbers, "including very recent data not available for review by the BRT," (USOFR 1998:11786) as well as protective efforts underway in the ESU to benefit chum and other salmon stocks (USOFR 1999b).

FWS found that Puget Sound/coastal bull trout include 34 separate subpopulations, which it categorized as strong, depressed, or unknown (USOFR 1999c:58927). It defined a strong population as having at least 5,000 individuals or 500 spawners, stable or increasing abundance, and no loss of historic life-history strategies. FWS found only one strong subpopulation in this DPS, in the lower Skagit River, while 10 were depressed and 23 were unknown. In contrast, bull trout were found historically in "immense or vast" numbers in Puget Sound estuaries. A recent study found they "were one of the most abundant fishes caught in marine fisheries of central Puget Sound from the 1880s to the early 1900s" (Goetz et al. 2004:120). Dolly Varden (like bull trout, a char native to Puget Sound and a member of the family salmonidae) are found among many bull trout subpopulations in the DPS, which adds to uncertainty regarding bull trout because the two species "are virtually impossible to differentiate visually," though they differ genetically and in some other characteristics (e.g., bull trout have far more variety in their life history strategies in both fresh and marine waters; Goetz et al. 2004). When FWS listed bull trout in November 1999, it had tested only 15 of the 34 subpopulations for the two species (USOFR 2001). It found that three subpopulations had only Dolly Varden, but it included all of the subpopulations in its listing action, since it could not exclude the possibility that all included bull trout, given the limited sample size of its tests. In basins where bull trout are found, they generally migrate through habitats used by Chinook salmon but spawn and rear at higher elevations with colder water. In January 2001, the similarity of bull trout and Dolly Varden and their frequent co-existence led FWS to propose listing Dolly Varden under the Similarity of Appearance provisions of the ESA (USOFR 2001), but it has not completed that action.

In March 2006, NMFS proposed that Puget Sound steelhead should be listed as threatened (USOFR 2006). This action followed a petition from Sam Wright, a biologist retired from the Washington Department of Fish and Wildlife, and reversed a decision NMFS had made 10 years before. The 1996 decision was heavily influenced by positive trends in abundance for the two largest steelhead runs in the Puget Sound region, in the Skagit and Snohomish rivers (USOFR 1996). More recent trends have been down in these rivers and nearly all others in the Puget Sound region, despite significant reductions in harvest. In both its 1996 decision and its latest proposal, NMFS also expressed concerns about high hatchery production. Nearly all hatchery stocks of Puget Sound steelhead originated outside of their current basins. While they are managed to produce early returning fish that can be harvested with minimal effect on wild runs, NMFS found this practice has likely led to high mortality for early returning wild fish, reducing their natural diversity. NMFS's listing proposal acknowledged that steelhead may benefit from the recovery plan developed for Puget Sound Chinook salmon (see pages 172–175 below) and from reforms recently proposed for hatcheries across the region (see pages 164–168 below). However, it found there was not enough certainty that these programs will be carried out or will provide sufficient benefit to steelhead to justify not listing them based on current threats. A final decision is expected in late winter or spring 2007.

The endangered listing for orcas was even more complex than the salmonid decisions. Orcas are found all over the world, in a multiplicity of distinct populations and behavioral patterns (Ford et al. 2002). Scientists generally agree that orcas should no longer be considered as one worldwide species with no distinct subspecies, but opinions regarding exactly how they should be classified are "in a state of flux" (Krahn et al. 2002). A BRT convened by NMFS in 2002 gave about equal support to four different subgroups to which the Southern Resident population of orcas found in Puget Sound might be assigned: resident orcas in the North Pacific (including British Columbia, Alaska, and Russia); North Pacific residents and other fish-eating "offshore" orcas, whose range includes waters further off the British Columbia and Washington coasts; fish-eating orcas worldwide; and a lineage based on mitochondrial DNA that includes resident and offshore orcas (Krahn et al. 2002). Without a formally recognized subspecies, NMFS chose not to list Southern Residents in June 2002 because they were not "significant" enough to orcas worldwide to list as a "distinct population segment" (NMFS 2002). That December, the Center for Biological Diversity and others filed a lawsuit asserting that this decision was "arbitrary and capricious," given the widespread scientific agreement that it was a mistake to continue treating all orcas worldwide as having no subspecies (Center for Biological Diversity 2005). A year later, a federal judge agreed, forcing NMFS to reconsider. The judge said that, even though scientists disagreed how orca subspecies should be defined, NMFS was obliged to make its own judgment, since the ESA requires giving "the benefit of the doubt to the species" (Environment News Service 2003). NMFS reconvened the same orca BRT in 2004. By a 5-to-1 margin, it concluded that

North Pacific resident orcas should be considered an unnamed subspecies of *O. orca*, partly based on improved genetic information (Krahn et al. 2004). By a 2-to-1 margin, it concluded that the Southern Residents qualified as a distinct population segment of this subspecies.

The orca BRT had always been concerned about the long-term viability of the Southern Resident population when considered on its own (Krahn et al. 2002, 2004). In 2004, the BRT's models predicted the likelihood of absolute extinction of the population within 100 years to be less than 5% based on trends since 1974, and 6%–19% based on the worsening trend over the previous 10 years (the higher end of the range depended on catastrophic events, such as oil spills). Based on that analysis, NMFS originally proposed in December 2004 to list Southern Resident orcas as threatened. After peer review and public comment, however, NMFS ultimately listed them in November 2005 as endangered (USOFR 2005b). This decision cited the ongoing and potentially worsening nature of the threats facing orcas in Puget Sound, including "the persistence of legacy toxins and the addition of new ones," increased vessel traffic, and reductions in food supply, particularly Chinook salmon (the orcas' favorite food). Orcas cannot metabolize polychlorinated biphenyls, or PCBs (Ford et al 2000), which are used as coolants and lubricants. Although PCBs were banned in the United States in 1979, they remain in the bodies of orcas for life and are passed on to new generations in concentrated form through the high fat content of mother's milk (P. Ross, Institute of Ocean Sciences, personal communication). PCBs also continue to be used in Asian industries, where they enter the atmosphere and are carried to the eastern Pacific (Ford et al 2000), entering the orcas' food chain. PCB levels in Southern Resident orcas are down dramatically since the 1970s but remain among the highest levels measured in any animals (Ross, personal communication). Moreover, other persistent organic pollutants, such as flame retardants and organochlorines, continue to be discharged into the environment (USOFR 2005b). These chemicals may be especially harmful to orcas' reproductive and immune systems (USOFR 2005b). All of these threats pose extra risk of extinction because of the naturally small population of Southern Residents.

Lawsuits Lead to Reconsidering the Chinook and Chum Salmons Listings and Critical Habitat

In February 2000, NMFS designated critical habitat for 19 ESUs, including Puget Sound Chinook salmon and Hood Canal summer chum salmon (USOFR 2000a). It designated all lakes and rivers occupied by listed fish, including areas potentially accessible above removable blockages, plus riparian areas, but excluded Indian lands and areas above naturally impassable barriers or impassable dams. It also designated marine nearshore areas for Puget Sound Chinook salmon, though it did not include marine areas elsewhere. As was standard practice at the time, NMFS found there was no economic impact from these designations, since both it and FWS contended that critical habitat added little or no additional protections to listed species. The National Association of Home Builders (NAHB) challenged this determination in district court in Washington, D.C. (*NAHB v. Evans* 2002). When the Tenth Circuit Court of Appeals decided another case consistent with NAHB's position (see *New Mexico Cattlegrowers' Association v. USFWS* 2001), NMFS sought and received a consent decree settling the suit. Under the decree, NMFS agreed to withdraw its critical habitat designations for listed fish and committed to issuing new ones that would take into account an analysis of their economic impacts (*NAHB v. Evans* 2002).

During this same period, NMFS lost another lawsuit, *Alsea Valley Alliance v. Evans*, which challenged its listing of Oregon coast coho salmon because NMFS had categorically excluded hatchery populations from the ESU (*Alsea Valley Alliance v. Evans* 2001a). Though NMFS did not appeal the decision, environmental and fishing groups did. In December 2001, the Ninth Circuit Court of Appeals agreed to stay the *Alsea* decision pending a final ruling on the appeal (*Alsea Valley Alliance v. Evans* 2001b[7]). Based on the *Alsea* decision, in 2001 and 2002 NMFS received petitions to delist 16 ESUs (including a petition filed jointly by the Kitsap Alliance of Property Owners and the Skagit County Cattlemen's Association to delist Puget Sound Chinook salmon and Hood Canal summer chum salmon; the Washington Farm Bureau also filed a petition for the same actions [see USOFR 2002a, 2002c]). It also received petitions from Trout Unlimited to define 14 ESUs (including Puget Sound Chinook salmon and Hood Canal summer chum salmon) as including only naturally spawned fish (USOFR 2002b). In February 2002, NMFS announced that it would reconsider its listing decisions for all salmon and steelhead ESUs that could potentially include hatchery fish (USOFR 2002a).

In June 2005, NMFS determined to maintain the listing of Puget Sound Chinook salmon as threatened (USOFR 2005c), as was widely expected. The only noteworthy change was to add four hatchery stocks to the ESU, based on a new policy to include hatchery stocks in listings if their "genetic divergence relative to the local natural population(s)…is no more than what would be expected between closely related natural populations within the ESU." NMFS's original status reviews had included hatchery fish in listed ESUs only if they were found "essential for recovery." NMFS also maintained its listing of Hood Canal of summer chum salmon as threatened (USOFR 2005c). NMFS included all eight hatcheries producing summer chum in Hood Canal as part of the ESU, recognizing that their primary purpose is conservation.

In September 2005, NMFS announced its final decision to revise critical habitat designations for Puget Sound Chinook salmon, Hood Canal summer chum salmon, and 17 other Pacific salmon species (USOFR 2005d[8]). The revised designations eliminated most unoccupied areas from designation (they include only 8 miles of unoccupied stream reaches in Puget Sound for Hood Canal summer chum salmon). NMFS now argues that there generally is insufficient information to determine whether currently occupied habitat is not adequate for recovery. The designation also removed all military areas, tribal lands, lands

---

[7] In February 2004, the court issued a final decision, dismissing the appeal based on NMFS's reconsideration of its listing of Oregon coast coho salmon based on the *Alsea* decision. This ruling did not remove Oregon coastal coho salmon from the ESA list but did prohibit enforcement of related ESA requirements until NMFS made a final listing decision. See Environment News Service 2004.

[8] A separate notice designated critical habitat for seven ESUs in California.

covered by habitat conservation plans, and a variety of areas where NMFS argued economic impacts outweigh conservation benefits. This includes much of the shoreline in central Puget Sound and Hood Canal and the entire watersheds of the Baker, Deschutes, Samish, and Sammamish rivers and a variety of smaller systems. As of March 2006, the revised critical habitat designations in the Puget Sound area have not been challenged in court. Their practical effect on federal actions may be relatively small, because federal agencies continue to be obligated to avoid jeopardizing the recovery of listed species, which extends to actions outside areas designated as critical habitat.

The 4(d) Rule: A Ground-Breaking Approach to Protecting Listed Salmon?

As discussed in Chapter 7, Section 4(d) of the Endangered Species Act allows special regulations to be issued for species listed as threatened instead of endangered. These regulations can allow for some take so long as, when considered as a whole, they "provide for the conservation of the species" (U.S. Code, volume 16, section 1533[d]]). NMFS has taken this approach to Puget Sound Chinook salmon, Hood Canal summer chum salmon, and 15 other threatened salmon and steelhead ESUs on the West Coast. NMFS articulated its strategy concisely in its rule-making decision:

> One of the primary reasons NMFS has taken this ground-breaking approach to publishing ESA 4(d) rules is to allow for a maximum of local input and Federal flexibility....A wide mosaic of activities affect salmon habitat. Those activities fall under the responsibility of a range of Federal, state and local authorities. The practical ability to make changes in those activities will depend in part upon the willingness and ability of those separate authorities to encourage change. Therefore, NMFS is attempting, to the greatest extent practicable, to build opportunities for state and local initiatives in the implementation of the ESA program. [USOFR 2000b:42468]

NMFS argued that this approach will lead to less take in actual practice than simply prohibiting all take, because it will demonstrate to all parties "that practical and realistic salmonid protection measures exist," allowing NMFS to "focus its enforcement efforts on activities and programs that have not yet adequately addressed the conservation needs of listed ESUs" (USOFR 2000b).

NMFS's 4(d) rule provides 13 exceptions to the ESA's general prohibition on take. Many are uncontroversial (for scientific research, rescuing injured or stranded fish, etc.[9]),

---

[9] The 13 exemptions are as follows:

1. ESA permits—those holding permits under the ESA (such as incidental take permits granted for habitat conservation plans or scientific research) are free of take prohibitions so long as they act in accordance with their permits and other applicable law. (This merely acknowledges what is legally required under Section 10 of the ESA.)
2. Ongoing scientific research—research that affected listed salmonids and was underway at the time NOAA published the 4(d) rule was allowed to continue with proper notification to NOAA.
3. Rescue and salvage actions—designated personnel may aid injured or stranded fish or salvage dead fish for scientific study.
4. Fishery management—discussed in more detail in the text.
5. Artificial propagation—discussed in more detail in the text.

but four have been the focus of lawsuits and ongoing scrutiny. These four establish conditions for NMFS's approval of harvest, hatcheries, forestry activities, and "Municipal, Residential, Commercial and Industrial development." The 4(d) rule for bull trout provides exceptions from take prohibitions only for fishing activities regulated by state governments, Indian tribes, and the National Park Service, in recognition that fishing for bull trout was already highly restricted and never involved the scale of salmon harvest (USOFR 1999c). FWS also proposed amending its rule to exempt habitat restoration "and other land and water management activities that are governed by enforceable regulations that provide substantial protection for bull trout" (USOFR 1999c:58934), which could potentially include forestry and development. FWS has, however, never finalized these changes to its rule, in part because of the same budget constraints that have kept it from other actions.

The next chapter will discuss how NMFS's 4(d) rule relates to forestry, but one central concept in its approach to habitat in the 4(d) rule—properly functioning conditions (or PFC)—is relevant to both forestry and urban and suburban development. Habitat conditions are "properly functioning" when they "create and sustain over time the physical and biological characteristics that are essential to conservation of the species, whether important for spawning, breeding, rearing, feeding, migration, sheltering, or other functions" (USOFR 2000b:42431). Properly Functioning Conditions are intended "to detect the health of underlying processes, not static characteristics," in recognition "that natural patterns of habitat disturbance, such as through floods, landslides and wildfires, will continue" (USOFR 2000b:42431). NMFS's evaluation standards for actions that affect salmonid habitat are clearly stated: they "must not impair properly functioning habitat, appreciably reduce the functioning of already impaired habitat, or retard the long-term progress of impaired habitat toward PFC" (USOFR 2000b:42480). NMFS uses a set of indicators for whether habitat is properly functioning, at risk, or not properly functioning . For example, the default indicator for maximum water temperature (an important aspect of water quality) that is properly functioning is 50–57°F; at-risk indicators are 57–60°F for spawning periods and 57–64°F for migration and rearing periods; and not properly functioning indicators are greater than 60°F for

6. Joint tribal/state plans—discussed in more detail in the text.
7. Scientific research—in addition to exempting research underway at the time the 4(d) rule was issued, the rule also exempts future research that is coordinated with state fishery management agencies and receives written approval from NMFS.
8. Habitat restoration—discussed in more detail in the text.
9. Water diversion screening—to receive an exemption, NMFS must agree in writing that a water diversion screen complies with technical criteria it issued previously.
10. Routine road maintenance—NMFS approved the Oregon Department of Transportation's road maintenance guide as a standard for other road departments.
11. Integrated pest management—NMFS similarly approved the pesticide program of the City of Portland's Parks and Recreation Department as a standard for others to follow.
12. Municipal, residential, commercial and industrial development and redevelopment—discussed in more detail in the text.
13. Forest management discussed in more detail in Chapter 9.

spawning and 64°F for migration and rearing. NMFS recognizes that even under natural conditions these indicators are not always met, due to periodic disturbances and inherent watershed characteristics (e.g., the outflow of lakes naturally tends to meet the not properly functioning temperature indicator in the summer and early fall, when lakes separate into a warm upper layer and a cool bottom layer). The important aspect of NMFS's analysis is whether an action will tend to improve, maintain, or degrade the various indicators (USOFR 2000b).

Another central concept in the 4(d) rule is that of viable salmonid populations, which applies to independent populations of salmon (e.g., a fall run of Chinook salmon returning to a particular river). Most ESUs group multiple, genetically related populations of listed salmon (there are 22 independent populations for Puget Sound Chinook salmon, listed in Table 8-3, on page 157). For each population, NMFS plans to establish viability criteria for abundance, productivity, spatial distribution, and diversity (some abundance and productivity criteria are complete; see Table 8-3). The criteria are supposed to equate to approximately a 5% likelihood that a population will go extinct over a 100-year timeframe (see Puget Sound Technical Recovery Team 2002). Working with the Washington Department of Fish and Wildlife and local Indian tribes (which co-manage harvest and hatchery issues in the Puget Sound area), NMFS also is establishing criteria for critical populations, which are "at a high risk of extinction over a short time period" (USOFR 200b). In general, NMFS has treated abundance as the most important statistic and has often allowed it to serve as a surrogate for the other variables (NMFS 2000).

In its 4(d) rule, NMFS said it would use the concepts of viable and critical populations to evaluate harvest and hatchery proposals as follows:

> *For harvests*: [A]ctions impacting populations that are functioning at or above the viable threshold must be designed to maintain the population or management unit at or above that level. For populations shown with a high degree of confidence to be above critical levels but not yet at viable levels, harvest management must not appreciably slow the population's achievement of viable function. Harvest actions impacting populations that are functioning at or below critical threshold must not be allowed to appreciably increase genetic and demographic risks facing the population and must be designed to permit the population's achievement of viable function, unless the plan demonstrates that the likelihood of survival and recovery of the entire ESU in the wild would not be appreciably reduced by greater risks to that individual population. [USOFR 2000b:42476]

> *For hatcheries*: Listed salmonids may be purposefully taken for broodstock only if the donor population is currently at or above the viable threshold and the collection will not impair its function; if the donor population is not currently viable but the sole objective of the current collection program is to enhance the propagation or survival of the listed ESU; or *if the donor population is shown with a high degree of confidence to be above critical threshold although not yet functioning at viable levels, and the collection will not appreciably slow the attainment of viable status for that population*...(USOFR 2000b:42477).When populations are at or below the critical level, the only hatch-

TABLE 8-3. Abundance goals for Puget Sound Chinook salmon populations.

Population	Mean spawner abundance, hatchery and wild, 1996–2000[a]	Low productivity[a] planning range for wild abundance	Low productivity[a] planning target for wild abundance	High productivity[b] planning target for wild abundance (productivity in parentheses)
Nooksack bioregion				
NF Nooksack	120	16,000–26,000	16,000	3,800 (3.4)
SF Nooksack	200	9,100–13,000	9,100	2,000 (3.6)
Whidbey basin bioregion				
Lower Skagit	2,300	16,000–22,000	16,000	3,900 (3.0)
Upper Skagit	8,920	17,000–35,000	26,000	5,380 (3.8)
Cascade[c]	330	1,200–1,700	1,200	290 (3.0)
Lower Sauk	660	5,600–7,800	5,600	1,400 (3.0)
Upper Sauk[c]	370	3,000–4,200	3,030	750 (3.0)
Suiattle[c]	420	600–800	610	160 (2.8)
NF Stillaguamish	660	18,000–24,000	18,000	4,000 (3.4)
SF Stillaguamish	240	15,000–20,000	15,000	3,600 (3.3)
Skykomish	1,700	17,000–51,000	39,000	8,700 (3.4)
Snoqualmie	1,200	17,000–33,000	25,000	5,500 (3.6)
Central/South Sound bioregion				
N. Lake Washington	194[d]	4,000–6,500	4,000	1,000 (3.0)
Cedar	398[d]	8,200–13,000	8,200	2,000 (3.1)
Green	7,191[d]	17,000–37,700	27,000	Unknown
White[3]	329[d]	Unknown	Unknown	Unknown
Puyallup	2,400	17,000–33,000	18,000	5,300 (2.3)
Nisqually	890	13,000–17,000	13,000	3,400 (3.0)
Hood Canal bioregion				
Skokomish	1,500[d]	Unknown	Unknown	Unknown
Mid-Hood Canal	389	5,200–8,300	5,200	1,300 (3.0)
Strait of Juan de Fuca bioregion				
Dungeness	123[d]	4,700–8,100	4,700	1,200 (3.0)
Elwha	1,319[d]	17,000–33,000	17,000	6,900 (4.6)

[a] The low productivity number in both the range and target represents one adult fish returning from the sea for each spawner, also called the equilibrium point (1:1).
[b] The high productivity number represents the number of spawners at the point where the population provides the highest sustainable yield for every spawner. The productivity ratio is in parentheses for each population and represents the relationship of fish returning from the sea for each spawner (e.g., 3.4:1 for NF Nooksack).
[c] Italicized populations are early runs, which return in the spring or summer rather than the fall and thus represent an important component of genetic diversity.
[d] Represents the geometric mean of spawner abundance from 1987 to 2001.
Source: Supplement to the Draft Puget Sound Salmon Recovery Plan, December 19, 2005, National Marine Fisheries Service.

> ery programs NMFS is likely to approve would be for the sole objective of enhancing the listed species' propagation and survival. [emphasis by the author, highlighting the most common case in NMFS's assessment; USOFR 2000b:42446]

Hatchery and harvest issues interact when harvests directed at hatchery fish (by far the dominant case within the Puget Sound region) incidentally catch fish that were naturally spawned. Even when hatchery marking programs (which typically clip the adipose fin of hatchery-produced fish) make it possible to identify and release naturally spawned fish, some percentage will not survive the experience. Nevertheless, in August 2005, NMFS amended its 4(d) rule to allow harvest of all fish with clipped adipose fins, including those produced at hatcheries whose salmon are part of ESUs, consistent with approved harvest management plans (USOFR 2005c).

Harvest: Conflicting Mandates and Pressures Allow Continued Take

One of the primary reasons Puget Sound Chinook salmon were listed under the ESA was the low abundance of many populations, due in no small part to high past harvest rates. In NMFS's listing decision, it noted that "total exploitation rates averaged 68% to 83%" and were more than 90% on some Puget Sound Chinook salmon stocks in the late 1980s, though it noted "some evidence" of decreased catch rates in the late 1990s (USOFR 1999a). The majority of this catch was in the ocean, predominantly off of British Columbia but also off of Alaska, Washington, and Oregon (USOFR 1999a; Puget Sound Indian Tribes and WDFW 2001). (Tagging studies have shown that it is extremely rare for Pacific Northwest salmon to be caught more than 200 miles from shore [NRC 1996].) Ocean harvests led the National Academy of Sciences to conclude in *Upstream* that sustainable salmon runs in the Pacific Northwest are not possible "without limiting the interceptions of U.S. salmon in Canada and obtaining the cooperation of Alaska" (NRC 1996:14).

Many find it curious, if not inexplicable, that harvest continues on listed fish, especially in American waters. James Connaughton, chairman of the White House Council on Environmental Quality, announced in January 2006 that the Bush administration would like to reduce or eliminate this harvest, noting "the luxury of eating threatened and endangered salmon that may be needed for recovery" (Rudolph 2006a). Commenting on this same irony, Oregon Congressman Greg Walden has remarked, "When I go out pheasant hunting, I don't get to take a spotted owl if my aim is off" (Rudolph 2006b). Yet in regulating salmon harvests, fishery managers work under conflicting mandates and agency missions. Complying with federal treaties with Canada and Indian tribes for salmon harvest is legally a coequal responsibility with the Endangered Species Act. Federal and state fishery agencies also face strong pressures to support non-tribal commercial and recreational fishing, especially in the face of treaty-protected Canadian and Indian fishing. Harvest in the Puget Sound area has declined dramatically since before the ESA listings, but continues because of these forces. Approved harvests are almost entirely directed at non-listed or hatchery fish but still incidentally catch tens of thousands of wild, listed salmon each year (NMFS 2004).

Besides tribal treaties (which are discussed at length in Chapter 13), the two most important documents for understanding how these harvests affect listed salmon are the 1999 Pacific Salmon Agreement with Canada and the Resource Management Plan for Chinook salmon developed by the Washington Department of Fish and Wildlife and Indian tribes, which NMFS approved in December 2004. The Pacific Salmon Agreement was a considerable improvement for conservation over the fixed maximum harvest levels previously allocated between the U.S. and Canada. Off of southeast Alaska, northern British Columbia, and the west coast of Vancouver Island, the agreement introduced "abundance-based fishing regimes," which vary based on the number of fish actually expected in different areas along the coast (see Appendix C of Pacific Salmon Commission 2001). However, these are still "mixed-stock" fisheries, where healthy and abundant stocks of salmon cannot be separated from depressed and endangered stocks. Most of the salmon caught off of the west coast of Vancouver Island (88% in 2003–2004) are from U.S. waters (*SSRA et al v. Gutierrez* 2005). Off of central and southern British Columbia (other than the west coast of Vancouver Island) and in the Pacific Northwest states, where fishing tends to be closer to the home rivers of salmon, fisheries are to be managed to protect individual stocks of salmon, with extra protections for weak stocks. Canada also agreed to require the live release of chum salmon in southern Canadian waters when Hood Canal summer chum salmon may be present. Canadian fisheries account for 25% to 80% of fishing-related deaths for most Chinook salmon populations in the Puget Sound area; this is expected to rise over the remaining years of the agreement, which extends through the 2009 fishing season (NMFS 2004). The large Canadian catch of listed U.S. salmon, primarily off of the west coast of Vancouver Island, has led U.S. negotiators to say they will "come out swinging" in talks to update the agreement (Rudolph 2006b). Canadian harvest has also led to two lawsuits by a coalition of fishing and conservation groups under the ESA. One case argues that any import of listed salmon from Canada violates the act (*SSRA et al. v. Bonner* 2005); the other argues that the biological opinion issued under the ESA for the Pacific Salmon Agreement was flawed and must be redone (*SSRA et al. v. Gutierrez* 2005).

The Puget Sound Chinook Harvest Resource Management Plan provides the protections for individual stocks required by the Pacific Salmon Agreement. It also has multiple other purposes: protecting treaty Indian fishing rights; conserving the "productivity, abundance and diversity" of Chinook salmon populations in the region; complying with the 4(d) rule for Chinook salmon; optimizing harvest of abundant Puget Sound salmon (including hatchery Chinook salmon and other salmon species); and managing risks from uncertainties regarding actual run sizes and harvest levels (NMFS 2004). Perhaps because a number of these purposes are legal mandates, management agencies are reluctant to state frankly that they can conflict with one another. This conflict was highlighted in NMFS's environmental impact statement (EIS) for its review of the plan, which identified a no fishing alternative as environmentally preferred. In fact, using criteria in the EIS, the harvest plan proposed by the state and tribes and approved by NMFS was the worst alternative for the environment of all those reviewed. Nevertheless, NMFS argued that it was the "most successful at balancing resource conservation, trust obligations to

Native American tribes, promotion of sustainable fisheries and prevention of lost economic potential associated with overfishing, declining species and degraded habitats" (NMFS 2004).

The approved resource management plan allows for harvest rates of naturally spawned Puget Sound Chinook salmon that vary by population, from up to 10% of returns to the Dungeness and Elwha rivers to up to 50% of the summer and fall returns to the Skagit River. If returns for a given population are projected to drop below a low abundance threshold, fishing would be restricted at certain places and times and with certain gear. This is projected to lower these percentages to 6% to 18%. NMFS acknowledges that allowing this much harvest of severely depressed populations is not driven "primarily by biological considerations." The driving factor is policy interpretation of what is an acceptable risk to listed Chinook salmon "to preserve an acceptable level of harvest opportunity on other salmon species and hatchery chinook stocks" (NMFS 2004). Beyond fishing allowed below the "low abundance threshold," the resource management plan's general practice of managing for a given harvest rate tends to increase fishing pressure on weaker populations, in comparison to managing for a target number of returning spawners, which was the traditional method into the 1990s.

In total, under the approved plan NMFS projects that an average of 45,249 naturally spawning Puget Sound Chinook salmon and 111,931 hatchery Chinook salmon would be caught annually in the Puget Sound area or coastal waters from 2005 through 2009 (NMFS 2004:4–33). This does not count fish caught in Canadian or Alaskan waters. NMFS argues that, given the available quality and quantity of habitat, providing greater numbers of natural spawners would be unlikely to lead to substantial increases in natural returns over time (the rationale for this argument is discussed in the next section). For any given population, NMFS argues that the approved harvest rates would have no more than a 10% chance of harming its ability to recover and only a 5% chance of causing it to fall to a critical threshold that would endanger its future. NMFS acknowledges, however, that not all harvests will stay under the proposed ceilings, but argues this is acceptable because not all populations must recover for the ESU to recover. On this basis, NMFS concludes that the harvest plan will "not appreciably reduce the likelihood of survival or recovery of listed Puget Sound chinook salmon" (NMFS 2004). Given that conclusion, the harvest plan met the 4(d) test. More restrictive alternatives also met the test, but because they would reduce opportunities for tribal harvests NMFS argued that they were inconsistent with its trust responsibility to the tribes.

The Scientific Critique of Harvest Policy

Scientists widely question the fundamental model for how salmon fisheries are managed, which NMFS used to argue that decreasing harvests in the short-term would not lead to substantially greater returns in the future. The logic of the model is as follows:

- As with most animals, under normal conditions, salmon have evolved to create more progeny than strictly necessary to sustain their numbers, to buffer against environmental risks.

- Beyond certain minimum levels, as more salmon return to spawn in a given system, the overall productivity of the population will decrease, because more individuals will be forced to spawn and rear in less favorable habitats.
- At a certain point along this curve (see Figure 8-1), productivity will fall to less than one-to-one—additional spawners will be unable to replace themselves. This is the equilibrium abundance for the salmon population, toward which it will naturally gravitate. When the amount or quality of habitat is decreased or degraded, this number declines.
- Fish caught above this equilibrium number will not reduce future returns.

The problem with the model, as the National Academy of Sciences said 10 years ago in *Upstream: Salmon and Society in the Pacific Northwest,* is that it "is fundamentally

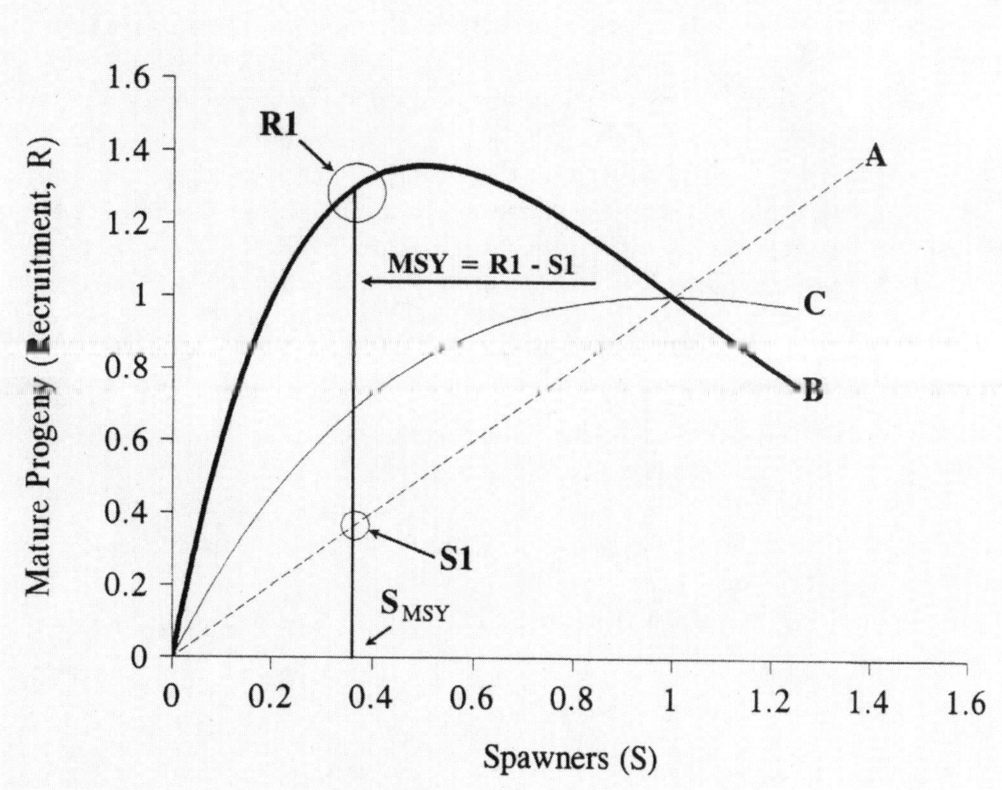

FIGURE 8-1. A prototypical fishery stock-recruitment curve. Line A is the "replacement line," where returning salmon exactly match their parents in number. Salmon populations can maintain themselves at several levels of abundance, and different salmon populations have different stock-recruitment curves. Curve B describes a population with greater productivity than curve C, but one with greater losses in productivity (greater "density-dependence") at larger returns. Populations with greater productivity can sustain their production at higher harvest rates. MSY is the theorized amount of maximum sustained yield for harvest. Source: National Research Council (1996:278).

inconsistent with historical data" (NRC 1996:285). It assumes a stable relationship between the number of spawning fish and the number of their progeny that will return, when "annual variation in the ratio of returns to spawners can vary by a factor of 10" (NRC 1996:280) because of floods, poor ocean conditions, and other factors. The model also assumes that existing data is sufficient to know what the equilibrium number is, though if salmon runs have been over-fished, by definition most data "will be from the lower range" of the model, when the real test for the model can only be from the upper range (NRC 1996). Seriously testing the model would require minimizing all harvest and holding environmental conditions relatively constant for decades. Moreover, the model does not consider the potential ecological benefits of salmon returns that may be surplus to humans, but that might otherwise feed wildlife and return nutrients to streams.

After receiving a thorough presentation on how salmon harvests were being managed across the Pacific Coast, NMFS's coast-wide scientific review panel commented, "we remain somewhat mystified concerning the scientific justification for current allowable harvests, especially the continuation of substantial or high allowable harvest rates on listed salmonid ESUs" (SRSRP 2001a:7). The panel noted that one of the primary reasons the ESUs were listed was that their populations had declined, meaning the ratio of returning salmon to spawners was less than one. In contrast to the harvest model's assumption, in every case that the panel reviewed the number of returning spawners was lower with existing levels of harvest than they were projected to be with no harvest, in some cases "by as much as 20% or 30%" (SRSRP 2001a:7). The panel said that fishery managers "were not making use of basic theories of harvesting fluctuating populations," which argue for the precautionary principle of erring on the side of lower harvests (SRSRP 2001a). Fishery managers told the panel that, after considering treaty obligations as well as the ESA, NMFS believed it must allow "the maximum harvest that does not 'substantially restrict recovery'" (SRSRP 2001a). However, the panel noted, "Substantial was never defined in this context." Fishery managers also told the panel that forgoing ocean harvests, where endangered and healthy populations are mixed, "would waste a valuable resource." The panel concluded,

> It appears to us that NMFS personnel involved in setting allowable harvest rates use subjectivity and legalism, and their inability to promote a transition to terminal fisheries [located near river mouths, where most harvestable salmon are known to be from that river], to justify biologically unsustainable harvest rates on several listed ESUs. [SRSRP 2001a:8]

The National Academy of Sciences was less judgmental in *Upstream* when it considered the challenge of limiting harvests on declining fish runs (NRC 1996). It noted that, even in 1996, before widespread fishing reductions under the ESA and the Pacific Salmon Treaty, the fishing industry's recent declines in income were "greater than that in any other major resource industry in the Pacific Northwest." The Academy noted that treaty obligations require that tribes not bear a disproportionate burden in recovering salmon, yet the fish reach them after substantial harvest has already occurred in mixed fisheries in the oceans, under the Pacific Salmon Treaty, which specifically cautions against "undue disruptions" of existing fisheries. Eliminating the mixed ocean fisheries would require that healthy wild populations either not be fished at all or be fished only in terminal areas.

Consumers may decide this issue. Alaskan and Canadian fishermen have argued that consumers find salmon less desirable if caught in terminal areas because as salmon prepare to spawn, they stop eating and begin drawing down energy reserves, which gradually reduces their oils and degrades their flesh. But this is not necessarily true prior to the ascent of salmon upriver, as demonstrated by the premium consumers pay for Alaska's Copper River salmon (which, by definition, have separated from fish returning to other areas). Fish in terminal areas are also larger than those in the ocean, simply because they have had more time to grow.

Through "eco-fish" certification programs, consumers could set a premium on fish caught in terminal areas. This would begin to support the enormous institutional change required to shift harvest practices. Eco-fish criteria have been developed for the amount and type of bycatch in a fishery (non-target species caught incidentally, the most famous example being dolphins caught in tuna nets).[10] Salmon from distant rivers are arguably a type of by-catch, but certification bodies have not recognized them as such and no interest groups have yet pressed for the change.[11]

In the 1930s, voter initiatives shut down fish traps in Puget Sound terminal areas because the traps were so efficient that they dominated the catch (see Chasan 1986). Now that the fishing industry has invested hundreds of millions of dollars in equipment to catch salmon in the ocean, the technological edge is reversed. Those who wait to fish in terminal areas may find that there are few fish left to catch, as Indian tribes have experienced for decades. The fundamental change must come from commercial fisheries governed by the Pacific Salmon Treaty, particularly off the coast of Vancouver Island. Change there, however, will not be possible without changes off the coasts of Alaska and mainland British Columbia, where many fish originating from Vancouver Island are caught. If the Puget Sound region is to prompt a transition to terminal fisheries, we will need to lead by example. It is worth noting that the key argument our fishery managers are currently making—that degraded habitat in the region justifies continuation of current regional harvest practices—weakens our ability to argue for reforms elsewhere.

Absent consumer pressure, the ESA may still force changes in harvest. After all, the ESA prohibits take, and the Supreme Court has never overturned its finding that "Congress intended endangered species to be afforded the highest of priorities" (*TVA*

---

[10] For selection criteria used in the eco-fish marketing program, see http://www.ecofish.com/selection criteria.htm.

[11] These were the reasons given when the author raised this issue in a question and answer period during a forum titled "The Growing Role of the Private Sector in Ocean Conservation: The *Seafood Choices* Movement," on May 5, 2004, at the Fourth World Fisheries Congress in Vancouver, British Columbia. Participants encouraged advocacy to include effects on weak stocks of salmon in future criteria, which continue to evolve.

v. Hill 1978:174). In January 2006, the same fishing and environmental groups that filed the two lawsuits regarding Canadian fisheries noted above submitted a notice to NMFS that they intended to sue the agency over approval of the Puget Sound Chinook harvest plan as a violation of the ESA (Brandt-Erichsen 2006). "Once a species—any species—is listed under the ESA, it is no longer a commercial resource to be exploited," the letter argued. As of June 2006, the groups were in negotiations with NMFS, the state and tribes over possible changes in harvest management that might obviate a lawsuit (S. Brandt-Erichsen, Heller Ehrman LLP, personal communication). In general, if individual populations of listed salmon begin to near extinction in Puget Sound or elsewhere, courts may require the federal government to stop all related fishing under its authority. As the National Academy of Sciences said, "fishing is the easiest mortality factor to control" (NRC 1996:12). However, the academy also concluded, "The control of fishing as a means to approach sustainability in salmon will only be as successful as our ability to address the freshwater habitat issues" (NRC 1996:300).

Hatchery Reform: Is It Enough?

There are approximately 130 state, tribal, and federal salmon hatcheries in Washington State, more than anywhere else on the Pacific Coast (Vanden Brulle and Gayeski 2003).[12] Together, they produce the majority of hatchery Chinook salmon, coho salmon, and steelhead in the world, along with some other species. Slightly more than half are in the Puget Sound area.

Hatcheries were mostly built to provide harvest opportunities to compensate for declines in naturally spawning fish. However, there is currently no serious debate that hatchery fish have harmed wild salmon through a variety of mechanisms, such as by competing with wild fish for food, shelter, and mates; by displacing wild fish from native habitats; by preying on wild fish; and, perhaps the two most notable factors, by modifying genetic adaptations through interbreeding and encouraging high harvest rates on mixed stocks of hatchery and wild fish (NRC 1996).

Hatchery fish differ genetically from wild fish for multiple reasons: (1) up until very recently and in some cases still today, hatchery managers have collected eggs from salmon in one system and transferred them to hatcheries elsewhere; (2) the very purpose of hatcheries—to reduce natural mortality rates for salmon eggs and juveniles—removes an important element of natural selection; (3) hatchery rearing environments can be dramatically different from natural environments, selecting different traits for survival; (4) hatcheries eliminate the process of salmon naturally choosing mates, which has some effect on fitness; and (5) hatchery managers have a strong motivation to collect eggs early in a salmon run, which increases their likelihood of collecting a tar-

[12] Vanden Brulle and Gayeski 2003 states that there are more than 130 state, tribal, and federal hatchery programs operating in Washington State and more than 300 from California to Alaska, so Washington has almost half the total. Pink salmon hatcheries in Alaska and chum salmon hatcheries in Japan produce more total juvenile salmon than Washington hatcheries, but northwest hatcheries produce the large majority of coho, Chinook, and steelhead juveniles. For details, see Mahnken et al. 1998.

geted number of eggs, though over time this modifies the run timing of offspring. In places where wild salmon runs have been completely lost, such as Japan, parts of New England, and eastern Canada, hatcheries have provided a way of maintaining salmon production for human consumption. Although hatchery advocates argue that they can be used to maintain wild salmon runs, there is no clear example where that has succeeded over the long term, and much evidence that it has failed (NRC 1996; Myers et al. 2004).

Given the importance of hatchery production for continued fisheries in Washington, problems with traditional hatchery management led Congress to fund the Western Washington Hatchery Reform Project beginning in 2000 (Mobrand et al. 2005). The goal of the project is "to determine how hatcheries can best support sustainable fisheries while, at the same time, assist with the conservation and recovery of naturally spawning populations." The project has included an independent scientific body, the Hatchery Scientific Review Group (HSRG), to review hatchery operations throughout Puget Sound and the Washington coast and to work with the state and Indian tribes to implement reforms. "Virtually all…previous assessments [of hatcheries] have focused on the problems and risks [of] hatcheries," members of the HSRG have argued; few "were tasked with developing scientifically defensible solutions to the problems they identified."

In its final report, the HSRG advocates for three principles of reform (Mobrand et al 2005):

1. *Every hatchery program must have well-defined goals in terms of its desired benefits and purpose.* While the two primary benefits of hatcheries are harvest and/or conservation, hatcheries can also serve research and education purposes. Goals should be quantified wherever possible. A common traditional measure of success—the number of juvenile fish released annually—does not necessarily further harvest goals and can be detrimental to conservation.
2. *Hatchery operations must be scientifically defensible.* This covers many issues: production should be sized based on the carrying capacity of marine and freshwater habitats; broodstocks should be locally-adapted and reared locally; hatchery salmon carcasses should be distributed to add nutrients to natural systems; and many other recommendations. Crucially, each hatchery operation should be defined as either "integrated" with natural populations in the same system or "segregated" from them (see below for details).
3. *Hatchery programs must respond adaptively to new information.* This would greatly boost commitments to monitoring and evaluation and to flexible hatchery designs and operations, so changes could be made as new information (e.g., regarding stray rates of hatchery fish into other streams) becomes available.

The HSRG termed the distinction between integrated and segregated operations to be a fundamental foundation of its recommendations. The goal of an integrated operation is to match the characteristics of the local natural population as closely as possible. This would include taking a representative sample of broodstock across the entire period of the run. It also would mean having a higher percentage of wild fish in the hatchery broodstock than the percentage of hatchery strays on the spawning grounds. This requires productive natural habitat because an integrated hatchery program needs, "as a long-term goal, a self-sustaining, naturally-spawning population capable of providing adult fish for broodstock each year" (Mobrand et al. 2005). The size of an integrated program "will necessarily be limited by the habitat available to the natural populations with which it is integrated and by the ability of the hatchery program to restrain natural spawning by hatchery-origin adults." In contrast, a segregated program would manage the hatchery population to be genetically distinct from the natural population. This would mean avoiding the use of wild fish in hatchery broodstock (i.e., collecting eggs only from returning hatchery fish) and limiting hatchery strays to no more than 5% of those that spawn in the wild. A segregated program is generally most appropriate when harvest is the primary goal "and the probability of hatchery-origin adults spawning naturally and reproducing successfully is very low." Managers must choose whether a hatchery will be integrated or segregated; it cannot be both.

Many, probably most, hatcheries in the Puget Sound area cannot currently meet the HSRG's criteria for either integrated or segregated operations. The numbers of straying hatchery fish are far too great, sometimes comprising a majority of fish on the spawning grounds. Returning wild salmon, in turn, are often in such small numbers that taking enough for broodstock at an integrated hatchery could seriously damage the wild population. This conflict may explain why NMFS has yet to act on the Hatchery Genetic Management Plans that the state and tribes submitted in 2003 and 2004, which are supposed to form the legal basis for NMFS approving hatcheries under the 4(d) rule. NMFS now plans to release a draft environmental impact statement regarding its action by the end of 2006 and a final EIS in June 2007 (A. Appleby, Washington Department of Fish and Wildlife, personal communication).

Washington Trout and the Native Fish Society, two environmental organizations that advocate for wild fish, sued the director of the Washington Department of Fish and Wildlife in 2002 and 2003 to spur completion of the 79 proposed HGMPs in the Puget Sound area and release them for public comment. When the HGMPs were proposed, Washington Trout had many criticisms. Most fundamentally, it argued that the overall size of the Chinook salmon, coho salmon, and steelhead hatchery programs in the Puget Sound area is far too large to justify under the ESA, given their effects on wild Chinook salmon (Vanden Brulle 2004). Similarly, the national group Trout Unlimited released a report in December 2003 that argued for changing hatchery operations from their historic "large agribusiness 'production-factory' model" to "a decentralized array of smaller-scale sustainable and diverse 'organic farm-like' facilities that are consistent with ESA responsibilities" (Williams et al. 2003).

Dramatic cutbacks in production would, however, raise serious issues for tribal treaty rights to harvest, which currently depend largely on hatchery fish. So far, changes to hatchery operations since the HSRG released its recommendations have been more modest, though not insignificant (LLTK 2005). Hatchery programs for Dungeness

River fall pink salmon, Garrison Springs chum salmon, Fox Island coho and Chinook salmons, Minter Creek chum and pink salmons, and Tulalip Bay spring Chinook salmon have all been discontinued. The McAllister Creek Hatchery on the Nisqually River was completely closed. There have been numerous facility and operational improvements across hatcheries throughout the region. The state hopes to implement changes to harvest practices that can better target hatchery fish, thus reducing their presence on the spawning grounds (H. Bartlett, Washington Department of Fish and Wildlife, personal communication). But it is questionable whether these practices can actually get hatchery stray rates below the HSRG's targets without reducing production levels. In any case, the improved harvest practices are not part of the current harvest plan, which has been approved through 2009.

The actual ability of hatcheries to provide meaningful conservation benefits remains unclear. Almost no studies have closely evaluated the performance of hatchery fish in the wild or the survival of their naturally produced offspring (Hulett et al. 2004). In June 2003, a scientific panel reviewing hatcheries in the Columbia River basin (separate from the HSRG) found that almost all hatchery operations offer "little chance for conservation benefit" and pose "some conservation risk" to any but the smallest wild populations (see ISAB 2003). The panel recommended that hatcheries attempt to supplement wild populations only when three conditions all hold: the wild runs are at risk of extirpation (becoming locally extinct) from habitat losses; supplementation from hatcheries would likely buy time for necessary habitat restoration; and funding is committed to that restoration (ISAB 2003). Even then, the panel supported supplementing natural runs with hatchery fish only "on a limited experimental scale." Without such conditions, it predicted that supplementation would reduce the genetic fitness and productivity of wild runs, while initial increases in abundance would encourage the continuation of unsustainable harvest rates and habitat degradation (ISAB 2003).

In 1996, the National Academy of Sciences lamented the lack of rigorous scientific study of hatcheries in *Upstream: Salmon and Society in the Pacific Northwest*, commenting, "Over the last century, the Pacific Northwest culture passed up the chance to learn adaptively about artificial propagation of anadromous Pacific salmon" (NRC 1996:304). NMFS's coast-wide scientific review panel agrees, saying its "highest priority" for research was treating all hatchery closures as opportunities for experiments, which could clarify the actual effects of hatcheries on wild salmon (SRSRP 2002). A simple example of such an experiment would compare two salmon stocks with similar histories of hatchery releases, where the releases stop for one and continue for the other (SRSRP 2001b). However, while the Washington Department of Fish and Wildlife is seeking more funds for monitoring to meet HSRG recommendations, it has not planned to study the results of closures or discontinued programs compared to control areas where hatchery production continues (Bartlett, personal communication). In addition, no federal funds are allocated to implement recommendations from the Hatchery Reform Project (LLTK 2006).

The ESA has clearly had a powerful effect on hatcheries in the Pacific Northwest. Only after widespread listing of salmon did hatchery managers undertake a serious scientific review of their operations and their ecological effects, despite years of outside calls for one. The lawsuit brought by Washington Trout and the Native Fish Society put hatchery managers and NMFS on notice that their actions will be closely scrutinized for compliance with the ESA. Pressures from fishing interests to maintain hatchery production remain strong, but the ESA is likely to force continued improvements in hatchery operations, especially as better information becomes available to compare actual results with HSRG standards and goals approved for individual hatcheries.

Salmon Farms: Less of a Concern Than Hatcheries?

There are 12 licensed salmon farms in Washington State, all in Puget Sound: four in Rich Passage (south of Bainbridge Island), three outside Anacortes, two by Port Angeles, and one each in Skagit Bay, in Discovery Bay, and on Hartstene Island in south Puget Sound.[13] In 2002, NMFS issued a report that reviewed the potential impacts of these farms on Puget Sound Chinook salmon and Hood Canal summer chum salmon (see Waknitz et al. 2002). It considered the multiple ways in which farmed salmon could potentially harm wild, native salmon. For example, escaped farmed salmon might prey on wild salmon, compete with them for food and habitat, and create weaker genetic hybrids through interbreeding; the concentration of farmed fish might introduce and transmit diseases, parasites, and antibiotic resistant bacteria to wild fish; fish wastes and the physical impacts of the farms might also damage nearshore habitat. The report concluded that these problems posed minor, if any, risks to wild salmon, especially in comparison to the potential effects of hatchery operations at their current scale. Assuming the farms remain at their present scale and continue to rear only the Atlantic salmon stocks they began with in the 1980s, the report found they are not a significant risk to listed salmon in the Puget Sound region. Regarding potential problems from escaped salmon, the report commented,

> If all the Atlantic salmon which have escaped into Puget Sound since 1980 (assume one million) were represented on a bar graph by a bar about 3 cm (1.2 inches) high, the total number of Pacific salmon released [from hatcheries] into Puget Sound and its river basins since 1980 would be depicted on the same graph by a bar about 76 meters (about 250 feet) high. [Waknitz et al. 2002:44]

As the report itself notes, however, NMFS as an agency has a vested interest in concluding that salmon farms pose little risk under the ESA: part of NMFS's mandate is "to advocate environmentally sustainable aquaculture through research, technology development, financial assistance, and regulatory programs" (Waknitz et al. 2002:ix). The report was also unable to take into account a study that was not completed until 2 years later on the transmission of parasitic sea lice from farm to wild salmon in the Broughton Archipelago, northeast of Vancouver Island (Krkosek et al. 2005). This

[13] From "The Hidden Cost of Your Salmon Fillet," at www.washingtontrout.org/salmonfarms.shtml.

study found that, as salmon passed one isolated farm, infection pressure was 70 times greater than background levels and remained unnaturally high for 30 km downstream. Considering the increased pressure across time and distance, the total direct contribution of sea lice from the farm was 30,000 times the background rate. Adding a second generation of sea lice born from those first infecting the wild salmon made the total direct and indirect contribution of lice from this one farm 200,000 times greater than natural levels across a 75-km migration route downstream.[14] Parasitic infection and disease is probably the most important concern that fish farms raise for wild salmon. In Norway, parasites from fish farms have been so devastating to wild fish that the government poisoned all aquatic life in dozens of rivers and streams in an effort to start over (Weiss 2002).

The NMFS study also did not review the potential effects of offshore fish farms, which may be built under legislation recently proposed in Congress. Pens for these farms would be placed in water between 100 and 200 feet (about 30 and 60 meters) deep, where they would float off of the ocean floor but well below the surface (Pope 2004). In the Northwest, the prime location for these farms is the Strait of Juan de Fuca, because of its deep, clean water and accessibility. The strait is also the primary migratory pathway for most salmon from Puget Sound and many from British Columbia's Fraser River. The Bush administration has proposed a regulatory system for offshore fish farms in federal waters, from 3 to 200 miles from shore (NOAA Offshore Aquaculture Program 2005). As of March 2006, the related legislation had been introduced in the Senate but no action had been taken on it.

Under the ESA, NMFS must consult with the Fish and Wildlife Service on the effects of any actions it might take to authorize new fish farms. Combined with the potential for citizen lawsuits to enforce the ESA's prohibition against take, this provides some assurance that fish farms will not become a considerably worse problem for listed salmon and the region's major ecosystems.

Habitat: The Failure of the 4(d) Rule

The 4(d) rule has clearly disappointed NMFS's expectations for habitat protection and restoration. From headwater areas to river mouths and the marine shoreline, NMFS hoped the rule would guide major reforms to regulations for all major land uses, falling broadly under the headings of development, forestry, and agriculture. For development, the rule highlighted the Tri-County effort in Snohomish, King, and Pierce counties in central Puget Sound as an example of the comprehensive regional proposals it hoped the rule would encourage to protect and restore habitat (USOFR 2000b). But Tri-County never submitted a formal proposal for approval, and neither has any other regional coalition or even a single local government across the Pacific Coast. The 4(d) rule noted that NMFS was working with the Washington Department of Ecology to develop a model program for development along

[14] Background summary of report on Transmission Dynamics of Parasitic Sea Lice from Farm to Wild Salmon, http://www.davidsuzuki.org/Oceans/Publications.asp.

shorelines (USOFR 2000b), but these regulations were overturned before they could be submitted to NMFS for approval (see Chapter 10, page 225). For forestry, NMFS supported the Forest and Fish regulations developed in Washington State, going so far as to say it would approve regulations that it found would protect habitat at least as well (USOFR 2000b). However, though Washington adopted these same regulations, it decided against submitting them for approval under the 4(d) rule (see next chapter, page 203). For agriculture, NMFS anticipated that farm management practices being negotiated under Washington's Agriculture, Fish, and Water would lead to future additions to the rule (USOFR 2000b), but the negotiations never led to such a proposal.

A brief review of the Tri-County process explains much of this failure. The executives of the three counties (which have a combined population of more than 3 million, more than three-quarters of the total population of the entire Puget Sound region) convened the process in 1998, working with leaders from Seattle, Tacoma, Bellevue, and Everett as well as Indian tribes and business and environmental groups.[15] By May 2001, the coalition had developed a standardized proposal for strict regulation of stream and wetland buffers and stormwater management, which went well beyond the existing regulations of any government in the coalition. The proposal also included improved road maintenance practices and commitments to watershed planning, habitat acquisition and restoration, and adaptive management. The package was reviewed by Parametrix, an environmental consulting firm, in coordination with NMFS and FWS. The review found that by definition the proposed regulations were not consistent with the 4(d) rule, since they did not "contribute to the attainment and maintenance" of Properly Functioning Conditions (see Parametrix 2002). As the review noted, site-scale regulations, even where they are much stricter than past practices, still lead to the "accumulation of residual impacts...at larger scales" (Parametrix 2002) because of the inevitable consequences of development and land clearing to natural processes. The review found that these impacts could potentially be addressed through habitat acquisition and restoration, but the Tri-County proposal provided few details on how this would be accomplished. In separate letters, the federal agencies agreed with this assessment (K. S. Berg and D. R. Lohn, 2002 letters to Tri-County chairs).

Tri-County never developed a more specific proposal to fund habitat projects. The coalition had come together in considerable part out of fear that lawsuits under the ESA would undermine the region's economy without protection for development through the 4(d) rule (R. Sims, R. Drewel, and D. Sutherland, 1999 letter to W. Stelle, National Marine Fisheries Service[16]). When no lawsuits were filed against local developments or development regulations (for reasons discussed in the last chapter), pressure to move forward with the proposal faded. The lack of legal pressure had a similar effect on other efforts to seek protection under the 4(d) rule for activi-

[15] See http://www.salmoninfo.org/TriCounty/tricounty.htm.

[16] http://www.salmoninfo.org/tricounty/tri-cresponse.htm.

ties affecting habitat, including aborted proposals from Kitsap County and the City of Snohomish.[17] Improved road maintenance practices, probably the least important part of the Tri-County proposal for salmon recovery, were approved under the rule, largely because many local governments and the state of Washington were prepared to implement them regardless. In contrast to development, road maintenance improvements did not require habitat projects to mitigate cumulative effects, since by definition road maintenance was considered good for salmon habitat if the alternative was not maintaining roads.

Water use, of course, can affect salmon habitat at least as much as land use, but the 4(d) rule contains fewer provisions for water. It establishes conditions for approving screens to keep fish out of water diverted from a stream or lake (USOFR 2002b), but does not provide for approval of municipal water withdrawals except as one of 12 conditions for approving development regulations, stating that new water supply demands must "be met without impacting flows needed for threatened salmonids" (USOFR 2000b:42480). Rather than pursue approval under this clause, which would have involved review of all their development regulations and policies, the cities of Seattle and Tacoma developed habitat conservation plans (HCPs) to protect their municipal water supply operations on the Cedar and Green rivers, respectively. Other jurisdictions in the Puget Sound area have also begun developing HCPs for water withdrawals, in some cases because of threatened lawsuits alleging take.

It is revealing that, as of March 2005, the only lawsuits in the region under the ESA that have successfully led to reforms of land-use practices to protect listed salmon have addressed federal actions—the Environmental Protection Agency's regulation of pesticide use and the Federal Emergency Management Agency's administration of flood insurance and related criteria for floodplain development (see *NWF v. FEMA* 2003). As discussed in the last chapter, the ESA's requirements are generally much easier to enforce against federal agencies than non-federal parties, especially for actions affecting habitat. The first lawsuit led to a court order restricting the use of pesticides until EPA completed consultations with NMFS. The order prohibited use of 54 pesticide chemicals within 20 yards of salmon streams and required that seven chemicals include "salmon hazard" warnings at points of sale in urban areas. The second lawsuit led to a settlement in which FEMA agreed to consult with NMFS on its floodplain insurance program, including minimum development standards for floodplains and floodplain mapping. FEMA standards have an enormous effect on floodplain development throughout the Puget Sound region, since local jurisdictions must meet them if private and public activities in their floodplains are to qualify not just for flood insurance but for any loans or financial assistance from a federally regulated lender or federal agency (Flood Protection Disaster Protection Act of 1973, U.S. Code, volume 42, section 4012[1]).

Though no lawsuits under the ESA have been filed to date against local develop-

[17] The author was in charge of the City of Snohomish's project, which still resulted in an Endangered Species Act strategy being implemented by the city.

ment regulations or policies in the Puget Sound region, this may change when urban growth boundaries are expanded under the Growth Management Act. To summarize related points from Chapter 7, lawsuits brought against development regulations face at least three fundamental challenges in proving take:

1. Most land-use regulations of concern are intended to protect salmon habitat, even if arguably they do not do so effectively enough;
2. The relationship between most land uses and harm to salmon is indirect and complex, making it difficult to predict that identifiable salmon will be harmed by one regulatory standard but not by another; and
3. The regulated activity, not the regulation, is the immediate cause of any potential take.

The first of these challenges does not apply to expanding urban growth boundaries, which cannot benefit salmon habitat. The second challenge applies weakly, if at all, since the science is clear about the ecological damage that can be predicted to result from dense urban development. The third challenge is a potential problem, but it would be far from insurmountable, given precedents in favor of vicarious liability (see Chapter 7, pages 128–131).[18] So, by stopping or conditioning the expansion of urban growth boundaries, ESA lawsuits may yet have significant effects on local land use in the Puget Sound region. Threats of lawsuits may also lead to negotiated settlements in specific cases where a relatively strong argument can be made that a land-use action is proximate to take of listed salmon. (For example, the Swinomish Indian Tribe threatened to sue Diking District 22 of Skagit County for operating tidegates that prevented fish from using estuarine habitat, which led to negotiated improvements; P. Goldman, EarthJustice, personal communication.)

The Shared Strategy: A Negotiated Settlement to Recover Puget Sound Salmon?

Efforts to address habitat issues in the region turned away from the 4(d) rule and instead focused on what came to be called the Shared Strategy for Puget Sound, which developed the recovery plan for listed salmon in the region. The Shared Strategy was conceived in meetings of regional leaders in 1999. It brings together top representatives of NMFS, the U.S. Fish and Wildlife Service, the Washington Department of Fish and Wildlife, Indian tribes, local governments, businesses, and environmental groups.[19] Probably the most influential participant is William Ruckelshaus, the first administrator of the Environmental Protection Agency and now a prominent businessman in the Seattle area.[20] The goal of the Shared Strategy's

---

[18] The author has discussed this point with environmental attorneys who have explored avenues for lawsuits against land-use practices under the ESA, who would prefer not to be named.

[19] See http://www.sharedsalmonstrategy.org/who-we-are.htm for members of the Shared Strategy's board and committees.

plan is "to recover self-sustaining, harvestable salmon runs in a manner that contributes to the overall health of Puget Sound and its watersheds and allows us to use this precious resource in concert with our region's economic vitality and prosperity" (Shared Strategy for Puget Sound 2005). NMFS is adopting the plan, with some key qualifications and conditions, as the official recovery plan for Puget Sound Chinook salmon under the ESA (NMFS 2005). NMFS is expected to do the same with a similar plan developed for Hood Canal summer chum salmon. While the Fish and Wildlife Service has developed its own draft recovery plan for Puget Sound bull trout, it expects to use the Shared Strategy plan as a vehicle for implementing some of its plan's recommended actions (J. Chan, U.S. Fish and Wildlife Service, personal communication). By developing a salmon recovery plan that meets federal standards, leaders of the Shared Strategy have hoped to attract hundreds of millions of federal dollars for implementation (see Wiley and Canty 2003).

The size and complexity of the Shared Strategy plan is enormous. The plan incorporates work done by 14 different watershed planning groups, as well as regional habitat actions that cross watersheds (e.g., for parts of the marine shoreline) and the harvest and hatchery plans discussed above. It envisions full recovery of Chinook salmon taking 50 to 100 years, but focuses on recommended actions for the first 10 years. The plan does not attempt to integrate actions across habitat, harvest, and hatcheries (except where individual watershed groups have done so), but identifies key issues for that effort, which it proposes to begin addressing in the first years of implementation. The plan stresses the importance of adaptive management—learning from the results of actions taken and adjusting priorities of further actions accordingly. It estimates the cost of implementing watershed plans, hatchery reforms, and regional habitat actions over the first 10 years to be approximately $1.55 billion, mostly for habitat acquisition and restoration (Shared Strategy for Puget Sound 2005). According to the plan, current regional spending for related actions is about $60 million a year, which translates to a gap of about $900 million over 10 years. To pay for this, the plan calls for four primary actions: increasing state funding for the Salmon Recovery Funding Board; diversifying federal and state funding sources; strategically seeking public and private grants; and redirecting 10% of existing mitigation funds for public and private construction projects to salmon habitat. This is a very optimistic view of what these actions can achieve. An additional weakness, as the plan acknowledges, is that "only about a third" of all these funds would be "available for distribution across the region." The plan's reliance on local funding and mitigation "means that urban watersheds with the largest population size have the potential to raise the most money." But that is not where the greatest needs are.

NMFS's review of the plan identified particular concerns in the Strait of Juan de Fuca bioregion (which includes the Elwha and Dungeness Chinook salmon populations), the Strait of Georgia bioregion (which includes the north and south fork Nooksack

[20] Mr. Ruckelshaus also chairs the state's Salmon Recovery Funding Board, which has overseen the distribution of more than $200 million in federal and state funds for salmon habitat projects and related work across the state since 2000.

River populations), and the Hood Canal bioregion (which includes the Skokomish and mid-Hood Canal populations). For the ESU to recover, NMFS's scientific advisory panel argues that all of the individual populations in these bioregions must recover, along with two to four individual populations in each of the Whidbey and central/south sound bioregions (see Table 8-3 for a list of populations by bioregion). All of the populations in the first three bioregions are currently small and far below recovery targets. Nevertheless, NMFS found that recommendations for these three areas meet ESA requirements for a recovery plan, assuming that "all the strategies identified in the [Shared Strategy] Plan are implemented, including adaptive management measures" (NMFS 2005). The plan offers little detail about how adaptive management will work.

Under the ESA, recovery plans must include the following three elements: (1) site-specific actions necessary to recover the species; (2) objective, measurable criteria for delisting the species; and (3) estimates of the time and cost required to achieve recovery and intermediate steps toward recovery (ESA, section 1533[f][1]). The plan clearly meets the second two criteria; the first is more problematic. The plan explicitly notes that "if there is a conflict between...this regional strategy" and individual chapters developed by watershed groups, "the individual watershed chapter shall take precedence" (Shared Strategy for Puget Sound 2005:437). Nevertheless, NMFS approved it conditioned on the opposite with respect to "enhancements" that NMFS's scientific advisory panel included in the plan (NMFS 2005). More generally, NMFS found "that this recovery plan is based on the best available science except for those specific issues where NMFS determines, through a critical assessment of all available scientific information, that alternative scientific conclusions are warranted" (NMFS 2005:38). As noted in Chapter 7, implementation of recovery plans is voluntary, though federal agencies arguably have an "affirmative duty" to contribute to recovery of listed species. NMFS has committed to use the Shared Strategy Plan to guide its regulatory reviews of federal actions and proposed habitat conservation plans, as well as allocations of federal funding.

If Puget Sound Chinook salmon are to be "delisted" under the ESA, NMFS requires that two to four populations in each of the five bioregions meet the planning ranges and targets shown in Table 8-3, and that further criteria be met for habitat functionality, the adequacy of regulations, management of harvest and hatcheries, and the control of exotic species (NMFS 2005). That means the region is a very long way from delisting Chinook salmon. Across the region, the average ratio of recent returns to the low end of the planning range recommended for recovery by NMFS's science advisory panel for just wild returns is 18.4 to 1. The ratio is even higher, 25 to 1, if it includes just those populations NMFS identified in its supplement as necessary for recovery. Although the ratios would be lower with greater productivity, the goals for productivity in the right-most column of Table 8-3 are ambitious and unlikely to be met. Moreover, these ratios count hatchery-bred salmon among recent returns, but the planning targets and ranges in Table 8-3 are based strictly on wild salmon.

It is interesting to note that when the National Academy of Sciences reviewed the Endangered Species Act in 1995, it found that "a species should be removed from the list [when] its risk of extinction has decreased to the point where it is no longer considered threatened" (NRC 1995:156).[21] Given that some members of NMFS's Biological Review Team for Chinook salmon believed that the Puget Sound ESU did not deserve to be listed as threatened in the first place, applying the Academy's standard would presumably lead to goals considerably less stringent than those in Table 8-3. The difference between these two standards is not accounted for merely by the fact that NMFS's delisting criteria for Puget Sound Chinook salmon seek to provide sustainable harvest as well as biological recovery, given that NMFS is allowing harvest even today. The difference fundamentally relates to the lack of quantifiable standards for risk of extinction in the ESA, and the lack of transparent, scientifically based models for calculating that risk for any particular species. The determination of risk is ultimately a matter of judgment, on which knowledgeable scientists disagree, as discussed on pages 143–144 above. Especially given the practical consequences, though, this judgment is more than a scientific one. As the National Academy of Sciences said in *Upstream*,

> There is no 'correct' answer to the question of precisely how much biological diversity and population structure should be maintained or can be lost to provide a long-term future for salmon. Scientific estimates—including uncertainties associated with them—are only part of the argument. Society must decide what degree of biological security would be desirable and affordable if it could be achieved, i.e., the desired probability of survival or extinction of natural populations, over what time and what area, at what cost. [NRC 1996:342]

A Shared Strategy for More than Just Salmon

The Shared Strategy's efforts are hampered by the very different ways the ESA applies to different activities. Risk of legal liability depends on how difficult it is to prove "take" under the Supreme Court's interpretation of the law, and whether the activity is conducted by a federal agency or not. Harvest reductions have already been dramatic since the 1990s, and are under continued pressure in considerable part because harvest is take by definition. Long-sought hatchery reforms are beginning and they will likely continue because hatcheries clearly can "harm" and "harass" listed salmon. But not that much has changed for habitat since before the listing. Watershed planning efforts have identified conservation priorities and have generally gotten the right people talking to one another, but the resulting plans almost entirely lack commitments for implementing either regulatory reforms or funding habitat acquisition and restoration projects. As discussed in Chapter 3, the plans also generally lack a long-term perspective that could keep site-by-site improvements from being overwhelmed by the effects of population growth and transformation of the landscape over time.

In addition to the inequities that result from the various ways the ESA applies to

---

[21] As noted previously, the National Academy of Sciences recommended that these judgments be put in terms of the "probability of extinction during a specified period (e.g., *x*% probability of extinction over the next *y* years)." It acknowledged that selecting particular degrees of risk and particular periods reflects both "scientific knowledge and societal values" (NRC 1995:174–175).

harvest, hatcheries and habitat, there is the larger inequity of how it applies to different species. As noted previously, for years budget and administrative obstacles have been keeping most terrestrial and freshwater species that might qualify for listing from even being considered, except under court order. Where listing decisions move forward, they remain matters of judgment, with no quantifiable criteria established by regulation or agreed on within the scientific community. Even more fundamentally, considering species one by one under the ESA can ignore more important questions, as NMFS's Biological Review Team for hake, cod, and pollock in Puget Sound argued:

> A significance emerges from consideration of these species collectively that is not apparent when any one is considered alone. Joint consideration...suggests ecosystem-level implications that are difficult or impossible to evaluate under terms of the ESA. It is possible, hypothetically, that the reduced or declining trends of each of the individual species in this group could be considered as insufficient for affording any of the species legal protection under the ESA. But taking no action, under such circumstances, might be a major mistake if this collective information is an indication that the Puget Sound area, as an ecosystem, is experiencing major change. Such changes could be of more far-ranging concern than could ever be recognized if any one species were considered individually. [Gustafson et al. 2000]

The National Academy of Sciences came to a similar conclusion when it evaluated the ESA in 1995. Although it said the ESA was "based on sound scientific principles" (NRC 1995:4), it also found that the ESA was not enough:

> [T]he task of managing each of the vast multitude of species on a case-by-case basis is beyond human capabilities. This is further compounded by the fact that many species remain undescribed. A challenge for the future is to find more integrated mechanisms to sustain both species and ecosystems that do not depend on case-by-case management. [NRC 1995[22]]

Ultimately, if we in the Puget Sound region are to protect our magnificent natural heritage, we must do so at the level of the region's major ecosystems—its forests, rivers, marine nearshore and distinctive habitats such as the south Sound prairies. As noted previously, much of the way we experience our heritage is at the level of these whole systems. Protecting them is also the most efficient way of addressing risks to individual species, from salmon and orcas to owls and butterflies. Salmon harvest restrictions and hatchery reform will be for naught if habitat continues to degrade. Lawsuits under the ESA that challenge the extension of urban growth boundaries or new water withdrawals may force some important habitat reforms. Indian treaty rights could ultimately force even greater changes, as Chapter 13 will discuss. But ultimately, given the pressures of population growth and climate change, habitat reforms that can conserve our natural heritage must be far more ambitious. That will require a much more serious

---

[22] This statement was written by the chair of the committee responsible for the report. The committee recommended ecosystem management as a better approach than managing for individual species, though it called the ESA a necessary safety net when other approaches are failing (NRC 1995: 200–202).

and widespread regional debate than the Shared Strategy has accomplished so far, despite its success at bringing so many different parties together.

Fortunately, one major land use in the region—forestry—has begun very substantial reforms already. Much can be learned from this experience, as discussed in the next chapter. Perhaps the most fundamental lesson, however, is that it started with a legal hammer.

References

Alsea Valley Alliance v. Evans, 143 F.Supp. 2d 1154 (D. Ore. 2001).

Alsea Valley Alliance v. Evans, No. 01-36071 (9th Cir. 2001).

Brandt-Erichsen, S.A. 2006. Sixty day notice of intent to sue over violations of sections 4(d), 7, and 9 of the Endangered Species Act—Puget Sound Comprehensive Chinook Management Plan: Harvest Management Component—ESA section 4(d) decision/determination. Heller Ehrman LLP, Seattle.

Center for Biological Diversity. 2005. Whale of a victory: five-year battle with Bush administration leads to protection for Puget Sound orcas. Endangered Earth (Winter 2006/2007):1, 8.

Chasan, D. J. 1986. The water link: a history of Puget Sound as a resource. University of Washington Press, Seattle.

Environment News Service. 2003. Judge orders feds to reconsider protecting puget sound orcas. Available: http://www.ens-newswire.com/ens/dec2003/2003-12-18-10.asp (December 2003).

Environment News Service. 2004. Appeals court denies Oregon coast coho salmon protection. Available: www.ens-newswire.com/ens/feb2004/2004-02-26-11.asp (March 2006).

Ford, J. K. B., G. M. Ellis, and K.C. Bascomb. 2000. Killer whales. University of Washington Press, Seattle.

Goetz, F. A., E. Jeanes, and E. Bea. 2004. Bull trout in the nearshore, preliminary draft, U.S. Army Corps of Engineers, Seattle.

Gustafson, R. G., W. H. Lenarz, B. B. McCain, C. C. Schmitt, W. S. Grant, T. L. Builder, and R. D. Methot. 2000. Status review of Pacific hake, Pacific cod, and walleye pollock from Puget Sound, Washington. National Marine Fisheries Service, Northwest Fisheries Science Center, Seattle. Available: www.nwfsc.noaa.gov/publications/techmemos/tm44/tm44.htm (March 2006).

Hulett, P. L., C. S. Sharpe, and C. W. Wagemann. 2004. Critical need for rigorous evaluation of salmonid propagation programs using local wild broodstock. Pages 253–262 *in* M. J. Nickum, P. M. Mazik, J. G. Nickum, and D. D. MacKinlay, editors. Propagated fish in resource management. American Fisheries Society, Symposium 44, Bethesda, Maryland.

ISAB (Independent Scientific Advisory Board). 2003. Review of salmon and steelhead supplementation. Northwest Power Planning and Conservation Council, Publication 2003-3, Portland, Oregon.

Krahn, M. M., P. R. Wade, S. T. Kalinowski, M. E. Dahlheim, B. L. Taylor, M. B. Hanson, G. M. Ylitalo, R. P. Angliss, J. E. Stein, and R. S. Waples. 2002. Status review of southern resident killer whales (*Orcinus orcha*) under the Endangered Species Act. National Marine Fisheries Service, NMFS-NWFSC-54, Seattle.

Krahn, M. M., M. J. Ford, W. F. Perrin, P. R. Wade, R. P. Angliss, M. B. Hanson, B. L. Taylor, G. M. Ylitalo, M. E. Dahlheim, J. E. Stein, and R. S. Waples. 2004. 2004 status review of southern resident killer whales (*Orcinus orca*) under the Endangered Species Act. National Marine Fisheries Service, NMFS-NWFSC-62, Seattle.

Krkosek, M., M. A. Lewis, and J. P. Volpe. 2005. Transmission dynamics of parasitic sea lice from farm to wild salmon. Proceedings of the Royal Society. Available: http://www.math.ualberta.ca/~mlewis/publications/SeaLice.pdf (March 2006)

LLTK (Long Live the Kings). 2005. Puget Sound and Coastal Washington Hatchery Reform Project, May 2005 Update. Available: http://www.lltk.org/pdf/HR_Update_May05.pdf (March 2006)

LLTK (Long Live the Kings). 2006. Puget Sound and Coastal Washington Hatchery Reform Project: 2006 work in progress. Report to Congress, March 2006. http://www.lltk.org/pdf/Report_To_Congress_06/HR_Report_to_Congress_Progress_Mar06.pdf (March 2006)

Mahnken, C., G. Ruggerone, W. Waknitz, and T. Flagg. 1998. A historical perspective on salmonid production from Pacific Rim hatcheries. Northern Pacific Anadromous Fisheries Commission Bulletin 1:38–53, Vancouver.

Middle Rio Grande Conservancy District v. Babbitt, No. CIV 99-870 (D.N.M. 2000).

Mobrand, L. E., J. Barr, L. Blankenship, D. E. Campton, T. T. P. Evelyn, T. A. Flagg, C. V. W. Mahnken, L. W. Seeb, P. R. Seidel, and W. W. Smoker. 2005. Hatchery reform in Washington state: principles and emerging issues. Fisheries 30(6):11–23.

Myers, J. M., R. G. Kope, G. J. Bryant, D. Teel, L. J. Lierheimer, T. C. Wainwright, W. S. Grant, F. W. Waknitz, K. Neely, S. T. Lindley, and R. S. Waples. 1998. Status review of Chinook salmon from Washington, Idaho, Oregon, and California. National Marine Fisheries Service, NOAA Technical Memorandum, NMFS-NWFSC-35, Seattle.

Myers, R. A., S. A. Levin, R. Lande, F. C. James, W. W. Murdoch, and R. T. Paine. 2004. Hatcheries and endangered salmon. Science 303:1980.

NAHB (National Association of Home Builders) v. Evans, WL 1205743 No. 00-CV-2799 (D.D.C. 2002)

Natural Resources Defense Council v. U.S. Department of Interior, 113 F.3d 1121 (9th Cir. 1997).

Nehlson, W., J. E. Williams, and J. A. Lichatowich. 1991. Pacific salmon at the crossroads: stocks at risk from California, Oregon, Idaho and Washington. Fisheries 16:4–21.

New Mexico Cattle Growers Association v. USFWS (U.S. Fish and Wildlife Service), 248 F.3d 1277 (10th Cir. 2001).

NMFS (National Marine Fisheries Service). 2000. Template for developing a fisheries management and evaluation plan (FMEP) under "4(d) Rules." National Marine Fisheries Service, Seattle.

NMFS (National Marine Fisheries Service). 2002. Questions and Answers About the National Marine Fisheries Service's June 2002 Endangered Species Act Decision for Southern Resident Whales. National Marine Fisheries Service, Seattle.

NMFS (National Marine Fisheries Service). 2004. Puget Sound Chinook Harvest Resource Management Plan, Final Environmental Impact Statement. National Marine Fisheries Service, Northwest Office, Seattle.

NMFS (National Marine Fisheries Service). 2005. Supplement to the Draft Puget Sound Salmon Recovery Plan. National Marine Fisheries Service, Northwest Region, Seattle.

NOAA Offshore Aquaculture Program. 2005. The National Offshore Aquaculture Act at-a-glance. National Marine Fisheries Service. Available: http://www.nmfs.noaa.gov/mediacenter/aquaculture/ (March 2006).

NRC (National Resource Council). 1995. Science and the Endangered Species Act. National Academy Press, Washington, D.C.

NRC (National Research Council). 1996. Upstream: salmon and society in the Pacific Northwest. National Academy Press, Washington, D.C.

NWF (National Wildlife Federation) v. FEMA (Federal Emergency Management Agency), Case No. 03-2824-Z (W.Wa Dist. 2003).

Pacific Salmon Commission. 2001. 1999/2000 Fifteenth Annual Report of the Pacific Salmon Commission. Pacific Salmon Commission, Vancouver. Available: http://www.psc.org/pubs/15th%20Annual%20Report.pdf (March 2006).

Parametrix. 2002. Biological review: Tri-County Model 4(d) Rule Response Proposal. Prepared for Tri-County Salmon Conservation Coalition, Seattle.

Pope, C. 2004. Offshore fish farming roils growing debate: supporters looking at Strait of Juan de Fuca as possible aquaculture site. The Seattle Post-Intelligencer (August 23):A1.

Puget Sound Indian Tribes and WDFW (Washington Department of Fish and Wildlife). 2001. Puget Sound Comprehensive Chinook Management Plan: harvest management component. Puget Sound Indian Tribes and Washington Department of Fish and Wildlife, Olympia.

Puget Sound Technical Recovery Team. 2002. Planning ranges and preliminary guidelines for the delisting and recovery of the Puget Sound Chinook salmon evolutionarily significant unit. National Marine Fisheries Service, Northwest Fisheries Science Center, Seattle.

Rudolph, B. 2006a. Feds call for less harvest of ESA fish—everywhere. NW Fishletter #209. Available: http://www.newsdata.com/fishletter/209/1story.html (March 2006).

Rudolph, B. 2006b. Politicians get earful on salmon harvest, Canadian interceptions. NW Fishletter #204. Available: http://www.newsdata.com/fishletter/204/1story.htm (March 2006).

Ruggerone, G.T. and F.A. Goetz. 2004. Survival of Puget Sound chinook salmon (*Oncorhynchus tshawytscha*) in response to climate-induced competition with pink salmon (*Oncorhynchus gorbuscha*). Canadian Journal of Fisheries and Aquatic Science. 61: 1756-1770.

Shared Strategy for Puget Sound. 2005. Draft Puget Sound Salmon Recovery Plan, volume 1, June 30,2005. Shared Strategy for Puget Sound, Seattle.

SRSRP (Salmon Recovery Science Review Panel). 2001a. Report for the meeting held August 27-29, 2001. National Marine Fisheries Service, Northwest Fisheries Science Center, Seattle.

SRSRP (Salmon Recovery Science Review Panel). 2001b. Report for the meeting held March 13-14, 2001. National Marine Fisheries Service, Northwest Fisheries Science Center, Seattle.

SRSRP (Salmon Recovery Science Review Panel). 2002. Report for the meeting held December 11-13, 2002. National Marine Fisheries Service, Northwest Fisheries Science Center, Seattle.

SSRA (Salmon Spawning & Recovery Alliance) et al v. Gutierrez. 2005. Complaint for Declaratory and Injunctive Relief. Case No. C05-1877. U.S. District Court of Western Washington, Seattle.

SSRA (Salmon Spawning & Recovery Alliance) et al v. Bonner. 2005. Complaint for Declaratory and Injunctive Relief. Case No. C05-1878. U.S. District Court of Western Washington, Seattle.

TVA (Tennessee Valley Authority) v. Hill 437 U.S. 153 (1978).

U.S. Department of the Interior. 2003. Endangered Species Act 'broken'—flood of litigation over critical habitat hinders species conservation. U.S. Department of Interior, press release, Washington, D.C.

USOFR (U.S. Office of the Federal Register). 1995. Endangered and threatened species: proposed threatened status for three contiguous ESUs of coho salmon ranging from Oregon through central California, Federal Register 60:142(25 July 1995):38011–38030.

USOFR (U.S. Office of the Federal Register). 1996. Endangered and threatened species: proposed endangered statues for five ESUs of steelhead and proposed threatened statues for five ESUs of steelhead in Washington, Oregon, Idaho, and California. Federal Register 61:155(9 August 1996):41549–41550.

USOFR (U.S. Office of the Federal Register). 1998. Endangered and threatened species; proposed threatened status and designated critical habitat for Hood Canal summer-run chum salmon and Columbia River chum salmon, Federal Register 63:46(10 March 1998):11774–11795.

USOFR (U.S. Office of the Federal Register). 1999a. Endangered and threatened species; threatened status for three Chinook salmon evolutionarily significant units in Washington and Oregon, and endangered status of one Chinook salmon ESU in Washington, Federal Register 64:56(24 March 1999):14307–14328.

USOFR (U.S. Office of the Federal Register). 1999b. Endangered and threatened species; threatened status for two ESUs of chum salmon in Washington and Oregon, Federal Register 64:57(25 March 1999):14507–14517.

USOFR (U.S. Office of the Federal Register). 1999c. Endangered and threatened wildlife and plants; determination of threatened status for bull trout in the coterminous United States: final rule, Federal Register 64:210(1 November 1999):58909-58933.

USOFR (U.S. Office of the Federal Register). 2000a. Designated critical habitat: critical habitat for 19 evolutionarily significant units of salmon and steelhead in Washington, Oregon, Idaho, and California, Federal Register 65:32(16 February 2000):7764–7787.

USOFR (U.S. Office of the Federal Register) 2000b. Endangered and threatened species; final rule governing take of 14 threatened salmon and steelhead evolutionarily significant units (ESUs), Federal Register 65:132(10 July 2000):42421–42481.

USOFR (U.S. Office of the Federal Register). 2001. Endangered and threatened wildlife and plants; proposed rule to list the Dolly Varden as threatened in Washington due to similarity of appearance to bull trout, Federal Register 66:6(9 January 2001):1628–1632.

USOFR (U.S. Office of the Federal Register). 2002a. Listing endangered and threatened species: findings on a delisting petition, and two listing petitions, concerning 16 evolutionarily significant units of Pacific salmon and steelhead, Federal Register 67:143(25 July 2002):48601–48603.

USOFR (U.S. Office of the Federal Register). 2002b. Endangered and threatened species; findings on petitions to delist Pacific salmonid ESUs, Federal Register 67:28(11 February 2002):6215–6220.

USOFR (U.S. Office of the Federal Register). 2003. Policy for evaluation of conservation efforts when making listing decisions, Federal Register 68:60(28 March 2003):15100–15115.

USOFR (U.S. Office of the Federal Register). 2005a. Endangered and threatened wildlife and plants: review of native species that are candidates or proposed for listing as endangered or threatened; annual notice of findings on resubmitted petitions; annual description of progress on listing actions. Federal Register 70:90(11 May 2005): 24870-24934.

USOFR (U.S. Office of the Federal Register). 2005b. Endangered and threatened wildlife and plants: endangered status for Southern Resident killer whales. Federal Register 70:222(18 November 2005):69903-69912.

USOFR (U.S. Office of the Federal Register). 2005c. Endangered and threatened species: final listing determinations for 16 ESUs of West Coast salmon, and final 4(d) protective regulations for threatened salmonid ESUs. Federal Register 70:123(28 June 2005):37160–37195.

USOFR (U.S. Office of the Federal Register). 2005d. Endangered and threatened species: designation of critical habitat for 12 evolutionarily significant units of West Coast salmon and steelhead in Washington, Oregon and Idaho. Federal Register 70:170(2 September 2005):52630–52858.

USOFR (U.S. Office of the Federal Register). 2006. Listing endangered and threatened species and designating critical habitat: 12-month finding on petition to list Puget Sound steelhead as an endangered or threatened species under the Endangered Species Act. Federal Register 71:60(29 March 2006):15666–15680.

Vanden Brulle, R. 2004. Making hatcheries safe for salmon recovery: WT challenges Puget Sound Hatchery Plan. Washington Trout Report 14(1):7–9.

Vanden Brulle, R., and N. Gayeski. 2003. An overwhelming body of evidence: how hatcheries are jeopardizing salmon recovery. Washington Trout Report 13(1):4–8, Washington Trout, Duvall, Washington.

Waknitz, F. W., T. J. Tynan, C. E. Nash, R. N. Iwamoto, and L. G. Rutter. 2002. Review of potential impacts of Atlantic salmon culture on Puget Sound Chinook and Hood Canal summer-run chum salmon evolutionarily significant units. National Marine Fisheries Service, NOAA Technical Memo, NMFS-NWFSC-53. Available: http://www.nwfsc.noaa.gov/publications/techmemos/tm53/Tm53.PDF (March 2006).

Waples, R. S. 1991. Definition of 'species' under the Endangered Species Act: application to Pacific salmon. National Marine Fisheries Service, Northwest Fisheries Science Center, Seattle.

Weiss, K. 2002. Learning from errors—or not? The Seattle Times (December 29):A3.

Weitkamp, L. A., T. C. Wainwright, G. J. Bryant, G. B. Milner, D. J. Teel, R. G. Kope, and R. S. Waples. 1996. Status review of coho salmon from Washington, Oregon and California. National Marine Fisheries Service, NOAA Technical Memorandum, NWFSC-24, Seattle.

West Coast Coho Salmon Biological Review Team. 1996. Draft status review update for coho salmon from Washington, Oregon and California. National Marine Fisheries Service, Seattle.

Wiley, H., and D. Canty. 2003. Regional environmental initiatives in the United States: a report to the Puget Sound Shared Strategy. Available: http://www.sharedsalmonstrategy.org/files/Final_regional%20initiatives.pdf (March 2006).

Williams, R., J. Lichatowich, P. Mundy, and M. Powell. 2003. A blueprint for hatchery reform in the 21st century: a Trout Unlimited special report. Available: http://www.tu.org/atf/cf/{0D18ECB7-7347-445B-A38E-65B282BBBD8A}/landscapemedia.pdf (March 2006).

Chapter 9. Applying the ESA (Continued): Owls, Forests, and Fish

> The most important thing we can do is to admit, all of us to each other, that there are no simple or easy answers. This is not about choosing between jobs and the environment, but about recognizing the importance of both and recognizing that virtually everyone here and everyone in this region cares about both. [President William Clinton, remarks at the Forest Conference in Portland, Oregon, April 2, 1993 (U.S. Forest Service and Bureau of Land Management 1994:S-5)]

Chapter Summary

Of all major land uses in the Puget Sound region, by far the biggest systematic improvements to protect habitat for listed salmon have been made by forestry. In part, this is a legacy of the fights over the spotted owl *Strix occidentalis*. The Northwest Forest Plan (NFP), which fundamentally reshaped management of federal forests in the Pacific Northwest, includes an Aquatic Conservation Strategy to protect and restore salmon habitat on federal lands. The shock of change caused by the plan was especially strong in the timber industry, with its large landholdings and the long-term orientation required by a crop that generally takes at least 40 years to reach harvestable size. Anticipating further effects on non-federal lands, many of the Puget Sound region's largest public and private forest owners negotiated habitat conservation plans (HCPs) to guarantee "no surprises" under the ESA for 50 or more years. In addition, the Washington Forest Protection Association (an industry trade group that includes large and small landowners) worked through a process known as Timber Fish and Wildlife to negotiate regulations for the entire industry, first for the spotted owl and other old-growth species, then for listed salmon. The latter regulations, known as the Forest and Fish agreement, have been approved by the Washington Forest Practices Board, an appointed body responsible for regulating forestry on state and private lands. They also have been approved by the National Marine Fisheries Service (NMFS) and the U.S. Fish and Wildlife Service as the basis for a habitat conservation plan that covers virtually all private timber harvesting in the state.

Environmentalists and some Indian tribes in Washington opposed the Forest and Fish regulations. Among their many concerns, probably the greatest is the lack of any protected buffer on seasonal streams not used by fish, which can greatly affect water quality and the supply of sediments and wood to downstream fish habitat. The buffer required in the NFP for such streams is generally at least 100 feet on each side. The environmentalists and tribes included a 70-foot buffer as part of an alternative they proposed to the Forest and Fish regulations, which also would have increased a wide variety of other habitat protections. However, a University of Washington study done for the state estimated that the Forest and Fish regulations were already projected to decrease the total value of non-federal forestlands in the state by 11%, or $2.7 billion. The environmentalist and tribal alternative would have decreased the value by 34%, or $8.4 billion. The Forest Practices Board had two fundamental goals for the regulations: compliance with the ESA and other federal requirements; and keeping the timber industry economically viable in the state. Largely with the second goal in mind, the board adopted the Forest and Fish regulations rather than the environmental and tribal alternative in 2001.

The calculation of costs for forest regulations highlights a critical dimension for any debate over the future of land uses and major ecosystems in the Puget Sound region. Without question, the proposal from environmental groups and tribes was better than the Forest and Fish regulations for fish and other species that depend on aquatic and riparian habitat in the state's forests, including a wide variety of birds, mammals, and amphibians. Something like their proposal may be necessary for the long-term health of the region's ecosystems. But who should pay for it, and what are the consequences of that decision?

On federal lands, though the NFP has largely been a success environmentally, some rural areas have borne major economic sacrifices, receiving considerably less help than the Clinton administration promised. The economic costs of the Forest and Fish regulations, as well as other state and private initiatives to protect forest habitat, have primarily been borne by the industry and landowners. Collectively, these federal and state efforts provide an extraordinarily valuable foundation for protecting the region's major ecosystems. To conserve the region's natural heritage, steps at least as great must be taken in other critical parts of those ecosystems, particularly floodplains, estuaries, and the Puget Sound shoreline. But sacrifices will have to be shared for a collaborative approach to succeed over time. There are, therefore, both positive and cautionary lessons to be learned from the experience in the region's forests, where the most important steps so far have been taken.

A Summary of the Northwest Forest Plan

Without a doubt, the northern spotted owl *Strix occidentalis caurina* has had the greatest effect of any listed species on ecosystem protection in the Pacific Northwest. Its listing as threatened, however, did not precipitate the enormous changes in how the region's old-growth forests were managed. As discussed in Chapter 7, the first lawsuits demanding protection of the owl and old-growth forests were filed under the National Forest Management Act, whose implementing regulations required maintenance of "viable populations of existing native and desired non-native vertebrate species" in national forests. Under these regulations, in 1985 the Forest Service identified the spotted owl as a "management indicator species" for old-growth forests. The Forest Service proposed protecting nearly 700,000 acres of old growth in national forests to support the spotted owl, 4 years before it was listed under the ESA. Nevertheless, the ESA played a powerful role in the final Northwest Forest Plan. The U.S. Fish and Wildlife Service initially identified 11.6 million acres as critical habitat for the owl, including land not currently occupied by the owl but potentially important for its recovery. Petitions to list numerous stocks of salmon in the Pacific

Northwest led to the Aquatic Conservation Strategy being added to the NFP, to protect salmon habitat and related riparian and upland areas. Concerns about potential ESA listings of rare or little known species associated with old-growth forests led to a Survey and Manage requirement in the NFP before harvest of old growth in unreserved areas could proceed.

Out of the 24.5 million acres of federal land in the range of the spotted owl, the final NFP established 7.4 million acres as "late successional reserves," which include mostly old-growth forest and mature forest that could become old growth in 50 to 100 years[1] (see map, Figure 9-1). This added to 7.3 million acres already protected from commercial timber harvest by Congress as national parks, wilderness areas, wild and scenic rivers, national wildlife refuges, and military reservations. The Aquatic Conservation Strategy added another 2.6 million acres in protected riparian areas for perennial and intermittent streams across all Forest Service and Bureau of Land Management forestlands, where the only harvest allowed is from thinning to enhance ecological functions. A further 1.5 million acres of federal forest was administratively withdrawn, including recreation areas, lands not suited for timber production, visual retention areas, and areas protected for locally endemic species. Four million acres of Forest Service and Bureau of Land Management land were identified as "matrix" lands for timber harvest, which could be cut only under numerous conditions. Another 1.5 million acres were identified as Adaptive Management Areas, intended "to develop and test new management approaches to integrate and achieve ecological and economic health, and other social objectives" (U.S. Forest Service and Bureau of Land Management 1994).

Though at the time of the NFP there were 10 species listed or proposed for listing under the ESA that depended on old-growth forests to some degree, it was primarily the northern spotted owl's needs that drove the size and location of the late successional reserves (U.S. Forest Service and Bureau of Land Management 1994). Alternatives for the plan were selected to meet or exceed conservation measures in a draft recovery plan for the spotted owl, which focused on federal land, where the majority of old-growth forest in the Northwest is located (U.S. Forest Service and Bureau of Land Management 1994). The marbled murrelet *Brachyramphus marmoratus*, a seabird that nests in older forests within 50 miles of marine waters, also affected the final selection of some reserves, but much less is known about its habitat needs (U.S. Forest Service and Bureau of Land Management 1994). In addition to riparian areas, the Aquatic Conservation Strategy added further protections in Key Watersheds, which were selected either for their importance to salmon conservation or as sources of high quality water (U.S. Forest Service and Bureau of Land Management 1994). No new roads are allowed in roadless areas within Key Watersheds. Before any timber harvest can take place, a watershed analysis linking land conditions to streams in the watersheds is required. That analysis also must prioritize restoration actions, which are to focus on removing and upgrading roads and restor-

[1] All land allocation information is from U.S. Forest Service and Bureau of Land Management 1994.

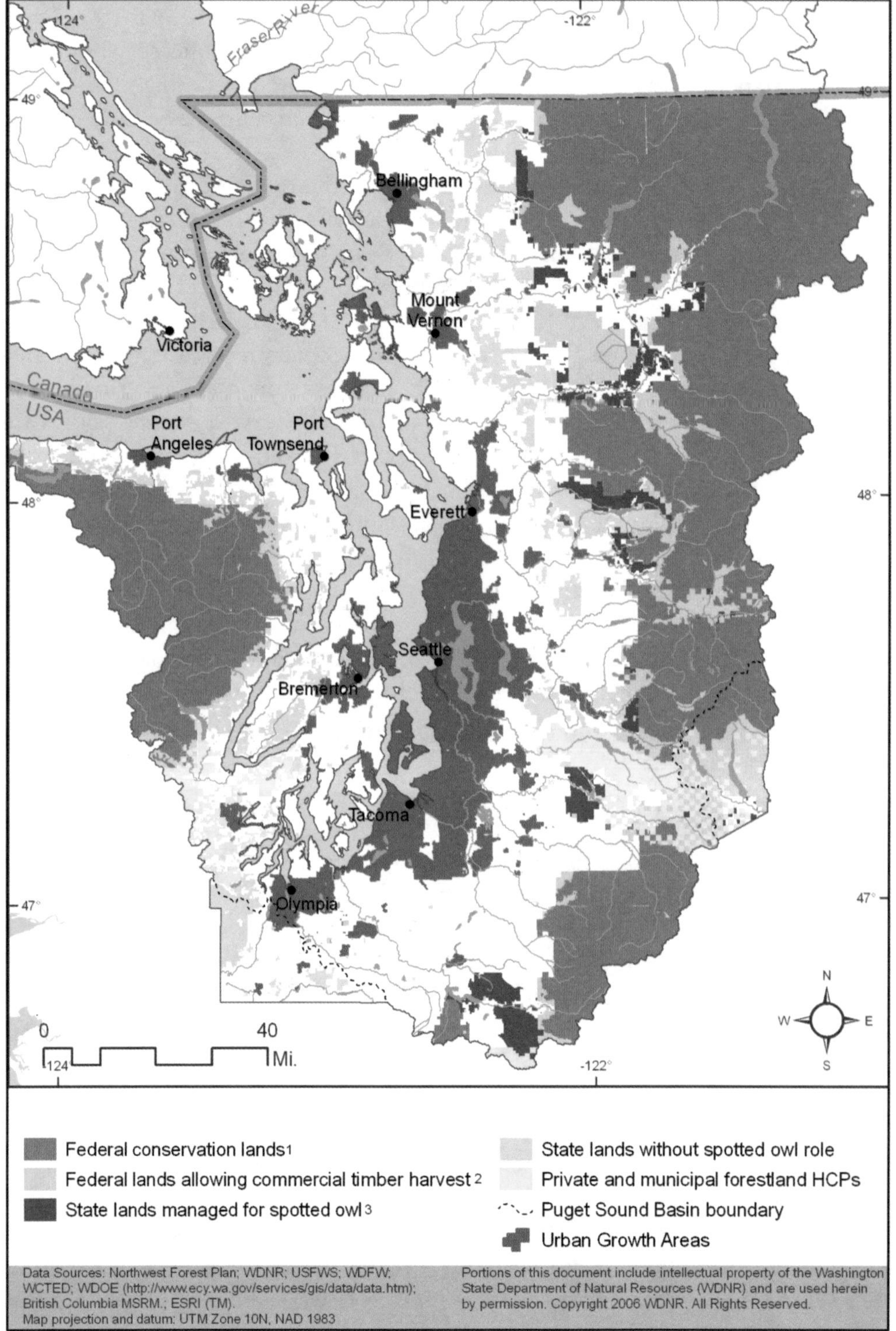

FIGURE 9-1. Conservation status of forest lands in the Puget Sound region. See notes, next page.

Notes, Figure 9-1

[1] Includes late-successional reserves, managed late successional areas, Congressional reserves, adaptive management reserves, and administratively withdrawn areas. Riparian reserves cannot be shown at this scale.

[2] Includes "matrix" lands, adaptive management areas, and forestlands with no designation.

[3] Includes areas managed for nesting, roosting, foraging, and dispersal, as well as natural resource conservation areas providing spotted owl habitat.

The map does not show lands covered by the "Forest and Fish" HCP, which would include all forested land subject to permits issued by the Washington Department of Natural Resources for forest practices.

ing riparian areas. (Restoration budgets were substantial in the early years of the plan, but have dropped to near zero since 2002.[2]) In a further impact of salmon on the NFP, NMFS issued a biological opinion on the plan that required no net increase in road impacts outside of Key Watersheds. Combined with the Aquatic Conservation Strategy, this opinion makes the construction of new roads in roadless areas unlikely in the Puget Sound region's national forests, whatever the outcome of the second Bush administration's efforts to overturn the nation-wide ban on new roads in national forests issued at the end of the Clinton administration (James Doyle, U.S. Forest Service, personal communication).

Economic Expectations for the Plan Are Disappointed

The NFP projected that timber sales from federal lands would average 958 million board feet per year from 1994 to 2004, mostly from thinnings and other partial harvests (U.S. Forest Service and Bureau of Land Management 1994). The plan also projected annual sales of approximately 100 million board feet of other wood not normally considered merchantable, including timber salvaged after fires and other disturbances. Combined, this was less than half the average federal harvest from 1990 to 1992, which court orders prohibited from continuing. It was less than a fourth the average during the 1980s—a rate which was unsustainable under any circumstances. Across Washing-

[2] In the Mt. Baker-Snoqualmie National Forest, for example, annual restoration budgets were \$3.5–\$3.9 million in the early 1990s but dropped to \$200,000 in 2002. In 2003, funding covered only flood repairs in the Darrington area; in 2004, funding was through a line item obtained by Congressman Norm Dicks to address fish-passage problems. From 1992 to 2002, the forest accomplished the following:

- 202 road miles decommissioned,
- 381 road miles storm-proofed,
- 230 road miles upgraded,
- 24 road crossing sites improved for fish passage,
- 1,092 acres of riparian/upland areas restored for improved watershed condition, and
- 82 miles of stream channel restored.

Information is from an e-mail to the author from C. Hansen-Murray (U.S. Forest Service).

ton, Oregon, and California, the NFP was projected to result in the loss of 10,000 jobs in timber harvest and processing relative to 1992 employment, which was already down 20,000 jobs from 1990 (U.S. Forest Service and Bureau of Land Management 1994). The eastern Puget Sound area was expected to be one of the harder hit regions, with a drop of more than 5,000 jobs relative to 1990; on the Olympic Peninsula, timber employment was projected to drop by more than 2,000. To address this economic dislocation, President Clinton proposed the Northwest Economic Adjustment Initiative, which guided $1.2 billion of federal funding to help communities hurt by the cutbacks in timber harvest.

Despite some successes, the initiative failed to meet most of the high expectations it generated, according to a 2002 assessment by Forest Community Research (FCR), a non-profit group in northern California focused on community-based approaches to ecosystem management (Forest Community Research 2002). Though the initiative was a federal program, FCR found that most federal agencies saw it as a unique case that had little effect on their organizational cultures. The most important positive legacy from the initiative was the more collaborative approach to meeting the economic development needs of rural communities at the state and regional levels, FCR concluded (Forest Community Research 2002). The initiative added regional processes to federal programs but little new staff or money (the $1.2 billion was mostly from existing programs), while final federal decisions continued to be made outside of the communities involved. Much of the federal funding was in the form of loans to help community infrastructure (such as water and sewer systems) meet federal requirements, providing little immediate relief to unemployed workers. Moreover, major losses in employment had already occurred by the time the initiative began. Re-training programs were overwhelmed, yet there was little local demand for the skills being taught. (FCR quoted one official as saying, "The administration never thought through where living-wage jobs were going to come from." [Forest Community Research 2002:84–85]) Ironically, forest restoration programs in the NFP were not closely tied to training programs in the economic initiative, in part because managers of the initiative wanted to appeal to local communities, which did not want to be seen as "buying into" the NFP (Forest Community Research 2002). The Clinton administration did not seek additional funding for the economic initiative because it saw Congress making the same linkage with the NFP (J. Kusel, Forest Community Research, personal communication).

Adding to continued distrust toward the NFP in rural communities, actual timber harvests from federal lands have been far below those projected in the plan. Details for both the Aquatic Conservation Strategy and the Survey and Manage program were added late in the plan (U.S. Forest Service and Bureau of Land Management 1994) and, after further analysis, decreased projected timber sales by about 15%, to 805 million board feet per year (see the settlement agreement *American Forest Resource Council v. Clarke* 2003). Lawsuits filed by environmental groups, largely to enforce these two programs, decreased actual harvests much further, to as little as 148 million board feet in 2000. (The Mt. Baker-Snoqualmie National Forest had a target of 12 million board feet that year but offered none for sale; the Olympic National Forest had a target of 17 million and offered 2 million[3] for sale). Over time, selective harvests intended to facilitate old-growth conditions in late successional reserves have become a larger, more reliable source of federal timber than the matrix lands originally designated for harvest, largely because of the Survey and Manage program and related lawsuits (Thomas et al. 2006).

This effect of lawsuits was not unique to the Northwest—nationally, the number of appeals of proposed timber sales from national forests tripled from 1995 to 2001, while board feet of timber sold dropped in half (see U.S. Forest Service 2002). Both the Clinton and the second Bush administrations proposed various internal reforms to reduce the associated costs and delays. The Clinton administration ultimately reported that "the Forest Service's decision-making process is broken and in need of repair." It said a solution would require changing the laws that govern the Forest Service to recognize "the increasing shift in emphasis...from producing timber to sustaining wildlife and fish" required by other laws, particularly the ESA (see Hill 1997). The Bush administration, though, argued that "the laws are not the problem....The problem lies in their implementation through a maze of rules and regulations that has evolved over the years" (U.S. Forest Service 2002:39).

Amendments to the NFP and Other Forest Regulations: The Bush Administration Emphasizes Harvest Management Goals

To help address these problems nationally, both the Clinton and Bush administrations issued amendments to regulations governing national forest plans. The National Forest Management Act requires these regulations to be consistent with the Multiple-Use Sustained-Yield Act of 1960. The 1960 act calls for management of national forests "for multiple use and sustained yield of the several products and services" obtained from them, which include timber, recreation, watershed protection, and fish and wildlife habitat. Despite a major critique of the regulations issued in 1990, they were not amended until late in the Clinton administration[4]. Sustainability was the key unifying principle of the new regulations issued by both the Clinton and Bush administrations, but the Clinton administration emphasized ecological sustainability, while the Bush administration viewed sustainability "as a single objective with interdependent social, economic, and ecological components" (USOFR 2002:72783). Most ominously for critics, the new Bush administration regulations eliminated the requirement to maintain "viable populations of existing native and desired non-native vertebrate species in the planning area" (USOFR 2005). Because this was the initial trigger for protection of the spotted owl, it generated great concern from all sides. The new regulations replaced the viability requirement with an emphasis on conserving ecosystem diversity, but further guidance as to what this

[3] Figures from Region 5 and 6 PTSAR Report (e-mail from P. Kain, U.S. Forest Service, Region 6, Forest Products and Vegetation Management).

[4] For a brief history of the regulations, see USOFR 2002.

may require was left to agency directives, which have not yet been released. The ecosystem approach, which still recognizes the importance of listed species and other species of interest, arguably makes sense from a scientific and a management perspective. It even could have led to a greater initial emphasis on conservation of old-growth forests than the spotted owl did as an "indicator species" before it was listed under the ESA. The true significance of this change will take experience to evaluate.

The new regulations also decreased the detail required for national forest plans, which the Bush administration described as "zoning documents" that identify the desired conditions for different parts of national forests and the general actions necessary to achieve them. Under the Bush regulations, harvest levels are no longer targets to be achieved, but are upper limits for long-term sustained yield. Forest plans can have less upfront scientific analysis, but are subject to independent scientific review and include more resources for monitoring to aid adaptive management (USOFR 2005). Notably, forest plans no longer require environmental assessments or impact statements under the National Environmental Protection Act. However, the same array of stakeholders that the Clinton administration identified must be involved in the development of forest plans. Furthermore, major actions to implement forest plans, such as a large timber sale or road construction in a roadless area, still require environmental impact statements. Objections can be filed before the Forest Service adopts plans, but once adopted, the plans cannot be appealed within the agency. The three national forests in the Puget Sound area—Olympic, Mt. Baker-Snoqualmie, and Gifford Pinchot—are scheduled to initiate new plans under this rule in 2008 and to complete their plans by 2012[5]. The plan for the Wenatchee National Forest, including the wildlife corridor east of Snoqualmie Pass, is currently being revised, with completion scheduled for 2007. The plans may propose modifications of the NFP to address fire risks, recreational demands, new ecological information, and other issues (Kain, personal communication).

Separate from these national changes to forest regulations, the Bush administration has also attempted to modify details in the NFP itself. In a friendly settlement to a lawsuit brought by the timber industry that was widely criticized by environmental groups, the administration committed to using its best effort to sell timber in amounts consistent with the plan—805 million board feet annually plus thinning sales of approximately 300 million board feet annually "to the extent that and for so long as such sales are consistent with the ecological objectives" of the plan (settlement agreement *American Forest Resource Council v. Clarke* 2003). Most of the specific actions the administration committed to take toward this goal are concentrated in Oregon and California, in part because the lawsuit alleged that the NFP violated a historic law that applies only in those states[6]. In a related effort, though, the ad-

[5] See "Schedule of Forest Service Land Management Plan Revisions and New Plans, October 1, 2003," at http://www.fs.fed.us/emc/nfma/index.htm.

[6] The Oregon and California Railroad and Coos Bay Wagon Road Grant Lands Act, U.S.Code, volume 43, section 1181(a).

ministration attempted to amend the Aquatic Conservation Strategy across the entire area, responding to a 1999 court decision that each project under the plan "must maintain the existing [ecological] condition or move it within the range of natural variability" (*Pacific Coast Federation of Fishermen's Association v. NMFS* 1999:1069). Under the amendment, which was consistent with direction from the Forest Service's Regional Ecosystem Office during the Clinton administration[7], the appropriate scale for evaluating a project's consistency with the Aquatic Conservation Strategy's objectives was a Fifth Field watershed, typically between 20 and 200 square miles (see U.S. Forest Service and Bureau of Land Management 2003). Since natural processes such as floods, fires, and landslides degrade habitat conditions at the site scale, both administrations argued that an action under the Aquatic Conservation Strategy that would degrade conditions in the short-term at the site scale was not necessarily inconsistent with the strategy. A project to thin a riparian area to help speed development of old-growth characteristics, for example, could be consistent with the strategy even if it increased sedimentation in the adjacent stream in the short term. Environmental groups sued to block this change. In March 2006, a federal magistrate recommended that the district court hearing the case require that NMFS and the U.S. Fish and Wildlife Service issue new biological opinions on this change in the straegy. As of April 2006, the future of this aspect of the NFP is not clear. In the meantime, little to no riparian logging is taking place, even though it would ostensibly facilitate old-growth characteristics.

As part of another friendly settlement to a lawsuit (see settlement agreement *Douglas Timber Operators Inc. v. Secretary of Agriculture and Secretary of Interior* 2003), the Bush administration also attempted to eliminate the Survey and Manage guidelines in the Northwest Forest Plan (U.S. Forest Service and Bureau of Land Management 2004). Instead, the administration proposed to protect rare or little known species under the existing Special Status Species Programs of the Forest Service and Bureau of Land Management. The administration acknowledged that, without mitigation, its proposal would risk the loss of 51 species (mostly fungi) from the area covered by the Northwest Forest Plan. Though the fundamental purpose of the Survey and Manage program had been to conserve rare and little-known species, the administration argued that enough was known about where these species are found that special management of known or anticipated sites would be sufficient to protect them from extirpation (U.S. Forest Service and Bureau of Land Management 2004). The administration also estimated that 142 species were likely to be extirpated from federal lands under both the Survey and Manage guidelines and its new plan because of factors outside the federal government's control (e.g., few populations of the species are found on federal lands, limited distribution, etc.[U.S. Forest Service and

[7] See C. A. Loop, U.S. Forest Service, 1999 memorandum to Regional Interagency Executive Committee members and California federal executives entitled "Regional Ecosystem Office Analysis and Interpretation of Three Issues Related to Northwest Forest Plan Requirements for Aquatic Conservation Strategy Consistency Determinations."

Bureau of Land Management 2004[8]). It estimated that its new plan would allow for 70 million board feet of additional timber annually, supporting about 635 timber-related jobs (though the plan would cut 328 jobs performing field surveys for rare species). The administration also estimated that its proposal would dramatically reduce the cost for forest thinning projects and prescribed burns intended to decrease the threat of catastrophic wildfires. (The final Healthy Forests Restoration Act of 2003, which addressed these issues more directly, maintains all protections of old growth in the Northwest Forest Plan. It requires that hazardous fuel reduction projects in old-growth stands should focus "largely on small diameter trees, thinning, strategic fuel breaks, and prescribed fire..." and maximize retention of large trees.[9]) Several conservation groups filed a lawsuit in Seattle to challenge the administration's elimination of the Survey and Manage requirements (NWEA sues to protect old growth and wildlife 2004). In August 2005, the court found in their favor on several points. As of April 2006, a final disposition of the case is still pending (Molina et al. 2006).

In a third friendly settlement of a lawsuit brought by timber interests, the Bush administration also committed to reviewing the status of the northern spotted owl and marbled murrelet under the Endangered Species Act. In September 2004, the U.S. Fish and Wildlife Service concluded that marbled murrelets in Washington, Oregon, and California did not qualify as a distinct population segment (USFWS 2004a). However, as of April 2006 their listing status had not changed because the agency had not yet concluded whether the species as a whole might deserve listing. In November 2004, the agency concluded that the northern spotted owl should continue to be listed as threatened (USFWS 2004b). In fact, owls in Washington State have been declining about 7% per year over the last decade; the rate of decline has been accelerating and appears to be greatest in the west Cascades (Owl loss accelerating, 2005). Declines have been much smaller in the southern portion of the owl's range, but the Fish and Wildlife Service has determined that even in Washington and northern Oregon the owl was not yet endangered (USFWS 2004b). Habitat loss on federal lands was no longer a primary threat; competition from barred owls *Strix vania*, which have been extending their range west for years) appears to be the new major threat to spotted owls. Other threats include West Nile Virus, Sudden Oak Death (a plant disease currently found in Oregon and California but with the potential to spread), and continued habitat losses on private lands (USFWS 2004b; U.S. Forest Service 2006). Although the Fish and Wildlife Service never finalized the draft recovery plan for spotted owls that it issued in 1992, it intends to complete the plan by the end of 2007 (USFWS 2006), when it also expects to make a final designation of critical habitat for the owl.

---

[8] Table S-1 in U.S. Forest Service and Bureau of Land Management 2004 summarizes the environmental and economic effects of different alternatives.

[9] See Healthy Forests Restoration Act: Summary and Analysis, http://www.fs.fed.us/spf/coop/library/HFRA.pdf.

To summarize, the Northwest Forest Plan has radically altered the management of national forests in the Puget Sound area and across the range of the spotted owl. So far, it has proven more effective at stopping actions that might harm old growth and other important habitats than it has at meeting goals for either restoration or harvest. The two major reasons for this are opposition from environmental groups and the general public to any continued harvest of old growth (which was originally expected to comprise as much as half of the projected timber sales) and large budget reductions for Forest Service operations, which depended in part on timber revenues. Larger budgets could have promoted habitat restoration and new, more ecologically sensitive approaches to harvest (Charnley 2006; Thomas et al. 2006). A commitment to avoid harvest of old growth, wherever it is found, could help speed development of a consensus to support logging that would promote restoration and harvest goals. That seems unlikely from the Bush administration, but realistically possible from a future administration, given the potential for broad public support of such a policy.

Non-Federal Forest (1): Lands Owned by the Washington Department of Natural Resources

Although the great majority of old growth in the Northwest is on federal land, most timber harvested in Washington State is on private land. About 13% is on state land managed by the Washington Department of Natural Resources (WDNR)[10]. Where state and private lands include or abut mature forest used by the northern spotted owl, timber harvest is constrained by the Endangered Species Act. This led WDNR and four large private landowners to negotiate Habitat Conservation Plans, which provide mitigation for incidental take of owls and other listed species as part of their timber harvest operations (see WFPA 2003). (The Cities of Seattle and Tacoma also negotiated HCPs for their watersheds, which include mature forest used by the spotted owl and other listed species.)

WDNR's HCP is by far the largest in the state. It covers 1.6 million acres, including all WDNR forestland within the range of the northern spotted owl (WDNR 1997). WDNR's HCP also covers Chinook salmon and all other species that use its land and are currently listed or may be listed through 2067, the end of the HCP's 70-year term (WDNR 1997:B3). Most of WDNR's forestland is currently in even-aged stands less than 80-years old. The main component of WDNR's conservation strategy for the spotted owl protects large blocks of forest adjacent to federal forest reserves in the Cascade Mountains (WDNR 1997:IV.26 and 36–37; see map, Figure 9-1). WDNR did not reserve forests specifically for spotted owls on the Olympic Peninsula, with the exception of parts of the Olympic Experimental State Forest toward the Pacific Coast. A federal analysis found WDNR's lands on the northeastern Olympic Peninsula were not crucial to maintaining spotted owl populations,

[10] Figures are from WFPA 2001.

which would benefit in any case from the HCP's protections for riparian areas and the marbled murrelet. (There are substantially more murrelets on the Olympic Peninsula than in the rest of the Puget Sound region[11]. See Table 9-1 for a comparison of riparian protections in the Northwest Forest Plan, WDNR's HCP, and Washington's Forest and Fish regulations.) Riparian protections in WDNR's HCP are primarily to benefit salmon, but should also benefit amphibians, which particularly depend on WDNR lands between the Olympic National Forest and Hood Canal. With the HCP's protections, the proportion of WDNR's lands older than 100 years is projected to increase dramatically over the next 50 to 100 years (see Figures 9-2, 9-3, and 9-4).

In areas not protected under its HCP, WDNR continues to harvest timber. Since WDNR is the trustee for federal lands granted to Washington upon statehood for the express purpose of supporting public schools, state universities, and other designated beneficiaries in perpetuity, it has a legal obligation to harvest timber[12]. Additionally, the legislature has directed WDNR to manage other forestland the state has acquired under the same trust responsibility (Revised Code of Washington [RCW] 79.22.040). The state supreme court has ruled that WDNR's trust responsibility requires that it act "with undivided loyalty" to the trust beneficiaries (see *County of Skamania v. State of Washington* 1984), who are represented on the Board of Natural Resources that oversees the department. These requirements limit the degree of environmental protection possible on WDNR land, but they also ensure WDNR does not subsidize timber sales, as the federal government has often done. (Congress sets annual targets for timber sales from the Forest Service independent of costs, which are budgeted separately [see GAO 1998][13].) The habitat provisions in WDNR's HCP were legally justified based on their providing the department regulatory certainty and protection from potential lawsuits under the ESA for 70 years.

Over the past few years, WDNR has been reviewing different strategies for its continuing timber harvest. Its original review of options ranged from 396 to 817 million board feet as an annual average for 2004 to 2013 (see WDNR 2003). Differences were based mostly on the intensity of management to meet harvest and habitat goals (e.g., active thinning can produce both faster forest growth and greater structural complexity to habitat, but entails some risks as well as short-term environmental impacts). In 2004, the Board of Natural Resources chose a preferred alternative that combined features from all alternatives, with total harvest approximately in the middle of the range. Environmental groups sued, arguing that WDNR's analysis did not adequately consider potential impacts on salmon and spotted owls (WEC 2005).

[11] A WDNR survey of 107 potential nesting sites on the Olympic Peninsula found 40 occupied; a survey of 56 sites in North Puget Sound found four occupied. South Puget Sound was not surveyed because murrelets, which spend much of their lives at sea, are not likely found there (P. Murphy, WDNR, personal communication).

[12] See WDNR 1997:II.1–3 for a succinct summary of WDNR's trust responsibilities.

[13] Continuation of this practice was confirmed in a phone interview with P. O'Day (U.S. Forest Service, Region 6, Budget and Financial Management).

TABLE 9-1. Riparian buffers: comparing federal, state, and private forestland.

Buffer size	Federal: aquatic conservation strategy	WDNR: habitat conservation plan	Private: forest and fish regulations[a]
Fish-bearing streams	300 feet or 2 SPTH[b]	150 feet or 1 SPTH[b], plus wind buffers[c]	1 SPTH[b], with inner and and outer zones[d]
Non fish-bearing perennial streams	150 feet or 1 SPTH[b]	100 feet	50 feet no touch for at least 50% of length of stream, including all sensitive sites (e.g., seeps, springs)
Non fish-bearing seasonal streams[e]	100 feet or 1 SPTH[b,f]	Width necessary to protect identifiable channels and unstable ground[g]	30 feet equipment limitation zone[h]
Buffer harvest restrictions	No harvest allowed until completion of a watershed analysis. After that, harvest allowed only from salvage, thinning, and fire reduction operations designed to attain desired ecological conditons.	First 25 feet no touch. From 25 to 100 feet, minimal harvest allowed, must not reduce ecological functions; beyond 100 feet, low harvest allowed (e.g., selective removal of single or small groups of trees, thinning for restoration; salvage requires additional mitigation).	First 50 feet no touch. If total trees in inner zone (including no-touch area) is greater than minimum for long-term desired condition, surplus can be harvested, starting with the smallest trees or trees farthest from stream. Harvest in outer zone must leave at least 20 trees per acre (can be reduced to 10 if surplus is kept in inner zone or woody debris is appropriately placed in stream).

Note: All buffers are on each side of the stream, measured from the edge of the streambank or, where the stream channel migrates, from the outside of the channel migration zone.

[a] Different rules apply to parcels ≤ 20 acres whose owners have < 80 acres of total forestland. For these owners, harvest is allowed in riparian areas with minimum numbers for trees remaining, based on size and substrate of stream.

[b] Width is greater of amount listed or Site-Potential Tree Height (SPTH)—the height of a mature tree of the dominant conifer species found in the upland portion of the riparian area. The Northwest Forest Plan based this on a 200-year-old tree; WDNR's HCP and the Forest and Fish regulations based it on a 100-year-old tree. As a reference, a 100-year-old Douglas fir may reach 215 feet on a highly productive site, but less than 100 ft on a site with low productivity.

[c] In areas with physical evidence that buffers have at least a moderate potential for windthrow, WDNR's HCP also requires wind buffers of an additional 100 feet on the windward side of buffers for fish-bearing streams.

[d] Inner zone is two thirds SPTH for streams ≤ 10 feet wide; three quarters SPTH for streams > 10 feet wide. Outer zone is remainder of SPTH.

[e] Seasonal streams must have a definable channel and evidence of annual scour or deposition. They have been estimated to make up approximately 40% of the overall stream network in forestlands.

[f] Riparian reserves for seasonal streams are adjusted after watershed analysis. Some may be considerably larger, some considerably smaller.

[g] WDNR's HCP includes detailed protections for areas prone to landslides, which are applicable for non fish-bearing streams on unstable slopes. WDNR committed to a 10-year research program to study the effects of forest management on unstable slopes, with the results to be incorporated into its HCP.

[h] Special rules to decrease soil disturbance; mitigation required if disturb more than 10%.

Sources: U.S. Forest Service and Bureau of Land Management 1994; WDNR 1997; WFPB 2001.

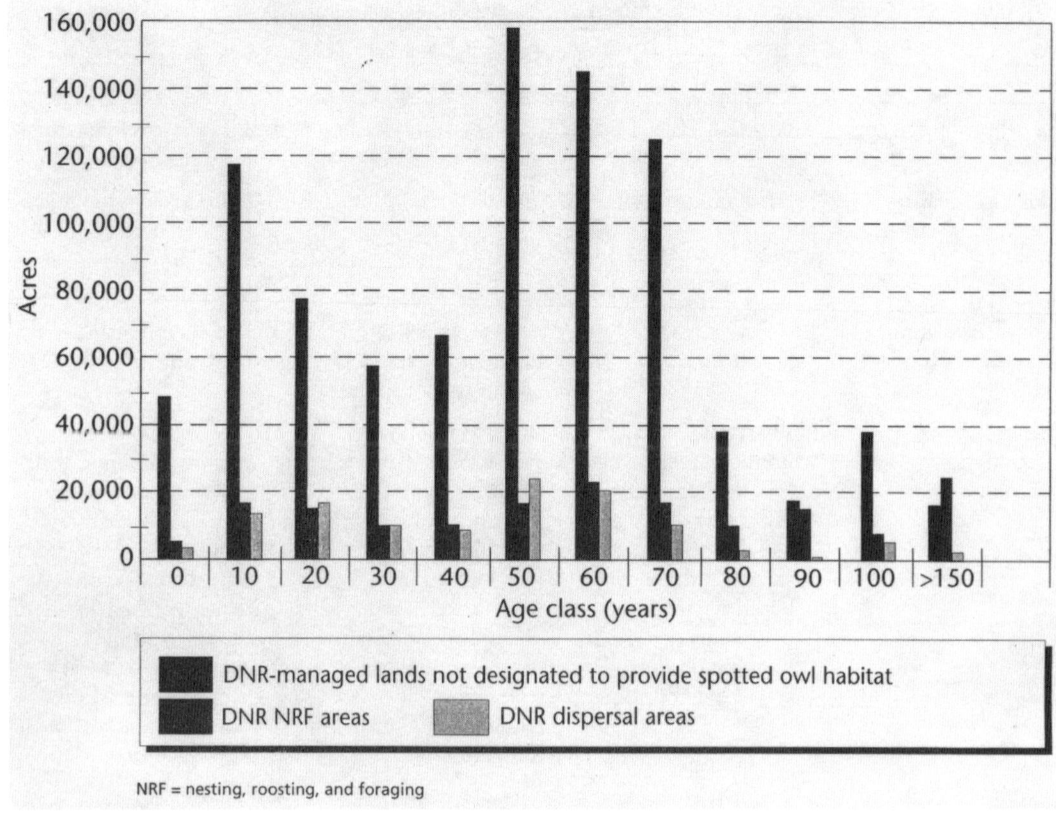

FIGURE 9-2. Forest age-class distribution in western Washington WDNR planning units, 1996. Source: WDNR (1997:IV.31).

After a King County Superior Court agreed in September 2005, settlement negotiations continued until March 2006, when WDNR and representatives from environmental groups and the industry agreed on a compromise. The compromise may still allow for the same level of overall harvest, but it obligates WDNR to improve and clarify protections for the spotted owl and riparian areas, including innovative and more labor-intensive approaches to harvests promoting ecological restoration (McClure 2006a; K. Ensenat, Washington Department of Natural Resources, personal communication). Environmental groups will also be more closely involved in monitoring implementation of the HCP.

In 2003, WDNR's forest practices were evaluated for possible certification as "well managed" under the international standards of the Forest Stewardship Council. Certification would authorize use of the council's endorsement and logo in the marketplace, potentially adding value to WDNR's forest products by allowing it to charge a premium or giving it access to buyers (such as Home Depot) that will buy only certified products. Although the review gave high ratings to most aspects of WDNR's management, some improvements were necessary for certification (Scientific Certification Systems 2003). Most importantly, aside from areas specifically pro-

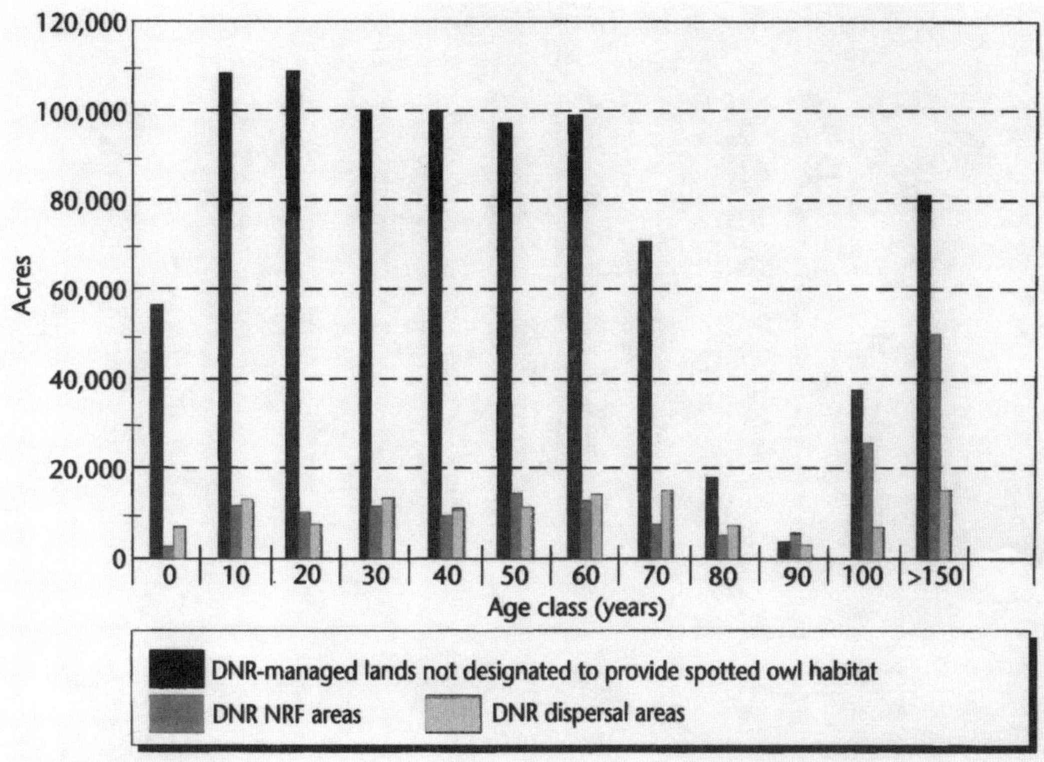

FIGURE 9-3. Projected forest age-class distribution in western Washington WDNR planning units, 2096. Source: WDNR (1997:IV.33).

tected by the HCP, the review found that WDNR had not designed a system that comprehensively defines, monitors, and protects areas of high conservation value. The review also expressed concerns about dramatic budget cuts in public lands management, including law enforcement, which affect protection of recreation and conservation areas. With these findings, WDNR originally did not pursue certification, but it may reconsider. The changes it is making under its settlement agreement with environmental groups may address most of the improvements needed for certification.Only a few other states in the country have certified management of their trust lands.

Non-Federal Forest (2): Private Land

About 40% of all forestland statewide is privately owned, divided almost equally between industrial landowners with 1,000 or more acres and smaller landowners (WFPA 2001[15]). These lands account for about three-quarters of all timber har-

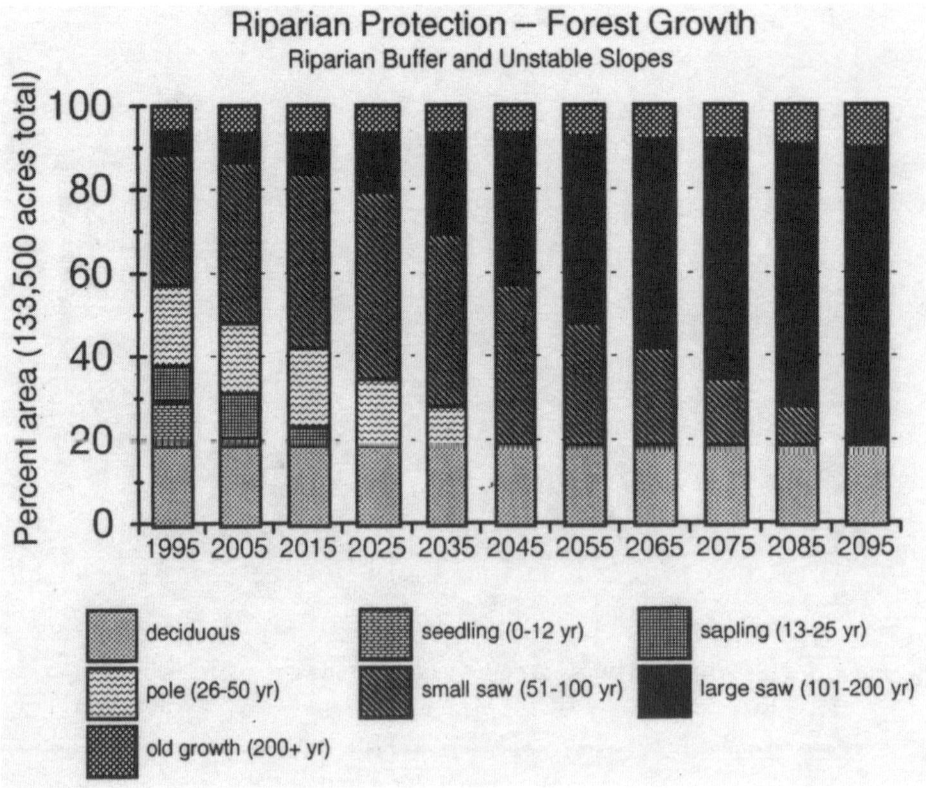

FIGURE 9-4. Projected forest composition of riparian buffers and unstable slopes under WDNR's HCP. Source: WDNR (1997:IV.60).

vested. Private forestland tends to be more productive than federal or state forestland, because it tends to be at lower elevations and is harvested earlier (typically on 40- to 60-year rotations [see WFPA 2001]), before tree growth begins to slow. Current harvest levels of about 3 billion board feet per year from private land are well below the near-historic highs of more than 4 billion board feet in the late 1980s[16]. Together with harvests from state, federal, and tribal land, this still makes Washington the second largest timber-producing state in the country, behind Oregon (see WFPA 2001).

Regulations governing private timber harvest in Washington have evolved since 1946, when the state first required replanting after harvest. In 1974, the state's Forest Practices Act established the Forest Practices Board, which is responsible for detailed regulations governing harvest on state and private land. The board adopted an initial

[15] The total land area for the state is 42.6 million acres; total forestland is 21.9 million acres, of which 8.5 million is privately owned, 4.3 million by industrial landowners (with 1,000 or more acres), and 4.2 million by nonindustrial landowners.

[16] See http://www.dnr.wa.gov/htdocs/obe/webtables.xls for details on timber harvests from 1899 to 2002.

set of forestry regulations in 1976 and has amended them numerous times since. In February 1987, representatives of industrial and small landowners, state agencies, tribes, counties, and environmental groups signed a Timber Fish and Wildlife (known by its initials, TFW) agreement, which established a consensus process for developing new regulations to be proposed to the Forest Practices Board. In the late 1980s, the TFW process led to major changes in regulations for riparian areas and other key issues. In 1992, concern that piecemeal rules were inflexible and did not address cumulative effects led to adoption of a recommendation from the TFW process for a voluntary program of watershed analysis (mandatory for WDNR), allowing protections for aquatic habitat to be tailored to the unique conditions of specific harvest areas[17]. In the mid-1990s, the TFW process also led to regulations to protect the spotted owl, allowing harvest in circles around known spotted owl nests as long as at least 40% of the circle remained suitable habitat[18].

In 2004, WDNR initiated a study of how harvests allowed under the TFW rules had actually affected spotted owl habitat. The study raised concerns that much of the remaining timber in owl circles did not meet criteria for structurally complex forests (Pierce et al. 2005). It also found that logging outside of the circles (even in Special Emphasis Areas designed to provide greater protection for owls) was fragmenting habitat across the landscape. Nevertheless, in November 2005 the Forest Practices Board rejected a proposal from WDNR staff to implement landscape planning that could address the fragmentation issue (Marsh 2006). Instead, the board set a temporary moratorium on logging near abandoned owl nests and called for a facilitated process that could work out differences between industry, WDNR, tribes, and environmentalists (McClure 2005). Frustrated with the lack of progress, in April 2006 the Seattle and Kittitas chapters of the Audubon Society announced that they intended to sue the state and the Weyerhaeuser Company for inadequate protection of spotted owl habitat (McClure 2006b).

Negotiations to update forestry regulations to protect salmon began in 1997 under the TFW process, which was expanded to include representatives of both NMFS and the U.S. Fish and Wildlife Service. Watershed analyses had shown that standard forestry regulations were generally insufficient to protect salmon habitat (see WFPB 2001, especially "Purpose and Need for Action"). Before negotiations were complete, however, representatives from environmental groups dropped out, joined by some tribes[19]. The final proposal, known as the Forest and Fish Report, was issued in April 1999. Though criticized by environmental groups and the tribes that left the negotiations, it was endorsed by the state legislature, which met in a special session to authorize emergency rules to adopt its recommendations (RCW 76.09.055). The emergency rules, which primarily focused on riparian protections, road restoration,

[17] For a discussion and critique of the watershed analysis program, see Collins and Pess 1997a, 1997b.

[18] The final regulations generally followed a draft 4(d) rule that the U.S. Fish and Wildlife Service proposed in May 1996 but never finalized. See USOFR 1996:21526.

[19] See WFPB 2001:S-4 for a list of participants.

unstable slopes, and the use of pesticides and herbicides, went into effect in March 2000. With the exception of provisions for pesticides and herbicides (which the federal government planned to regulate through other processes), NMFS endorsed the new forestry regulations in its 4(d) rule for Chinook salmon. The lack of any buffer for seasonal streams came under particular criticism, but NMFS emphasized its support for commitments to road restoration and adaptive management in the Forest and Fish Report (see USOFR 2000). (Forest roads can have enormous impacts on streams, particularly on the delivery of sediment, which can increase 10 to nearly 100 times above background rates in roaded areas, especially from increased landslides [see Beechie et al. 2003].) Under the Forest and Fish agreement, standards for forest roads were dramatically improved. Forest owners were required to complete assessment plans of all their roads within 5 years and to bring them all into compliance within 15 years. The legislature later provided exemptions for some of these requirements for forest owners with less than 80 acres (see RCW 76.09.420)[20]. In contrast to forestry regulations in Oregon and California, NMFS said that Washington's regulations would contribute to the recovery of listed salmon (USOFR 2000).

Before the Forest Practices Board took final action on permanent rules in 2001, the environmental groups and tribes proposed an alternative that differed from the emergency rules on many points, including riparian protections, categorization of streams, road restoration, wetland protections, timber harvest in areas with large rain on snow effects, monitoring, and adaptive management[21]. The most dramatic difference concerned riparian protections for seasonal streams, which a study done for the Forest and Fish negotiations calculated made up a little under half of all stream miles in forested areas[22]. In areas adjacent to seasonal streams, the Forest and Fish regulations limit the use of heavy equipment and disturbance of soils but provide no permanent buffer. (See Table 9-1 for a detailed comparison of riparian protections in the Northwest Forest Plan, WDNR's HCP, and the Forest and Fish regulations. Also see Figure 9-5 for a diagram of how the Forest and Fish regulations apply to different streams.) Environmental groups and tribes proposed a 70-foot no-cut buffer on either side of seasonal streams without fish. These streams, particularly in steep areas, are a major source of sediments and large wood to downstream areas used by fish. The final environmental impact statement (FEIS), which compared the Forest and Fish proposal with existing regulations and the proposal from environmental groups and tribes, concluded that the Forest and Fish regulations appeared

---

[20] See WAC 222-24-050 to -052 for detailed regulations on road maintenance and abandonment.

[21] See WFPB 2001 for detailed comparisons between the alternatives.

[22] The analysis, done by the WFPA using WDNR data field-checked against lands owned by Weyerhaeuser and Champion Pacific, estimated that 43% of forest stream miles in the north Puget Sound area were seasonal and non-fish-bearing and 28% were perennial and non-fish-bearing; in south Puget Sound, the numbers were 39% and 31%; in the "North Coast" area of Clallam and Jefferson counties, they were 45% and 21%. More recent research is increasing the mileage for perennial streams and reducing it for seasonal streams (C. Mitchell, WFPA, and J. Ehrenreich, WFPA, Forest Tax and Economics, personal communications).

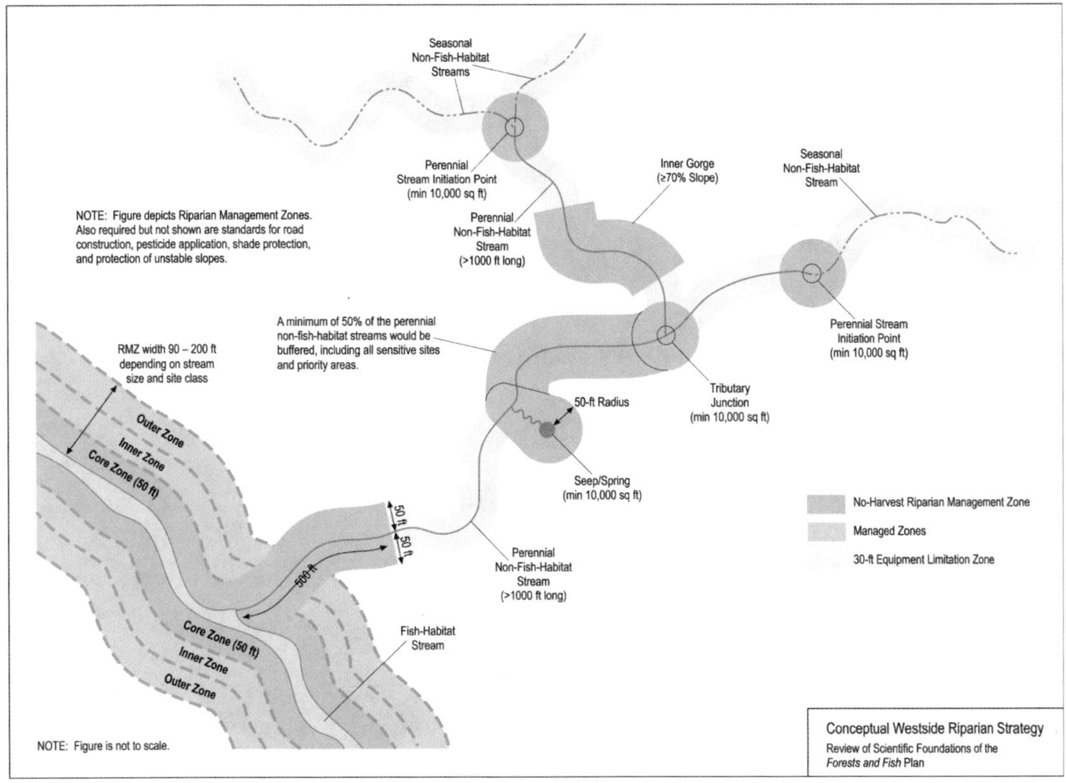

FIGURE 9-5. Riparian protections in Forest and Fish regulations for western Washington forests. Source: CH2M Hill (2000:1–5).

> to provide adequate protection for most riparian functions except for those along many small streams which have no riparian management zones....There is a high degree of uncertainty regarding the impact of insufficient LWD recruitment, leaf/needle litter recruitment, shade, and microclimate along small nonfish-bearing streams on downstream fish habitat. [WFPB 2001:S-10]

The FEIS found that risks to fish habitat were greater in watersheds that had been previously degraded by substantial timber harvest, since there were no provisions in the new regulations to account for cumulative effects (WFPB 2001; in contrast to the old watershed analyses). Risks were also greater in watersheds with a high proportion of small landowners, since they have fewer requirements for riparian protections under the Forest and Fish regulations (WFPB 2001). Overall, the FEIS concluded that the new regulations posed "a low to moderate risk of continued habitat degradation over the short-term" for fish, with a better outlook over the long term based on adaptive management and road improvements. The other group of species the FEIS focused on was amphibians, which it said were at moderate risk from continued habitat degradation along larger streams and at high risk along smaller streams (WFPB 2001). Amphibians also would be harmed by harvest of forested wetlands, which was allowed outside of stream riparian areas under existing regulations and the Forest and Fish proposal (WFPB 2001). The FEIS found that the proposal from environmental groups and tribes posed a "low to very low risk" of continued habitat degradation for fish and a low risk for amphibians (WFPB 2001:S-12–S-13).

The Forest Practices Board did not make its final decision based solely on environmental concerns. The goals it set for the new rules included keeping the timber industry "economically viable in the state of Washington" (WFPB 2001:S-2[23]). Under state law, the board was required to determine that the new rules were the least burdensome means of achieving the board's goals and that their probable benefits exceeded their probable costs (RCW 34.05.328). Regarding the latter requirement, a study by a professor from the University of Washington's College of Forest Resources concluded that the proposed regulations decreased the value of timber assets by $2.7 billion compared to existing regulations (about 11% of their total value of $24.8 billion), and would also cause from $2.4 billion to $3.4 billion of lost wages over 20 years (discounting losses from future years to create a single net present value figure [see Perez-Garcia 2001[24]; J. Ehrenreich, Washington Forest Protection Association, personal communication]). The study found that the alternative proposed by the environmental groups and tribes would have decreased timber asset values by another $5.7 billion (for a total reduction of 34% of their existing value). It did not calculate the cost of the proposal in lost wages, though it suggested that they could be proportionate to the lost value of timber (Perez-Garcia 2001). The study found that there was no reliable means of estimating how many additional fish would be produced by improved habitat under the alternatives. It also did not try to calculate economic benefits from improved habitat for wildlife, improved water quality, or other positive consequences of either alternative over existing regulations. Nevertheless, the study found that benefits of the proposed regulations exceeded costs if they increased state fish populations by 5% or more above existing levels (Perez-Garcia 2001). It found that the cost of the environmentalist and tribal alternative would exceed this benefit level, but it did not consider whether that alternative would have greater benefits than the Forest and Fish regulations. To compensate affected businesses for the cost of the Forest and Fish regulations, the legislature gave them a 16% credit against timber excise taxes. A state study later found this averaged about one-eighth the cost of lost timber harvest from the new regulations (though the credit for any individual business is not tied to the cost of compliance with the regulations; Rice 2002).

Provisions for adaptive management in the Forest and Fish regulations were crucial to the positive conclusions that NMFS and the FEIS reached concerning

[23] Quoting minutes from the Washington Forest Practices Board meeting of 22 September 1998.

[24] The report might have overstated costs by using conservative assumptions regarding the percentage of forest streams that were fish-bearing or perennial. It assumed that 57% of forest stream miles in western Washington were fish-bearing, 14% were perennial and non-fish-bearing, and only 29% were non-fish-bearing and seasonal. The Washington Forest Practices Association estimated considerably higher percentages for both types of non-fish-bearing streams—see footnote 21.

their benefits to fish. However, the detailed studies that will ultimately be necessary to support adaptive management for the regulations are just beginning. Top priorities include determining the actual extent of perennial versus seasonal streams and evaluating the effects of harvesting the entire buffers of seasonal streams on local amphibian populations as well as downstream salmon habitat (D. Martin, Cooperative Monitoring Evaluation and Research Committee for the Forest and Fish Regulations, personal communication). Early indications are that far more stream miles are perennial than originally estimated, which would dramatically increase the amount of riparian forest that must be left standing. Studies will attempt to frame Forest and Fish regulations by comparing their effects to considerably greater or lesser restrictions. The studies will be conducted in coordination with research and monitoring for WDNR's HCP and the Northwest Forest Plan (in some cases, federal forests will serve as reference conditions). Major study results should be available in the next few years, but some studies will take up to 50 years to include a full timber harvest rotation. The studies are developed and overseen by a Cooperative Monitoring Evaluation and Research Committee of scientists (CMER), based on priorities established by the Forest Practices Board, which appoints the committee[25]. Findings are to be reviewed by an independent Scientific Review Committee. Representatives from the TFW process serve on a policy committee that will make recommendations by consensus to the Forest Practices Board for changes to regulations or other elements of the Forest and Fish agreement based on this research. (Environmental groups rejoined this committee in late 2003.) If the policy committee disagrees with recommendations from CMER or cannot reach consensus among its own members, a dispute resolution process begins, which can include formal arbitration. The Forest Practices Board makes final decisions on all changes to regulations.

Despite NMFS's expressed support for the Forest and Fish regulations, they were never formally approved under the 4(d) rule. Instead, the state of Washington negotiated terms with the federal government for a Habitat Conservation Plan, which has been approved as the basis for a 50-year incidental take permit for forestry activities in compliance with the regulations. This heightens concerns among environmental groups about how the federal government's guarantee of no surprises would relate to adaptive management provisions over the length of the permit.

Beyond Forest Regulations: The Cascade Agenda and the Cascades Conservation Partnership

Washington's forestry regulations are arguably the strictest in the country, but they also arguably do not deserve endorsement or approval under a 4(d) rule or a habitat conservation plan, especially given their lack of any buffer required for seasonal streams. Nevertheless, the industry's commitment to major and comprehensive improvements to forest roads deserves recognition, as does its commitment to a formal adaptive man-

[25] See WAC 222-12-045 for details of the adaptive management process.

agement process. The latter may prove to be a valuable example far beyond the timber industry, especially if it is strengthened as part of a final HCP. In time, it could conceivably reverse the policy on seasonal streams, based on sound scientific research. The fact remains that in 2001 the state's timber industry accepted restrictions on its practices to benefit salmon that cut the total value of its land by $2.7 billion. No representatives of any other major land use in the state have accepted anything remotely similar.

The lack of similar sacrifices for other land uses is not just a concern for equity. While much of the Puget Sound region's best remaining salmon spawning habitat is in forestland under state regulation, most of the best floodplain habitat (used for both spawning and rearing) is in agricultural use; most other important spawning and rearing habitat is in rural residential use. Urban uses dominate many estuaries and large portions of the Puget Sound shoreline, which are crucial transitional habitats as salmon adjust to saltwater, where they must grow rapidly to survive. Protecting spawning habitat in forested areas alone will not reverse the decline of the region's salmon. Imposing restrictions on the timber industry without requiring similar sacrifices from other land uses also increases the pressure to convert forestland to uses that are typically worse for salmon over the long term. Maintaining the viability of the state's timber industry is not just an economic issue. From an ecological perspective, forestry is the preferred land use for large portions of the Puget Sound area, if land is going to be put to economic use at all. This ecological consideration is even stronger when considered globally, given continued increases in demand for forest products from the region's growing population. If that demand is not met by the region's own industry—in one of the most productive locations for forestry in the world—it will come from elsewhere, potentially at even greater ecological cost.

To avoid losing the ecological benefits of forestland, the region must develop mechanisms to compensate forest owners for at least part of the benefits that it now receives for free from their land. In 2003, the World Forestry Congress recognized this as an international need for forests in developed and developing countries alike (see World Forestry Congress 2003). In the Puget Sound region, this need has been recognized most profoundly in the Cascade Agenda, developed by the Cascade Land Conservancy working with civic leaders and interested citizens (Cascade Land Conservancy 2005a). The agenda calls for a variety of near- and long-term measures to maintain working forests and preserve ecologically sensitive lands in Snohomish, King, Pierce, and Kittitas counties, where the Cascade Land Conservancy is based. The most fundamental recommendation is for widespread use of transfers of development rights from forested lands to urban areas, so forest owners can realize the economic benefits from potential development without sacrificing the public benefits of keeping their land in forest production. Because these transactions can be costly, the agenda anticipates that they will focus on larger tracts.[26] Maintaining forestry on smaller woodlots (which are most prominent at the forest fringe, where development pressures are greatest) would depend on programmatic support, tax benefits, and other incentives. These approaches are consistent with my call for compensation to property owners for restrictions that go beyond a regulatory baseline. The agenda also calls for technical support to help small woodlot owners meet regulatory requirements and qualify for tax benefits; group certification for woodlots in a particular area under the Forest Stewardship Council (discussed for WDNR lands on pages 196–197) or the Sustainable Forestry Initiative; group Habitat Conservation Plans that could emulate Lewis County's proposed Family Forest HCP in the Cowlitz and Chehalis basins; mechanisms for woodlot owners to pool revenues so they do not depend strictly on a 40-plus year rotation for funds; and other innovative actions that could help maintain working forests among small and large landowners.

In a separate campaign, the Cascades Conservation Partnership acquired many of the important checkerboard lands in the wildlife corridor near Snoqualmie Pass between 2000 and 2004. The partnership grew out of an alliance between the Northwest Ecosystem Alliance (now Conservation Northwest) and the Sierra Club, which formed after a land exchange brokered by the Sierra Club created controversy over trades of lowland forest for previously harvested land near Snoqualmie Pass (see The future in sight: how the Cascades Conservation Partnership saved a landscape, 2004). The partnership aimed to acquire the rest of the most important lands in private ownership near Snoqualmie Pass and key properties near Stevens Pass to transfer them to federal ownership. It set a goal of raising $125 million of public and private funds by 2004. The crash of the stock market and the end of federal budget surpluses kept the partnership from meeting these goals, but it raised more than half the total amount and acquired nearly half of its target properties. The I-90 Wildlife Bridges Coalition, which includes leadership from the Partnership, Biodiversity Northwest, the Seattle and Kittitas Audubon Societies, and others, is continuing the effort to acquire the remaining parcels[27]. The coalition is also advocating for improved wildlife passage under and over Interstate 90 as part of highway improvements planned for the area.

A conservation strategy for the ecoregion should complete the work of the Cascades Conservation Partnership and support the work of the I-90 Coalition. It should also support the Cascade Agenda, which is developing strategies that will be necessary to protect major ecosystems across the Puget Sound area as the region's population continues to grow. To date, the most important sacrifices made in the region to comply with the Endangered Species Act have come from rural areas, first with dramatic reductions in timber harvest from federal lands to support the spotted owl and more recently with further restrictions on forestry to protect listed salmon. Expectations in rural communities that sacrifices in the Northwest Forest Plan would be balanced with other support were largely disappointed. For rural areas to maintain or increase their ecological services to the region as their population grows, property owners must receive greater financial incentives and assistance for habitat protection and restoration.

---

[26] In September 2004, King County made an enormous contribution to this effort by purchasing the development rights on the 90,000-acre Snoqualmie Tree Farm from the Hancock Timber Resource Group for $22 million. (Cascade Land Conservancy 2005b)

[27] See the organization's homepage: http://www.i90wildlifebridges.org/index.htm.

The Cascade Agenda also includes recommendations for conserving agricultural and rural lands and for improving environmental and open space values in urban areas. Its geographic focus, however, excludes many of the ecologically most important parts of the region, which lie outside of Snohomish, King, Pierce, and Kittitas counties. A conservation strategy that considers the Puget Sound area as an ecosystem must have a broader geographic vision. As discussed in the following chapters, it also must include amendments to Washington's Growth Management Act and other key state laws governing land use and water management.

References

American Forest Resource Council v. Clarke. Civil No. 94-1031-TPJ (D.D.C), appeal pending No. 02-5024 (D.C. Cir. 2003).

Beechie, T. J., G. Pess, E. Beamer, G. Lucchetti, and R. Bilby. 2003. Role of watershed assessments in recovery planning for salmon. Pages 194–225 in D. R. Montgomery, S. Bolton, D. B. Booth, and L. Wall, editors. Restoration of Puget Sound rivers. University of Washington Press, Seattle.

Cascade Land Conservancy. 2005a. The Cascade Agenda: a 100 year vision for Pierce, King, Kittitas, and Snohomish counties. Cascade Land Conservancy, Seattle. Available: http://www.cascadeagenda.org/ (April 2006).

Cascade Land Conservancy. 2005b. Conservation Report 2004-2005. Cascade Land Conservancy, Seattle.

Charnley, S. 2006. The Northwest Forest Plan as a model for broad-scale ecosystem management: a social perspective. Conservation Biology 20(2):330–340.

Collins, B. D., and G. R. Pess. 1997a. Critique of Washington's Watershed Analysis Program. Journal of the American Water Resources Association 33(5)997–1010, Middleburg, Virginia.

Collins, B. D., and G. R. Pess. 1997b. Evaluation of forest practices prescriptions from Washington's Watershed Analysis Program. Journal of the American Water Resources Association 33(5):969–996, Middleburg, Virginia.

County of Skamania v. State of Washington, 102 Wn.2d 127, 685 P.2d 576 (1984).

Douglas Timber Operators Inc. v. Secretary of Agriculture and Secretary of Interior, Case No. 01-CV-6378-AA (D. Or. 2003).

Forest Community Research. 2002. Assessment of the Northwest Economic Adjustment Initiative. Sierra Institute for Community and Environment, Taylorsville, California.

The future in sight: how the Cascades Conservation Partnership saved a landscape. 2004. Northwest Ecosystem News (Winter):12–14.

GAO (General Accounting Office). 1998. Forest Service: barriers to generating revenue or reducing costs. General Accounting Office, GAO/RCED-98-58, Washington, D.C.

Hill, B. T. 1997. Forest Service decision-making: greater clarity needed on mission priorities. Statement of Barry T. Hill, Associate Director of the Forest Service, in testimony before the Subcommittee on Forests and Public Lands Management, Committee on Energy and Natural Resources, U.S. Senate, February 25, 1997. General Accounting Office, GAO/T-RCED-97-81, Washington, D.C.

Marsh, M. 2006. Conservation update: forests—spotted owls, old growth forest and Washington's Forest Practices Board. Douglasia 30(1):4–5.

McClure, R. 2005. Tighter review of owl habitat rejected: state board instead suggests 'facilitator' role. Seattle Post-Intelligencer (November 10):B1.

McClure, R. 2006a. Accord reached on state forests: deal creates process for timber planning. Seattle Post-Intelligencer (March 22):B1.

McClure, R. 2006b. With spotted owl falling, lawsuit is planned: Audubon Society tells Weyerhaeuser, state they are violating species act. Seattle Post-Intelligencer (April 19):A1.

Molina, R., B. G. Marcot, and R. Lesher. 2006. Protecting rare, old growth, forest-associated species under the survey and manage program guidelines of the Northwest Forest Plan. Conservation Biology 20(2):306–318.

NWEA sues to protect old growth and wildlife. 2004. Northwest Ecosystem News (Summer):5

Owl loss accelerating. 2005. Northwest Ecosystem News (Spring):8.

Pacific Coast Federation of Fishermen's Association v. NMFS (National Marine Fisheries Service), 71 F.Supp.2d 1063, at 1069 (W.D.Wash. 1999).

Perez-Garcia, J. 2001. Cost benefit analysis for new proposed forest practices rules implementing the forests and fish report. Final report to the Washington Department of Natural Resources, Agreement #FY00-133, Seattle.

Pierce, D. J., J. B. Buchanan, B. L. Cosentjno, and S. Snyder. 2005. An assessment of the status of spotted owl habitat on non-federal lands in Washington between 1996 and 2004. Washington Department of Fish and Wildlife, Olympia.

Rice, W. N. 2002. Comparing the value of 'forest and fish' leave-trees with the forest excise tax credit. Report to the Legislature. Washington Department of Revenue, Olympia.

Scientific Certification Systems. 2003. Available: http://www.pinchot.org/policy_change/certification/Washington_DNR_2003_Update_Audit_Report.pdf (May 2006).

Thomas, J.W., J.F. Franklin, J. Gordon and K.N. Johnson. 2006. The Northwest Forest Plan: Origins, Components, Implementation Experience, and Suggestions for Change. Conservation Biology 20(2):277–287.

U.S. Forest Service. 2002. The process predicament: how statutory, regulatory and administrative factors affect national forest management. U.S. Forest Service, Washington, D.C.

U.S. Forest Service. 2006. Sudden oak death. Available: http://www.na.fs.fed.us/sod/ (April 2006).

U.S. Forest Service and Bureau of Land Management. 1994. Final supplemental environmental impact statement on management of habitat for late-successional and old-growth forest related species within the range of the northern spotted owl. U.S. Forest Service and Bureau of Land Management, Portland, Oregon.

U.S. Forest Service and Bureau of Land Management. 2003. Final supplemental environmental impact statement, for clarification of language in the 1994 Record of Decision for the Northwest Forest Plan; national forests and Bureau of Land Management districts within the range of the northern spotted owl, proposal to amend wording about the aquatic conservation strategy. U.S. Forest Service and Bureau of Land Management, Portland, Oregon.

U.S. Forest Service and Bureau of Land Management. 2004. Final supplemental environmental impact statement, to remove or modify the survey and manage mitigation measure standards and guidelines. U.S. Forest Service and Bureau of Land Management, Portland, Oregon.

USFWS (U.S. Fish and Wildlife Service). 2004a. Five-year review of marbled murrelet completed. Available: news.fws.gov/NewsReleases/ (April 2006).

USFWS (U.S. Fish and Wildlife Service). 2004b. Northern spotted owl still threatened despite progress in addressing habitat needs. Available: news.fws.gov/NewsReleases/ (April 2006).

USFWS (U.S. Fish and Wildlife Service). 2006. Recovery plan for northern spotted owl to be developed. Available: news.fws.gov/NewsReleases/ (April 2006).

USOFR (U.S. Office of the Federal Register). 1996. Endangered and threatened wildlife and plans: proposed special rule for the conservation of the northern spotted owl on non-federal lands, Federal Register 61:92(10 May 1996):21426–21430,

USOFR (U.S. Office of the Federal Register). 2000. Final rule: endangered and threatened species: final rule governing take of 14 threatened salmon and steelhead evolutionarily significant units, Federal Register 65:132(10 July 2000):42421–42481.

USOFR (U.S. Office of the Federal Register). 2002. National forest system land and resource management planning; proposed rules, Federal Register 67:235(6 December 2002):72769–72816.

USOFR (U.S. Office of the Federal Register). 2005. National forest system land management planning, Federal Register 70:3(5 January 2005):1023–1061.

WDNR (Washington Department of Natural Resources). 1997. Final Habitat Conservation Plan, Washington Department of Natural Resources, Olympia.

WDNR (Washington Department of Natural Resources). 2003. Draft environmental impact statement, alternatives for sustainable forest management of state trust lands in western Washington, November. Available: http://www.dnr.wa.gov/htdocs/fr/sales/sustainharvest/sustain_sepa.htm (March 2006).

WEC (Washington Environmental Council). 2005. Court halts harmful increase in logging of state forests. Washington Environmental Council newsletter (Winter):3.

WFPA (Washington Forest Protection Association). 2001. Forest facts and figures. Washington Forest Protection Association, Olympia.

WFPA (Washington Forest Protection Association). 2003. Forest management, salmon recovery and watershed planning. Washington Forest Protection Association, Olympia.

WFPB (Washington Forest Practices Board). 2001. Final environmental impact statement on alternatives for forest practices rules for aquatic and riparian resources. Washington Forest Practices Board, Olympia.

World Forestry Congress. 2003. XII World Forestry Congress, final statement: forests, source of Life. Food and Agriculture Organization, Rome.

Chapter 10. Land Use: Growth Management and Beyond

> Land use regulations are "the most fundamental and pervasive environmental laws of all." [Settle and Gavigan 1993:875]

Chapter Summary

Washington's Growth Management Act (GMA) is the "integrating framework" for all its other land-use laws, in the words of the state legislature (Legislative finding, 1995 code 347, section 1). Because land use is so fundamental to how ecosystems function, this makes the GMA the single most important law for conservation in the Puget Sound region. Compared to the land-use laws that came before it or that still apply in most of the rest of the country, the GMA provides an invaluable foundation for conservation. It is the primary reason the region has decreased its per capita consumption of land and increased protections for important fish and wildlife habitats since the early 1990s.[1] But as a foundation for conserving the state's major ecosystems, it is still fundamentally flawed.

The GMA divides the landscape into categories of urban, rural, farming, forestry, or mining areas based almost entirely on human uses of the land. It actually refers to "ecosystems" only once, in its definition of "critical areas," which it generally treats at the small scale of wetlands, shellfish beds, stream reaches, and the like. The GMA mandates regulation of development to protect the ecological functions of critical areas using "best available science." But it also mandates the accommodation of growth, without acknowledging that the best available science is clear that these mandates cannot be accomplished together—at least if protecting functions and values is interpreted to mean "no net loss," as state agencies have articulated the standard. Furthermore, the GMA does not require that planning for land uses be connected to the water needed to support them. Disconnecting land and water uses and relying on the fiction that all ecological functions can be protected as growth continues avoids the hardest land and water management choices that a regional conservation strategy must make to succeed over the long term. These are

- Where should new human land uses and water withdrawals be avoided or strictly limited to protect the most important characteristics of regional ecosystems?
- Where should environmental losses be allowed because of growth?
- Where should restoration be targeted to mitigate for these losses?
- To what degree should that restoration restrict or eliminate existing human land uses?
- How should owners of land and water rights be compensated for limits on both new and existing uses?

In addition to potential reforms of the GMA, this chapter also explores two other topics: Washington's vesting laws, which provide developers certainty at the expense of other

[1] For an analysis of trends in densities under the GMA, see Growth Management Services 2003.

public interests; and public subsidies for roads and development, with their enormous cost in higher taxes, decreased quality of life, and environmental degradation.

Without question, amending Washington's land-use laws to address all of these issues would face enormous political challenges. In evaluating those challenges, however, we can take considerable inspiration in how far the region has already come in little more than the past decade.

Sprawl: A National Trend with National Pressures

Since at least World War II, metropolitan areas across the United States have been consuming land far faster than their populations have been growing. A study in 2000 summarized the statistics:

> The 1950 census reported that 69 million people resided in 157 urbanized areas covering almost 13,000 square miles. By 1990, the population of these same 157 areas had grown to over 130 million people occupying almost 46,000 square miles. While urbanized population grew 88 percent, urbanized land expanded 255 percent (almost three times the rate of population growth). By 1990 the average resident of these 157 communities was consuming 90 percent more land area than just 40 years before. [Rusk 2000:80]

This trend continues in most parts of the country. It is worst, ironically, in the regions growing most slowly (Fulton et al. 2001). Between 1982 and 1997, the West actually grew the most compactly of any region in the country, increasing in total population by 32.2% and in urbanized land by 48.9%. During that time (when development in Washington was largely unaffected by the Growth Management Act), the Seattle-Tacoma metropolitan area grew at a roughly average pace for the West, increasing 33.1% in population and 50.9% in urbanized land (Fulton et al. 2001). In 1997, it was tied with the Portland region as the 27th most densely populated metropolitan area in the country, at 5.10 persons per urbanized acre. Many regions often considered to exemplify sprawl are actually much more densely populated, including Los Angeles (8.31 persons per urbanized acre in 1997, Phoenix (7.20 persons per urbanized acre), and Las Vegas (6.67 persons per urbanized acre) (Fulton et al. 2001). Honolulu topped the list in 1997 a, at 12.36 persons per urbanized acre.

The pressures on metropolitan areas to consume more land per person are many and generally well known. Some of the most important pressures have resulted from automobiles becoming the dominant mode of transportation in the United States over the past century. The sprawling effect of transportation by car was exacerbated in the 1960s and 1970s as interstate highways became the dominant means of travel *within* urban regions, allowing for relatively rapid transportation even to decentralized destinations. Other pressures include the federal tax deduction for mortgage interest, which subsidizes homeownership and thereby reduces development of rental housing (which is typically denser and more concentrated in central cities); federal mortgage programs and guarantees for mortgage insurance, which also mostly support single-family homes;

changes in the racial mix of central cities; declines in central city school districts; the desire of consumers for larger homes on larger lots as incomes have risen; and a variety of other factors, including the public subsidies for growth discussed in this chapter. Given how powerfully these forces combine to encourage the consumption of land even in regions where population is not growing, fast-growing regions face an immense challenge in trying to curb their land consumption. Across the nation, progress has typically required leadership from state governments to overcome regional conflicts and to authorize new approaches for local land-use laws. Oregon was the first state to take up this challenge, adopting the country's first major growth management laws in 1973. Since then, Maryland, Florida, Minnesota, Utah, and other states have implemented aspects of growth management. Washington, however, has been the only state in the country to match the comprehensiveness of Oregon's approach.[2]

Washington Land-Use Law Before the Growth Management Act

In comparing the approaches that Washington and Oregon have taken to growth management, the most important difference is the much stricter top-down approach in Oregon. Local land-use plans in Oregon must be approved by the state. In the most heavily populated part of Oregon, a regional government, Portland Metro, directly governs land-use decisions. (This top-down approach was not changed by the November 2004 passage of Oregon's Measure 37, which would have at least temporarily invalidated most land-use regulations adopted after a landowner's family first purchased a given property, unless the regulating government paid full compensation for lost value. The measure, which was overturned in court in October 2005, was itself a top-down directive, though obviously with a different purpose than Oregon's growth management laws. Arguably, the top-down approach of these other laws partly provoked Measure 37.)

In contrast, state government in Washington sets goals but gives local governments considerable discretion in meeting them. This is consistent with Washington's long tradition of limiting the power of state government. It also reflects the will of state voters in response to the two most important initiatives environmentalists have ever placed on a state-wide ballot—Initiative 43, which prompted the Shoreline Management Act (SMA) in the early 1970s, and Initiative 547, which addressed issues not covered by the legislature in the first version of the Growth Management Act (GMA 1) in 1990. As written by environmentalists, both initiatives set high standards for local plans and regulations and their approval processes. Both failed at the polls but prompted legislative action that approached the same issues with much greater deference to local control. In 1972, voters approved the legislature's alternative version of the Shoreline Management Act at the same time as they rejected Initiative 43. In 1990, voters rejected Initiative 547 after the governor and legislative leaders promised to address limitations in GMA 1 in the next legislative session.

---

[2] For a detailed review of growth management efforts in these states, see Calthorpe and Fulton 2001.

Legislators had previously debated amending the state's general land-use laws in the early 1970s, when the legislature passed not only the SMA but the State Environmental Policy Act (SEPA). Both laws were overlays, which left other land-use laws intact. The SMA established planning and regulatory requirements for the use and development of most of the state's shorelands. At least nominally, it placed a higher priority on preservation of "the natural character" and "the resources and ecology" of shorelines than on development. SEPA authorized a potentially rigorous review process for all state and local actions that might harm the natural or built environment, including permit approvals for development. It was modeled in considerable part on the National Environmental Policy Act (NEPA); both SEPA and NEPA can require environmental impact statements for actions with major environmental consequences, SEPA for actions taken by state and local governments, NEPA for federal actions. SEPA confers broad authority to local governments and state agencies to condition or reject projects with substantial adverse environmental effects, even if the projects meet other existing regulations. In 1973 and 1974, the house of representatives passed a State Land Planning Act that would have addressed many of the same issues as the GMA. Both times, however, the act failed in the senate, in part because legislators were anticipating generous planning subsidies from the federal government, which never materialized after federal attention turned to the Middle East oil embargo and its impacts on the nation's economy (Settle and Gavigan 1993). The legislature never seriously took up these issues again until the GMA. The situation was akin to remodeling a house "elaborately... without repairing a faulty foundation and leaky roof," as noted by Seattle University Law Professor Richard Settle (Settle and Gavigan 1993:875), author of the leading textbook on Washington land-use law.

Before the GMA, there was no requirement that cities and counties coordinate zoning and land-use regulations across jurisdictions to meet regional goals. (One state supreme court decision required local governments to consider the effects of their land-use actions outside of their jurisdictions, but it was isolated and "too general to provide meaningful guidance to local governments and lower courts" [*SAVE v. Bothell* 1978; see Settle and Gavigan 1993 and Clement and Krogh 1970].) Under the Planning Commissions Act, requirements for Washington cities and counties to plan for land use were "trivial," as Richard Settle has said (Settle and Gavigan 1993:876). The act did not apply at all to local governments with home rule charters (typically the largest cities and counties), which permitted planning and zoning free of any state limitations or requirements. Not only did state law not require that public infrastructure such as roads and utilities be coordinated with private development, but state courts and the legislature also blocked local efforts to raise funds for infrastructure through fees tied to the impacts of new development (Settle and Gavigan 1993). Other innovative approaches to land-use issues, such as transferable development rights or planned unit developments, were discouraged because of uncertain legal authority. Cities and counties were not required to provide for low- and moderate-income housing. The SMA provided some protection for shorelines but also encouraged water-dependent and water-related development. SEPA requirements were fundamentally procedural. The only other important environmental obligations that local governments had were based on federal laws, such as the Clean Water Act, or court precedents that protected public health and safety.

In 1957, the four central Puget Sound counties of King, Kitsap, Pierce, and Snohomish created the Puget Sound Governmental Conference to develop long-range regional plans. By the late 1960s, 14 cities had joined the conference, which had developed regional plans for open space, transit, streets, and highways (Clement and Krogh 1970). However, the conference never had authority over local decisions and declined in importance during the 1970s and early 1980s. In the late 1980s, just as national urban affairs critic Neal Pierce recommended abolishing the agency (by then renamed the Puget Sound Council of Governments), it regained prominence by developing Vision 2020. This plan, which ultimately guided much of the thinking behind the GMA (Calthorpe and Fulton 2001), integrated transportation and land-use planning across the central Puget Sound region. It proposed to concentrate growth in existing urban centers and other areas most easily served by extensions of existing infrastructure, thus protecting farms, forests, and open space. Without changes in state law, however, it had few mechanisms for implementation and none of its proposals were binding.

At about this same time, public concern over the effects of growth on the Puget Sound region was becoming intense. In 1989, Governor Booth Gardner responded by appointing a Growth Strategies Commission to provide preliminary recommendations on new state laws before the 1990 legislative session and to give final recommendations by June 30, 1990 (Washington Executive Order 89-08; see Settle and Gavigan 1993). Sensing public impatience, legislative leaders decided not to wait for the preliminary report. They created their own committee to develop proposed growth management legislation in advance of the 1990 session. The house and senate could not agree on terms for the legislation during the regular session, and so Governor Gardner called them back to Olympia to focus on these issues. On the last day of this special session, the legislature passed the initial version of the Growth Management Act (GMA 1). GMA 1 established the goals and many of the requirements that remain in the act today, but it contained major omissions. It required that comprehensive plans of adjacent counties and cities be coordinated and consistent, but provided no process for meeting that requirement. It required that counties consult with cities in designating Urban Growth Areas, but provided no process to resolve differences other than state mediation. GMA 1 provided no process for ensuring that local plans and regulations complied with its requirements. It also did not address whether state agencies should follow local plans. Recognizing these and other weaknesses, the legislature asked the Growth Strategies Commission to recommend how to address them by October 1, 1990.[3]

Environmental groups, skeptical that these issues would be addressed to their satisfaction, decided to take advantage of public frustration over growth and pushed Initiative

[3] Summary of GMA 1 is from Settle and Gavigan 1993:888–889.

547. Though the initiative ultimately lost, its initial popularity helped influence the Growth Strategies Commission to make more ambitious recommendations than many observers had expected (Settle and Gavigan 1993[4]). The governor incorporated many of these recommendations in proposed legislation in 1991. Legislative leaders, who had promised during the Initiative 547 campaign to address the shortcomings of GMA 1, strove to keep their word. Negotiations on the new legislation again extended beyond the regular session, ultimately involving business and local government leaders. In June, the legislature passed the second version of the GMA. It addressed all of the issues above and, together with GMA 1, remains the foundation of the act today.

The Growth Management Act: An Overview

The primary purposes of the GMA, the legislature wrote, are to provide "certainty for development decisions, reasonable environmental protection, long-range planning for cost-effective infrastructure, and orderly growth and development" (Settle and Gavigan 1993). Since this book focuses on how the GMA relates to protecting native habitat and ecosystems, a thorough review of the act as a whole is beyond this book's scope, but a summary of the act's goals and most important requirements provides necessary context for that discussion.

The GMA applies to all fast-growing parts of the state (including all counties in the Puget Sound area and the cities within them), as well as other areas where county governments have chosen to plan under its rules (Revised Code of Washington [RCW] 36.70A.040[1]). For all of these areas, the GMA establishes 14 goals to guide local planning and regulations: (1) encourage development in urban areas; (2) reduce sprawl; (3) encourage efficient and coordinated transportation systems; (4) encourage affordable housing; (5) encourage economic development; (6) protect private property rights; (7) encourage timely and predictable permitting for development; (8) conserve natural resource industries; (9) protect open space; (10) protect the environment; (11) encourage citizen participation in planning; (12) coordinate the provision of public facilities and services with development; (13) preserve historic sites; and (14) meet the collective goals of the Shoreline Management Act, which the legislature added in 1995 in an attempt to integrate requirements of the two laws. Though the 14 goals can be mutually competitive, the GMA sets no priorities between them (RCW 36.70A.020). The two goals in the GMA that directly relate to the natural environment read as follows:

(9) Open space and recreation. Encourage the retention of open space and development of recreational opportunities, conserve fish and wildlife habitat, increase access to natural resource lands and water, and develop parks.

(10) Environment. Protect the environment and enhance the state's high quality of life, including air and water quality, and the availability of water. [RCW 36.70A.020]

---

[4] Comparing the expectations of Growth Strategies Commission (GSC) Chair Richard Ford and member James Ellis, as reported in The difficult politics of growth management, 1989, and Governor Gardner's reaction to the GSC's preliminary report, quoted in Land use plan stuns, 1990.

Building on its goals, the GMA contains five core substantive mandates, as described by Richard Settle:

> First, new growth must be concentrated in Urban Growth Areas (UGAs) that are contiguous with existing urbanized areas and meet other specified standards. Second, new development may not be allowed unless adequate transportation, and perhaps other public facilities [unspecified in the Act], will be available concurrently with the development. Third, counties and cities may not exclude regionally essential public facilities and must accommodate affordable housing. Fourth, environmentally critical areas must be designated and protected. Finally, natural resource lands of long-term commercial significance for agricultural, forest product and mining industries must be designated and protected. [Settle 1999:12]

In addition to its substantive mandates, the act also has extensive procedural requirements. Counties and cities must develop comprehensive plans that address issues of land use, housing, capital facilities, utilities, and transportation. "The comprehensive plan" of each jurisdiction, Settle says, "is the central nervous system of the GMA. It receives and processes all relevant information and sends policy signals to shape public and private behavior" (Settle 1999). Each plan must be guided by the GMA's 14 goals and must be internally consistent (RCW 36.70A.070). (There is some irony to this, as Settle notes, given the GMA's unwillingness to set priorities between its own competing goals [Settle 1999].) A jurisdiction's development regulations and capital budget must conform with its comprehensive plan (RCW 36.70A.120). Local jurisdictions that share borders or regional problems must ensure that their plans are coordinated and consistent (RCW 36.70A.100, 210), accomplishing this through countywide planning policies, which are ultimately adopted by county governments after extensive cooperative processes with cities (RCW 36.70A.100). An analogous process is required to achieve consistent policies across counties with contiguous urban areas and populations exceeding 400,000—presently just King, Pierce, and Snohomish counties (RCW 36.70A.210[7]). Working with cities, counties must designate Urban Growth Areas and must allocate 20-year population projections made by the state to these designated areas (RCW 36.70A.110[2]). Urban Growth Areas must include "a range of urban densities and uses" as well as "greenbelt and open space areas" (RCW 36.70A.110[2]). Three Growth Management Hearings Boards—for eastern Washington, central Puget Sound (King, Kitsap, Pierce, and Snohomish counties), and the rest of western Washington—are to adjudicate compliance with the GMA's substantive and procedural requirements (RCW 36.70A.250). Disputes over whether local legislative actions or inactions comply with the GMA (or the Shoreline Management Act) must be taken through the boards, whose members are appointed by the governor and are experienced with land-use planning and policy (Settle 1999).[5] Board decisions may be appealed to the courts,

[5] See RCW 36.70A.260 regarding the qualifications for members of hearings boards. The process for hearings applies the principle of exhaustion of administrative remedies, RCW 34.05.534.

but they are given substantial deference and have been upheld without change nearly 95% of the time (Trohimovich 2002).

The three "fundamental building blocks" of land-use planning under the GMA are urban, rural, and natural resource lands, in the words of the Central Puget Sound Growth Management Hearings Board (CPSGMHB; *Upper Green Valley Preservation Society v. King County* 2001:10). All lands must be designated in one of these categories (the last category includes land designated for agriculture, forestry, or mining). The act does not specify allowable densities for these areas, but starting in the mid-1990s hearings boards developed some general rules governing density requirements. These rules were recently put into some doubt by a state supreme court decision, which found that the boards did not have authority to impose "bright line" rules for density if the GMA itself contains no such rules (*Viking v. Holm* 2005). In the Puget Sound region, the rule for urban areas has been a minimum density of at least four dwelling units per acre, with limited exceptions allowed for some pre-existing developments and for environmental protection (see Settle 1999, citing *Litowitz v. Federal Way* 1996 and *Benaroya v. Redmond* 1996). The rule for rural areas has been no more than one unit per 5 acres, with exceptions allowed for pre-existing lots and tightly restricted rural commercial areas (see *Sky County v. Snohomish County* 1996 and Settle 1999). Rules for natural resource lands—which the GMA defines based on their "long-term commercial significance"[6] for agriculture, forestry, or mining, and not on their ecological value (RCW 36.70A.170)—have required even less density. With exceptions for pre-existing lots and small clustered developments, agricultural resource areas have been limited to no more than one unit per 10 acres and forestry resource areas to no more than one unit per 20 acres, while zoning for mineral resource areas can be more site-specific (see *Friday Harbor v. San Juan County* 1999 and *Abenroth v. Skagit County* 1998). Following the *Viking* decison, further actions by the state supreme court or the legislature may be necessary to clarify the rules for density across the building blocks of the GMA.

Because local governments are mandated to establish urban growth areas and designate and conserve natural resource lands, the Western Washington Growth Management Hearings Board (WWGMHB) once described rural lands as "the leftover meatloaf in the GMA refrigerator" (*Achen v. Clark County* 1995)—these lands are what remains after the other designations are made. In 1997, the legislature amended the GMA to provide greater direction about the purposes of rural areas (RCW 36.70A.030 and 070). As later summarized by the WWGMHB, policies for rural areas in comprehensive plans "must protect...rural character...by containing and controlling rural development, assuring visual compatibility, reducing low-density sprawl, protecting critical areas and surface water and ground water resources and protecting against conflicts with the use of designated resource lands" (*Butler v. Lewis County* 2000).

---

[6] The precise phrase "long-term commercial significance" is used only in the definition of agricultural land in RCW 36.70A.030, but the words and their meaning are applied to all three industries in RCW 36.70A.170.

Critical Areas: "No Net Loss" of Functions and Values?

The GMA defines "critical areas" to include "the following areas and ecosystems: (a) wetlands; (b) areas with a critical recharging effect on aquifers used for potable water; (c) fish and wildlife habitat conservation areas; (d) frequently flooded areas; and (e) geologically hazardous areas."[7] This definition is the only use of the word "ecosystem" in the act. Before taking any other actions under the GMA, local governments must designate critical areas and natural resource lands and adopt regulations to protect them. Designating and protecting these areas comes first for two reasons: "to preclude urban growth area status for areas unsuited to urban development and, in the case of critical areas, to prevent irreversible environmental harm during the lengthy preparation process of GMA comprehensive plans and development regulations" (Settle and Gavigan 1993). However, in the words of the CPSGMHB, the GMA gives "virtually no direction as to the appropriate level of protection" for critical areas (*Pilchuck Audubon Society v. Snohomish County* 1995). Settle agrees, saying that the GMA is "nearly mute on substantive standards for local protection of critical areas" (Settle 1999).

Both of the last two observations came *after* the legislature amended the GMA in 1995 to clarify requirements for protection of critical areas. This amendment was part of the Regulatory Reform Act of that year, which attempted to integrate requirements of the GMA, the SMA, and SEPA to help streamline permits for new development. A brief digression concerning the Regulatory Reform Act provides valuable context for understanding the legislature's approach to critical areas. The act, which passed both houses of the legislature unanimously, was praised by *The Seattle Times* as part of "common sense reforms" reflecting "two years of bipartisan efforts to tame the regulatory process, to make government more sensitive to the legitimate needs of small business and property owners, and to measure costs against the potential benefits of any new regulation" (see State rules reforms are worth the risks, 1995 and Land use law reforms a lesson in persistence, 1995). In the election prior to the 1995 legislative session, Republicans gained control of the state house of representatives, offering voters a "Contract with Washington" modeled on the national party's "Contract with America" (which was even more successful nationally than in the state, helping Republicans win majorities in both houses of the U.S. Congress). Prior to passing the Regulatory Reform Act, the 1995 legislature approved Initiative 164, the Private Property Regulatory Fairness Act, which required that private property owners be fully compensated for any regulatory limits on use of their property that served a purpose other than preventing a public nuisance (Washington Law 360-61, section 4[1], 1995). Saying that Initiative 164 was adopted "by ignorance or political trickery," *The Seattle Times* called the "two distinctly different approaches" to reforming land-use regulations "one of the oddest legacies of this Legislature" (Legislature 1995, 1995). Opponents of Initiative 164 quickly gathered

[7] RCW 36.70A.030 for definition, RCW36.70A.170 for designation requirement.

signatures for a referendum to overturn the new law, which passed in November 1995 with 59% of the statewide vote.[8]

The Regulatory Reform Act added the following new language on critical areas to the GMA, now codified as RCW 36.70A.172(1):

> **Critical areas—Designation and protection—Best available science to be used.** In designating and protecting critical areas under this chapter, counties and cities shall include the best available science in developing policies and development regulations to protect the functions and values of critical areas. In addition, counties and cities shall give special consideration to conservation or protection measures necessary to preserve or enhance anadromous fisheries.

Only a few appellate court decisions have clarified how this language is to be applied. The two most significant are *HEAL v. CPSGMHB* (1999), and *WEAN v. Island County* (2004). The *HEAL* decision addressed the requirement of using best available science, ruling that "evidence of the best available science must be included in the record and must be considered substantively in the development of critical areas policies and regulations" (*HEAL v. CPSGMHB* 1999:532). The court recognized that these policies and regulations must balance multiple goals, noting that the legislature gave local governments "the authority and obligation to take scientific evidence and to balance that evidence among the many goals and factors to fashion locally appropriate regulations based on the evidence not on speculation and surmise" (*HEAL v. CPSGMHB* 1999:532). However, the court concluded

> While the balancing of the many factors and goals could mean the scientific evidence does not play a major role in the final policy in some GMA contexts, it is hard to imagine in the context of critical areas..., which are deemed "critical" because they may be more susceptible to damage from development. The nature and extent of this susceptibility is a uniquely scientific inquiry. It is one in which the best available science is essential to an accurate decision about what policies and regulations are necessary to mitigate and will in fact mitigate the environmental effects of new development. [*HEAL v. CPSGMHB* 1999:532–533]

As the growth management hearings boards have applied this decision, they have determined whether best available science was "considered substantively" based on the requirement to protect the functions and values of critical areas. Where local regulations have applied at least the low end of recommendations in the scientific literature to protect the functions and values of critical areas (such as the width of stream or wetland buffers), the hearings boards have typically upheld the regulations (see, for example, *FSC v. Skagit County* 1997:4). Where local regulations have not done so, the boards have typically invalidated them (see, for example, *PPF v. Clallam County* 2000:6). In general, the hearings boards have applied the functions and values requirement as a non-degradation standard, as the CPSGMHB articulated in an important January 1997 decision:

---

[8] Referendum 48 was passed 769,869 to 544,788; see RCW 64.42.

> The Act's requirement to protect critical areas, particularly wetlands and fish and wildlife habitat conservation areas, means that the values and functions of such ecosystems must be maintained. While local governments have the discretion to adopt development regulations that may result in localized impacts upon, or even the loss of, some critical areas, such flexibility must be wielded sparingly and carefully for good cause, and in no case result in a net loss of the value and functions of such ecosystems within a watershed or other functional catchment area. [*Tulalip Tribes of Washington v. Snohomish County* 1997]

The second appellate court decision, *WEAN v. Island County* (2004), modified this standard, though without specifically acknowledging it had done so. *WEAN v. Island County* (2004) accepted Island County's assertion that it must balance multiple goals under the GMA, environmental protection being only one of them. The decision allowed a local government to adopt regulations that best available science indicates would not protect functions and values if the government provides "findings explaining the reasons for its departure from BAS [best available science] and identifying the other goals of GMA which it is implementing by making such a choice." Environmental advocates have argued that *WEAN v. Island County* requires that a local government demonstrate that it *must* depart from best available science to meet other GMA goals, but the court did not appear to set so high a standard (2004:173/894). In the same case, while the court found a 25-foot buffer for Type 5 (non-fish-bearing, seasonal) streams to fail the GMA test for protection, it found a 50-foot buffer for Type 4 (non-fish-bearing, perennial) streams and a 100-foot buffer for Type 3 (salmon-bearing, 5-foot or wider) streams to comply with the GMA (*WEAN v. Island County* 2004:174/894, 178/896). The best available science is clear that *none* of these buffer widths is sufficient to protect all functions and values of streams and riparian areas, particularly for wildlife habitat.

Since the GMA does not define "fish and wildlife habitat conservation areas," the hearings boards have allowed local governments to adopt their own definitions, so long as they are consistent with the goals and requirements of the act (*Pilchuck Audubon Society v. Snohomish County* 1995). Noting that the GMA refers to fish and wildlife habitat *conservation areas*, the CPSGMHB found in an early decision that the Act does not require that all fish and wildlife *habitat* be protected—only areas that are important to conserve, which the boards have given local governments considerable discretion to define. However, since the legislature "did not limit the protection of fish and wildlife habitat conservation areas to just certain species," the boards have found that local development regulations must protect *all* species within these areas (*Pilchuck Audubon Society v. Snohomish County* 1995:32), since that is among their ecological functions and values.

The requirement to give special consideration to effects on anadromous fisheries adds a further dimension to the requirements to include best available science and protect functions and values. As the Western Washington Growth Management Hearings Board (WWGMHB) stated in a December 1996 decision,

> This part of the statute directs measures for both preservation and enhancement. It therefore limits the discretion available to local governments when dealing with anadromous fish. In balancing the scientific evidence against issues of practicality and economics, the result must be more heavily weighted toward science when dealing with anadromous fish. The "special consideration" language directs that local governments must go beyond what might otherwise be done in designating and protecting other kinds of critical areas. [*Clark County Natural Resources Council v. Clark County* 1996]

Critical Areas as Ecosystems: Larger Scales Provide Some Flexibility

At least prior to the *WEAN v. Island County* decision in June 2004, the growth boards generally allowed other goals of the GMA to justify decreased protections for critical areas in only very limited cases. The WWGMHB approved exempting agricultural activities that pre-date the GMA from critical areas regulations, but only under two conditions: the activities must be in designated agricultural resource lands and they must use best management practices (designed for environmental protection), which potentially require improving past practices (*PPF v. Clallam County* 2000:7; also see *FOSC v. Skagit County* 1997:6–7). The CPSGMHB had been at least as strict regarding protection of critical areas in urban areas:

> The GMA requires designation and protection of critical areas and makes no qualifying statement that, for example, urban wetlands are any less important or deserving of protection than rural ones. As a practical matter, past development practices may have eliminated and degraded wetlands in urban areas to a greater degree than rural areas, but the Board rejects the reasoning that this provides a GMA rationale for not protecting what is left. [*Pilchuck Audubon Society v. Snohomish County* 1995]

Because the GMA allows wetlands and fish and wildlife habitat conservation areas to be defined as ecosystems, the CPSGMHB found that a local government may permit

> the loss of all or a portion of an individual site-specific critical area, so long as the values and functions of the ecosystem in which the critical area is located are not diminished. The nature of ecosystems necessitates that such site-specific judgments, e.g., whether to allow filling in a small wetland, be made in the context of the likely impact on the functions and values of the larger system. This means that, in the circumstances that a local government permits elimination of a wetland, for example, it has a duty to assure that the net values and functions of the ecosystem are not diminished. How far afield it must look to make this determination is dependent on the specific circumstances, whether it is the level of an entire watershed ecosystem, a sub-basin, or other functional catchment area. [*Tulalip Tribes of Washington v. Snohomish County* 1997:8–9][9]

[9] The *Everett Shorelines Coalition v. City of Everett* (2003) decision similarly defined shorelines as ecosystems, allowing site-specific losses if the net functions and values of the ecosystem were protected.

The ecosystems of wetlands and fish and wildlife habitat conservation areas are "frequently...larger in scope than individual parcels, and may even extend beyond the boundaries of individual jurisdictions" (*Tulalip Tribes of Washington v. Snohomish County* 1997) the CPSGMHB acknowledged. It therefore commended the "broader geographic scope of a county-wide comprehensive plan" as "a logical framework to examine certain critical areas on an ecosystem/watershed basis, where appropriate, and to establish appropriate localized policies and interjurisdictional coordination" (*Tulalip Tribes of Washington v. Snohomish County* 1997).

An important CPSGMHB decision in 2003, which applied the GMA to an intensively developed urban shoreline, also tested the relationship of the GMA to the Shoreline Management Act. In *Everett Shorelines Coalition v. City of Everett*, the board found that shorelines of state-wide significance are necessarily critical areas "subject to both the GMA and the SMA" (*Everett Shorelines Coalition v. City of Everett* 2003:24) since they are "constituted" by wetlands, fish and wildlife habitat conservation areas, frequently flooded areas, and aquifer recharge areas, all of which are critical areas under the GMA. Based on this understanding, the board found that the City of Everett "failed to meet three fundamental duties":

> The first is a duty to recognize that all Shoreline Master Program policies and regulations [under the Shoreline Management Act] for "shorelines of state-wide significance" are also critical area policies and regulations and thus are subject to the substantive requirements of the Growth Management Act, including the use of Best Available Science. The second is a duty to adopt critical areas regulations for shorelines of state-wide significance that will *assure* no net loss of the functions and values of shoreline ecosystems. The third duty is to adopt shoreline policies that, through their implementation, will *assure* actual restoration, over time, of ecosystem values and functions, including those necessary to sustain anadromous fish. [Emphasis in original; *Everett Shorelines Coalition v. City of Everett* 2003:3]

In a later clarifying order, the board noted that "where a strongly developed and committed land use pattern of intensive urban uses exists, it is within the discretion of a local government to allow the continued operation and even redevelopment of such uses." Nevertheless, because the shoreline is a critical area, the board said that local governments have "a duty to evaluate and take necessary actions to assure protection of these ecosystems" (*Everett Shorelines Coalition v. Washington State Department of Ecology* 2003:5). Largely in response to this decision, the legislature amended both the GMA and the Shoreline Management Act (discussed further below), but the substance of the duties the board identified remains largely in place today.

State Guidelines Generate Controversy and Lawsuits

The GMA requires that state agencies adopt "minimum guidelines" for designating critical areas and natural resource areas, which local governments must "consider" (RCW 36.70A.050 and 36.70A.170). The actual guidelines have gone beyond issues relating to designation and have also attempted to represent the best available science for protecting the functions and values of critical areas. The hearings boards, while noting "the strange nature of regulations that are a 'minimum' but yet only 'guidelines'" (*Pilchuck Audubon Society v. Snohomish County* 1995), have consistently found them to be only advisory and not binding. Nevertheless, the boards have consulted the guidelines concerning both designation and protection of critical areas and, at least in some cases, have required that local governments justify deviations from the guidelines (see *Diehl v. Mason County* 1996).

The state guidelines provide a lengthy definition of "fish and wildlife habitat conservation areas," which includes a variety of freshwater and marine habitats as well as the seasonal ranges and habitats of "endangered, threatened and sensitive species" and "species of local importance."[10] The guidelines recommend "cooperative

---

[10] WAC 365-190-080(5) reads as follows:

Fish and wildlife habitat conservation areas. Fish and wildlife habitat conservation means land management for maintaining species in suitable habitats within their natural geographic distribution so that isolated subpopulations are not created. This does not mean maintaining all individuals of all species at all times, but it does mean cooperative and coordinated land use planning is critically important among counties and cities in a region. In some cases, intergovernmental cooperation and coordination may show that it is sufficient to assure that a species will usually be found in certain regions across the state.

(a) Fish and wildlife habitat conservation areas include:
(i) Areas with which endangered, threatened, and sensitive species have a primary association;
(ii) Habitats and species of local importance;
(iii) Commercial and recreational shellfish areas;
(iv) Kelp and eelgrass beds; herring and smelt spawning areas;
(v) Naturally occurring ponds under twenty acres and their submerged aquatic beds that provide fish or wildlife habitat;
(vi) Waters of the state;
(vii) Lakes, ponds, streams, and rivers planted with game fish by a governmental or tribal entity; or
(viii) State natural area preserves and natural resource conservation areas.
(b) Counties and cities may consider the following when classifying and designating these areas:
(i) Creating a system of fish and wildlife habitat with connections between larger habitat blocks and open spaces;
(ii) Level of human activity in such areas including presence of roads and level of recreation type (passive or active recreation may be appropriate for certain areas and habitats);
(iii) Protecting riparian ecosystems;
(iv) Evaluating land uses surrounding ponds and fish and wildlife habitat areas that may negatively impact these areas;
(v) Establishing buffer zones around these areas to separate incompatible uses from the habitat areas; and
(vi) Restoring of lost salmonid habitat.
(c) Sources and methods
(i) Counties and cities should classify seasonal ranges and habitat elements with which federal and state listed endangered, threatened and sensitive species have a primary association and which, if altered, may reduce the likelihood that the species will maintain and reproduce over the long term.
(ii) Counties and cities should determine which habitats and species are of local importance. Habitats and species may be further classified in terms of their relative importance.

Counties and cities may use information prepared by the Washington department of wildlife to classify and designate locally important habitats and species. Priority habitats and priority species are being identified by the department of wildlife for all lands in Washington state. While these priorities

and coordinated land use planning" across jurisdictions to connect habitats "so that isolated subpopulations are not created" (WAC 365-190-080[5]). They note that the Washington Department of Fish and Wildlife (WDFW) has identified priority habitats and species, though local governments are not bound by these priorities.

In April 2002, the Washington Department of Community Trade and Economic Development (CTED) published "Citations of Recommended Sources of Best Available Science for Designating and Protecting Critical Areas" (Washington State Office of Community Development 2002). Prominent among the 109 citations listed

---

are those of the department, they and the data on which they are based may be considered by counties and cities.

(iii) Shellfish areas. All public and private tidelands or bedlands suitable for shellfish harvest shall be classified as critical areas. Counties and cities should consider both commercial and recreational shellfish areas. Counties and cities should at least consider the Washington department of health classification of commercial and recreational shellfish growing areas to determine the existing condition of these areas. Further consideration should be given to the vulnerability of these areas to contamination. Shellfish protection districts established pursuant to chapter 90.72 RCW shall be included in the classification of critical shellfish areas.

(iv) Kelp and eelgrass beds; herring and smelt spawning areas. Counties and cities shall classify kelp and eelgrass beds, identified by department of natural resources aquatic lands division and the department of ecology. Though not an inclusive inventory, locations of kelp and eelgrass beds are compiled in the *Puget Sound Environmental Atlas, Volumes 1 and 2*. Herring and smelt spawning times and locations are outlined in WAC 220-110-240 through 220-110-260 and the *Puget Sound Environmental Atlas.*

(v) Naturally occurring ponds under twenty acres and their submerged aquatic beds that provide fish or wildlife habitat.

Naturally occurring ponds do not include ponds deliberately designed and created from dry sites, such as canals, detention facilities, wastewater treatment facilities, farmponds, temporary construction ponds (of less than three years duration) and landscape amenities. However, naturally occurring ponds may include those artificial ponds intentionally created from dry areas in order to mitigate conversion of ponds, if permitted by a regulatory authority.

(vi) Waters of the state. Waters of the state are defined in Title 222 WAC, the forest practices rules and regulations. Counties and cities should use the classification system established in WAC 222-16-030 to classify waters of the state.

Counties and cities may consider the following factors when classifying waters of the state as fish and wildlife habitats:

(A) Species present which are endangered, threatened or sensitive, and other species of concern;
(B) Species present which are sensitive to habitat manipulation;
(C) Historic presence of species of local concern;
(D) Existing surrounding land uses that are incompatible with salmonid habitat;
(E) Presence and size of riparian ecosystems;
(F) Existing water rights; and
(G) The intermittent nature of some of the higher classes of waters of the state.

(vii) Lakes, ponds, streams, and rivers planted with game fish.

This includes game fish planted in these water bodies under the auspices of a federal, state, local, or tribal program or which supports priority fish species as identified by the department of wildlife.

(viii) State natural area preserves and natural resource conservation areas. Natural area preserves and natural resource conservation areas are defined, established, and managed by department of natural resources.

for fish and wildlife habitat conservation areas are management recommendations from WDFW for priority habitat and species. In November 2003, CTED incorporated these recommendations into example regulations it included in a handbook to assist local governments in meeting their responsibilities for critical areas (see Washington State Department of Community, Trade and Economic Development 2003a). The Example Code would require a habitat assessment for all proposed developments within 300 feet of wetlands, shorelines, floodplains, streams, or other habitat conservation areas or their buffers (see Washington State Department of Community, Trade and Economic Development 2003a). A habitat assessment must include a "detailed discussion of the potential impacts" of the proposed development on these areas. Impacts must be mitigated so that each biological function affected would "achieve functional equivalency or improvement on a per function basis" (Washington State Department of Community, Trade and Economic Development 2003a:A102). Buffer widths for habitat conservation areas must "reflect the sensitivity of the habitat and the type and intensity of human activity proposed to be conducted nearby, and shall be consistent with the management recommendations issued by [WDFW]" (Washington State Department of Community, Trade and Economic Development 2003a:A118). Recommended buffers can be quite large, including 250 feet for shorelines of the state, 200 feet for other fish-bearing streams, and 225 feet for intermittent streams with potential for high mass wasting (landslides that would generate large amounts of sediment; Washington State Department of Community, Trade and Economic Development 2003a:A123[11]). Recommended buffers can be larger in urban areas, to protect critical areas from higher intensity land uses (Washington State Department of Community, Trade and Economic Development 2003a:A53,[12] A110[13]).

Although the WDFW and CTED recommendations have been controversial, since they are merely advisory they have not received the degree of opposition that was directed at the Washington Department of Ecology's proposed guidelines for updating local shoreline master programs, first issued for public review in 1999.[14] Under the Shoreline Management Act, local shoreline programs must be approved by Washington Department of Ecology (WDOE); in jurisdictions without an approved program, WDOE's guidelines apply directly. The same Regulatory Reform Act that added the new critical areas language to the GMA in 1995 also directed WDOE to review the SMA guidelines every 5 years. WDOE's 1999 proposal would have updated the guidelines for the first time since 1972, the year voters approved the SMA.[15] After conduct-

[11] Riparian buffer recommendations cited in model code.

[12] CTED's recommended buffers for wetlands of all sizes and ecological importance were larger for areas with higher intensity land uses.

[13] Its recommendations for riparian buffers were explicitly intended to apply to "all natural resource lands, rural areas, and lands within urban growth areas."

[14] The historical review in this paragraph comes from "History of Washington's Shoreline Management Act and Regulatory Guidelines" on Washington State Department of Ecology's Web site at http://www.ecy.wa.gov/programs/sea/sma/guidelines/downloads/SMA_History.pdf.

ing nine public hearings and receiving about 2,500 comments (which included strong opposition from agriculture, development, and property rights interests), WDOE decided in late 1999 to withdraw its proposed guidelines in favor of a revised version the next year. Its new proposal provided two options for local governments to update their shoreline plans, Path A and Path B. The latter included strict measures that federal agencies had determined were consistent with the Endangered Species Act. WDOE adopted the new guidelines in November 2000. The next month, the Association of Washington Business (representing a coalition that included local governments) and the Washington Aggregates and Concrete Association appealed the guidelines to the Shoreline Hearings Board (a state agency with a quasi-judicial role under the SMA). The Washington Environmental Council intervened in the appeal in support of the new guidelines. The board ruled in August 2001 that WDOE had not properly conducted the review process and that certain provisions of Path B exceeded its statutory authority. Since this ruling invalidated WDOE's new guidelines and WDOE had previously repealed the old guidelines, it left the state with no shoreline guidelines, though local plans were still in effect. The next month, the Association of Washington Business, the Association of Washington Cities, and the Washington Environmental Council entered mediated negotiations on the guidelines, supported by the governor, the state attorney general, and the director of WDOE. In December 2002, the negotiating parties agreed to a new set of guidelines and a proposed process for their implementation. The process required that the legislature approve state funding to help local governments update their shoreline plans over an extended time, with the first updates due in 2005 and the last due in 2014, after which they would be updated every 7 years, concurrent with updates of critical area regulations (Washington Department of Ecology and Department of Community, Trade and Economic Development 2004). The legislature approved these actions, and the guidelines were adopted in December 2003 (Washington Administrative Code [WAC] 173-25, Shoreline Master Program Guidelines). Under the new guidelines, previously adopted local shoreline plans remain valid until they have been replaced by new plans.

The new, 100-page guidelines note that shoreline master program goals and policies are part of local comprehensive plans, and so must be consistent with GMA requirements (WAC 173-26-191). The guidelines also note,

> Nearly all shoreline areas, even substantially developed or degraded areas, retain important ecological functions....Also, ecosystems are interconnected.... Therefore, the policies for protecting and restoring ecological functions generally apply to all shoreline areas, not just those that remain relatively unaltered....Where uses

[15] The sequence of events began in 1970 when the Washington Environmental Council collected enough signatures to send Initiative 43 to the legislature. The legislature adopted an alternative shoreline law the next year and placed both Initiative 43 and its alternative on the ballot in 1972 (general elections were held only in even-numbered years at the time). Ecology began drafting its guidelines in 1971, after the legislature initially approved the Shoreline Management Act. It formally adopted the guidelines in July 1972. They were affirmed that November when the voters approved the legislature's alternative to Initiative 43.

or development that impact ecological functions are necessary to achieve other objectives of [the SMA], master program provisions shall, to the greatest extent feasible, protect existing ecological functions and avoid new impacts to habitat and ecological functions before implementing other measures designed to achieve no net loss of ecological functions. [WAC 173-26-201{2}{c}]

The guidelines recognize that the policy goals of the SMA "may not be achievable by development regulation alone," particularly given constitutional protections for private property (WAC 173-26-186[5]). They also recognize "that shoreline ecological functions may be impaired not only by shoreline development subject to [permits under] the Act but also by past actions, unregulated activities and development that is exempt from the Act's permit requirements" (WAC 173-26-186[8]). Similar to the GMA's critical areas provision, the guidelines provide that

> Local master programs shall include policies and regulations designed to achieve no net loss of...ecological functions....[M]aster programs shall include goals and policies that provide for restoration of...impaired ecological functions....To ensure no net loss of ecological functions and protection of other shoreline functions and/or uses, master programs shall contain policies, programs, and regulations that address adverse cumulative impacts and fairly allocate the burden of addressing cumulative impacts among development opportunities....[WAC 173-26-186{8}{b–d}]

In 2003, the legislature amended both the GMA and SMA to clarify requirements for protecting the ecological values of shorelines (see Engrossed Substitute Senate Bill [ESHB] 1933, chapter 321, laws of 2003). When shoreline plans are updated under the new shoreline guidelines, critical areas that are within shoreline areas and their buffers are to be governed under the new plans. Until then, these areas remain subject to GMA requirements. However, since the GMA and the shoreline guidelines require no net loss of ecological functions using the best available science (the shoreline guidelines use the phrase "the most current, accurate, and complete scientific and technical information available" [WAC 173-26-201{2}{a}], which has the same meaning), the substantive standard for protection is the same. If anything, the standard is higher under shoreline plans, since the 2003 law requires them to provide a level of protection for critical areas within shorelines "at least equal" to that required by the GMA (RCW 36.70A.480[4], as amended by ESHB 1933), and the shoreline guidelines require plans to provide for restoring impaired ecological functions.

The Best Available Science: At Odds with the GMA and the SMA Guidelines

Unfortunately, the best available science concerning streams and wetlands is clear that it is *not possible* to fully protect their ecological functions and values from degradation caused by surrounding development and the removal of native vegetation:

> Hydrologically and biologically, there are no truly negligible amounts of clearing or watershed imperviousness....Almost every increment of cleared land, and of constructed pavement, is likely to result in some degree of resource degradation or

loss. [Booth et al. 2002]

Regardless of location or variables considered, relatively high levels of biological integrity cannot occur without comparatively low urbanization and intact natural cover. However, these conditions do not guarantee fairly high integrity and should be regarded as necessary but not sufficient conditions for its occurrence. In contrast, comparatively high urbanization and natural cover loss make relatively poor biological health inevitable. [Horner et al. 2001]

The GMA does not limit the functions and values of critical areas that local governments must protect. Accordingly, growth management hearings boards and state agencies have, at least prior to the *WEAN v. Island County* (2004) decision interpreted the GMA to require protection of *all* functions and values of wetlands and fish and wildlife habitat conservation areas; any diminution must be made up elsewhere within their ecosystems. Applying this rule faithfully in all cases, however, is either impossible or at least highly impractical for four reasons, which typically act in combination:

- *Some functions cannot be made up elsewhere.* In an important example for salmon, degraded ecological functions in estuaries, where our largest cities are located, cannot be replaced in rural areas upstream, where salmon spend different parts of their life cycle. Similarly, if a migratory corridor for wildlife is broken or drastically narrowed in one place, widening it elsewhere cannot substitute for the lost function. Such irreplaceability can apply to time as well as space—the loss of mature trees, for example, cannot be made up by planting saplings.
- *Similarly, different ecological functions and values cannot be traded for one another.* Changing the hydrology of a stream, for example, changes ecological functions and values that cannot be made up through other means, such as by improving physical habitat with woody debris or by removing noxious weeds in a riparian area, however valuable the latter two actions may be.
- *Some functions require very large buffers to be fully protected, particularly in urban areas.* State guidelines for bald eagles, for example, recommend against constructing roads or even trails within as much as three-quarters of a mile of eagle nests (Larsen et al. 2004). Wetland buffers protecting amphibians, which typically spend most of their lives on land, are often estimated in the range of 300 meters (984 feet) (King County 2004). Best available science generally calls for larger buffers in areas with higher intensity land uses, such as urban areas (for example, see Washington State Department of Community, Trade and Economic Development 2003a), precisely where other growth management goals (including the protection of high quality environments in rural areas) encourage concentration of development.
- *Lastly, even very large buffers are not enough—some ecological functions and values are inextricably tied to conditions in a larger landscape.* The functions and values of streams and wetlands, for example, can be degraded by essentially any loss of natural land cover within their entire drainage basins, largely because that almost inevitably changes their hydrology. Clearing and development beyond buffer areas also can degrade or eliminate connectivity between habitat conservation areas, reducing their

ability to support species that must migrate to new areas to maintain healthy, genetically diverse populations.

The complexities and conflicts created by a potential standard—no net loss of functions and values—that generally cannot be met in developing areas have created some controversy (particularly with the update of King County's critical area ordinance), but less than might have been predicted for three reasons. First, the legislature has granted local governments generous deadlines for compliance with the 1995 amendment on critical areas, which some governments still have not met, so in much of the region local regulations have only recently changed or have yet to change to meet the new requirements.[16] Second, *WEAN v. Island County* (2004) now provides a legal basis for balancing these requirements with other GMA goals. Third, no one ever seriously proposed regulations that could have actually met the no net loss standard. Even the state Example Code, which nominally calls for development to mitigate for lost functions on a per function basis, proposed buffers for streams, wetlands, and other habitat areas that would have led to the loss of functions—and very few jurisdictions adopted buffers as big as the Example Code proposed.

It is interesting to note that the legislature's report on the Regulatory Reform Act does not even mention the requirement to protect the functions and values of critical areas, despite this being the most difficult of the new critical area requirements for local governments to meet (at least if it was to mean no net loss). The legislature's report notes only that the act requires that best available science be used to protect critical areas and that special consideration be given to anadromous fisheries.[17] If the legislature had understood what was actually required to fully protect the ecological functions and values of critical areas in the face of growth, presumably it would not have made that a requirement—let alone by unanimous vote. The legislature's action on this amendment has similarities to Congress's near-unanimous approval of the ESA in 1973. When an absolute ecological standard is put into law, as a general rule one may suspect that either the standard is not mandatory or the legislative body does not comprehend the meaning of its action.

Comprehensive Plans: A Better Way for Environmental Protection

Scientists describe ecosystems as "hierarchical," meaning that they can be defined at many different scales, with smaller ecosystems nested in larger ones. A wetland, for example, may feed a tributary to a major river, which flows into Puget Sound. The

[16] Legally, the deadlines relate only to the eligibility of local governments for a variety of state grants and loans. As the hearings board decisions quoted above illustrate, local governments have been obligated to protect the functions and values of critical areas ever since the 1995 amendment went into effect. Nearly all local governments in the Puget Sound area, however, had adopted critical area regulations under the GMA before the 1995 amendment. Environmental groups and others that might challenge local regulations on this basis have generally chosen to wait and see what improvements local governments choose to make within the state's schedule.

[17] Report on ESHB 1724, chapter 347, law 95, page 119, of the House of Representatives report on the 1995 legislative session.

wetland, tributary, and river are all part of Puget Sound's ecosystem; the wetland and tributary are part of the river's ecosystem; the wetland is part of the tributary's ecosystem (typically best understood to include its whole drainage basin); and the wetland itself may be said to be an ecosystem, connected to but distinct from the area that drains to it.

The GMA is therefore scientifically correct in stating that wetlands and fish and wildlife habitat conservation areas can be considered ecosystems. But by never using the word again, the act does not recognize this hierarchical nature of ecosystems or their connections to the surrounding landscape. The GMA's focus on development regulations to protect critical areas concentrates attention on the small-scale ecosystems of individual wetlands or streams. The hearings boards have supported broader approaches, but the act is fundamentally not structured to address the needs of ecosystems at a larger scale. In addition to development regulations, a landscape approach toward protecting larger ecosystems would work through comprehensive plans, countywide planning policies, capital improvement plans (for both protection and restoration), and designated land uses. Since the GMA currently defines urban growth areas, natural resource lands, and rural areas almost entirely by their human uses, a landscape approach would likely require a new building block in the GMA—a category for large parts of the landscape to be conserved primarily for their ecological importance.

Currently, the act does not mention any ecological goal for how comprehensive plans must address land use, other than requiring open space and controlling water pollution:

> Each comprehensive plan shall [designate]...the proposed general distribution and general location and extent of the uses of land, where appropriate, for agriculture, timber production, housing, commerce, industry, recreation, open space, general aviation airports, public utilities, public facilities, and other land uses....The land use element shall provide for protection of the quality and quantity of ground water used for public water supplies. Where applicable, the land use element shall review drainage, flooding, and storm water run-off in the area and nearby jurisdictions and provide guidance for corrective actions to mitigate or cleanse those discharges that pollute waters of the state, including Puget Sound or waters entering Puget Sound. [RCW 36.70A.070{1}]

By nearly ignoring all other ecological aspects of the land uses determined through comprehensive planning, the GMA currently cannot provide long-term protection for the Puget Sound area's natural heritage. Ecologically, the land does not really "speak first," as the CPSGMHB once said it did, referring to the initial designation of critical areas and natural resource lands (*Bremerton v. Kitsap County* 1995:31). The GMA has been crucial in helping the region grapple with fundamental decisions as to where and how it should grow. But it is essentially blind to how these choices will determine the future of the region's ecosystems. Simply mandating that the functions and values of critical areas be protected conveniently ignores that this is impossible at the scale the GMA defines ecosystems, particularly while complying with the GMA mandate to accommodate growth. Some ecological functions and values must inevitably be lost at local scales as areas are converted to urban and suburban development. These losses can be effectively compensated for only by acting on a larger scale to reverse past impacts in other parts of the landscape. Over time and across substantial areas, this would mean that the region must let rivers again take over some farmland in floodplains. We must strategically remove floodplain developments that never should have been allowed to build there in the first place. We must purchase land or development rights to ensure that some stream basins and forests can serve as refuges for the long-term protection and restoration of fish and wildlife. We must purchase and remove some development along the Puget Sound shoreline. Since the impacts of a greater human population will be unavoidably substantial in some places, we can make up for them only by substantially reducing impacts elsewhere. The details of exactly which actions should be taken where require both scientific analysis and practical negotiations, including compensation for affected landowners. But at a conceptual level it is clear what must be done.

Beyond the GMA: Vesting Laws Are Critical

Besides the GMA, other land-use laws must also be amended for a regional conservation strategy to succeed. Prominent among these are vesting laws, which determine the point in the development process after which the laws that apply to a development cannot be changed. Washington vests development (freezing these other laws) earlier in the process than any other state in the country—as early as when a developer makes a preliminary application to subdivide land. This "virtually invites subversion of the public interest," Richard Settle commented in his textbook on Washington land-use law (Settle et al. 1983). Washington's vesting laws create considerable challenges for meeting even the current goals of growth management. If left unchanged, they could doom a more ecological approach to the landscape, given the need to adapt conservation strategies to new scientific understanding over time.

Across the country, about 40 states provide developers no protection from changes to land-use laws until developers have "made substantial changes to their property or otherwise committed [themselves] to [their] substantial disadvantage" in reliance on existing laws or government decisions (comparisons of states in this paragraph are from Overstreet and Kirchheim 2000:1061, note 92, citing Delaney and Vaias 1996) . This approach has subtle differences between states, making the exact number of states that apply it a matter of interpretation. At least six states protect property developers from changes to the law made after their projects have been formally approved by relevant permitting agencies.[18] California and Texas are similar to Washington but do not go so far in granting property owners the right to develop under the laws in effect when they *apply* for initial permits.

[18] Arizona, Colorado, Massachusetts, North Carolina, New Jersey, and Pennsylvania; see Overstreet and Kirchheim 2000:1065, note 123.

As is true for most other states, Washington's vesting doctrine was developed in the courts, not the legislature. The legislature codified some important aspects of it in the 1980s, but much of the doctrine remains based on rules developed by the state supreme court. Even defenders of the vesting doctrine acknowledge that the 1954 supreme court decision that is generally seen as the doctrine's first appearance, *Odgen v. City of Bellevue* (1954), "did not claim to be directly interpreting the [federal or state] constitution, a statute, or previous Washington cases; it simply announced a new rule of law" (Overstreet and Kirchheim 2000:1075). This decision concerned an application for a building permit that complied with all relevant laws at the time it was submitted. The court found that once the city council had performed its "discretionary" function of establishing the laws applicable to the permit, the permit's issuance was a "ministerial", non-discretionary function. In the second foundational case for Washington's vested rights doctrine, *Hull v. Hunt* (1958), the state supreme court specifically rejected the approach followed in the majority of other states:

> Notwithstanding the weight of authority, we prefer to have a date certain upon which the right vests to construct in accordance with the building permit. We prefer not to adopt a rule which forces the court to search through…'the moves and countermoves of…parties….' to find that date upon which the substantial change of position is made which finally vests the rights. The more practical rule to administer, we feel, is that the right vests when the party…applies for his building permit. [*Hull v. Hunt* 1958:130]

In a 1994 decision, the state supreme court acknowledged that vesting protection comes at a cost to the public interests that would be furthered by applying land-use laws adopted after this "date certain":

> The practical effect of recognizing a vested right is to sanction the creation of a new nonconforming use. A proposed development which does not conform to newly adopted laws is, by definition, inimical to the public interest embodied in those laws. If a vested right is too easily granted, the public interest is subverted. This court recognized the tension between public and private interests when it adopted Washington's vested rights doctrine. The court balanced the private property and due process rights against the public interest by selecting a vesting point which prevents "permit speculation," and which demonstrates substantial commitment by the developer, such that the good faith of the applicant is generally assured. The application for a building permit demonstrates the requisite level of commitment. In *Hull v. Hunt*, this court explained, "the cost of preparing plans and meeting the requirements of most building departments is such that there will generally be a good faith expectation of acquiring title or possession for the purposes of building…." [*Erickson and Associates v. McLerran* 1994:874; quoting *Hull v. Hunt* 1958:130]

However, land-use laws and the development process have both grown more complicated in the decades following *Hull v. Hunt*, frequently requiring substantial costs to developers well before they apply for building permits. This led to a series of court decisions that extended vesting rights to prior steps in the development process. Partly because the new rules were established incrementally, they became complex and potentially confusing. In 1987, the legislature codified key parts of the vesting doctrine, but instead of clarifying it the new laws created contradictions that worsened these problems. The key new language is in RCW 58.17.033(1):

> A proposed division of land…shall be considered under the subdivision or short subdivision ordinance, and zoning or other land use control ordinances, in effect on the land at the time a fully completed application for preliminary plat approval of the subdivision, or short plat approval of the short subdivision, has been submitted….

A "plat" is the map that depicts a subdivision of land into distinct lots (see RCW 58.17.020[2]). For a large subdivision, a preliminary plat application may include a considerable amount of detail concerning streets, drainage, utilities, parks, open space, and other issues (see RCW 58.17.110). For smaller subdivisions—particularly for short plats (which have four or fewer lots)—a preliminary plat application may be more sketchy. Though a final plat application is separate from a preliminary one, a key aspect of the new law is that it freezes the regulations that apply to the *final* approval based on the timing of the *preliminary* application. When the legislature codified this amendment it also adopted RCW 19.27.095, which freezes the regulations for a building permit based on the timing of the *building permit* application (which is not made until after approval of the final plat; RCW 19.27.095[1]). The legislature left in place a 1969 law governing long subdivisions, which had two relevant clauses: final plats must be evaluated based on the laws "in effect at the time of *preliminary plat approval*"; and vesting of final plats terminates 5 years after final plat approval (RCW 58.17.170).

In 1997, the state supreme court attempted to resolve most of the conflicts in these laws in *Noble Manor Co. v. Pierce County* (1997). The court determined that all relevant state and local laws that apply to a proposed land use vest at the time a complete preliminary plat application is made. For short subdivisions, these rights vest for perpetuity; for long subdivisions, they vest for 5 years after final plat approval. The court noted that granting longer vested rights to short plats than to large subdivisions could be questioned as a policy decision, since short plats involve a less rigorous approval process. However, the court determined that this was a legislative decision and that there were conceivable reasons for the legislature's apparent choice (*Noble Manor Co. v. Pierce County* 1997:282). The court did not mention the potential contradiction between these rules and the law that requires building permits to be judged based on the laws in effect at the time of *building permit* (not plat) applications. (Pierce County argued in *Noble Manor Co. v. Pierce County* [1997] that, reading RCW 58.17.033 and RCW 19.27.095 together, the former only vested the division of land, not development rights. The court disagreed, pointing to a legislative report that said, "The vesting of rights doctrine is extended to applications for preliminary or short plat approval" [*Noble Manor Co. v. Pierce County* 1997:277–278].) In a concurring opinion that expressed regret over the legislature's actions, Justice Philip Talmadge wrote:

> ...a right to use land that vests in perpetuity may cause intractable planning problems. Polyglot development of small plats, creating a patchwork quilt of legal, nonconforming uses, is antithetical to sound land use planning. [*Noble Manor Co. v. Pierce County* 1997:287–288]

Futurewise (formerly known as 1000 Friends of Washington, the leading citizen group advocating for growth management in Washington) strongly agreed with this criticism in a 2002 review of the GMA, saying, "In some counties, it will be years before the effects of GMA are seen on the ground because so much of the rural lands are already platted into urban-style lots that are vested under the State's permissive vesting laws" (Trohimovich 2002). Though the *Noble Manor Co. v. Pierce County* decision noted that short plat applications typically do not require that a developer identify a proposed use, later appellate decisions have extended the decision's vesting protection to uses that a developer merely discusses with local government staff (*Westside Business Park v. Pierce County* 2000). Critics see this as an incentive to "blurt out a proposed 'use' to a local planner...in the hope of using that disclosure to stave off any new land use laws (even ones that do not prevent realization of the proposed use)" (Wynne 2001:916).

Counterbalances to Vesting: Three Not-So-Good Alternatives

Local governments have three legal options to counter the potentially adverse effects of vested development rights. They may strictly regulate nonconforming uses to achieve at least some of the goals intended by current laws; they may adopt regulations that provide for substantial administrative discretion, giving them more flexibility as circumstances change; and they may use their authority under SEPA to condition or deny developments that have adverse impacts on the natural or built environment, even if the developments would otherwise be legal based on their vested rights. All three of these options have considerable drawbacks.

Ironically, given the approach of Washington courts toward vesting, they have "consistently...acknowledged the desirability of eliminating nonconforming uses, and usually [have] applied traditional deferential review to local zoning ordinance provisions which terminate or limit such uses," Richard Settle notes (Settle et al. 1983:46). Nevertheless, local governments rarely exercise their power to restrict nonconforming uses, for both political and legal reasons. A simple but common example illustrates why. Consider a set of homes that is built much closer to a salmon stream than current law would allow (which is probably true at least somewhere on every stream with development along it in the Puget Sound area). Few elected officials would be tempted to threaten that the homes must be moved or torn down, even if this might only be triggered by major repairs or additions. Not only would such threats likely create a political backlash that could spread well beyond the immediate neighborhood, but also they would raise constitutional issues over "unduly oppressive" restrictions that balance the public interest against those of the property owners (see Chapter 6). Proposing restrictions on nonconforming commercial land uses could be even more challenging. Not only might business owners have more resources than homeowners to fight the restrictions, they also frequently have the added incentive that the nonconforming status of their property enhances its economic value by limiting competition (Settle et al. 1983).

If a local government uses the second option above (limiting vested rights by adopting regulations that allow substantial administrative discretion), its approach could be challenged legally for not assuring that critical areas are sufficiently protected. Such a challenge would have a basis in experience, since administrative discretion has more typically been used to *decrease* restrictions on property development, not increase them. As Settle notes regarding variances granted from existing regulations:

> Too often lay members of boards of adjustment or other bodies assigned the variance function have regarded the variance as a general dispensing device available to relieve landowners of inconvenient zoning restrictions whenever neighbors fail to resist loudly enough. The promiscuous, unprincipled granting of variances is assigned much of the blame for the often dismal performance of traditional zoning....It is the cumulative effect of hundreds or thousands of variances in a community which undermines the regulatory purpose and principles of the zoning ordinance and comprehensive plan. [Settle et al. 1983:49]

SEPA: A More Flexible Tool, but with Important Limitations

The third alternative (using SEPA to limit vested rights) provides the most popular strategy available to local governments (R. Settle, Seattle University Law School, personal communication). SEPA's broad goals include fulfilling "the responsibilities of each generation as trustee of the environment for succeeding generations" (RCW 43.21C.020[2]). The act directs local governments and state agencies to interpret and administer their policies, regulations, and laws consistent with its goals to "the fullest extent possible" (RCW 43.21C.030[1]). Courts have regularly approved using SEPA as a basis for setting conditions on proposed development, not only when the conditions have conflicted with vested property rights but also when conditions have gone beyond what *current* laws would require if the development were not vested (Settle et al. 1983).[19] As an example of the latter case, after Puget Sound Chinook salmon were listed under the Endangered Species Act, Snohomish County used SEPA to require buffers along Chinook salmon streams that were larger than the County's standard regulations would have required based on SEPA policy to protect species listed under the ESA (W. Hall, Snohomish County Surface Water Management Division, personal communication). There are, however, important limitations on using SEPA to override vested development rights. First, most smaller developments are exempt from SEPA, including all short plats. Second, substantive requirements based on SEPA are largely discretionary, so they have the general weaknesses of discretionary regulations discussed above. Third, restrictions based on SEPA must still refer to policies adopted by the permitting government (RCW 43.21C.060). It is not entirely clear when these

[19] Cites two cases as examples: *Polygon Corp. v. Seattle* 1978 and *Cook v. Clallam County* 1980.

policies vest—some court decisions have ruled that they vest with all other land-use laws, but administrative regulations issued by the Washington Department of Ecology vest them later in the process, when a draft environmental impact statement is issued or when a project is determined to have no major environmental impact (see Wynne 2001 for a discussion of this point; WDOE's regulation is WAC 197-11-660[1][a]).[20] A fourth problem with using SEPA to limit vested property rights is that it can reduce the predictability and timeliness of permitting, which are goals shared by the GMA, the vesting doctrine, and the Regulatory Reform Act. Delays and uncertainty add costs to development, which potentially also conflict with GMA goals for affordable housing and economic development.

A study of SEPA done in 2003 for the state of Washington noted that "getting to 'yes' quickly and with certainty" is commonly even more important to developers than the financial cost of permitting (Washington State Department of Community, Trade and Economic Development 2003b). Richard Settle notes that Oregon, which has no comparable law to SEPA, has viewed definitive standards under its growth management laws as a primary means to reduce regulatory delay (Settle and Gavigan 1993). The Regulatory Reform Act provided one means to address these issues by authorizing "planned actions" in areas targeted for growth in local comprehensive plans. Under a planned action, the environmental consequences of development in targeted areas are reviewed comprehensively under SEPA in advance of particular developments, which then would not be subject to their own SEPA reviews. In three of the nine cities reviewed in the 2003 state study, major developments would not have proceeded without such protection against the potential costs and delays of SEPA appeals. In most of the other cities reviewed, planned actions were an important contributing factor that encouraged new development in targeted areas (Washington State Department of Community, Trade and Economic Development 2003b). In Everett, the study estimated a typical project that would otherwise require an environmental impact statement under SEPA would save 9 months and at least $288,000 through a planned action. The study also noted, however, that predicting the cumulative impacts of anticipated projects in a plan-level EIS is easier for "built environmental impacts like traffic and public services" than for natural resources

> because the systems are simpler and have fewer variables. The predictive models for natural resources, such as groundwater, fish and wildlife habitat, and wetlands, are less accurate because the natural systems are far more complex, and we have less understanding of the variables that influence them. [Washington State Department of Community, Trade and Economic Development 2003b:10]

The study noted that watershed planning and similar more systematic approaches to evaluating natural resources may help future planned actions to predict these impacts more reliably.

---

[20] Court cases include *Victoria Tower Partnership v. City of Seattle* 1987 and *Adams v. Thurston County* 1993.

Public Investments and Subsidies: Major Influences on Development

The state study of planned actions found that public investment in infrastructure or cleaning up environmental hazards was often at least as important as plan-level SEPA processes to encourage development in targeted areas. The public investments not only had inherent benefits for new development, they also communicated a jurisdiction's commitment to supporting development (Washington State Department of Community, Trade and Economic Development 2003b) in the targeted areas, which developers anticipated would carry over to other issues. More broadly, Futurewise has urged that the state adopt a Smart Growth Investment Strategy for similar reasons. The strategy would target state and federal spending "to existing downtowns, town centers, industrial areas and other smart growth sites throughout the state" (Trohimovich et al. 2001). The state of Maryland is widely seen as a national model for this approach. Its "Priority Funding Areas" law "limits most state public facility, economic development, housing and other funding programs to smart growth areas that local governments designate consistent with state criteria" (Trohimovich et al. 2001). This would not restrict addressing health and safety problems in other areas, but would direct funding for new capacity and most new state facilities to targeted areas. Futurewise notes that Washington's Public Works Trust Fund has taken an important step in this direction by awarding additional points to low-interest loan applications for infill development (Trohimovich et al. 2001).

In the 1990s, the federal government adopted new policies for transportation funding consistent with this philosophy. The policies require urban regions to link their proposed transportation projects to local comprehensive plans.[21] They also removed what had been an important encouragement for sprawl by allowing federal transportation funds to pay for maintenance, which had previously been mostly a state and local responsibility. The central Puget Sound area has been a national leader in using these policies to further Smart Growth principles (Calthorpe and Fulton 2001). The first priority of the Puget Sound Regional Council (PSRC), the metropolitan transportation planning agency for the area,[22] is "to maintain, preserve, make safe, and optimize existing transportation infrastructure and services" (Puget Sound Regional Council 2001:28). One of its six investment principles states:

> Compact development of designated urban centers, high capacity transit station areas, and other communities should be supported through direct investment. Investments within, or connecting, designated Urban Centers and high capacity transit

[21] The significance of the Intermodal Surface Transportation Efficiency Act of 1991 and the 1998 Transportation Equity Act for the 21st century that reauthorized it is discussed in Destination 2030, the metropolitan transportation plan for the central Puget Sound region, issued by the Puget Sound Regional Council, May 24, 2001.

[22] The PSRC is responsible for regional transportation planning in King, Kitsap, Pierce, and Snohomish counties and their cities. It is the latest incarnation of the Puget Sound Governmental Conference, discussed on page 209. Thurston, Island, and Skagit counties also informally coordinate some transportation planning with the PSRC.

station areas that demonstrate support for urban center physical design guidelines are high regional priorities. [Puget Sound Regional Council 2001:28]

These changes in federal, state, and regional investment strategies encourage Smart Growth, but the way local and state funds are raised for transportation still provides substantial indirect subsidies for sprawl, as the PSRC acknowledges. Since the 1980s, an increasing proportion of funds for the region's roads has come from sales and property taxes and other general revenues (Puget Sound Regional Council 2001), rather than taxes on gasoline. (Local roads, as opposed to state or interstate highways, are mostly funded through non-transportation related sources.[23]) Even gasoline taxes do not account for the fact that demand for road capacity is based on where and when vehicles are driven rather than how much they are driven. Charges on roadway use that would increase at peak hours and in congested corridors, though recommended by a PSRC task force, are probably still years away even as a pilot project (Puget Sound Regional Council 2001).

Impact Fees: A Mechanism to Reduce Subsidies for Development (and Reduce General Taxes)

State and local funding for roads are far from isolated subsidies for sprawl. In general, private development pays relatively little of the cost for the new public infrastructure and services necessary to serve it. In four studies cited by Futurewise, the estimated capital cost of new public facilities necessary to serve one new single-family home ranged from a low of $23,011 to a high of $83,216. (The wide range was largely due to assumptions concerning the density of development—less dense development is generally more expensive to serve—and transportation costs—only the high estimate attempted to maintain traffic capacity with no increase in congestion. [Fodor 2000; Trohimovich et al. 2001].) These estimates included the cost of additions to existing arterials, highways, utilities, schools, and other services needed to support the development. They excluded costs that developers paid for utilities, roads, and other elements of new subdivisions that directly serve the new homes. Most of the public costs are borne by general taxes, largely sales, property or business taxes.

Washington law authorizes local governments to charge "impact fees" to defray some of the costs for new roads, schools, parks, open space, and fire protection facilities necessary to serve new development.[24] In contrast to California and some other states, however, Washington law specifically does not allow local governments to collect fees for all of the impact of new development on these costs,[25] nor does it authorize impact

[23] A 1999 study for the Puget Sound Regional Council found that local taxes unrelated to transportation paid for 67% of the cost for city streets and 61% of the cost for county roads (Transportation Pricing Task Force 1999).

[24] RCW 82.02.050 authorizes impact fees; RCW 82.02.090(7) defines which public facilities may be supported by impact fees.

[25] RCW 82.02.050(2) "...the financing for system improvements to serve new development must provide for a balance between impact fees and other sources of public funds and cannot rely solely on impact fees."

fees for other local government capital expenses necessary to serve development, such as police, corrections, and other criminal justice facilities. Washington law also authorizes transportation impact fees only for roads, not for transit or trip reduction programs (Fodor 2000; Siegel et al. 2000; Trohimovich et al. 2001). Impact fees in Washington can be complex to calculate and challenging to administer; they also can be viewed as making a city less competitive for economic development. Partly for those reasons, local governments often do not charge them. In a survey by the Association of Washington Cities in 2002, only 7 of the 175 cities responding charged impact fees for all authorized services (D. Catterson, Association of Washington Cities, personal communication).[26] Most charged only a small fraction of the actual cost to serve new development. Issaquah had the highest total charges, at $11,433 per single family home, about half of the lowest estimate for actual costs cited above (Catterson, personal communication).[27]

If the state legislature mandated impact fees instead of merely authorizing them, it would remove much local concern over their potentially anti-competitive effects. To address broader concerns over the state's competitiveness as a whole, the legislature could also mandate reductions in general taxes to balance new revenues from fees (though fee revenues will rise and fall with development activity, and so are more variable than general taxes). The state could reduce the administrative burden of impact fees by providing standardized methods for calculating them; this would also help local governments defend their charges against legal challenges. Standardized methods could include lower fees for developments that are less costly to serve, such as infill developments that use existing, underutilized infrastructure. Such differential charges are currently not explicitly authorized under state law, discouraging their use.

In California, state law authorizes local governments to charge impact fees to recover the full cost of infrastructure to serve growth (except for schools, whose impact fees are capped, with additional costs paid by state and local bonds). After Proposition 13 reduced and capped California property taxes in 1978, most local governments began to use impact fees to the maximum extent possible to pay for capital improvements needed to serve new development. The combination of limiting property taxes and authorizing impact fees is similar to my suggestion of mandating full impact fees along with a reduction in general taxes. In many cases, local governments in California charge over $30,000 for a typical new single family home, and more for large and expensive homes. If anything, some governments may have gone beyond their authority to charge for the costs of growth and have used impact fees to pay for general operating and capital expenses. Such governments may be

[26] The seven were Issaquah, Mt. Vernon, Olympia, Renton, and Stanwood in the Puget Sound area, plus Battle Ground and Camas.

[27] Fees collected for new school facilities ranged from $634 per single family home in Stanwood to $6,131 in Issaquah; for new fire protection facilities, they ranged from $94 per single family home in Redmond to $488 in Renton; for new park facilities, they ranged from $300 per single family home in Sultan to $3,147 in Issaquah; and for new transportation facilities, they ranged from $517 per single family home in Gig Harbor to $2,710 in Duvall.

sued and forced to reduce their fees (California Government Code 66000–66018; Institute of Local Self Government 2004; D. Carigg, League of California Cities, personal communication).

There are two primary arguments for using general tax revenues to subsidize public facilities that are only needed because of new development: the entire existing tax base arguably benefits from economic growth; and, on average, about half of new development in our region is constructed to serve the children of existing taxpayers.[28] But new residential development does not benefit the tax base—it costs substantially more to serve new homes on an ongoing basis than they return in local tax revenues (for an example, see American Farmland Trust 1999). Impact fees that charge the full cost of serving new development would raise the cost of new housing, but most affordable housing is not built new. If higher impact fees were balanced by reductions in general taxes, these fees would make most housing *more* affordable.[29] Moreover, such charges would still not account for the non-financial costs of growth borne by the general public, including degradation of the environment, increased traffic congestion, and greater densities than some communities want.

Even without impact fees, many critics have argued that growth management laws increase the cost of housing because they restrict the supply of land. National studies on this issue have had mixed results. Restrictions on land supply that come with growth management do appear to increase costs for housing and economic activity, as the economic laws of supply and demand would predict.[30] However, growth management typically involves more than restrictions on land, and many other aspects of the GMA counter this effect. The act requires local governments to accept a fair share of low-income housing and to promote "a variety of residential densities and housing types" to support "all economic segments of the community." National research emphasizes the importance of such inclusionary housing requirements in keeping housing affordable in areas with growth management laws (Nelson et al. 2002). Denser housing typically required by growth management is also generally less expensive, because smaller units are less costly to build and land costs are lower per unit. Growth management also reduces the total cost of private and public infrastructure, which is ultimately passed on to homebuyers and taxpayers. (The National Research Council found that the combined private and public cost for infrastructure to serve compact development is appreciably less than the cost for traditional sprawl, averaging approximately 75% for transportation infrastructure, 80% for utilities, and 95% for schools [Burchell et al.

---

[28] See population projections in Chapter 1, page 3.

[29] Because Proposition 13 not only reduced property taxes and rolled back assessments but did not allow reassessments until property changes ownership, it has distributed tax benefits very unequally, rewarding long-time homeowners at the expense of new ones and thus providing far less benefits to most people for housing affordability. This is not possible in Washington, where all property must be taxed at the same rate, under Article VII, Section 1 of the state constitution.

[30] For a survey of the literature, see Nelson et al. 2002, page 21: "…we can conclude that when traditional land use regulations and certain growth controls act as supply constraints, especially in closed regional land markets with strong demand for new housing, housing price inflation can be substantial."

1998; Trohimovich et al. 2001].) The cost difference was greater in a study for the Salt Lake City area, which estimated the combined public and private infrastructure cost of future growth to be $37.6 billion for traditional development and $22.1 billion for smart growth (Envison Utah estimates quoted in Calthorpe and Fulton 2001). Growth management may also reduce other costs of living, such as transportation costs and even health-related costs (by improving air quality and increasing options for pedestrian travel, for example), which may balance higher housing costs. Finally, it is worth noting that successful efforts at growth management will increase the relative costs of residential and commercial real estate in a region simply by making it a more desirable place to live.

Land-Use Reform: Essential Components of a Regional Conservation Strategy

Primarily because of the GMA, Washington land-use laws provide much greater protection for the environment than they did before the early 1990s. But state guidelines and hearings board decisions that assume all ecological functions and values can be protected as growth continues are based on a fiction. As long as this fiction is accepted, there is little pressure to debate the difficult choices raised by the ecological consequences of growth, let alone to make hard decisions and follow through with action.

Ultimately, eliminating or dramatically reducing subsidies for growth must be part of the answer, since the cumulative loss of land to development is the root cause of decline for the region's ecosystems. This requires higher impact fees. If the legislature mandated such fees, it could help ensure that housing remains affordable and the state remains economically competitive by also mandating corresponding reductions in general taxes. (Since commercial development generally provides a net gain in local tax revenues relative to services provided, some subsidy might even be retained for it.)

A second part of the answer must be to recognize the needs of major ecosystems in designating land uses across the landscape. This might require adding a new category to the GMA's three existing building blocks of urban, rural, and natural resource (farming, forestry, or mining) lands, where natural processes are given priority. Such a category would not necessarily exclude human uses, but would require they be consistent with ecological goals for the land. The GMA currently defines critical areas at too small a scale to accomplish this. Under the GMA, buffers are the primary tool that local governments use to protect the functions and values of critical areas. But even large buffers cannot protect all functions and values as surrounding areas develop. Moreover, buffers alone do not address connectivity between protected habitats, whether adjacent land uses are complementary or in conflict with protected areas, or the hydrologic relationship between aquatic habitats and the entire area that drains to them. Ecosystems need protection through *both* land-use designations and development regulations.

A third part of the answer must be to compensate for the fact that substantial growth, even if sensitively located and regulated, will inevitably degrade some environmental values in its vicinity. The cumulative effects of growth must be mitigated at a broader geographic scale, by restoring ecologically more important places that have been degraded by past land uses. These may be not only off site but also perhaps 100 or more miles away from where growth is occurring.

All of these elements of a conservation strategy can only succeed with a change in state vesting laws, so that public goals for the region's future are not undermined by rights granted years ago with different goals in mind. Changing these rights might require compensation in some cases. Not changing them, however, virtually guarantees that a regional conservation strategy will fail.

Lastly, reform in land-use laws must be connected to reform in water laws. However, as the next two chapters discuss, many of the most fundamental reforms in water law circle back to land use. Growth puts further pressure on limited water supplies, while stormwater runoff from developed areas threatens the hydrology and water quality of streams, lakes, wetlands, and Puget Sound itself. Ecologically, everything is connected.

References

Abenroth v. Skagit County, WWGMHB Case No. 97-2-0060, Final Decision and Order (1998).

Achen v. Clark County, WWGMHB Case No. 95-2-0067, Final Decision and Order (1995).

Adams v. Thurston County, 70 Wash. App. 471 (1993).

American Farmland Trust. 1999. Cost of community services: Skagit County, Washington. Available: www.farmland.org/pnw/Skagit_County_COCS.pdf (March 2996).

Benaroya v. Redmond, CPSGMHB No. 95-3-0072c, Final Decision and Order (1996).

Booth, D. B., D. Hartley, and R. Jackson. 2002. Forest cover, impervious-surface area, and the mitigation of stormwater impacts. Journal of the American Water Resources Association 38:835–845.

Bremerton v. Kitsap County, Central Puget Sound Growth Management Hearings Board Case 95-3-0039c, Final Decision and Order (1995).

Burchell, R. W., N. A. Shad, D. Listokin, H. Philips, A. Downs, S. Seskin, J. S. Davis, T. Moore, D. Helton, and M. Gall. 1998. The costs of sprawl—revisited. Transit Cooperative Research Program Report 39. National Academy Press, Washington, D.C.

Butler v. Lewis County, WWGMHB Case No. 99-2-0027c, Final Decision and Order (2000).

Calthorpe, P., and W. Fulton. 2001. The regional city: planning for the end of sprawl. Island Press, Washington, D.C.

Clark County Natural Resources Council v. Clark County, WWGMHB No. 96-2-0017, Final Decision and Order (1996).

Clement, G. B., and E. Krogh, Jr. 1970. Regional planning and local autonomy in Washington zoning law. University of Washington Law Review 45:593–622.

Cook v. Clallam County, 27 Wn. App. 410 (1980).

Delaney, J. J., and E. J. Vaias. 1996. Recognizing Vested Development Rights as Protected Property in Fifth Amendment Due Process and Takings Claims. Washington University Journal of Urban and Contemporary Law 49.

Diehl v. Mason County, WWGMHB Case No. 95-2-0073, Final Decision and Order (1996).

The difficult politics of growth management. 1989. The Washington Journal (December 11):A5.

Erickson and Associates v. McLerran, 123 Wn.2d 864 (1994).

Everett Shorelines Coalition v. City of Everett, CPSGMHB Case No. 02-3-0009c, Final Decision and Order (2003).

Everett Shorelines Coalition v. Washington State Department of Ecology, Order Granting Tribes' Motion to Reconsider and Clarify (2003).

Fodor, E. 2000. The cost of growth in Washington State. The Columbia Public Interest Policy Institute, Bellevue, Washington.

FOSC (Friends of Skagit County) v. Skagit County, WWGMHB Case No. 96-2-0025, Final Decision and Order (1997).
Friday Harbor v. San Juan County, WWGMHB Case No. 99-2-0010, Final Decision and Order (1999).
Fulton, W., R. Pendall, M. Nguyen, and A. Harrison. 2001. Who sprawls most? How growth patterns differ across the U.S. The Brooking Institution Survey Series, Washington, D.C.
Growth Management Services. 2003. Buildable Lands Program: 2002 evaluation report-a summary of findings. Washington Department of Community, Trade and Economic Development, Olympia.
HEAL (Honesty in Environmental Analysis and Legislation) v. CPSGMHB (Central Puget Sound Growth Management Hearings Board), 96 Wn. App. 522, 979 P.2d 864 (1999).
Horner, R., C. May, E. Livingston, D. Blaha, M. Scoggins, J. Tims, and J. Maxted. 2001. Structural and non-structural BMPs for protecting streams. Watershed Management Institute, Crawfordville, Florida.
Hull v. Hunt, 53 Wash. 2d 125 (1958).
Institute of Local Self Government. 2004. Fees and dedications. Available: http://www.cacities.org/resource_files/22002.Dedications%20and%20Fees.pdf (December 2004).
King County. 2004. Best available science, volume 1: a review of science literature. King County Department of Natural Resources and Parks, Water and Land Resources Division, King County Executive Report, Seattle. Available: http://www.metrokc.gov/ddes/cao/ (March 2006).
Land use law reforms a lesson in persistence. 1995. The Seattle Times (May 17):B4.
Land use plan stuns. 1990. The Seattle Times (July 10):D1.
Larsen, E. M., J. M. Azzerad, and N. Nordstrom. 2004. Management recommendations for Washington's priority species. Volume 4: Birds. Washington Department of Fish and Wildlife, Olympia.
Legislature 1995. 1995. The Seattle Times (May 26):B6.
Litowitz v. Federal Way, CPSGMHB No. 96-3-0005, Final Decision and Order (1996).
Nelson, A. C., R. Pendall, C. J. Dawkins, and G. J. Knaap. 2002. The link between growth management and housing affordability: the academic evidence. The Brookings Institution Center on Urban and Metropolitan Policy, Washington, D.C.
Noble Manor Co. v. Pierce County, 133 Wn.2d 269 (1997).
Odgen v. City of Bellevue, 45 Wash. 2d 492, 275 P.2d 899 (1954).
Overstreet, G., and D. M. Kirchheim. 2000. The quest for the best test to vest: Washington's vested rights doctrine beats the rest. Seattle University Law Review 23:1043–1095.
Pilchuck Audubon Society v. Snohomish County, CPSGMHB No. 95-3-0047, Final Decision and Order (1995).
Polygon Corp. v. Seattle, 578 P.2d 1309 (1978).
PPF (Protect the Peninsula's Future) v. Clallam County, WWGMHB Case No. 00-2-0008, Final Decision and Order (2000).
Puget Sound Regional Council. 2001. Destination 2030. Puget Sound Regional Council, Seattle.
Rusk, D. 2000. Growth management: the core regional issue. Pages 78–106 in B. Katz, editor. Reflections on regionalism. Brookings Institution Press, Washington, D.C.
SAVE (Save a Valuable Environment) v. Bothell, 89 Wash. 2d 862 (1978).
Settle, R. L. 1999. Washington's growth management revolution goes to court. Seattle University Law Review 23(1):12.
Settle, R. L., P. L. Buck, and J. E. Haggard. 1983. Washington land use and environmental law and practice. Butterworth Legal Publishers, Seattle.
Settle, R., and C. Gavigan. 1993. The growth management revolution in Washington: past, present, and future. University of Puget Sound Law Review 16:875.
Siegel, M. L., J. Terris, and K. Benfield. 2000. Common problems in fiscal impact analysis. Chap-

ter 4 *in* Development and dollars: an introduction to fiscal impact analysis in land use planning. Natural Resources Defense Council, New York. Available: www.nrdc.org/cities/smartGrowth/dd/chap4.asp (March 2006).

Sky County v. Snohomish County, CPSGMHB Case No. 95-3-0068 (5368c), Final Decision and Order (1996).

State rules reforms are worth the risks. 1995. The Seattle Times (May 10):B4.

Transportation Pricing Task Force. 1999. The effects of the current transportation finance structure: paper 2. Puget Sound Regional Council, Seattle. Available: http://www.psrc.org/datapubs/pubs/pricing2.pdf (March 2006).

Trohimovich, T. 2002. The Growth Management Act after more than 10 years: another look and a response to criticisms. 1000 Friends of Washington, Seattle.

Trohimovich, T., D. Hursh, and R. Thorsten. 2001. Pricing growth. 1000 Friends of Washington, Seattle.

Tulalip Tribes of Washington v. Snohomish County, CPSGMHB Case 96-3-0029, Final Decision and Order (1997).

Upper Green Valley Preservation Society v. King County, CPSGMHB, Green Valley, 8308c (2001).

Victoria Tower Partnership v. City of Seattle, 49 Wash. App. 755 (1987).

Viking v. Holm, 155 Wn.2d 112 (2005).

Washington Department of Ecology and Department of Community, Trade and Economic Development. 2004. Questions and answers on ESHB 1933. Critical areas protection under the Growth Management Act and Shoreline Management Act. Available: http://www.ecy.wa.gov/programs/sea/sma/laws_rules/90-58/1933_Guidance.pdf (March 2006).

Washington State Department of Community, Trade and Economic Development. 2003a. Example code provisions for designating and protecting critical areas. Appendix A *in* Critical areas assistance handbook: protecting critical areas within the framework of the Washington Growth Management Act. Washington State Department of Community, Trade and Economic Development, Olympia.

Washington State Department of Community, Trade and Economic Development. 2003b. SEPA and the promise of the GMA: reducing the costs of development. Washington Department of Community, Trade and Economic Development, Olympia.

Washington State Office of Community Development. 2002. Citations of recommended sources of best available science for designating and protecting critical areas. Washington State Office of Community Development, Olympia. Available: http://qa.cted.wa.gov/_CTED/documents/ID_874_Publications.pdf (March 2006).

WEAN (Whidbey Environmental Action Network) v. Island County, 122 Wn. App. 156, 93 P.3d 885 (2004).

Westside Business Park v. Pierce County, 100 Wash. App. 599 (2000).

Wynne, R. D. 2001. Washington's Vested Rights Doctrine: how we have muddled a simple concept and how we can reclaim it. Seattle University Law Review 24:851–939.

Chapter 11. Not Enough Water: Planning Can Only Do So Much

> Subject to existing rights all waters within the state belong to the public, and any right thereto, or to the use thereof, shall be hereafter acquired only by appropriation for a beneficial use and in the manner provided and not otherwise; and, as between appropriations, *the first in time shall be the first in right*....[Emphasis added; Washington State Water Code, Revised Code of Washington 90.03.010]

Chapter Summary

Washington poses some of the most difficult challenges for managing water of any state in the country. No other state has a wider range of rainfall: from 120 or more inches annually along the coast to less than 10 inches in the interior Columbia basin.[1] Water is also used very differently across Washington. A study by the U.S. Geological Survey of water use in Washington in 2000 estimated that domestic use accounted for 63% of all withdrawals in the Puget Sound area; industry consumed 77% of withdrawals in southwest Washington; and agriculture dominated with 87% of withdrawals in eastern Washington (Lane 2004; R.C. Lane, U.S. Geological Survey, personal communication). This enormous variation makes it extremely difficult to set statewide standards for water management. Balancing human and ecological needs in Washington is further challenged by bad timing.Unlike much of the rest of the country, the greatest demand for water in Puget Sound and most of the state is when water is least naturally available (see Figure 11-1).

That being said, Washington's heritage of water law—which it largely shares with other western states—mostly adds to these problems. As stated in Washington's water code, the most fundamental principle of this heritage is that "the first in time shall be the first in right" (Revised Code of Washington [RCW] 90.03.10). This means early users of water always have priority over later users. The latter include fish and wildlife, since their needs were recognized by state law only beginning in the early 1970s. Known as the "prior appropriation" doctrine, this policy was developed to encourage early settlement and economic development in the West. It assured miners and irrigators who invested in putting scarce water to use that other people would not come along later and cut off their supplies.

Most western states have done a better job than Washington in adapting western traditions to address contemporary concerns, such as increased demand from growing populations, requirements of the Endangered Species Act and Clean Water Act, and the rights of Indian tribes to river flows that support treaty rights to fish or farm (see Chapter 13). In recent years, Washington has made some relatively minor reforms to

[1] For details on precipitation across the state, see http://www.wrcc.dri.edu/summary/climsmwa.html. For a state map showing ranges of precipitation, see http://www.ocs.orst.edu/pub/maps/Precipitation/Total/States/WA/wa.gif.

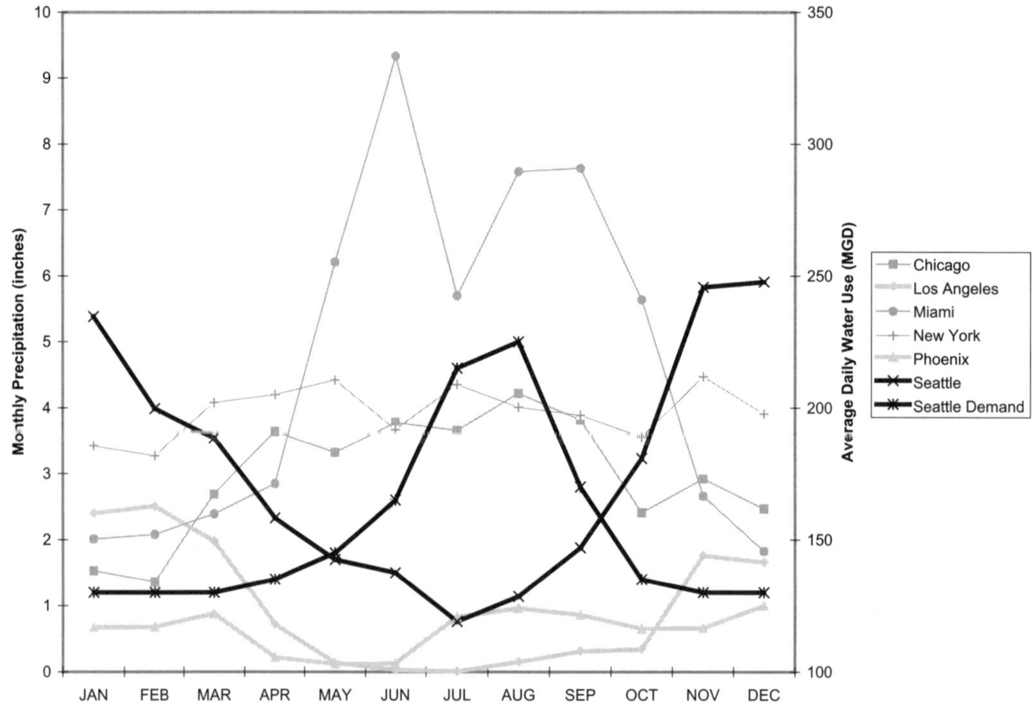

FIGURE 11-1. Average monthly precipitation and water demand in Seattle, compared to precipitation in other cities of the country. Only on the Pacific Coast does precipitation decline in the summer. This not only reduces water supplies, but also leads to greater irrigation demands for crops and non-native plants. Note that average summer precipitation in Phoenix is about the same as in Seattle. Precipitation data are averages from 1961 to 1990 from the National Climatic Data Center. Available: http://lwf.ncdc.noaa.gov/oa/ncdc.html (June 2006). Seattle water demand is averaged from 1990 to 1998 (except for the drought year of 1992) and includes suburban utilities that purchase water from Seattle. Available: http://dnr.metrokc.gov/wlr/watersup/precipuse.htm (June 2006).

its water laws, but mostly it has invested in watershed planning, which has been heavy on process but short on solving water resource disputes. Watershed planning groups are crippled by their lack of authority over key issues, lack of critical information, lack of adequate funding, and lack of legislative decisions that would free them from fighting battles ultimately rooted in state law. Washington's reliance on watershed groups follows a period when the Washington Department of Ecology (WDOE), trying to implement the legislature's most recent comprehensive reforms, attempted to decide fundamental questions regarding the future of water resources across the state. That approach never really had a chance. Wherever water is scarce, its future is inseparable from that of the communities that depend on it. As Washington State's population grows and the needs of fish and wildlife receive greater legal recognition (under federal law or tribal treaties), water will become increasingly scarce across most of the state.

Climate change will make it even scarcer (see Chapter 2, pages 36–37). A state agency working alone, without clear laws, strong political support, and the close involvement of affected communities, cannot decide the most fundamental questions regarding the future of the state's water. Who has a right to withdraw water? How much water must be left in streams? How will goals for stream flows be met? Watershed groups also cannot answer these questions alone. They may help opposing interests reach some compromises, but the hardest decisions ahead will almost certainly require action by the legislature, the courts, and potentially the voters through citizen initiatives.

A Brief History of Washington Water Law to 1971

Since Roman times, European law has recognized water as "a public or community resource, owned by no one" (Pharris and McDonald 2000:1). American law adopted this same principle. In the eastern and central United States, where water is generally plentiful and nearly all landowners have access to some surface water or groundwater to meet their needs, water law has followed the riparian doctrine, carried over from Great Britain (Pharris and McDonald 2000). Under this doctrine, landowners adjacent to bodies of water have an equal right to use it, sharing equally if there is a shortage. All landowners also have a right to groundwater beneath their property; this right is typically tempered by reasonable use criteria to protect their neighbors' rights to shared groundwater sources (Pharris and McDonald 2000). However, in the arid western United States this doctrine proved unworkable and was replaced by the prior appropriation doctrine, discussed above. As federal lands were privatized, Congress recognized the rights of western states to modify water law to their different circumstances (Fish and Wildlife Coordination Act [FWCA], U.S. Code, volume 43, section 661[2]).

Washington State courts initially recognized both the riparian and the prior appropriation doctrines. Although the legislature supported principles of the prior appropriation doctrine as early as 1891 (2 years after statehood; Pharris and McDonald 2000), it was not until 1917 that the legislature passed the state's first comprehensive water management law. It came down clearly on the side of prior appropriation for all future water rights:

> Subject to existing rights all waters within the state belong to the public, and any right thereto, or to the use thereof, shall be hereafter acquired only by appropriation for a beneficial use and in the manner provided and not otherwise; and, as between appropriations, the first in time shall be the first in right. Nothing contained in this act shall be construed to lessen, enlarge, or modify the existing rights of any riparian owner, or any existing right acquired by appropriation, or otherwise. [RCW 90.03.10].

The prevalence of private disputes regarding the seniority of rights under the previously unregulated system prompted the 1917 Water Code (Pharris and McDonald 2000),

[2] First passed in 1866.

which is still in place today. New surface water withdrawals require a permit from the state. The state (today acting through WDOE) can deny the permit if it finds that there is no unappropriated water available, the proposed use would impair existing water rights, or the proposed use is otherwise "detrimental to the public interest," giving due regard to "the highest feasible development" of the use of state waters (RCW 90.03.290[3]). The state issues water rights not only for the amount of water to be used but also for the purpose and place of use (see RCW 90.03.240), assigning a priority date of when the application for the right was filed (see RCW 90.03.340). Water rights are attached to the land where they are used unless they are formally transferred (which can include changing either the purpose or the place of use). Transfers must be approved by the state, which must find that they would not harm other existing rights (RCW 90.03.380). For those claims that date to before 1917, the Water Code authorized state courts to adjudicate priority dates and establish actual rights; this is still the only means available to establish the actual rights of these claims (see *Rettkowski v. Department of Ecology* 1993). An adjudication is triggered by a petition from one or more persons who claim a water right affecting a particular waterbody (which may be as small as a spring or creek or as large as a major river basin; RCW 90.03.110). Adjudication involves a comprehensive review of all water rights and claims for that waterbody and results in a final determination of all water rights and their relative priority dates (Pharris and McDonald 2000). Though this process applies statewide, in 1917 it was most important to farmers in eastern Washington, where water was scarce and many claims dated to well before the state code. Even today, almost all completed adjudications have been in eastern Washington (see map, Figure 11-2).

The next major development in state water law came in 1945, when the legislature extended the rules for surface water to groundwater, adding a few special rules only for groundwater. The groundwater code recognized that surface water and groundwater can be connected. (In fact, it is now understood that they are *always* connected. Depending on the relative elevations of a surface water body and the water table in its vicinity, water flows from one to the other.) For this reason, the state supreme court has interpreted the groundwater code to apply "the paramount rule of 'first in time, first in right'" across both surface and groundwater withdrawals in the same basin (*Rettkowski v. Department of Ecology* 1993).

One rule unique to groundwater is that new groundwater rights are allowed to infringe on senior groundwater rights if the existing rights depend on shallow wells that can be dug deeper to reach sufficient water within a "reasonable" pumping distance (Pharris and McDonald 2000). Another unique rule states that changes to the location or purpose of use for groundwater must meet all of the criteria for a new right, including public interest criteria (Pharris and McDonald 2000), which do not apply to transfers of surface water rights. The most important rule unique to groundwater is that specified small uses are exempt from even needing a water right. These uses are

> [A]ny withdrawal...for stockwatering purposes, or for the watering of a lawn or of a noncommercial garden not exceeding one-half acre in area, or for single or group

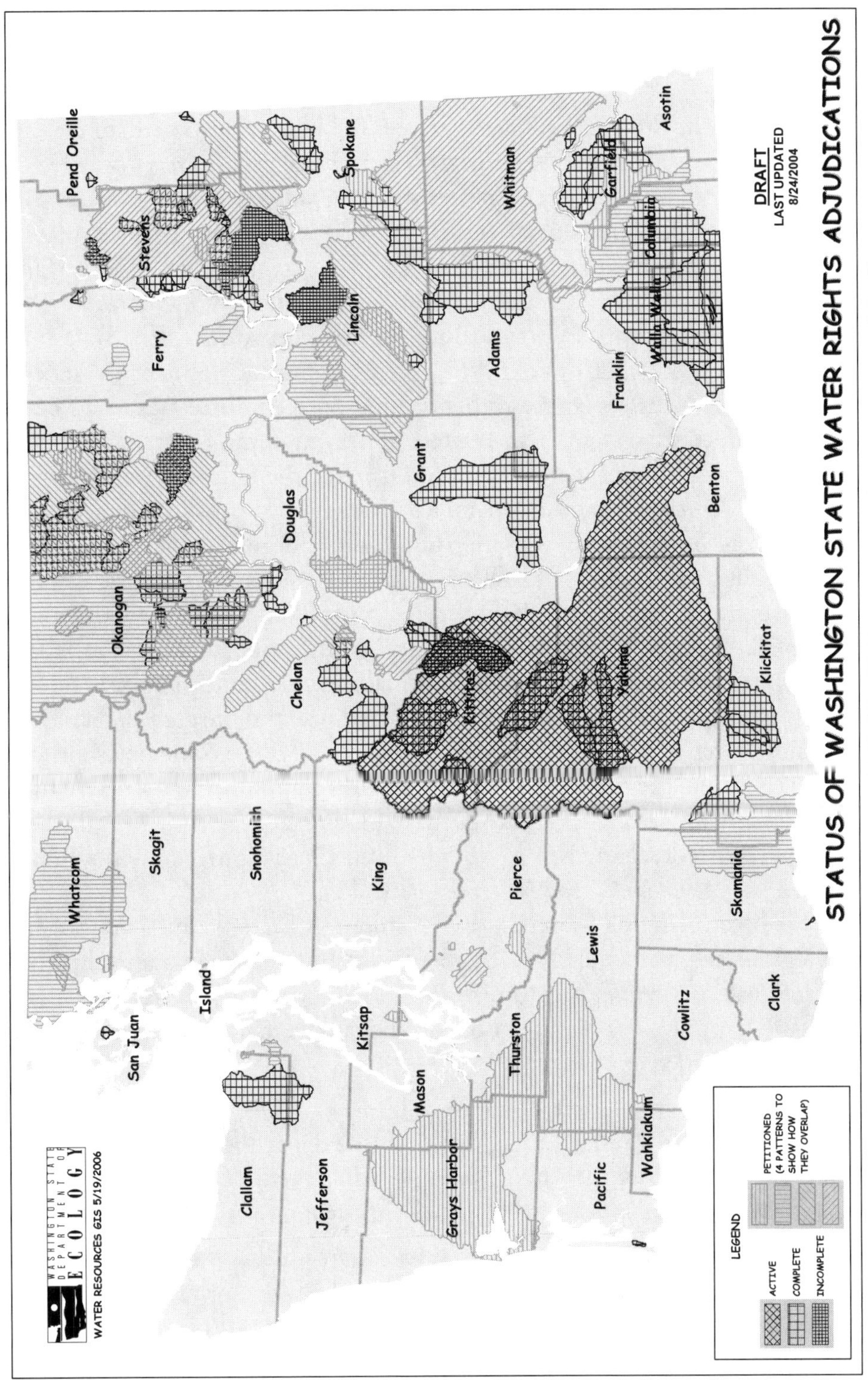

FIGURE 11-2. Status of Washington water rights adjudications. The Dungeness River basin is the only part of the Puget Sound region with a completed adjudication.

> domestic uses in an amount not exceeding five thousand gallons a day, or for an industrial purpose in an amount not exceeding five thousand gallons a day....[RCW 90.44.050]

Cumulatively, exempt users can withdraw large amounts of water (there are currently estimated to be more than 750,000 exempt wells in Washington, serving approximately 1.5 million people, about one-quarter of the state's population; see CELP 2004).

The next major development affecting Washington water law took place at the federal level. In 1952, Congress passed the McCarran Amendment, which waived the federal government's right to immunity from state adjudication processes for water rights (FWCA, section 666). In practical terms, this means that if the state initiates a general adjudication of water rights in state court, the water rights of the federal government and Indian tribes whose rights depend on federal treaties—can be adjudicated in the state court system. The United States Supreme Court later determined that this amendment did not merely allow but *required* the federal government to defer to state court processes to establish federal water rights and tribal treaty rights to water in the context of comprehensive adjudications. The Supreme Court recognized that Indian tribes have some reason to fear adjudication of their rights by elected state judges.[3] However, the Court said that allowing federal adjudication would create "the possibility of duplicative litigation, tension and controversy between the federal and state forums, hurried and pressured decision making, and confusion over the disposition of property rights," thus defeating what it said was the purpose of the McCarran Amendment (*Arizona v. San Carlos Apache Tribe* 1983). State court decisions on tribal water rights can still be appealed to the United States Supreme Court, where the Court said tribal rights would receive "a particularized and exacting scrutiny commensurate with the powerful federal interest in safeguarding those rights from state encroachment" (*Arizona v. San Carlos Apache Tribe* 1983:571).

The next noteworthy development in Washington State water law came in 1967, when the legislature passed the Water Rights Registration, Waiver and Relinquishment Act. The act's ostensible goal was to provide clarity and finality in relating established water rights to water claims dating to before the surface and groundwater codes. The heart of the act provided as follows:

> All persons [without a permit] using or claiming the right to withdraw...surface or ground waters of the state...shall file with the department of water resources [now WDOE] not later than June 30, 1974, a statement of claim for each water right asserted on a form provided by the department. [RCW 90.14.041]
>
> Any person claiming the right to divert or withdraw waters of the state as set forth [above] who fails to file a statement of claim...shall be conclusively deemed to have waived and relinquished any right, title, or interest in said right. [RCW 90.14.071]

[3] State supreme court judges have lost elections in Idaho and Colorado based on their decisions in favor of federal water rights; see Hobbs 2001.

This law also established the "use it or lose it" principle, under which water right holders who fail to "beneficially use all or any part" of their right for five consecutive years relinquish their right, which reverts to the state (RCW 90.14.160–180). (Since municipal users typically serve growing populations, the legislature clarified in 2003 that they are allowed to "grow into" their water rights; Second Engrossed Second Substitute House Bill 1338, chapter 5, laws of 2003; see pages 263–264, below.) The requirement of beneficial use theoretically provides a legal basis for using conservation standards to eliminate rights to wasted water (Pharris and McDonald 2000). In practice, however, the use it or lose it principle has generally been a disincentive for conservation, since not using all of an existing right for five years poses the threat of losing any amount not used.

The 1967 act has failed to provide clarity and finality for water claims. Initially, this was because the legislature did not appropriate sufficient funds to administer it, which caused the director of Water Resources to take the extraordinary step of making an administrative ruling that his agency could not implement the new law. The legislature re-enacted the law in 1969 with a larger appropriation for administration (C. Roe, former water law attorney to both the legislature and the Washington Department of Ecology, personal communication). More importantly over the long term, the legislature has not encouraged systematic adjudications to determine the validity of water claims and has reopened opportunities to file claims for short periods in 1979, 1985, and 1997 (RCW 90.14.043, RCW 90.14.067, and RCW 90.14.068). To date, WDOE has recorded about 169,000 claims. As the Attorney General's Office has said, "Short of litigation, it is impossible to assess how many of these claims represent vested water rights. Many claims may be invalid, overstated, overlapping, abandoned, reduced, or modified in their scope" (Pharris and McDonald 2000:VI, 17). In areas that have not been adjudicated (including almost all of the Puget Sound area), it is impossible to know how much water can legally be withdrawn.

In 1967, the legislature also passed the Minimum Water Flows and Levels Act (which it also reenacted with amendments in 1969). This act granted the Department of Water Resources (now WDOE) broad authority to establish minimum flows in streams, lakes, or other public waters to protect fish and wildlife or recreational or aesthetic values (RCW 90.22.010). However, it specified that these rights would have a priority date as of when the Department established minimum flow rules, leaving these rights junior to all water rights established before them (WDOE 2001).

Little was done to implement the Minimum Flows Act prior to passage of the Water Resources Act of 1971, which is still the most significant water legislation enacted in recent times. This act established 11 fundamental policies to guide water management, including

> Uses of water for domestic, stock watering, industrial, commercial, agricultural, irrigation, hydroelectric power production, mining, fish and wildlife maintenance and enhancement, recreational, and thermal power production purposes, and preservation of environmental and aesthetic values...are declared to be beneficial. [RCW 90.54.020{1}]

> Allocation of waters among potential uses and users shall be based generally on the securing of the maximum net benefits for the people of the state. Maximum net benefits shall constitute total benefits less costs including opportunities lost. [RCW 90.54.020{2}]
>
> Perennial rivers and streams of the state shall be retained with base flows necessary to provide for preservation of wildlife, fish, scenic, aesthetic and other environmental values, and navigational values. Lakes and ponds shall be retained substantially in their natural condition. Withdrawals of water which would conflict therewith shall be authorized only in those situations where it is clear that overriding considerations of the public interest will be served. [RCW 90.54.020{3)(a}]

The act directed WDOE to "develop and implement...a comprehensive state water resources program" to ensure that "future water resource allocation and use" was consistent with these policies.

In Search of "Optimum" Flows: WDOE Tries to Implement the Water Resources Act

In 1976, WDOE adopted regulations for a comprehensive state water program. It established 62 Water Resource Inventory Areas (WRIAs) as planning units across the state, generally following the watershed boundaries of major rivers (Washington Administrative Code [WAC] 173-500-040; see Figure 11-3). Within each WRIA, WDOE anticipated developing a plan for managing water with the following goals:

1. Identify and foster development of water resource projects;
2. Declare preferences or priorities of use by categories;
3. Set forth streams closed to future appropriation;
4. Establish flows on perennial streams of the state in amounts necessary to provide for preservation of wildlife, fish, scenic, aesthetic, and other environmental values, and navigational values;
5. Allocate quantities for beneficial uses;
6. Reserve water for future beneficial use;
7. Withdraw waters from additional appropriation when sufficient information or data are lacking for the making of sound decisions;
8. Establish criteria for limit beyond which further appropriation will not be made;
9. Designate areas within the state to be used for management purposes; and
10. Be guided by the declaration of fundamentals contained in RCW 90.54.020 [the Water Resources Act]. [WAC 173-500-029]

The Water Resources Act required WDOE to coordinate with Indian tribes and local governments and to encourage "all persons and private groups and entities showing an interest in water resources programs" to participate in its planning processes (RCW 909.54.060[1]). Ultimately, however, WDOE was legally responsible to propose and adopt a plan for each WRIA to meet the above sweeping goals, which obviously could have profound consequences for the futures of affected communities.

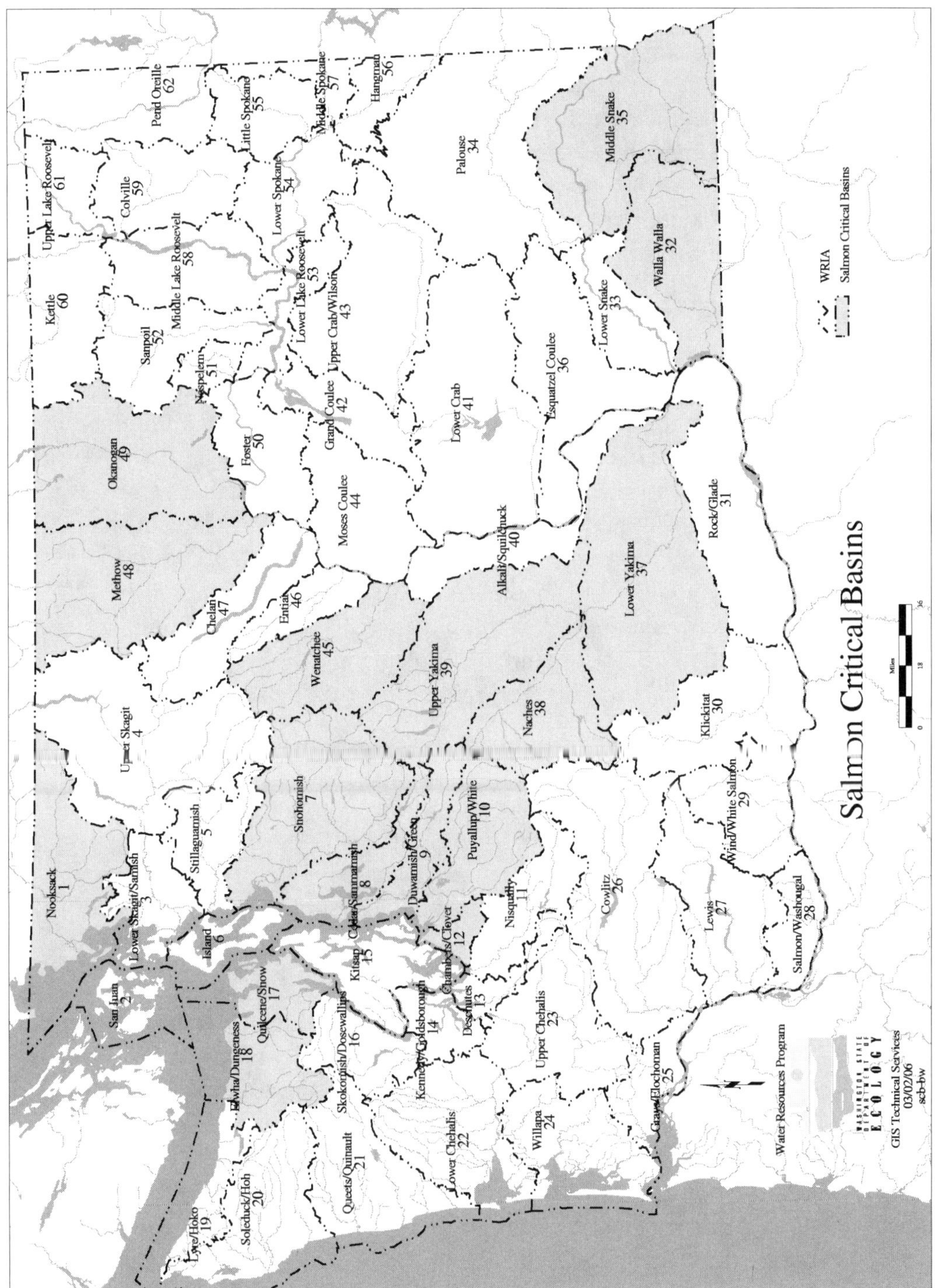

FIGURE 11-3. Water Resource Inventory Areas in Washington. "Salmon critical basins," where existing water withdrawals are considered to be in the greatest conflict with flows needed for fish, are shaded.

By 1985, WDOE had adopted instream resource protection programs for 20 of the 62 WRIAs, establishing minimum flows on main-stem rivers and some larger tributaries (H. Adelsman, Washington Department of Ecology, personal communication). In that year, the state Ecological Commission (an appointed body of citizens with authority to disapprove some regulatory actions proposed by WDOE) rejected the department's proposal for instream flows for WRIA 16, which includes both the Skokomish and Dosewallips rivers at the south end of Hood Canal. While some local interests thought WDOE's proposed flows for the WRIA were too restrictive of other uses, the commission ruled that they were not restrictive enough to protect instream values (Dyer 1993:145). This led WDOE to undertake a comprehensive administrative review of its instream flow and water allocation program (see Joint Select Committee on Water Resource Policy 1989). A 20-member advisory committee helped WDOE develop a new proposal for the program. After a draft environmental impact statement in February 1987 received widespread criticism, the department revised its proposal and issued a new preferred alternative in November of that year.

WDOE's preferred alternative called for "optimum" flows to protect fish and wildlife and other instream values (such as recreation); however, WDOE still would evaluate proposals for new withdrawals by their effects on current conditions (see WDOE 1987). It proposed to evaluate flows using a "state-of-the-art" methodology that focused on minimum flows for fish habitat, supplemented by other information where available. Watersheds would be placed in one of five different classes:

Class 1: Current flows exceed optimum levels; excess water is available for appropriation.
Class 2: Suboptimum flows are allowed; to maintain current instream resources, mitigation is required fornew withdrawals.
Class 3: Pristine streams, closed to new appropriations
Class 4: Current flows are optimum and no new appropriations are allowed.
Class 5: Current flows are suboptimum and should be improved through water conservation and transfers of water rights (WDOE 1987).

Under WDOE's preferred alternative, no reduction in existing instream resources would be allowed. Proponents for new withdrawals would bear all associated costs to protect public resources (WDOE 1987). No new wells would be exempt from restrictions "except for in-house domestic use only when no alternative supply is available" (WDOE 1987:6). Existing diversions could be increased only after conservation measures were taken. Conservation might also be required to transfer existing rights or for new water rights (WDOE 1987). Though WDOE might form advisory committees to help it develop proposals for water resources in a planning area, it would not be bound by their recommendations (WDOE 1987). WDOE would evaluate allocations of water for future uses or instream flows against the Water Resources Act test of "maximum net benefits for the people of the state," using administrative rules still to be developed (WDOE 1987). In "high priority planning areas," WDOE might temporarily close WRIAs to new withdrawals until it adopted new regulations.

In its final environmental impact statement for this proposal, WDOE acknowledged that its regulations "would affect new urban and industrial development, because strong instream flow protection measures would limit the acceptable sources for obtaining new water supplies" (WDOE 1987:20). It also acknowledged that new agricultural production would be inhibited in Class 1, 3, and 4 watersheds, and existing agricultural production and income might be affected by conservation requirements in Class 5 watersheds (WDOE 19987). WDOE said that fish and other aquatic resources would benefit from flow restoration efforts in Class 5 streams and (in a twist not supported by today's science) that they would also "probably" benefit from new withdrawals that reduced "higher than optimum flows" in Class 1 streams.

Though citizen letters "almost unanimously supported preservation of instream resources, optimum flows for fisheries and recreation, and mandatory water conservation," interest groups attacked WDOE's preferred alternative from all sides (WDOE 1987[4]). WDOE published sample excerpts from written comments in an appendix to its environmental impact statement:

> Although the preferred alternative may be an improvement over current state practices and policies, it is fatally flawed by its failure to comply with federal law. The state improperly proposes to qualify a treaty right. [Northwest Indian Fisheries Commission]
>
> It appears that D.O.E. has completely ignored all of the public comments of the Washington State Water Utilities who represent by far the majority of the people in the State of Washington....[D.O.E.'s past] balance has obviously tilted to greatly favor the instream flow needs. [Federal Way Water and Sewer]
>
> Our major concern is the freezing of optimum flow levels at the existing flows. Although DOE is justifiably protecting existing fish habitat, additional flows will be needed for fish enhancement efforts. [Washington Council of the Federation of Fly Fishermen]
>
> We support Ecology's objective of maintaining existing levels of instream resources (including fish habitat provided by natural flows) within planning regions, but we believe that adopting optimum flow as the flow standard is, in effect, requiring out-of-stream users to enhance, rather than maintain, existing levels of instream resources. [City of Seattle]
>
> We support the Preferred Alternative but believe that the method for establishing instream flows should be broadened beyond a basis in fisheries needs only. Many of our members are river boaters who want their river flow needs taken into consideration in setting instream flows. [Northwest Rivers Council]
>
> The law declares that instream values such as fish and wildlife maintenance are beneficial uses of water in the same context as consumptive uses—neither holds a

[4] All following quotes from Appendix G-4 of WDOE 1987, Sample excerpts from written comments regarding the Department of Ecology's preferred alternative.

> preference. The law further requires that potential uses, without exception, be allocated on the basis of maximum net benefits. Unfortunately, the elements of the preferred alternative are not consistent with these fundamentals. [Washington Water Power]

> The water and electric rate impacts which would result from implementation of the preferred alternative and the outright limitations which could be imposed on future development if this proposal is implemented, make the preferred alternative a program which should undergo legislative review prior to implementation. [Association of Washington Cities]

> Our industry—agriculture—appears to be the primary target for obtaining necessary flows to optimize the fish habitat! Water is the *lifeblood* of many Eastern Washington communities. The direction being taken by the Department of Ecology *needs* legislative oversight—*now*. [Emphasis in original; Washington State Water Resources Association]

"The Moratorium" and Initial Legislative Recommendations

The calls for legislative action were answered swiftly and emphatically in 1988. What came to be known as "the moratorium" prohibited WDOE from altering its existing standards for instream flows and water allocation, reserving any blocks of water for future instream or out-of-stream uses, or issuing any permanent new water rights through June 30, 1989 (1988 Senate Bill 6724). The legislature also established a Joint Select Committee on Water Resource Policy, with representatives from the state house and senate representing both political parties, to make recommendations on changes to state water law and policy prior to the legislature's 1989 session. The same bill called for a "neutral…Independent Fact Finder" to assist the Joint Select Committee "by gathering opinions from interested parties, reviewing relevant documents, and analyzing existing laws and policies" (Appendix G in Joint Select Committee on Water Resource Policy 1989).

That summer, the Fact Finder reported that the biggest problem was the lack of clear policy guidance from the legislature:

> With undefined terms interspersed among old water statutes and with new laws often overlaid on existing ones, it has been difficult for interested parties to have productive discussions—let alone reach consensus….The message [from] the fact-finding process was repeated time and time again: Washington needs a clearly articulated water policy, with all key terms precisely defined, inconsistencies eliminated from prior statutes, and with new provisions that address the complex issues that have arisen in recent years.

> Does the public interest extend to maintaining family farms and the character of rural communities supported by irrigated agriculture? Does it mean keeping costs down to water ratepayers who are trying to make ends meet? Is the public interest served by accommodating hydropower development as an alternative to fossil fuel and nuclear power plants? Does it mean honoring treaties for sharing the region's resources among Indian people and new settlers? Each person may have different

answers to these questions—and the legislature has yet to define the scope of the public interest as it is used in water policy statutes. [Appendix G in Joint Select Committee on Water Resource Poligy 1989]

The Joint Select Committee agreed that amendments were needed to state law to provide "clear and precise guidance" on setting instream flows and other issues. Ultimately, the committee determined that "the magnitude and complexity of issues involving the 'fundamentals of water policy' would make it extremely difficult" to complete its work before the 1989 legislative session (Joint Select Committee on Water Resource Policy 1989:12). It decided instead to focus on making "as much progress as possible...on two of the most significant issues, instream flows and water allocation."

The committee agreed with the Fact Finder that existing laws provided several different "public interest tests" for allocating water, with "no specific criteria or definitions" to help decide them (Joint Select Committee on Water Resource Policy 1989:17). It generally supported the non-degradation standard for instream resources proposed by WDOE, with selective restoration of instream resources that need greater flows "where the costs and impact upon other activities are not excessive" (Joint Select Committee on Water Resource Policy 1989:14).[5] The general public, the committee found, should bear the cost of restoring historic losses, while new water rightholders should pay to mitigate adverse impacts from new withdrawals. New allocations of water generally should be deferred until the flows needed to protect the existing abundance and quality of instream resources are determined. These flows should take into account recreation and other values in addition to fish and wildlife habitat. The "best available scientifically recognized method" should be used to quantify each of these instream needs by 1995, using flows for the previous 10 years as the standard for measuring existing resources. Where there was a compelling need to approve a new allocation before minimum flows were determined, it should be provisional, to be modified "once complete information is obtained." The committee recognized, however, that there is a "fundamental conflict" between instream resources that depend on a dynamic hydrologic system and economic activities that depend on the "certainty and security of water rights." Balancing these needs, it recommended that *all* future permits for offstream uses be for a fixed term, following which they would be "reviewed under the same standard and criteria as first issued." The term for new rights should be no less than "the time required to recover the applicant's investment." New allocations should be allowed to bring flows below established instream needs "only in the rare circumstance" where the proposed use "is essential to meet public health and safety needs; there are no feasible alternative means of supply, including conservation measures" and mitigation is provided. The committee recommended that all future allocations must provide the best overall benefit to society by balancing the following factors:

[5] Most of the following recommendations are from page 14 or Appendix F, Draft policy recommendations, of Joint Select Committee on Water Resource Policy 1989.

- The benefit of the allocation to the applicant;
- Impacts upon the state's economy, recognizing the primary goal of providing future economic stability to the region where the diversion occurs;
- The current and future benefit and cost to the people in the basin considering their cultural beliefs and traits; [and]
- The loss of alternative uses of water, including both offstream and instream, that might otherwise be made within a reasonable time.

> Any future allocations of water must not detrimentally effect [sic] the current and future need for an adequate and high quality supply of domestic water satisfactory to that region's planning priorities and consistent with the policies of the state. [Appendix F of Joint Select Committee on Water Resource Policy 1989]

The committee found that improvements in conservation and the efficient use of existing withdrawals offered "the quickest path to development of additional water" (Joint Select Committee on Water Resource Policy 1989:28). Like WDOE, it considered spring flood waters as excess that "may be stored for later use in low-flow months," potentially benefiting both instream resources and new offstream uses (Joint Select Committee on Water Resource Policy 1989:27).

The committee recognized that "the enormous diversity of water sources and uses in the state requires that statutory standards and procedures allow for flexibility to resolve unique water use conflicts considering both the state's interest and local circumstances" (Joint Select Committee on Water Resource Policy 1989). Though it made no specific recommendations to address this issue, it urged "improved planning and coordination between state, local and federal agencies, Indian tribes, water purveyors, and instream and offstream water users" and noted its interest in a tiered approach "that would permit regional or local water resource planning with variations tailored to local circumstances" (Joint Select Committee on Water Resource Policy 1989).

The committee issued these draft recommendations in December 1988. After widespread fears were expressed that enacting them into law "could result in severe restrictions upon future offstream diversions," the committee withdrew them as "too much, too fast" (Joint Select Committee on Water Resource Policy 1989:12). It recommended that the legislature defer major changes in state water law until the 1990 session, giving the committee more time to refine its proposals.

Trying to Build on the Existing System: The Chelan Process

About this same time, Governor Booth Gardner organized a subcabinet to review water policy. The governor's liaison to the group later described the next steps as follows:

> In early 1990, the Subcabinet met with Tribal leaders and Legislative members to discuss the potential of developing a cooperative planning process for water resources. Based on that meeting, the Joint Select Committee drafted legislation which was enacted during the 1990 legislative session calling for a cooperative approach to water resources planning among interest groups, local governments, tribes and water users....One of the critical elements leading to the emphasis on cooperative planning

> was the interest of the state and the Indian tribes in cooperatively resolving environmental issues, including water resource issues, relating to their treaty right to harvest fish.
>
> The two state government efforts, executive and legislative, were combined and the state, together with the tribes, formed a common effort to hold a water resources planning retreat. Over 160 participants from a broad range of interests [state, local, and tribal governments; environmentalists; the business community; the agricultural community; commercial and sport fishing interests; and recreational boaters] met in May 1990...to collectively decide whether cooperative water resource planning might be an acceptable and effective way to deal with the complex issues surrounding our decisions on water. [Cottingham 1993]

After the group met again in the fall of 1990 at Chelan, the process they proposed for deciding water resource issues became known as the Chelan Agreement. It proposed that a new Water Resources Forum be established to shape state water policy, clarify existing terms and policies, recommend changes to state law, and provide policy guidance on critical water resource issues as needed (Dyer 1993). Recommendations would "build on the existing system of water rights" and would "in no way affect existing water rights without the consent of the water rights holder" (Dyer 1993:155). The forum would include six representatives of Indian tribes; three representatives each from state government, local government, business, agriculture, and environmental interests; and one representative each from recreation and sport and commercial fishing interests. The three fishing representatives would serve together as a caucus. Decisions would be made by consensus, defined as no negative votes from any caucus of representatives (Dyer 1993; K. Cottingham, attorney at law, personal communication).

The Chelan Agreement set out principles for at least two pilot watershed planning processes, one in the Puget Sound area and one in eastern Washington, each on the scale of at least one WRIA. Though the processes would operate within the Water Resources Act of 1971, a participating government from the planning area, not WDOE, would coordinate the planning effort. WDOE would have authority to approve or remand the plan that resulted, but could not amend it directly. A planning committee would include at least the same caucuses as the forum and would also operate by consensus, except that decisions could be made with a consensus of the government caucuses and support from a majority of the interest group caucuses. The committee would determine the scope of its planning effort, which could be comprehensive or could focus on groundwater, surface water, consumptive needs, or non-consumptive needs. Guidelines regarding the outcomes to be sought from the plans were to be developed before pilot planning processes got underway. All plans would be required to include a statement that "nothing herein authorizes the impairment of any treaty or other right of an Indian tribe or member under federal law" (Dyer 1993).

In an addendum to the Chelan Agreement, each caucus described its goals for the process. Tribes wanted instream flows for fish and wildlife to be a mandatory element of every plan, and argued that such flows should have a priority date of "time immemorial," making them paramount to all other uses of water. Agriculture wanted assurance of "a plentiful and quality water supply to accommodate future needs" (Dyer 1993). Businesses wanted certainty and predictability that water supplies would sustain economic growth. Local governments wanted assurance that water supplies would be sufficient to meet growth management targets, habitat protection would be realistic, and costs would be equitably shared. Environmentalists and recreational and fishing interests sought a net improvement in water-dependent ecosystems, including restoration of instream flows in overallocated streams.

Post-Chelan: Putting Watershed Planning "in the Hands of the People"

The Chelan Agreement governed only process. Though some of its principles were ultimately inserted in the state's Watershed Planning Act, the Chelan process was never really applied. Governor Booth Gardner's office coordinated development of the Agreement, but Governor Mike Lowry was elected in 1992 and was not similarly committed to supporting its implementation. Pilot processes applying the Chelan principles were proposed for the Methow River and the Dungeness River portion of WRIA 18. Though the process had some success in the Dungeness, this took advantage of work that the Jamestown S'Klallam Tribe had already begun with local farmers (P. Crain, Clallam County, personal communication). (The Dungeness is also the only major river basin in Puget Sound that has been adjudicated, at the request of farmers in the 1920s.) Guidelines for plan results under the Chelan Agreement were never completed. A task force recommended to develop proposed legislation on water conservation never submitted a proposal to the legislature. The Water Resource Forum was created, but its recommendations were largely ignored and it ultimately disbanded. Consensus among the caucuses proved difficult, in part because of an impression among most other interests that the tribes had the most to gain from the process (Adelsman, personal communication).

In September 1993, as faith in the Chelan Agreement was fading, the Washington State Supreme Court issued what came to be known as "the Sinking Creek decision," which made resolving state water issues even more difficult (*Rettkowski v. Department of Ecology* 1993). The decision grew out of WDOE's attempt to enforce the seniority of water claims, which ranchers in the case said dated to before the 1917 Water Code, allowing them to water their cattle in Sinking Creek and adjacent ponds and springs, about 65 miles west of Spokane. After a WDOE study showed that the creek and ponds were drying up from groundwater pumping by nearby irrigators (under permits issued in the 1950s), WDOE ordered the irrigators to stop pumping "to protect senior surface water rights" (*Rettkowski v. Department of Ecology* 1993:223). A majority of the state supreme court found that WDOE did not have authority to enforce the seniority of water claims without a formal adjudication of water rights. The court acknowledged that adjudication was not a "cheap and easy" solution (*Rettkowski v. Department of Ecology* 1993:225). In fact, since the 1970s the only large-scale adjudication of water rights in the state has been in the Yakima River basin, which had been underway for 16 years at the time of the supreme court decision and continues today, 13 years later. (The State Attorney General's Office estimates that the case will conclude between 2007 and 2012 [Pharris et al. 2002].) In a dissenting opinion, Justice Richard Guy said that the majority's solution was "bad law and bad policy," which required "prohibitively expensive and interminable litigation" instead of allowing WDOE to make initial determinations of seniority, which WDOE already had to do when issuing new permits (*Rettkowski v. Department of Ecology* 1993:237, 238, 243). Guy hoped that the "absurdity" (*Rettkowski v. Department of Ecology* 1993:238) of the decision would lead to comprehensive reforms from the legislature:

> The Legislature must consider whether western water law meets today's societal needs, given the understanding that water is not an infinite resource. The Legislature must now examine the water resources of this state and determine, for example (1) who controls those resources; (2) the extent of all government allocations of those water resources; (3) the present water usage from all sources, allocated and unallocated; (4) what water resources will be available in the future; (5) what future water needs will be; (6) how water allocations should be made; (7) what public interest is involved in water allocations and use; and, (8) if water allocations are to be changed as to existing users, whether under existing law that constitutes a taking for which compensation must be paid. [*Rettkowski v. Department of Ecology* 1993:243]

In the 13 years since the *Sinking Creek* decision, the legislature has not taken up Guy's challenge. In 1994, Republicans gained a majority of the state house of representatives and a near-majority of the state senate (where a 25–24 Democratic majority included a number of rural conservatives, who were aligned with Republicans on many issues[6]). In what many saw as retribution for WDOE's denial of groundwater applications and its attempts to enforce state water laws, the 1995 legislature cut WDOE's Water Resources budget dramatically and cut it still more 2 years later, after Republicans gained control of the state senate in the 1996 elections (CELP and WEC 2002). This led to the legislature nearly eliminating WDOE's enforcement program and causing a major slowdown in processing water rights applications. The huge resulting backlog (CELP and WEC 2002; Adelsman, personal communication) of applications further angered legislators, though they were primarily responsible for the problem.

With Republicans in control, the legislature approved its initial version of the Watershed Planning Act in 1997. Governor Gary Locke vetoed most of it but supported its initial sections, which he said "set the tone for how we will resolve many of our water problems."[7] The approved sections included the following findings:

> The local development of [watershed] plans serves vital local interests by placing

---

6 Numbers from Legislative Information Center; comment on Democrats from H. Adelsman, personal communication, and author's own observations.

Governor's explanation of partial veto of Second Senate House Bill 2054, chapter 442, laws of 1997.

> it in the hands of people: Who have the greatest knowledge of both the resources and the aspirations of those who live and work in the watershed; and who have the greatest stake in the proper, long-term management of the resources. The development of such plans serves the state's vital interests by ensuring that the state's water resources are used wisely, by protecting existing water rights, by protecting instream flows for fish, and by providing for the economic well-being of the state's citizenry and communities. [RCW 90.82.010]

The sections of the act that Locke approved established a watershed planning process under which WDOE provides grants to organize and support local planning but otherwise has a very limited role. Before the next legislative session, the director of WDOE worked with legislative leaders and water interests to craft language to replace the vetoed sections. Indian tribes and environmental groups generally opposed the result, but the legislature passed it with little change in 1998 and it guides the state's approach to water resources planning today.

State-authorized watershed plans, for one or more WRIAs, must be initiated with the concurrence of all counties in the planning area as well as the largest city and largest water utility (RCW 90.82). Initiating governments must invite all tribes with reservations in the planning area to participate. If the tribes agree to participate, they are also to be treated as initiating governments. State agencies are required to assist watershed plans "at the request of and to the extent desired" by the local planning body. Watershed plans must quantify the amount of water available, the amount being used, the amount of water rights and claims, and other key data for the planning area (though adjudication remains the only means to determine the validity of water claims and to confirm priority dates for all rights and claims that draw from a particular waterbody). Watershed plans must also include strategies for increasing the amount of water available for both instream and out-of-stream uses. At the discretion of the initiating governments, watershed plans may include habitat and water quality elements and may recommend instream flows for adoption by WDOE. The planning body may also recommend establishing small reserves of water for future use, which are given priority over adopted instream flows (Blomstrom et al. 2005 and K. Allston, Quinalt Indian Nation, personal communication). If the planning body approves instream flows or these reserves, WDOE cannot change them. If the planning body has not approved a flow within 4 years of receiving funding, WDOE may proceed establishing flows as otherwise authorized by law. As in the Chelan Agreement, plans can only be adopted by a consensus of participating government representatives and a majority vote of non-government representatives on the body overseeing the plan.

This system has failed in Central Puget Sound, from Skagit County in the north to Pierce County in the south as well as in Kitsap County (Blomstrom et al. 2005). It was never even attempted in the Stillaguamish, Snohomish, Lake Washington, Green/Duwamish, and Puyallup/White watersheds. In the upper and lower Skagit River watershed, the Chambers/Clover Creek watershed in Pierce County, the Deschutes

River watershed in Thurston County, and on the Kitsap Peninsula, planning groups were established under the law but the process was terminated, typically because Indian tribes opposed key recommendations. The opposition of tribes was a major reason the process never began in the other watersheds. Among other reasons, tribes have been concerned that approving instream flows through this process could diminish their treaty rights to flows that would support salmon harvests (Allston, personal communication; see Chapter 13, pages 309–311, for a discussion of treaty rights to water).

The watershed planning process has progressed in about half of the Puget Sound ecoregion, including the Nooksack and Nisqually watersheds, San Juan and Island counties, and all watersheds on the Olympic Peninsula within the ecoregion except for the Kitsap Peninsula (Blomstrom et al. 2005). In the Nooksack, the planning group is working through a mediated settlement process to quantify treaty reserved water rights for the Lummi and Nooksack tribes. The Nisqually Tribe led development of the Nisqually plan, which did not attempt to change existing instream flow rules set for the Nisqually River in 1981. The plan did recommend further stream flow analysis to improve flows on the Mashell River, the Nisqually's largest tributary. The plan also recommended additional efforts in water conservation, reuse, and reclamation, as well as processing of new water rights applications in selected sub-basins. The two island counties did not address flow issues for their streams, which tend to be small, and instead focused on water supply challenges. On the Olympic Peninsula, planning groups recommended flows for the Dungeness River and its lower tributaries, the Quilcene River and for some of the smaller systems emptying into the western Strait of Juan de Fuca. At this stage, though, no new flows have been adopted for any streams on the Olympic Peninsula or anywhere else in Puget Sound under the watershed planning process.[8] Recommendations for the Dungeness have run into opposition, as did WDOE's process to adopt an instream flow rule for the Quilcene.

Bringing the Story Up to Date

The most important change to state water law since the Watershed Planning Act came in 2003 with adoption of the Municipal Water Law (Second Engrossed Second Substitute House Bill 1338). This law authorized all public water suppliers that serve 15 or more connections (including both public and private purveyors) to "grow into" their water rights and use them across their entire approved service areas—even in over-appropriated basins where their service areas have grown substantially since their rights were originally approved. While utilities lobbied hard for this authority, the final law balanced it with new obligations, most importantly a schedule to develop and implement regulations for conservation by the State Department of Health, which oversees utilities providing drinking water. The regulations, originally scheduled for adoption in 2005, are now scheduled for public review in summer 2006, with adoption in the fall. As of May

[8] WDOE established a new instream flow rule for the Stillaguamish River in 2005, but did so outside of the watershed planning process.

2006, the Health Department was proposing regulations with three key elements:

1. Planning Requirements: evaluate rate systems that would encourage conservation (i.e., higher rates for higher usage); implement a specified number of water use efficiency measures deemed cost-effective, the number varying based on the size of the water system, or explain why these measures were not adopted.
2. Leakage Standard: by 2016, install meters to calculate actual usage and leakage from the distribution system; limit leakage to 10% or less of water used (not counting losses in transmission to the system); implement Water Loss Control Plans to bring substandard systems into compliance.
3. Goal-Setting and Reporting: establish water conservation and efficiency goals in a public process; report annually on performance to customers, the state and the public (WDOH 2006).

Environmental groups and tribes are concerned about these regulations on a number of grounds, including the few substantive requirements, the length of time allowed before metering is required, and the uncertainty of enforcement, in part due to limited funding (S. Nixon, Center for Environmental Law and Policy, personal communication). These concerns are grounded in experience. Since 1993, for example, the state has required metering for all new surface water withdrawals and, in areas with a depressed stock of salmon, for *all* withdrawals greater than 1 cubic foot per second. Yet even after a successful lawsuit against the state for not implementing this law, the court order recognized that the legislature was not prepared to fund full implementation, and so called for metering only users responsible for 80% of total withdrawals in 16 "fish critical" watersheds across the state (see map, Figure 11-3; *American Rivers v. Washington State Department of Ecology* 2001).

In the Central Puget Sound area, local governments and other water interests have been searching for a workable alternative to the state's watershed planning process for years now. WRIA-based salmon conservation plans have typically mentioned instream flows as a concern, but at most have identified possible actions that might help improve flows, with few specifics and no commitments. Seattle and Tacoma developed Habitat Conservation Plans with flow provisions for their watersheds in the Cedar and Green river basins, respectively.[9] In 2001, the Central Puget Sound Water Suppliers Forum (including water utilities and county governments from Snohomish, King and Pierce counties) developed projections for future demand across the region, identifying areas that would likely experience shortages over the next 20 to 50 years (CPSWSF 2001). The forum also identified options for addressing increased water demands, acknowledging that this should include alleviating priority flow problems for fish. So far, however, the region has not even prioritized these flow problems, let alone begun to address them. In 2003, environmental groups, utilities, local govern-

[9] The Muckleshoot Indian Tribe did not endorse Seattle's HCP and later sued the city over flow issues. The parties reached a settlement agreement that limited future water withdrawals and gave the tribe access to the watershed for hunting.

ments and the state proposed the Central Puget Sound Regional Water Initiative to develop a comprehensive solution to these issues, but it fizzled before it even formally began because of tribal opposition (Allston, personal communication).

In 2005, King County and the Cascade Water Alliance (a coalition of suburban utilities that receive water from Seattle's system but that must find new sources for future needs) chartered an agreement (Cascade Water Alliance and King County 2005), which has grown into a broader water supply planning process that may ultimately cover the entire county (King County 2005). By the end of 2007, participants hope to update the forum's demand forecasts; use improved environmental criteria to evaluate all supply options, including reclaimed water (particularly from King County's new Brightwater wastewater treatment plant) and the possible use of Lake Tapps as a new regional source (see Figure 11-4); prioritize tributary streams for flow improvements; and evaluate the potential impacts of climate change on all options. This is an ambitious agenda. If this process is successful, it will set important precedents for solving challenging water issues throughout the region, especially for urbanized areas.

The Hardest Decisions Remain: Adjudication, Tribal Rights, and Water Conservation

The Central Puget Sound Regional Water Initiative failed in part because of larger challenges that still face water planning processes in King County and across the region. Without adjudicating the thousands of water claims in each WRIA, it is impossible to know how much water can legally be withdrawn from them. Without monitoring the thousands of exempt wells in each WRIA and metering all permitted withdrawals, it is impossible to know how much water actually *is* being withdrawn. More science may help set instream flows for fish, but legally those flows will continue to be junior to all rights granted before them—unless they are protected by tribal treaty rights (which must be confirmed either by negotiations or litigation) or by the Endangered Species Act (whose role in protecting flows remains untested in the region; see Chapters 7 and 8, especially page 171). Scientific approaches to setting flows are complex, expensive, and still hold many uncertainties. It is therefore practically difficult to set flows for tributaries as well as major rivers, though tributaries are inherently more sensitive to water withdrawals, simply by being smaller. Ecologists increasingly recognize the value of natural flows throughout the year (e.g., floods are necessary to create new habitats, high spring flows help move juvenile salmon out to sea; Currens et al. 2002). Groundwater is hydraulically linked to surface water and also supports microbiological communities that are key to filtering pollutants from aquifers (B. Richter, The Nature Conservancy, personal communication). Scientifically, it can no longer be argued that withdrawing "surplus" water does not harm fish or other native species if it leaves minimum stream flows. *All* water withdrawals involve environmental tradeoffs.

Washington's emphasis on watershed plans is in part a reasonable response to the

FIGURE 11-4. Lake Tapps, in north Pierce County, illustrates the complex challenges of water management in a heavily developed area. The lake's current size was created by diverting much of the base flow of the White River at river mile 24.3 to create a reservoir used by Puget Sound Energy for a hydroelectric dam. Flow is returned at river mile 3.5. The dam ceased operation in January 2004, providing an opportunity to restore these flows to the river. However, residents around the lake oppose lowering lake levels. The Cascade Water Alliance is seeking to withdraw 100 cubic feet per seond from the lake to serve growing King County suburbs, opposed by the Puyallup and Muckleshoot Indian Tribe and some cities. Negotiations continue regarding future flow diversions. Courtesy of the U.S. Geological Survey.

wide variation in the availability and use of water in the state. Nevertheless, Washington can learn much from other western states that have at least begun to take on some of the more fundamental contemporary problems raised by western water law. Idaho is systematically adjudicating water claims throughout the Snake River basin, which covers nearly 90% of the state (WDOE and Office of the Attorney General 2002). Oregon has given considerable authority to its water resource agency to determine the validity of water claims and to negotiate flows reserved by treaty to Indian tribes; aided by this, more than 75% of its watersheds have been adjudicated. Montana has established a Reserved Rights Compact Commission to negotiate treaty-reserved flows with Indian tribes. Once proposed flows are approved by the Montana legislature, tribal councils, and federal agencies, they will be incorporated into a long-term, statewide adjudication of water rights that is underway (Pharris et al. 2002). States in the southwest have also successfully negotiated flows reserved for Indian tribes and, at least in particular regions, have demonstrated the potential for saving water through aggressive conservation and reuse programs (R. Paschal, Center for Environmental Law and Policy, and B. Bennett, King County Department of Natural Resources and Parks, personal communications).

The state's proposal to require that utilities at least evaluate rate structures that would encourage conservation is both a disappointment and an opportunity. Experience in the City of Seattle and elsewhere has shown that changes in rate structure can lead to substantial conservation at little cost to most customers.[10] More fundamentally, the region should ask whether water should continue to be given away for free. Water is publicly owned, but water right holders pay only for the cost of withdrawing, transporting and, as necessary, treating it to drinking water standards. Their right is recognized as a form of property—a right to use—but it is not taxed. They may sell this right for large sums of money, while the public receives nothing. The practice of giving water away reflects many historic beliefs that are no longer widely held: water has no value unless it is put to human use; there is more than enough water to meet all human needs (a once-common view at least in the first parts of this country to be settled); and withdrawing surplus water causes no harm or even may benefit the environment (asserted by both WDOE and the legislative Joint Select Committee less than 20 years ago). Arguably, the lack of any charge for water withdrawals is also justified because water is a necessity for human life (though users are still charged for all other costs to deliver clean water to their taps).

Economists note that when something is sold at less than its true cost, demand will tend to overwhelm supply. The International Conference on Water and the Environment (held in Dublin, Ireland in 1992) concluded that water has an economic value in all its competing uses and should be recognized as an "economic good" (Gustanski 2003). Effectively, this would require a tax on water use. To send the most meaningful market signals, the amount of such a tax should relate in some way

[10] For examples of reductions due to changes to rate structures and a good discussion of price elasticity, see Chesnutt et al. 1997. For an example from Texas of how rates reduced consumption by 15%, see Nieswiadomy and Fox 1996.

to the ecological cost of withdrawing water. It therefore should allow for some variation between different parts of the state and different times of the year (since the ecologiocal cost of withdrawals varies across the state and withdrawals during the low flow season, from summer through early fall, generally come at greater ecological cost than at other times of the year). This could be a powerful motivation toward conservation; it could also discourage the use of existing water rights for low-value purposes. Given the very different political, economic, and environmental circumstances across the state, it might be best to propose such a tax only for the Puget Sound area.

Since at least the 1980s, conservation has consistently been the least costly and most popular option to meet increasing demands for water in Washington, but there has been relatively little state or regional action to implement it. In 1987, citizen letters on WDOE's instream flow proposal "almost unanimously supported preservation of instream resources, optimum flows for fisheries and recreation, and mandatory water conservation" (WDOE 1987:25). In 1989, the legislature's Joint Select Committee called conservation "the quickest path to development of additional water" (Joint Select Committee on Water Resource Policy 1989:28). A statewide poll in 2002 found that 65% of voters supported mandatory water conservation standards for water utilities, with only 27% opposed.[11] Numerous partnerships have developed over recent years to promote and facilitate water conservation programs in the region, including the Partnership for Water Conservation, the Water Conservation Coalition of Puget Sound, and the Saving Water Partnership. But much more can be done.

With increasing demand for water from a growing population, the only alternatives to conservation are transferring water from less populated areas (which would have considerable environmental consequences, potentially where ecological values are greater), increasing storage (which also would have major environmental consequences, at a cost of hundreds of millions of dollars for major new supplies), and reusing wastewater or stormwater (both of which are feasible only in certain places, typically costing the most of all these alternatives). The first and second alternatives also bring a serious risk of litigation, under either the Endangered Species Act, tribal treaties, or both. For the foreseeable future, increased conservation remains the obviously preferred option.

References

American Rivers v. Washington State Department of Ecology, Thurston County Superior Court No. 99-2-00480-6, Ecology's Compliance Plan (2001).

Arizona v. San Carlos Apache Tribe, 463 U.S. 545 (1983).

Blomstrom, G., W. Bolender, and B. Anderson. 2005. Progress on Watershed Planning and Setting Instream Flows: A Report to the Washington State Legislature. Washington Department of Ecology, Publication #05-11-038. Olympia, Washington.

[11] As reported in CELP (2002:footnote 140), the firm of Fairbank, Maslin, Maullin and Associates polled 500 voters statewide between May 18 and 21, 2002 for the Washington Environmental Council.

Cascade Water Alliance and King County. 2005. Memorandum of understanding on water resource and supply planning between Cascade Water Alliance and King County, Washington. February 8, 2005. Seattle.

CELP (Enter for Environmental Law and Policy). 2002. Washington's wa$ted water. The Center for Environmental Law and Policy, Seattle.

CELP. 2004. H2Grow: Washington's burgeoning population leads us to ask: where will they get their water. Washington Waterwatch 21:4, Center for Environmental Law and Policy, Seattle.

CELP (Center for Environmental Law and Policy) and WEC (Washington Environmental Council). 2002. Dereliction of duty: Washington's failure to protect our shared waters. Available: http://www.wecprotects.org/streams/pdfs/waterreport.pdf (March 2006)

Chesnutt, T. W., J. A. Beecher, P. C. Mann, D. M. Clark, W. M. Hanemann, and G. A. Raftelis. 1997. Designing, evaluating, and implementing conservation rate structures. California Urban Water Conservation Council, Sacramento.

Cottingham, K. 1993. Developing a water resource process. Pages 141–154 *in* P. Dyer, editor. Whose water: past, present, future. University of Washington, Institute of Environmental Studies, Seattle.

CPSWSF (Central Puget Sound Water Suppliers Forum). 2001. Central Puget Sound Regional Water Supply Outlook, Seattle.

Currens, K. P., H. W. Li, J. D. McIntyre, W. F. Megahan, and D. W. Reiser. 2002. Instream flows for salmon. Independent Science Panel, Technical Memorandum 2002-1, Olympia, Washington. Available: http://www.governor.wa.gov/gsro/science/documents.htm (March 2006).

Dyer, P. 1993. Whose water? Past; present; future. University of Washington, Institute for Environmental Studies, Seattle.

Gustanski, J. 2003. How does water fit in your wallet? Center for Environmental Law and Policy, Washington Waterwatch No. 19, Seattle.

Hobbs, Jr., G. 2001. State water politics versus an independent judiciary: the Colorado and Idaho experiences. Quinnipiac Law Review 20:669–696.

Joint Select Committee on Water Resource Policy. 1989. Report to the legislature. Joint Select Committee on Water Resource Policy, Olympia, Washington.

King County. 2005. King County water supply planning process: planning framework summary. October 31, 2005. Seattle.

Lane, R.C. 2004. Estimated domestic, irrigation, and industrial water use in Washington, 2000. U.S. Geological Survey. Scientific Investigations Report 2004-5015. Tacoma, Washington.

Nieswiadomy, M., and T. Fox 1996. Calculating water savings using a spreadsheet program. Pages 105–110 *in Proceedings of Conserv96:* Responsible water stewardship. American Water Works Association, Denver.

Pharris, J. K., and P. T. McDonald. 2000. An introduction to Washington water law. Washington State Office of Attorney General, Olympia.

Pharris, J., M. S. Wilson, and A. Reichman. 2002. Federal and Indian reserved water rights. A report to the Washington State Legislature by the Office of the Attorney General, State of Washington, Olympia.

Rettkowski v. Department of Ecology, 122 Wn.2d 219, 858 P.2d 232 (1993).

WDOE (Washington Department of Ecology). 1987. Preferred alternative: instream resources and water allocation program review. Washington Department of Ecology, Olympia.

WDOE (Washington Department of Ecology). 2001. Setting instream flows in Washington State. Washington Department of Ecology, Publication No.1813-WR, Olympia.

WDOE (Washington Department of Ecology) and Office of the Attorney General. 2002. Streamlining the Water Rights General Adjudication Procedures. Washington Department of Ecology and the Office of the Attorney General, Publication No. 02-11-019, Olympia.

WDOH (Washington Department of Health). 2006. Fact Sheets, Water Use Efficiency Rule. Washington Department of Health, Publications #331-302, 331-303, 331-304, 331-305, 331-306, 331-340, Olympia, Washington.

Chapter 12. Water Quality: Inseparable from the Land Around It

> The objective of [the Clean Water Act] is to restore and maintain the chemical, physical, and biological integrity of the Nation's waters. [Clean Water Act, U.S. Code, volume 33, section 1251(a)]

Chapter Summary

Laws regarding water quality and water withdrawals have generally developed separately from each other—so much so that Washington is unusual among western states in placing responsibility for both issues in the same agency, the Washington Department of Ecology (WDOE; Reisner and Bates 1990; Pharris and McDonald 2000). In contrast to the federal government's general deference to state law for water withdrawals, the federal Clean Water Act (CWA) is the fundamental framework for most state laws protecting water quality, in Washington and elsewhere. Since the CWA was passed in 1972, it has helped bring about enormous reductions in pollution across the country, particularly from industries and sewage plants. Largely as a result, waters near the most intensely developed marine and river shorelines of the Puget Sound region are generally much cleaner and healthier today than they were 30 years ago.

Nationally and regionally, the most serious water pollution problems that remain are the most intractable. The large majority relate to stormwater runoff from land that humans have altered. Effective solutions must typically address combinations of issues, including land use, development practices, transportation systems, and the daily choices of thousands or even millions of people (whether to fix leaks in car engines, use fertilizer or herbicides, pick up pet wastes, etc.). Solutions are generally best crafted for whole watersheds. Where should growth go? Where should technical assistance and education programs be targeted? Where is it most important to retain or restore native vegetation? Watershed planning groups across most of the region are debating these issues, in attempts to meet requirements of the CWA, the Endangered Species Act (ESA), state laws, and local and regional goals. Participating organizations—which commonly include local governments, state and federal agencies, businesses, community groups, and Indian tribes—individually can address some of the issues. But the watershed groups themselves generally have no authority to enforce their recommendations and little, if any, money to assist implementation. Regional processes to coordinate land-use decisions were similarly hamstrung before the Growth Management Act (see Chapter 10). Just as the legislature ultimately gave such authorities to regional planning bodies for land use, it may give watershed groups more authority and funding as the problems they are trying to address become more visible and urgent. In fact, since the futures of water and land are inseparable, recommendations of watershed planning *must* ultimately be embodied in growth management plans and land-use decisions to succeed.

As discussed in Chapter 10, there are no known ways to avoid some degradation of water quality and ecological values when surrounding areas develop. Nevertheless, the

CWA's goals for waterbodies make no distinctions based on surrounding land uses. For the most part, neither do the goals of WDOE's stormwater regulations, which constitute the state's most important effort to address the relationship between land development and water quality. Setting the same goals for all streams may sound noble, but it can have counterproductive consequences. WDOE's regulations do not yet apply across the region, but if they did, they could create economic incentives for development in less urbanized areas, where it would be less expensive to meet state standards. If state courts find these regulations place what should be a public burden on some private developments, the courts could throw out the regulations for violating substantive due process (see Chapter 6, pages 97–99). An independent scientific review criticized WDOE's "one size fits all" approach, arguing that watershed analyses could target stricter requirements where they will do the most good (Currens et al. 2003). WDOE acknowledges the validity of this criticism (E. O'Brien, WDOE Water Quality Program, personal communication), but such analyses are currently available for very few places.

WDOE's regulations generally remain the best available across the Puget Sound area, as the independent scientific review found. But they are not the best the region can do. If the region is to meet its goals for water quality and aquatic ecosystems as it continues to grow, it must develop effective alternatives to WDOE's regulations that are more affordable and equitable and do not create counterproductive economic incentives. Such regulations cannot be "one size fits all" in either the goals they set for different streams or the means they choose to achieve them. This is challenging, technically and politically, but the current approach risks spending even more money while the region's major aquatic ecosystems continue to decline.

The Clean Water Act: A Necessary First Step

After a long campaign from fishing interests and oyster growers in the Puget Sound area, Washington State passed its first water pollution control law in 1945 (Chasan 1981). Proponents were most concerned about discharges from pulp and paper mills, which came to the shores of Puget Sound in the 1920s. The mills were generally located on sheltered bays, which offered safe anchorage for ships but also tended to concentrate mill effluents, deoxygenating nearby waters and suffocating marine life (Chasan 1981). Canneries, smelters, and other industries had freely polluted the sound for decades, but pulp and paper mills introduced water pollution on a scale the region had never experienced before (Chasan 1981). A state study in the 1930s found that decomposing wood wastes from a single large mill could draw as much oxygen from the water as untreated sewage from a city of 1.4 million people (Eriksen and Townsend 1940, cited in Brown 1995). During the Depression, however, the politically powerful mills provided much needed jobs and they continued to avoid serious regulation even after the state water pollution act was passed. In 1951, the federal government identified Puget Sound as the sixth most polluted area in the country (Chasan 1981). Well into the 1950s and 1960s, discharges of metals and many other toxins continued to increase at industrialized locations across Puget Sound (MacDonald and Crecelius 1994). Partly as a result, by 1956 the annual harvest of Olympia oysters was less than a tenth of its 1935 level, which already had fallen well below pre-mill days (Chasan 1981).

Some regional efforts to reduce water pollution succeeded. Most notably, in 1958 voters in the Seattle area created a new agency, Metro, to transport and treat sewage that had been fouling Lake Washington and other parts of the area. The project was "the first major commitment to fighting pollution made in any metropolitan area in the United States," as a historian of Puget Sound later said (Chasan 1981). Within a few years of Metro's operation, water quality in the lake and other affected areas had obviously improved. The new treatment plants discharged effluent deep into Puget Sound, where the water is less sensitive to the nutrients in sewage, particularly since powerful currents quickly mix and dilute them (Edmondson 1991).

As the environmental movement grew nationally in the 1960s, two events in 1969 focused concerns on water pollution. On January 29, an oil rig off the coast of Santa Barbara, California, accidentally opened holes in a fault below the ocean, releasing some 200,000 gallons of crude oil that spread across 800 square miles of ocean and 35 miles of coastline, killing seabirds, whales, and other marine life.[1] On June 22, the Cuyahoga River in Cleveland, Ohio, gained infamy by bursting into flames, fueled by oil and other industrial wastes (Adler et al. 1993). Two years later, the Second Annual Report of the President's Council on Environmental Quality found that one-third of U.S. waters were "characteristically polluted." Late the following year, an overwhelming and bipartisan majority of Congress approved the CWA of 1972 over the veto of President Nixon, who had objected to its cost. Senator Edmund Muskie of Maine, who led the fight for the act, stated the case for the final vote as follows:

> Can we afford clean water? Can we afford rivers and lakes and streams and oceans which continue to make possible life on this planet? Can we afford life itself? Those questions were never asked as we destroyed the waters of our Nation, and they deserve no answers as we finally move to restore and renew them. These questions answer themselves. And those who say that raising the amounts of money called for in this legislation may require higher taxes, or that spending this much money may contribute to inflation simply do not understand...this crisis. [Adler et al. 1993:2]

The objective of the CWA "is to restore and maintain the chemical, physical, and biological integrity of the Nation's waters." To meet this objective, Congress laid out an ambitious set of goals, including

(1) It is the national goal that the discharge of pollutants into the navigable waters be eliminated by 1985;
(2) It is the national goal that wherever attainable, an interim goal of water quality which provides for the protection and propagation of fish, shellfish, and wildlife and provides for recreation in and on the water be achieved by July 1, 1983 [this goal is popularly described as requiring that all waters be "fishable and swimmable"]; and

[1] For details, see http://www.geog.ucsb.edu/~jeff/sb_69oilspill/69oilspill_articles2.html.

(3) It is the national goal that the discharge of toxic pollutants in toxic amounts be prohibited....[CWA, section 1251{a}]

The Environmental Protection Agency (EPA) was put in charge of administering most aspects of the act. The U.S. Army Corps of Engineers was given the lead over permits for dredging and filling. These permits notably evolved within a few years to include actions affecting wetlands (see pages 280–283, below). However, Congress anticipated that state governments would actually implement most of the CWA's key provisions:

> It is the policy of the Congress to recognize, preserve, and protect the primary responsibilities and rights of States to prevent, reduce, and eliminate pollution, to plan the development and use (including restoration, preservation and enhancement) of land and water resources, and to consult with the Administrator [of the EPA] in the exercise of his authority under this chapter....[CWA, section 1251{b}]

Consistent with the Tenth Amendment to the U.S. Constitution (see Chapter 6, pages 87–88), states cannot be mandated to implement the CWA. Instead, they are given the choice of having the EPA implement it within their jurisdiction or doing it themselves, with EPA financial assistance and oversight. States have generally chosen the latter option for most elements of the CWA. In Washington, as in most states, the state has assumed four broad responsibilities under the act:

1. Administering a system of permits to limit the discharge of water pollutants (known as the National Pollution Discharge Elimination System, or NPDES, though only in rare cases do the permits require the complete elimination of pollutants);
2. Monitoring and evaluating the quality of waterbodies to determine if they are capable of supporting desired uses;
3. Developing and supporting plans and actions to improve water quality, including the distribution of federal and state grants and loans; and
4. Certifying that actions requiring federal permits or licenses will not cause violations of water quality standards or contribute to continuing violations.

Implementing the Clean Water Act: Point Sources Receive the Initial Focus

NPDES permits are typically the strongest regulatory tool available to clean up water pollution.[2] Largely for that reason, they received the greatest initial attention from the EPA and state agencies. NPDES permits are required for all "point" sources of pollution (individual sources that discharge potentially large amounts of pollutants, such as factories or sewage treatment plants; "non-point" sources, such as automobiles or fertilized lawns, contribute small amounts of pollution individually, though cumulatively they may be large sources). NPDES permits restrict the amounts of specified pollutants that a point source may discharge. The limits must be at least as strict as national guidelines EPA establishes for specific industries, based on the "best available technology economically achievable" (in Washington State, the operative phrase is "All known, available and

[2] For an overview of the NPDES Permit program, see USEPA (2006a).

reasonable methods of prevention, control and treatment" [Washington Administrative Code {WAC} 173-220-020], but the effect is the same). Congress envisioned that the EPA guidelines would get stricter over time, as better technology became available and affordable (see Adler et al. 1993). Point sources are not allowed to discharge more than the guidelines for their industry. The guidelines are not based on a cost-benefit analysis, but require EPA to determine that affected industries can reasonably bear their costs (*CPC International Inc. v. Train* 1976). If a receiving waterbody does not meet water quality standards, the CWA allows NPDES permits to be stricter than EPA guidelines, based on a point source's allocation of the total amount of a given pollutant allowed into the waterbody (USEPA 2006a). NPDES permits may also be stricter than EPA guidelines, if that is necessary to keep a point discharge from substantially degrading the quality of a waterbody, even if the waterbody currently meets water quality standards (as might be the case for a factory discharging pollutants to a pristine stream, for example; USEPA 2006a). If the economic impacts of stricter standards in either of these cases are judged to be "substantial" and "widespread," the CWA allows a variance (USEPA 2006b). (In actual practice in Washington, WDOE issues few NPDES permits that are stricter than industry guidelines [G. Bailey, WDOE, personal communication], even when EPA would prefer tougher standards to help address known water quality problems downstream [R. Smith, updated letter to M. White, WDOE[3]].)

This permitting system has dramatically decreased the amount of pollution entering the nation's waters. It is a major reason why much of Puget Sound and at least parts of the area's river systems are considerably cleaner today than they were 30 or more years ago.[4] But non-point sources of water pollution have not seen similar improvements. In many cases, non-point pollution is probably far worse today than before passage of the Clean Water Act, principally because of increases in population and automobile use. Across the country, the EPA now estimates that point sources are solely responsible for about 10% of all violations of water quality standards, while non-point sources are solely responsible for 43%; for the 47% of cases where both are responsible, non-point sources are typically the more serious problem (USEPA 2006a). The relative importance of non-point sources is probably even greater in Washington (R. McBride, WDOE, personal communication), where bacterial pollution and high water temperatures are the two most frequent violations.

The CWA declares "it is the national policy that programs for the control of non-point sources of pollution be developed and implemented in an expeditious manner" (CWA, section 1251[a][7]). Nevertheless, the CWA provides EPA no regulatory authority over non-point pollution, nor does the CWA require states to establish regulations to address it (USEPA 2006a). The act authorizes federal funding to

[3] The letter concerned the Environmental Protection Agency's comments on proposed Section 3.3.11 "TMDL's and WLA's and 303(d) – Interim Permitting" of WDOE's Permit Writer's Manual.

[4] WDOE and other agencies have also overseen many different projects to clean up contaminated sediments (mostly due to pollutants discharged prior to NPDES permits) at sites throughout Puget Sound.

help implement state plans to address non-point pollution that have been approved by EPA, but the funds are small compared to the scale of the problem ($237 million was budgeted for the entire country in 2002 [USEPA 2006a]). In Washington, the state Water Pollution Control Act provides legal authority for enforcement against non-point sources of pollution (RCW 90.48). In practice, though, the state generally emphasizes voluntary compliance, technical assistance, and referral to local authorities before taking enforcement action against non-point sources. Statewide in 2001, WDOE took 10 formal enforcement actions against non-point sources of pollution, while making 542 partnering contacts (see Bernath 2003). Most of the enforcement actions as well as the contacts involved farms. Major sources of non-point pollution in urban areas—typically including automobiles, pet wastes, and lawn and yard care products (see, for example, Thornton Creek Watershed Management Committee 2001)—are particularly ill-suited to enforcement actions, since any one contributor is responsible for an extremely small part of the problem.

The CWA does, however, provide a means to address non-point pollution in urban areas. In 1987, Congress amended the act to require NPDES permits for large municipal stormwater programs, stormwater from industry (including construction sites), and combined sewer overflows (which result when sewage systems designed to carry stormwater—a common arrangement in older cities—are overwhelmed during large storms, forcing them to discharge untreated sewage at overflow points; CWA, section 1342[p]–[q]). All three activities were defined as point sources of pollution. The 1987 amendment required large municipal stormwater programs (in jurisdictions with more than 100,000 people) to "reduce the discharge of pollutants to the maximum extent practicable, [using] management practices, control techniques and system, design and engineering methods, and such other provisions as the [EPA] Administrator or the State determines appropriate" (CWA, section 1342[p][3][B]). Subsequent EPA regulations required municipal programs to

- map the locations of their outfalls;
- test water quality at a representative sample of their outfalls;
- eliminate non-stormwater connections (e.g., sewer drains) to their stormwater systems;
- describe current and projected land uses in their service area;
- develop and implement a strategic plan to reduce polluted runoff from current land uses and from new development or redevelopment; and
- estimate the effects of implementing their plans (USEPA 2006b).

A second phase of these regulations, issued in January 2000, extended a subset of these requirements to all other municipal stormwater programs in urban areas (i.e., in jurisdictions with fewer than 100,000 people; see USEPA 2000). Phase II municipal stormwater programs were required to include at least the following elements:

- Public education and outreach;
- Public participation and involvement (in developing stormwater control programs and regulations);

- Elimination of non-stormwater connections to stormwater systems;
- Pollution prevention guidelines;
- Stormwater controls for construction sites (which the Phase II regulations extended for all jurisdictions to sites as small as 1 acre); and
- Control of post-construction runoff from developed areas (USEPA 2000).

The last requirement is the most expensive and controversial. As of May 2006, how it and the others will be applied in Washington are still being negotiated between WDOE and the jurisdictions. Final permits are expected to be issued before the end of the year (O'Brien, personal communication). The jurisdictions must fully comply with requirements by the end of their permit terms, which typically last 5 years.

Toward the "Fishable and Swimmable" Goal: Water Quality Standards and TMDLs

Under the CWA, a state's most fundamental responsibility in monitoring and evaluating water quality is to identify the "designated" uses for its waterbodies, which the act requires states to protect. Designated uses may include drinking water, agricultural water supply, water-based recreation, and habitat for fish, shellfish, and wildlife.[5] Designated uses must include any use of a waterbody that has been feasible since the CWA's regulations went into effect in November 1975 (this was intended to ensure that the quality of the nation's waters did not worsen after the CWA[6]). Designated uses may also include other desired uses that could be attained through restoration efforts. Economic considerations are allowed when determining desired uses for restoration, but if a waterbody (or a particular section within it) would naturally be fishable or swimmable without man-made pollution, economic impacts must be substantial and widespread to justify not including fishing and swimming among its designated uses.[7] EPA establishes criteria for the water quality that each designated use requires; the CWA requires these to be based on science, and without economic considerations (USEPA 2006b). States must follow EPA criteria or demonstrate that state standards will protect uses at least as well. States must then monitor actual conditions to document whether their waters are meeting relevant standards. If even one standard for one use is not being met, the state must develop a "Total Maximum Daily Load" (TMDL) for the waterbody (USEPA 2006a). A TMDL sets the total amount of a pollutant that can enter a waterbody while meeting water quality standards (including a margin of safety and, in some cases, a reserve for future growth) and allocates this amount among different sources (including non-point sources).

[5] Where not otherwise specified, the summary of the act's provisions are from USEPA 2006a.

[6] See Code of Federal Regulations, volume 40, section 131.3(e): "Existing uses are those uses actually attained in the water body on or after November 28, 1975, whether or not they are included in the water quality standards." Even if an actual use has not occurred, if water quality capable of supporting it has been achieved, then that use is "existing" (B. Painter, Environmental Protection Agency, personal communication).

[7] See USEPA 2006b for details of how substantial and widespread economic impacts are evaluated.

After states and the EPA ignored TMDL requirements for two decades, citizen lawsuits in 1992 led EPA to issue guidance and an ambitious timetable for states to develop TMDLs to clean up waterbodies not meeting EPA standards. Since early 2000, when EPA attempted to update these rules, this program has been in disarray. In March 2000, the General Accounting Office (GAO) reported that most states had less than half the data they needed to assess whether their waters met CWA standards. Nationally, the GAO found that only 19% of river and stream miles, 10% of ocean shoreline, 40% of lake area, and 70% of estuary area had been assessed at all; only about half of these assessments were based on current, site-specific information (GAO 2000). Even for water quality problems that the states identified, the GAO found "a vast majority of states" had less than half the data needed to identify the sources of problems and to develop TMDLs (see GAO 2000). Following this study, Congress suspended EPA's new regulations in October 2000 and asked the National Research Council to report on the scientific basis for the TMDL program. After a short study, the council said the budget requirements to address the national backlog of TMDLs were "staggering" (NRC 2001a:2). Counting only those waterbodies where data was available, EPA estimated the backlog was greater than 40,000 TMDLs. A comprehensive and current assessment of all the country's waterbodies might dramatically increase this number (though probably not in proportion to the total number of waterbodies monitored, since current monitoring is generally focused on areas of known problems as well as areas used by the public). In March 2003, the Bush administration withdrew the rules for TMDLs that Congress had suspended (see Pegg 2003).

In November 2001, EPA issued new guidance to the states for monitoring and assessing water quality. Noting that a majority of the nation's waters "remain unmonitored and unassessed," the guidance agreed with the National Research Council in recommending a statistical approach to estimating the state of the nation's waters:

> It is not necessary nor practicable for states and territories to do site-specific monitoring of all waters to be able to make...an assessment of all waters [as the CWA requires]. EPA believes that a probabilistic monitoring design applied over large areas, such as a state or territory, is an excellent approach to producing, with known confidence, a "snapshot" or statistical representation of the extent of waters that may or may not be impaired. [Wayland 2001:2]

This would provide an overview of the condition of the nation's waters, but it would not provide the information necessary to know if a TMDL was needed to clean up a specific waterbody, unless it was part of the statistical sample. EPA called for all waterbodies to be placed in one of five categories:

1. Meeting standards and likely to continue doing so.
2. Meeting some standards but information is insufficient to determine if all are being attained.
3. Information is insufficient to determine if any standard is being met.

4. Not meeting one or more standards but no TMDL is required because
   a. a TMDL has already been completed; or
   b. other pollution control requirements are reasonably expected to result in meeting all standards in the near future; or
   c. the impairment is not caused by a pollutant [note: habitat degradation, flow modifications, channel alterations, the effects of previously introduced exotic species, or other actions that do not involve a "discharge" into water are not "pollutants" under the CWA].[8]
5. One or more water quality standards are being violated or likely will be violated within 2 years (Wayland 2001).

A TMDL is required only for waterbodies in Category 5.[9] However, under EPA's new policy, if a waterbody was previously found to require a TMDL, it may be removed from Category 5 only for good cause, including "more recent and accurate data, more sophisticated water quality modeling, flaws in the original analysis…or changes in conditions, e.g., new control equipment, or elimination of discharges" (Wayland 2001:3).

"TMDLs do not create any new federal regulatory authority over any type of sources" the EPA notes (USEPA 2006a). For point sources, TMDLs are supposed to include pollutant allocations that can be incorporated into NPDES permits. For non-point sources, however, EPA says that TMDLs are simply a source of information that, for a given waterbody, should answer such questions as the following:

- Are nonpoint sources a significant contributor of pollutants to this impaired waterbody?
- What are the approximate total current loads of impairment-causing pollutants from all nonpoint sources in the watershed?
- What fraction of total loads of the pollutant(s) of concern come from nonpoint sources vs. point sources?
- What are the approximate loadings from the major categories of nonpoint sources in the watershed?
- How much do loads from nonpoint sources need to be reduced in order to achieve the water quality standards for the waterbody?
- What kinds of management measures and practices would need to be applied to various types of nonpoint sources, in order to achieve the needed load reductions? [USEPA 2006b]

The regulations proposed by the Clinton administration in 2000 would have required implementation plans for TMDLs, with a schedule for actions to bring waterbodies into compliance with standards (N. Bell, Northwest Environmental Advocates, personal communication). Though the Bush administration's proposed TMDL regulations do

[8] See CWA, section 1362[6] for definition of "pollutant."

[9] This category corresponds to the water bodies listed as violating water quality standards under section 303(d) of the Clean Water Act, popularly known as "the 303(d) list."

not contain these requirements, in 1997 EPA and the state of Washington accepted a court settlement that included a timetable to complete TMDLs with implementation plans (see "TMDLs and Water Quality Standards in Washington State" below). Non-point plans typically must rely on at least some voluntary actions, but recommendations for urban stormwater programs can be required through NPDES permits. As noted previously, Washington can also take enforcement actions against non-point sources under state law (though it rarely does), and state and federal funding for nonpoint programs can prioritize actions recommended in implementation plans for TMDLs (though actual funding has never matched the scale of the problems). TMDLs can also lead to special conditions being placed on federal actions that would affect water quality. Probably the two most important such actions are the relicensing of dams (which may set flow requirements to address water quality issues downstream; *PUD No. 1 of Jefferson County v. WDOE* 1994; C. Maynard, WDOE, personal communication), and the issuing of permits for impacts to wetlands (L. Randall, WDOE Shoreland Environmental Assistance Program, personal communication).

Wetlands: Slowing but Not Stopping Losses

Before the CWA, regulatory protections for wetlands were nearly non-existent at the federal level and minimal at the Washington State and local levels. Wetland protections under the CWA are based on its requiring a permit "for the discharge of dredged or fill material into the navigable waters" (CWA, section 1344[a]). At first, the Corps of Engineers resisted extending this requirement beyond traditionally navigable waterways, which it had regulated to prevent obstructions since the Rivers and Harbors Act of 1899. However, though the CWA borrowed the term "navigable waters" from the Rivers and Harbors Act and earlier versions of federal water pollution control laws, it broadened the definition to encompass all "waters of the United States" (CWA, section 1362[7]). After federal courts, the Environmental Protection Agency, and leaders in Congress made it clear that the Corps of Engineers' narrow approach was inconsistent with this new definition and the goals of the CWA, the corps revised its initial regulations in 1975. The corps requires that three different factors—soils, vegetation, and hydrology—all demonstrate wetland characteristics to determine that a particular area is a wetland (USACE 2006). Its new regulations, finalized in 1977, broadened its permitting authority to include actions affecting even isolated wetlands and intermittent streams.[10] More recent federal court decisions have restricted this authority for isolated wetlands and other waterbodies that are not navigable themselves and that are not directly associated with navigable waters (see Chapter 6, pages 87–89).

Other recent court decisions have narrowed the corps' permitting authority in

[10] For a summary of this process, see *Solid Waste Agency of Northern Cook County v. Army Corps of Engineers* 2001:183–184.

another way, questioning whether the CWA's restriction against "the discharge of dredged or fill material" provides a sufficient basis for federal regulation of activities that affect the integrity and ecological functions of wetlands, if they do not introduce foreign material to them.[11] The Supreme Court deadlocked, 4–4, on a case from the Ninth Circuit Court of Appeals that would have helped answer this issue, when Justice Anthony Kennedy recused himself from the decision because of his acquaintance with the plaintiff.[12] The tie vote resulted in affirming the Court of Appeals' decision, which supported the CWA's authority in the case (which required a permit for "deep ripping" of wetlands[13]). The Ninth Circuit includes the Puget Sound area, so its broader approach to the CWA should generally apply to similar cases in the region. However, since other circuits have read the CWA more narrowly, this issue is likely to return to the Supreme Court, where Judge Kennedy's vote may lead to a different result.

Regardless, the CWA remains the primary basis for federal regulation of actions affecting wetlands. It is also the primary mechanism that Washington and most other states use to regulate these actions (McMillan 1998), through their responsibility to certify that federal permits will not contribute to violations of water quality standards. The CWA allows states to administer regulations against discharges to wetlands and other non-tidal waters directly, but nearly all states choose to let the corps take the lead,[14] in part because this saves them money while they retain approval authority under the certification process. However, for isolated wetlands no longer covered by the CWA, Washington has established its own regulatory system, issuing permits under administrative orders (WDOE 2001). The ultimate legal foundation for these orders is the state's Water Pollution Control Act, which gives WDOE authority "to control and prevent the pollution of…surface and underground waters of the State of Washington" (RCW 90.48.030). The act does not specifically include wetlands in its list of such waters, but a Thurston County Superior Court decision in 1993 ruled that all wetlands "bigger than puddles" are waters of the state (*Building Industries Association of Washington v. City of Lacey* 1993). Accordingly, since 1997 state water quality standards have defined wetlands as surface waters of the state to be governed by the state's anti-degradation policy, which generally follows that of

[11] See, for example, *National Mining Association v. U.S. Army Corps of Engineers* 1998, which found that the redeposit of dredged materials that incidentally fall back in the course of dredging operations did not require a 404 permit; *United States v. Wilson* 1997 found that sidecasting ditch materials in a wetland did not require a 404 permit.

[12] See *Borden Ranch Partnership v. U.S. Army Corps of Engineers* 2002 for the one sentence decision affirming the Court of Appeals decision because of an equally divided court. For the circuit court decision, which found that deep ripping of wetlands required a 404 permit, see *United States v. Nubour* 2001. Also see Egelko 2002.

[13] "Deep ripping" involves plowing up to seven or more feet through impermeable soils, such as clay or glacial till, to drain a wetland.

[14] Michigan and New Jersey are the only states in the country that have assumed direct responsibilities to regulate wetlands under Section 404 (C. Stark, Corps of Engineers, personal communication).

the CWA.[15] The state also regulates activities affecting wetlands under the Shoreline Management Act, the Hydraulic Code, and the Forest Practices Act.[16] However, in practice the most important non-federal wetland regulations affecting development are typically local regulations to protect critical areas under the Growth Management Act (see Chapter 10), which tend to focus on the size of wetland buffers. The other regulations apply only when direct impacts are proposed to wetlands themselves, rather than to their buffers; the latter is far more common.

In 1989, both Washington Governor Booth Gardner and the first President Bush set goals of "no net loss" of wetlands for the state and the nation, respectively (McMillan 1998; NRC 2001b). Neither goal has been achieved. A study by the U.S. Fish and Wildlife Service found that the nation lost an average of 58,545 acres of wetlands a year between 1986 and 1997 (NRC 2001b). That was, however, a vast improvement over the previous decade (the first under the corps' initial wetland regulations), when annual losses averaged more than four times that much (NRC 2001b). One reason dramatic losses continue is that projects to create or restore wetlands as mitigation for actual wetland impacts have frequently failed. In a 2001 study of this issue, the National Research Council found that some types of wetlands, such as fens and bogs, "cannot be effectively restored with present knowledge" (NRC 2001b:4). A 2002 WDOE study of 24 wetlands that were created or restored as mitigation for other wetland impacts found only three that fully met performance measures (Johnson et al. 2002). Federal guidelines for wetland permits have a strong preference for compensation as near to the impact as possible, but the National Research Council's study noted that these sites are often both constrained by development and permanently altered by changes to surrounding land (NRC 2001b). The National Research Council called for watershed evaluations at a landscape scale to help determine where and how wetland impacts are best mitigated (NRC 2001b). WDOE's study made similar recommendations. It argued in favor of wetland mitigation banks, which can "address regional concerns or identified management problems within a specific basin or watershed, such as sedimentation, water quality degradation, or flood control" (Johnson et al. 2002:92). A "banked" wetland is restored or created for the purpose of selling mitigation credits to other projects that impact wetlands within a specified area. Ideally, banked wetlands are larger, higher functioning, and ecologically more

---

[15] See WAC 173-201A-020 for definitions, and WAC 173-201A-300 to -330 for the antidegradation policy. For a general discussion of how these regulations are applied, see McMillan 1998. Complicating matters further, the state definition excludes artificial wetlands that are intentionally created and do not serve as mitigation for other wetland impacts, as well as wetlands unintentionally created by roads constructed after July 1, 1990. The CWA does not exempt these wetlands, so the corps' definition is based strictly on the characteristics of the site. See Code of Federal Regulations, volume 40, section 230.3(t); for a discussion of the corps' approach to recognizing wetlands, see www.usace.army.mil/inet/functions/cw/cecwo/reg/rw-bro.htm.

[16] The Shoreline Management Act (RCW 90.58) applies only to wetlands within 200 feet of shoreline water bodies and wetlands associated with these water bodies and is mostly administered locally. See Chapter 10 as well as McMillan 1998. The Hydraulic Code (RCW 77.55.100) requires a permit from the Washington Department of Fish and Wildlife for wetland actions that would affect the bed or flow of a stream. The Forest Practices Act (RCW 76.09) regulates forest practices that affect wetlands.

important than impacted wetlands, and have binding commitments for their ongoing maintenance and monitoring. Banked wetlands also can be built in advance, so their performance can be known before credits are sold (though even successfully restored or created wetlands may need 20 years or more to achieve their functional goals [NRC 2001b]). Wetland banks have much promise, but the ingredients for their success are not easy to bring together. Meanwhile, wetland losses continue incrementally, though far more slowly than before the CWA.

TMDLs and Water Quality Standards in Washington State

In October 1997, EPA and WDOE settled a lawsuit filed by two environmental organizations, Northwest Environmental Advocates and Northwest Environmental Defense Center, over the slow progress of TMDLs in Washington. The agreement requires WDOE to develop TMDLs for 1,566 violations of state water quality standards, which equals the number on the state's 1996 list (EPA, 1997 Memorandum of Agreement to the WDOE, regarding the implementation of Section 303(d) of the Federal Clean Water Act). Largely because Washington committed to develop detailed implementation plans for these TMDLs, the agreement gives WDOE until 2013 to complete them, with interim goals of 249 TMDLs by 2003 and 801 TMDLs by 2008 (Attachement A of EPA, Memorandum of Agreement). Low priority violations on the 1996 list can also be replaced by higher priority violations identified later. As of May 2006, WDOE was on schedule, having submitted 501 TMDLs to EPA (with EPA funding about three-fourths of the cost [McBride, personal communication]). While 336 of these had detailed implementation plans, at best they have just begun implementation (McBride, personal communication). Even where implementation plans have been completed, Northwest Environmental Advocates has a number of concerns about them. First, non-point recommendations may be implemented sporadically, if at all, given lack of funding to support voluntary solutions and the state's record of limited enforcement. Second, NPDES permits for point sources may be too lax, based on optimistic assumptions regarding pollution reductions from non-point sources. Third, if the plans have long implementation periods, interim targets may require so little improvement that stronger actions are not triggered even if little progress is being made (Bell, personal communication). The settlement agreement is vulnerable on this last point: it endorses an approach where "locally-driven programs [have] a chance to be successful before more restrictive measures are applied"; water quality standards need not be met until the end of the implementation planning period, which the agreement does not limit and which WDOE believes could extend 50 years in some cases. Northwest Environmental Advocates had little leverage to require faster implementation, since federal regulations do not require that TMDLs have implementation plans at all (McBride, personal communication). Federal regulations also set no standards for what will be accepted as best management practices to reduce non-point sources of pollution (Bell, personal communication).

The National Research Council's report on TMDLs warned against focusing on "administrative outcomes [e.g., the number of TMDLs developed] as measures of success for the TMDL program" (NRC 2001b:3). Instead, it stressed that "first and foremost" the focus should be on "improving the condition of waterbodies as measured by attainment of designated uses." By this measure, even non-point plans that Washington began implementing before the settlement agreement have not been successful so far. Not one plan has yet led to a waterbody coming into compliance with water quality standards (McBride, personal communication). The blame for this cannot simply be assigned to WDOE, since it has little funding to assist implementation, no authority to require land-use changes, and little political support for enforcement actions. When the agency has tried to identify implementation responsibilities in TMDLs, it has commonly run into strong local objections (McBride, personal communication). Watershed groups are in the best position to win support for voluntary actions to address water quality violations, but they, too, have no authority over land-use decisions and little funding to assist implementation.

Despite these weaknesses in implementation, water quality standards remain important as legally recognized criteria that can bring attention to water quality issues and lead to development of clean-up plans. In July 2003, WDOE proposed changing a variety of key water quality standards for the state, which it submitted for EPA approval.[17] Most fundamentally, WDOE proposed changing how it designates uses for waterbodies. As discussed above, water quality standards are based on these uses. Instead of continuing to group all bodies of freshwater under five generic classes (AA, A, B, C, and lakes), with each having a pre-defined set of characteristic uses, WDOE proposed to designate each waterbody for specific uses for humans, fish, and wildlife.[18] For human uses, the key questions would be whether a waterbody provides a source for domestic water supply and whether it provides recreation opportunities involving secondary, primary, or "extraordinary primary contact" with water. In waterbodies designated for secondary recreation, humans are not likely to be fully submerged during recreation either in that waterbody or downstream, so bacterial pollution is less likely to put them at risk of serious gastrointestinal illness (M. Hicks, WDOE, personal communication). Waters designated for extraordinary primary contact provide extraordinary protection against waterborne disease; the designation also applies to streams flowing into extraordinary quality shellfish harvesting (WAC 173-201A-020). WDOE proposed to designate all waterbodies for providing wildlife habitat. For fish, in the Puget Sound area WDOE proposed to assign waterbodies to one of four designations: spawning and rearing by char (bull trout *Salvelinus confluentus* and Dolly Varden *S. malma*); spawning and "core" rearing for salmon and trout; spawning and "noncore" rearing for salmon and trout (the primary distinction between these two designations is whether the fish tend to rear in the

[17] For details, see www.ecy.wa.gov/programs/wq/swqs. In particular, see WAC 173-201A-200 for the new criteria and WDOE's Focus Sheets for explanation of its changes.

[18] See WAC 173-201A-600 for designations; see WAC 173-201A-020 for definitions of uses. For WDOE's explanation of its changes, see WDOE 2002.

waterbody during the summer; Hicks, personal communication); and rearing and migration (i.e., not spawning) for salmon and trout (see WAC 173-201A-200[1][c]).

Since most waterbodies could fit in more than one of the categories for fish use, they would be assigned to the most restrictive category for water quality standards, which primarily relate to temperature. All salmonids need cold water, but WDOE's proposal recognized that their tolerance for high temperatures varies by species and life stage. Farm and business groups argued that WDOE's temperature standards were unrealistically low, but in March 2006 EPA disapproved parts of the proposal where it found the standards were not low enough (M. Gearhard, EPA, letter to D. Peeler, WDOE). WDOE did not apply its proposed standards based on known fish distribution, but instead placed waterbodies in the new designated use categories based on their past classification (e.g., all Class AA waters were automatically designated for "Salmon and trout spawning, core rearing and migration," except where high elevation and smaller size placed them in the "Char" designation, based on the general habitat needs of bull trout and Dolly Varden). EPA found that this frequently placed streams in a category that would allow higher temperatures than needed to support known fish distribution, based on records from the Washington Department of Fish and Wildlife and tribes (USEPA 2006c). EPA's other major concern was that, while WDOE acknowledged its proposed temperature standards were not always protective of summer spawning or egg incubation, WDOE did not identify where it would apply stricter criteria. EPA used state, tribal and federal records to show where it believed stricter temperature criteria should apply (USEPA 2006c). EPA acknowledged that a variety of factors might make it difficult or impossible to meet the standards it recommended. EPA offered to work with WDOE to identify where natural conditions, limitations caused by dams, or a use attainability analysis could justify higher temperatures (Gearhard, letter). The two agencies are now working together to resolve their differences, with a goal of implementing new standards by spring 2007 (M. Hicks, WDOE, and K. Collins, EPA, personal communications).

In revising its standards for water quality, WDOE did not follow prominent scientific critics who argue that biological criteria should be added to the chemical criteria traditionally used to define water quality. Jim Karr and Richard Horner, two professors at the University of Washington who are nationally recognized experts on the relationship of water quality to biological integrity,[19] argue that biological indices are better than chemical criteria for predicting the health of salmon streams (Karr et al 2003). A third of the streams in the region that Karr and Horner reviewed in 2003 met WDOE's proposed chemical criteria, yet did not meet biological criteria to protect and sustain native salmonids. Biological criteria, however, are much better at indicating the presence of a problem than determining what the problem actually is. WDOE uses biological information to support its chemical criteria and to improve its understanding of problems caused by chronic lower levels of pollutants, but the agency does not believe it currently has sufficient data to use biological criteria as water quality standards for regulatory purposes (Hicks, personal communication).

[19] Karr served on the committee responsible for NRC 2001a.

WDOE's Stormwater Manual: Trying to Address the Most Difficult Non-Point Issue

Since the largest source of human-caused water pollution in the Puget Sound area is stormwater from developed landscapes, it should not be surprising that of all WDOE's regulatory actions to protect water quality, the one that affects the most citizens is its Stormwater Management Manual for development (WDOE 2005). The manual's standards for preventing stormwater pollution during construction are intended to apply to all new development and redevelopment in the region. Above low thresholds (e.g., 2,000 square feet of new or replaced impervious surface), the manual calls for all development and redevelopment to infiltrate as much stormwater as possible into the ground and to control pollution at its source. Above higher but still relatively low thresholds (e.g., 5,000 square feet of new impervious surface, approximately two homes), the manual calls for all developments and most redevelopments to meet all of its minimum requirements, which include modeling the amount of stormwater expected to flow off site during and after storms of varying sizes and constructing facilities to detain and clean this stormwater to specified levels.

Although WDOE issued an initial version of its latest manual in August 2001, most development projects in the Puget Sound area have not had these requirements applied to them. The manual has no independent regulatory authority—it is implemented through laws or regulations adopted by individual local governments and through permits tailored to specific projects (WDOE 2005). However, in negotiations for Phase II NPDES permits for municipal stormwater programs (which, as discussed earlier, will apply to jurisdictions in urban areas with populations below 100,000), WDOE is advocating that local governments be required to adopt its latest manual or the substantive equivalent (with the key exception that, for these smaller jurisdictions, the thresholds would all be raised to 1 acre of disturbed land, rather than 7,000 square feet of disturbed land or 5,000 square feet of impervious surface [WDOE 2006a]). Arguably, permits for Phase I governments (above 100,000 population) already require them to follow the new manual. (None currently do so, but in October 2004 the Puget Soundkeeper Alliance sued Snohomish County to seek compliance; in October 2005, the two sides settled [Smith, personal communication], with Snohomish County committing to adopt the Puget Sound Action Team's Technical Guidance Manual for Low Impact Development [PSAT 2005].[20] Regardless, WDOE is advocating that permit renewals for Phase I governments explicitly include the new manual [WDOE 2006b].) Thus, within the next few years, WDOE's latest stormwater requirements may be affecting developments across much of Puget Sound.

---

[20] The permits call for Phase I jurisdictions to adopt WDOE's stormwater manual (1992 editions, as amended by its replacement). WDOE staff are not sure that this requirement to comply with the manual's replacement is enforceable, since Phase I governments could not have known what it would involve at the time their permits were issued. Environmental attorneys disagree. (O'Brien, and R. Smith, Washington Trout and Native Fish Society, personal communications).

If NPDES permits require compliance with the new manual, citizen lawsuits to enforce the manual's standards would be relatively straightforward. Unlike, for example, a lawsuit alleging "take" under the ESA, a lawsuit to enforce an NPDES permit would not have to show site-specific data concerning impacts on listed species from stormwater, nor would it rely on a local government's vicarious liability for impacts caused by the developments they regulate (see Chapter 7, pages 128–131). If a court found that a local government was out of compliance with its NPDES permit, the only question would be what remedy the court would order (Smith, personal communication). Presumably, the government would be given a certain amount of time to bring its stormwater program into compliance; in the meantime, it might be enjoined from issuing new permits under its old standards.

Currently, most local governments in the region require that developments at least meet the stormwater requirements in WDOE's 1992 manual. That manual was written to help implement the state's 1991 Puget Sound Water Quality Management Plan. In contrast, the latest manual (issued in May 2005) is intended to meet requirements of the CWA and to support recovery of salmon listed under the Endangered Species Act; the manual also applies across all of western Washington, not just to Puget Sound (WDOE 2005). Though the legal authority for enforcing the stormwater manual is ultimately the CWA, neither manual focuses just on water pollutants. The manuals also address stormwater quantity, which affects the size, frequency, and duration of high flows in receiving streams. In turn, this affects the quality and quantity of fish habitat (a designated use) and how much sediment the streams carry (since high flows can cause substantial erosion and high levels of sediment are a common cause of water quality violations).

The 2005 manual, which includes five volumes totaling nearly 1,000 pages,[21] provides a detailed review of Best Management Practices (BMPs) designed to

- reduce the amount of water pollution generated by different land uses;
- maximize infiltration of stormwater into the ground; and
- detain and clean stormwater that still is discharged to waterbodies even after the first two sets of BMPs are applied.

Detention ponds, which collect stormwater runoff from a site and discharge it at a slower rate, are typically the most expensive BMPs in the manual, especially when taking into consideration the amount of otherwise developable land they require. The 2005 manual calls for much larger ponds than the 1992 manual, primarily to minimize the time that streams experience flows high enough to cause erosion. The complex calculation for determining the size of these ponds is based primarily on half the 2-year peak stormwater discharge that leaves a given site; this relates to the

[21] Volume I reviews minimum technical requirements and site planning; volume II reviews pollution prevention BMPs during construction; volume III reviews requirements for analyzing and minimizing the impacts of development on water quantity downstream; volume IV reviews BMPs for minimizing the amount of pollutants generated from different land uses; and volume V reviews BMPs for removing pollutants from stormwater runoff.

typical storm that would cause erosion in area streams.[22] The manual requires that the *duration* of erosive discharges that are half the 2-year peak and larger (up to a 50-year event) leaving a development match the duration for the same site in a *predeveloped* condition, which the manual defines as "a forested land cover unless reasonable, historic information is provided that indicates the site was prairie prior to settlement" (WDOE 2005:2–31). This requires that detention ponds must be 60% to 300% larger than under the 1992 manual,[23] which did not have a predevelopment standard and which focused only on limiting peak flows, not the duration of erosive flows. Combining these and other costs to meet the new requirements (including the cost of land as well as the cost of constructing facilities), compliance with the new manual could cost an additional $10,000 to well over $20,000 for a typical new house, based on a 1996 King County study adjusted for inflation (Johnson 1996).[24] Increases in stormwater management costs for new roads and most commercial development are even greater (O'Brien and C. Crawford, King County Water and Land Resources Division, personal communications).

The 2005 manual's requirements for stormwater quantity apply to all discharges to streams and lakes in the Puget Sound area except direct discharges to large lakes and lower mainstem rivers, which are identified in the manual. The lack of detention for discharges to lakes has little effect on downstream flows. A lack of detention for discharges to lower rivers may actually help reduce downstream flooding, since high flows from upper reaches take time to arrive at lower reaches (O'Brien, personal communication). The manual's requirements for discharges to wetlands are similar to its requirements for streams, with a goal of maintaining their "natural hydroperiod"—the fluctuation of their water elevations both seasonally and in response to storms (WDOE 2005). Water quality BMPs must be designed "to capture and effectively treat about 90% to 95% of the annual runoff" from a developed site; TMDLs or basin plans can require even higher levels of treatment (WDOE 2005).

Meeting the new requirements can be especially expensive for redevelopments in highly urbanized areas, though that is generally where growth management and water-

---

22 The discharge includes both surface runoff and shallow subsurface runoff or "interflow." The latter is important because it is the primary contributor to rapid rises in streamflows in naturally forested environments, which in western Washington typically have little or no surface discharge even after very large storms, well beyond the 2-year event, because of their high rates of evapotranspiration and groundwater infiltration (O'Brien, personal communication). Research supporting the focus on flows above 50% of the 2-year event is compiled in an unpublished manuscript by Derek Booth, "Rationale for a 'Threshold of Concern' in Stormwater Release Rates," University of Washington, Center for Water and Watershed Studies.

23 The Building Industry of Washington estimates that the ponds must be 200–300% larger than under the 1992 manual (see Meilleur and Mower 2002). King County and the WDOE believe that 60% more accurately describes the lower end of the range, which they also believe is the most typical case (O'Brien, personal communication).

24 Costs given are for elements of WDOE's manual that were part of King County's latest manual. The Building Industry Association's study estimated that complying with the new requirements is 300%–600% more expensive than the 1992 standards.

shed goals would want to encourage growth. For this reason, the manual provides some exceptions for heavily urbanized areas and redevelopment (WDOE 2005). Most controversially, the manual proposes a lower discharge standard in stream basins that have had at least 40% total impervious surface for at least 20 years. Arguing that these stream channels have irreversibly adapted to urbanized flows, WDOE proposes a standard based on the existing condition (i.e., not making things worse) rather than the historic condition in these basins (WDOE 2004). All redevelopment with less than 5,000 square feet of new or replaced impervious surface, or that adds less than 50% to the assessed value of an existing site, would be exempted from new flow control and pollutant removal requirements. A local government may allow redevelopments to pay a fee in lieu of constructing stormwater facilities, though this fee must at least equal the cost they would have incurred for construction.

WDOE argues that applying the manual's requirements to redevelopment is "consistent with other utility standards," where local governments require major remodeling to meet new code requirements for fire systems, sewage disposal, and the like (WDOE 2005). The situations are not necessarily parallel, however, since building code requirements often benefit building occupants or directly address public health and safety problems, while new stormwater facilities may contribute only a small increment toward addressing shared environmental problems, which require extensive actions from many others to show observable improvement. Less expensive investments may be considerably more cost-effective at improving water quality than new or retrofitted stormwater facilities (vacuum street sweeping, for example, can be very effective at removing pollutants and fine sediments from stormwater runoff [G. Minton, Resource Planning Associates, personal communication]). Moreover, courts may find that requiring redevelopments—or new developments—to mitigate for more than the stormwater impacts of the incremental effects of their own development is an unfair burden to place on a private party to meet a public goal, for reasons discussed in Chapter 6 (B. Johns, Master Builders Association of King and Snohomish Counties, personal communication).

Scientific Assessment Gives Manual Mixed Reviews; WDOE Acknowledges Its Limitations

In June 2003, the state's Independent Science Panel issued a review of the 2001 version of WDOE's stormwater manual (Currens et al. 2003). Although it complimented the manual as "one of the most comprehensive in the United States and...impressive in its scope, coverage and quality," the review raised a number of critical concerns. Most fundamentally, it warned against "applying a 'one size fits all' project level approach to all watersheds across western Washington" (Currens et al. 2003:8). The review found that the actual benefit from applying the manual's requirements would vary based on a large number of factors, including the size and location of a proposed development, the amount and location of existing development in the basin, the soils and precipitation patterns of a basin, the size of substrate downstream (e.g., sand erodes at much lower flows than large cobble), background levels of sediment, the condition of riparian areas, and the amount and quality of woody debris downstream. The review found that roads, particularly in rural areas, deserve their own distinct requirements for stormwater management, in part because they affect the routing as well as the quantity and quality of stormwater (Currens et al. 2003). A watershed-scale approach to stormwater requirements could allow consideration of all these factors, the review found, providing "a means to optimize the application costs of stormwater management in locations with the potential for greatest benefits" (Currens et al. 2003:7).

The review also challenged the manual's approach to stormwater quality. It questioned whether many of the BMPs for stormwater quality would actually provide as much treatment as the manual indicates (Currens et al. 2003). (Other critics have added that a treatment standard based on annual runoff will not necessarily address water quality problems when they are most acute, typically after storms in late summer. Discharges in the summer create higher concentrations of pollutants in streams because base flows are low. Fish are also more susceptible to harm from pollutants in the summer because higher water temperatures increase their stress levels and metabolism [Minton, personal communication].) The Independent Science Panel's review also warned that "the combined effects of all toxicants in stormwater cannot be predicted accurately" (Currens et al. 2003:13). At most, tests to establish acute and chronic levels of toxicity for pesticides, metals, and hydrocarbons from road runoff and other toxicants have generally evaluated the direct and indirect effects of single chemicals, using national test species that are not necessarily the most relevant for Northwest ecosystems. Furthermore, the effects of many potential toxicants have not been evaluated at all (D. Lester, King County Water and Land Resources Division, personal communication). For all of these reasons, the review found that information to design adequate guidelines for stormwater pollution control "is not likely to be available for the foreseeable future" (Currens et al. 2003:13). It recommended incorporating research on these issues into a wider strategy of monitoring and adaptive management (Currens et al. 2003).

Despite these criticisms, the Independent Science Panel still concluded, "we believe that individually or collectively the scientific issues [we raise] are insufficient to preclude use of [WDOE's stormwater] manual" (Currens et al. 2003:i). Few streams in the Puget Sound region have had watershed analyses that approach what the panel recommended to correct the "one size fits all" problem (O'Brien and Minton, personal communications). Across Puget Sound, the total societal cost to comply with stormwater requirements will easily exceed $1 billion over the next decade,[25] but neither WDOE nor most watershed groups or local governments have the millions of dollars needed to do the detailed analyses that could ensure these funds are being spent most effectively.

In April 2006, five environmental groups in the region[26] notified EPA of their intent to sue the agency for allegedly failing to consult with NMFS regarding its delegation

[25] At $10,000 per house (a very low estimate), this would require only 100,000 houses, without counting costs for commercial development and public works.

[26] National Wildlife Federation, Public Employees for Environmental Responsibility, Puget Soundkeeper Alliance, People for Puget Sound, and Washington Trout.

of Clean Water Act responsibilities to WDOE (Smith 2006). The groups argued that the state's NPDES stormwater permits (for boatyards and construction sites, as well as the proposed permit for municipal programs) authorized a variety of actions that harm Puget Sound Chinook. They cited comments from NMFS on WDOE's stormwater manual, which argued for requiring low impact development in urban areas, stricter requirements to prevent stormwater pollution, and advanced water quality treatment for all roads (Berg and Landino 2004). The groups' concerns regarding the construction site permit included its allowing continued contributions of fine sediments, alkaline water, phosphorus, metals, toxics, and warm water that harm salmon (Smith 2006). Their concerns with the boatyard permit focused especially on discharges of copper, as well as weak enforcement mechanisms. This lawsuit is not likely to be resolved soon (Smith, personal communication).

WDOE acknowledges that even universal implementation of its stormwater manual under ideal conditions would be insufficient to protect fish habitat because it still would not address non-hydrologic sources of degradation (such as poor riparian areas or lack of structural habitat), nor would it remove all introduced pollutants or address all of the hydrologic effects of removing forest cover (the total volume of stormwater would be greater because of decreased evapotranspiration from trees, while summer baseflows would be lower because of decreased infiltration). As WDOE says, "despite the application of appropriate practices and technologies identified in this manual, some degradation of urban and suburban receiving waters will continue, and some beneficial uses will continue to be impaired or lost due to new development" (WDOE 2005:1–25).

To address these issues, WDOE advocates retaining 65% to 75% of the natural soils and land cover in a drainage basin, together with low-impact approaches to development, such as permeable pavement, green roofs, reduced road widths, and site designs that use natural topography and vegetation to manage stormwater (WDOE 2005:1–25). The manual provides some incentives for these approaches, but it does not mandate them. Doing so would probably go beyond WDOE's legal authority under the CWA and almost certainly would go beyond the authority the legislature would choose to give the agency. Moreover, as WDOE says, even if all of these low-impact approaches were applied together, whether they would be sufficient to ensure that development does not alter the natural qualities of receiving waterbodies is "the question yet to be answered" (WDOE 2005:1–26).

In summary, WDOE's stormwater manual would achieve its objective of restoring natural rates of erosion only if its generic assumptions are correct for particular watersheds and its requirements are applied to all new and existing development. The latter would not only be expensive, particularly in urbanized areas, but also might not be legal, since it would require new developments and redevelopments to mitigate for more than their own incremental impacts. (It also would never happen simply because smaller developments are exempt from its requirements.) Even if the manual's standards were met everywhere, this would not address other hydrologic and non-hydrologic impacts of development. Preserving natural land cover is more effective than engineered approaches for reducing stormwater impacts of development, but the stormwater manual cannot mandate preserving or restoring natural land cover and provides only limited incentives to do so. At a larger scale, the manual may actually encourage the loss of natural land cover, since the cost of complying with the manual's requirements is generally greater in urbanized areas, which may push growth into less developed areas. Rather than taking a "one size fits all" approach, a watershed-scale approach to stormwater management could address many of these issues by evaluating the actual costs and benefits of different requirements for different areas. However, such detailed watershed analyses have been done in only a few relatively small areas. For most of the region, WDOE's manual—despite its many shortcomings—remains the best tool available to address the impacts of stormwater from development.

A Better Way: Beyond "One Size Fits All"

The region must address stormwater impacts effectively to keep its water quality and aquatic ecosystems from continued decline in response to growth. Especially if this is to be done affordably and equitably, we must develop better approaches than WDOE's stormwater manual. This would partly be a technical exercise, evaluating different ways of managing stormwater and the characteristics of specific watersheds to determine the costs and benefits of alternatives for particular places. Doing this well would cost millions of dollars, but that is probably less than 1% of what the region will pay over the next decade to implement stormwater requirements that everyone agrees are not sufficient to protect aquatic resources. The current approach adds $10,000 or more to the cost of the average new house and even more to new commercial development, yet fails to provide that protection. It thus reduces the affordability of housing and the state's economic competitiveness to gain limited environmental benefits; it also creates incentives to develop in rural areas, where the cost of compliance is lower but the damage to natural resources from development is higher.

The challenges for a better approach are mostly political and institutional, not technical. Studies to target stormwater requirements where they will do the most good require funding. It can be difficult to allocate money from state and local budgets to stormwater programs, even though it would provide an enormous return on the much larger expenditures that private and public projects must make to meet stormwater requirements. The region also needs to experiment on a large scale with low-impact approaches to development. This frequently requires revising parts of local building codes that were adopted with other goals in mind (e.g., parking requirements, or road widths that are designed for emergency vehicles not just to pass through but to turn around; PSAT 2005). It requires crediting low-impact developments for their decreased runoff by reducing or eliminating standard requirements for stormwater facilities, even when low-impact approaches may still be experimental. Setting aside forested land for stormwater benefits may require public subsidies or special incentives. For low-impact development to succeed on more than just a pilot basis, it will also require educating developers, finance companies, and potential customers of its benefits, which can be economic as well as environmental. (Green roofs, for example, provide insulation that reduces heating costs in the winter and cooling costs in the summer, while extending the life of roofs by protecting them from ultraviolet light and temperature extremes. Preservation of natural soils and vegetation during construction lowers long-term landscaping and irrigation costs and provides aesthetic benefits that may add to the market value of new developments.)

Targeting stricter and more expensive requirements for stormwater management where they will do the most good would require the region to set different goals for different waterbodies, including urban and rural streams. As some of the Pacific Northwest's leading hydrologists have said,

> We cannot find any basis to expect that the full range of hydrological and ecological conditions can be replaced in a now-degraded urban channel. The key tasks facing watershed managers, and the public that can support or impede their efforts, are therefore (1) to identify those watersheds where existing low urbanization, and associated high-quality stream conditions, warrant the kinds of development conditions that may protect much of the *existing* quality of these systems; and (2) to develop a new set of management goals for those watersheds whose surrounding development precludes significant ecosystem recovery. Following the same strategy in all watersheds, developed and undeveloped alike, simply makes no sense. [Booth et al. 2002]

WDOE's new use-based approach to streams begins to recognize some of these distinctions. However, the CWA's goal that all waters be "fishable and swimmable" can make it difficult to vary goals among streams. The act's requirement that there be no loss of designated uses after November 1975 does not acknowledge that there may be unavoidable consequences of development and land clearing to downstream areas.[27] A law that simply prohibits these consequences is meaningless if it treats water quality and land use as separate topics and deals only with the former. In this, the CWA has important parallels to the Growth Management Act's prohibition against losses in the functions and values of critical areas. Both ignore the best available science, which indicates there will be some inevitable losses in urbanizing areas.

Accepting lower goals for the ecology and water quality of urban streams does not mean writing them off. The goals would be lower compared to rural streams, not to the way most urban streams have been treated in the past. The region should ensure that urban streams pose no major human health risks, limit their delivery of pollutants to ecologically more productive areas downstream, recognize and protect their value as natural amenities for urban areas, and protect and restore the habitat they provide to fish and wildlife. Regarding the last goal, however, it is important to acknowledge that those species benefiting most from protection and restoration of urban habitats may

---

[27] Given the relationship between standard development and degraded water quality in receiving waters, this could possibly be used as a basis for using NPDES construction permits to stop all developments in a basin that are greater than 1 acre, or to approve them only on the condition that they use low-impact approaches.

not have been numerous or even present in the same places before development. Most of these species will be capable of tolerating considerable degradation and fragmentation of native habitats. In the Puget Sound region, for example, cutthroat trout have proven capable of surviving and even thriving in urban streams, where other salmonids are rarely found in sizable numbers. Cutthroat trout, however, are a major predator of other fish, including less tolerant salmonids listed under the Endangered Species Act. Improving habitat for more tolerant species can be a mixed blessing to a larger ecosystem. The goals for any particular area need to be set within that larger context, including both its watershed and the ecoregion.

References

Adler, R. W., J. C. Landman, and D. M. Cameron. 1993. The Clean Water Act: 20 years later. Island Press, Washington, D.C.

Berg, K.S. and S.W. Landino. 2004. Letter to Ed O'Brien, Washington State Department of Ecology. December 23, 2004. Lacey, Washington.

Bernath, S. 2003. Water Quality Program Annual Compliance Report, calendar year 2001. Washington Department of Ecology, Publication 03-10-018, Olympia.

Booth, D., D. Hartley, and R. Jackson. 2002. Forest cover, impervious-surface area, and the mitigation of stormwater impacts. Journal of the American Water Resources Association 38:835–845.

Borden Ranch Partnership v. U.S. Army Corps of Engineers, 537 U.S. 99 (2002).

Brown, B. 1995. Mountain in the clouds: a search for the wild salmon. University of Washington Press, Seattle.

Building Industries Association of Washington v. City of Lacey, Thurston County Superior Court, Case No. 91-2-02895-5 (1993).

Chasan, D. J. 1981. The water link: a history of Puget Sound as a resource. University of Washington Press, Seattle.

CPC International Inc. v. Train, 540 F.2d 1329 (8th Cir. 1976), certiorari denied 430 US 966 (1977).

Currens, K. P., H. W. Li, J. D. McIntyre, W. F. Megahan, and D. W. Reiser. 2003. Review of "Stormwater Management Manual for Western Washington." Independent Science Panel, Report 2003-1, Olympia, Washington. Available: http://www.governor.wa.gov/gsro/science/documents.htm (March 2006).

Edmondson, W. T. 1991. The uses of ecology: Lake Washington and beyond. University of Washington Press, Seattle.

Egelko, B. 2002. Wetland penalty is upheld by Supreme Court: Sacramento-area rancher slapped for use of 'deep-ripping' plowing. The San Francisco Chronicle (December 17):15.

Eriksen, A. and L. Townsend. 1940. The occurrence and cause of pollution in Grays Harbor. Washington Pollution Control Commission, Bulletin Number 2, Olympia.

GAO (General Accounting Office). 2000. Water quality: key EPA and state decisions limited by inconsistent and incomplete data. General Accounting Office, GAO/RCED-00-54, Washington, D.C.

Johnson, B. 1996. King County surface water design manual update: cost analysis. King County Department of Public Works, Surface Water Management Division, Seattle.

Johnson, P., D. Mock, A. McMillan, L. Driscoll, and T. Hruby. 2002. Washington State Wetland Mitigation Evaluation Study, phase 2: evaluating success. Washington Department of Ecology Publication No. 02-06-009, Olympia.

Karr, J. R., R. R. Horner, and C. R. Horner. 2003. EPA's review of Washington's water quality criteria: an evaluation of whether Washington's criteria proposal protects stream health and designated uses. National Wildlife Federation, Seattle.

MacDonald, R. W., and E. A. Crecelius. 1994. Marine sediments in the Strait of Georgia, Juan de Fuca Strait and Puget Sound: what can they tell us about contamination? Pages 101–137 in R. C. H. Wilson, R. J. Beamish, F. Aitkens, and J. Bell, editors. Review of the marine environment and biota of Strait of Georgia, Puget Sound and Juan de Fuca Strait. Canadian Technical Report of Fisheries and Aquatic Sciences 1948.

McMillan, A. 1998. How ecology regulates wetlands. Washington Department of Ecology, Shorelands and Environmental Assistance Program, Publication No. 97-112, Olympia.

Meilleur, A., and D. Mower. 2002. Addendum to the technical review of the Washington State Department of Ecology stormwater management manual for the Building Industry Association of Washington. DBM Consulting Engineers, Auburn, Washington.

National Mining Association v. U.S. Army Corps of Engineers, 145 F.3d 1399 (D.C. Cir. 1998).

NOAA Fisheries Service. 2003. HCD stormwater online guidance: ESA guidance for analyzing stormwater effects. NOAA Fisheries Service, Northwest Region, Seattle. Available: http://www.nwr.noaa.gov/1habcon/habweb/habguide/stormwater_032003.pdf (July 2003).

NRC (National Research Council). 2001a. Assessing the TMDL approach to water quality management. National Academy Press, Washington, D.C.

NRC (National Research Council). 2001b. Compensating for wetland losses under the Clean Water Act. National Academy Press, Washington, D.C.

Pegg, J. R. 2003. Panel debates how to fix holes in the Clean Water Act. Environment News Service (September 16). Available: *http://www.ens-newswire.com/ens/sep2003/2003-09-16-10.asp* (March 16).

Pharris, J. K., and P. T. McDonald. 2000. An introduction to Washington water law. Office of the Attorney General, Olympia.

PUD No.1 of Jefferson County v. WDOE (Washington Department of Ecology), 511 U.S. 700 (1994).

PSAT (Puget Sound Action Team). 2005. Low Impact Development: Technical Guidance Manual for Puget Sound. Revised May 2005. Puget Sound Action Team. Olympia, Washington. Available: http://www.psat.wa.gov/Publications/LID_tech_manual05/lid-index.htm (October 2005).

Reisner, M., and S. Bates. 1990. Overtapped oasis: reform or revolution for western water. Island Press, Washington, D.C.

Smith, R. 2006. Notice of intent to sue for violation of Endangered Species Act – failure to consult on effects of NPDES delegation and oversight on threatened Puget Sound Chinook salmon. Smith & Lowney, P.L.L.C., Seattle.

Solid Waste Agency of Northern Cook County v. Army Corps of Engineers, 531 U.S. 159 (2001).

Thornton Creek Watershed Management Committee. 2001. Thornton Creek Draft Watershed Action Plan. Thornton Creek Watershed Management Committee, Seattle Public Utilities, and Washington Department of Ecology, Seattle.

United States v. Nubour, 274 F.3d 435, 444 (7th Cir. 2001), petition for cert. filed, No. 01-10947 (U.S. 2002).

United States v. Wilson, 133 F.3d 251 (4th Cir. 1997).

USACE (U.S. Army Corps of Engineers). 2006. Recognizing wetlands: an informational pamphlet. Available: www.usace.army.mil/inet/functions/cw/cecwo/reg/rw-bro.htm (March 2006).

USEPA (U.S. Environmental Protection Agency). 2000. Storm Water Phase II Final Rule: an overview. U.S. Environmental Protection Agency, EPA 833-F-00-001, Fact Sheet 1.0, Washington, D.C.

USEPA (U.S. Environmental Protection Agency). 2006a. Introduction to the Clean Water Act. Available: http://www.epa.gov/watertrain/cwa/ (March 2006).

USEPA (U.S. Environmental Protection Agency). 2006b. Policy and guidance: interim economic guidance for water quality standards. Available: www.epa.gov/waterscience/econ/chaptr1.html (March 2006).

USEPA (U.S. Environmental Protection Agency). 2006c. Basis for EPA's partial disapproval of Washington's 2003 water quality standard revisions. Available: http://yosemite.epa.gov/R10/WATER.NSF/Water+Quality+Standards/WA+WQS+EPA+Disapproval (August 2006).

USFWS (U.S. Fish and Wildlife Service). 1999. A framework to assist in making Endangered Species Act determinations of effect for individual or grouped actions at the bull trout subpopulation watershed scale. U.S. Fish and Wildlife Service, Portland, Oregon.

Wayland, III, R. H. 2001. 2002 Integrated water quality monitoring and assessment report guidance. U.S. Environmental Protection Agency, Office of Wetlands, Oceans and Watersheds, Washington, D.C. Available: www.epa.gov/owow/tmdl/2002wqma.html (March 2006).

WDOE (Washington Department of Ecology). 2001. Isolated wetlands—changes in the regulatory process. Washington Department of Ecology, Publication No. 00-06-020, Olympia

WDOE (Washington Department of Ecology). 2002. Changing the surface water quality standards from a 'class-based' to a 'use-based' format. Washington Department of Ecology, Publication No. 00-10-064 (revised), Olympia, Washington.

WDOE (Washington Department of Ecology). 2004. Proposed flow control standard for highly urbanized drainage basins: a Department of Ecology discussion paper. Development Services Section, Water Quality Program, Washington Department of Ecology. Olymia, Washington.

WDOE (Washington Department of Ecology). 2005. Stormwater management manual for western Washington. Washington Department of Ecology, Publication No. 05-10-029 to 05-10-033, Olympia, Washington.

WDOE (Washington Department of Ecology). 2006a. Western Washington Phase II Municipal Stormwater Permit: Preliminary Draft. Washington Department of Ecology, Olympia, Washington.

WDOE (Washington Department of Ecology). 2006b. Western Washington Phase I Municipal Stormwater Permit: Preliminary Draft. Washington Department of Ecology, Olympia, Washington.

Chapter 13. Tribal Treaty Rights: A "Unique Obligation"

> The Indians understood, and were led by Governor Stevens to believe, that the treaties entitled them to continue fishing in perpetuity and that settlers would not qualify, restrict, or interfere with their right to take fish. The most fundamental prerequisite to exercising the right to take fish is the existence of the fish to be taken. [*United States v. Washington* 1980:203]

Chapter Summary

In the next 5 to 10 years, federal courts will begin to determine whether Puget Sound Indian tribes have a treaty right to the protection of habitat necessary to produce harvestable salmon runs and, if so, what legal powers this grants them. For more than 20 years, the tribes have asserted this right. Initially, they sought to have it recognized as an abstract principle they could apply to future land-use actions. After giving their arguments some degree of support, the courts ultimately declined to rule in the abstract, deciding in 1985 that the principle was best established in light of specific circumstances. Nearly 16 years passed before the tribes filed a lawsuit for that purpose. In January 2001, 20 tribes sought a court order requiring the state of Washington to accelerate its repair of road culverts that block salmon from hundreds of miles of spawning and rearing habitat. No decision in that case has yet been reached; whatever decision is made will most likely be appealed, potentially delaying a legal resolution for years. If the courts ultimately recognize a treaty right to habitat protection, it could become one of the strongest legal tools available to protect habitat, for a number of reasons:

- It would apply to all salmon and shellfish, not just listed species;
- It would require that populations of these fish be raised enough to allow at least some harvest, not just avoid extinction;
- It could provide a legal basis for mandating at least some of the actions in the recovery plan for Puget Sound salmon developed under the Endangered Species Act (ESA); and
- It could prove easier to enforce against state and local development regulations than the ESA.

Tribal treaties could thus become a critical tool for protecting important parts of the Puget Sound ecoregion in ways the parties who signed them more than 150 years ago never could have imagined.

A Short History of Northwest Indian Fisheries

It is difficult to estimate how many Indians lived in the Puget Sound region 500 years ago, before foreign diseases introduced by European and American explorers and traders (principally smallpox, measles, whooping cough, mumps, cholera, and gonorrhea) began to decimate Indian populations across the Northwest (Lackey et al. 2006). The decline in the Indian population continued well into the 19th century, as Euro-American settlers grew in number and competed with Indians for land and resources. From 1770 to 1870, the Indian population across the northwest is estimated to have fallen from about 100,000 to under 10,000 (*Washington v. Washington State Commercial Passenger Fishing Vessel Association* 1978:664), but even the higher number was probably well below historic levels, when the northwest was "one of the most densely populated nonagricultural regions of the world," based on archaeological evidence (Boyd 1990, cited in NRC 1996).

Salmon made this dense population possible. There were many other foods available, but throughout the northwest Indian diets were based on salmon, a source of protein that was both abundant and reliable, returning to predictable places at predictable times (Taylor 1999). It was long assumed that Indian fisheries could never have been large enough to appreciably affect salmon populations in the region, but increasing estimates for both the pre-contact population and their per capita consumption of salmon have challenged this assumption. At its height, the Indian harvest may have approximated the size of industrial harvests near the beginning of the twentieth century (Taylor 1999)—possibly 42 million pounds annually on the Columbia River, for example, about 28% to 57% of the estimated biomass of salmon available. The much larger numbers than earlier estimates are consistent with the hypothesis that Indian populations would have approximated the carrying capacity of their food sources (Taylor 1999). They also are consistent with the universal taboo among northwest Indian cultures against over-harvest. Such a taboo would only be necessary if the cultures could, in fact, over-harvest salmon runs.

Indian fishing techniques could be "frighteningly" efficient: "weirs blocked all passage to spawning grounds; seines corralled large schools of salmon; and basket traps collected without discrimination" (Taylor 1999). Indian harvests were, however, dispersed across time, space, and different salmon species. Indians fished throughout most of the year, targeting different species as they returned, with harvests located close enough to spawning grounds that fishermen could modify the catch as necessary to ensure that enough spawners would sustain large runs, gauging this number based on generations of experience. Except for the Indians' use of fire to clear vegetation, they lacked the technology to greatly affect salmon habitat (Lackey et al. 2006). In contrast, industrial fisheries were concentrated near canneries, were generally oblivious to losses from bycatch and waste, focused on the most commercially desirable species (Chinook salmon *Oncorhynchus tshawytscha* above all), and made little if any adjustment for variations in returns (Taylor 1999). Moreover, by the time industrial fisheries reached their height, Euro-Americans had been radically altering habitat in the Northwest for decades, first by the mass-trapping of beavers (whose dams had created great complexes of stream and off-channel habitats), then by the clearing of land, the construction of channel-blocking dams, and the pollution of water from mining, timber, agriculture, and cities. These changes substantially reduced the number of fish the region could produce (Taylor 1999). Thus, the total size of the Indian and industrial fisheries might have been comparable when each fishery was at its peak, but the two had vastly different effects on salmon populations.

In 1854 and 1855, Isaac Stevens, the first governor and superintendent of Indian Affairs of Washington Territory, negotiated treaties with Indians across the state to acquire land title for American settlement and construction of a transcontinental railroad (*United States v. Washington* 1974:354; Montgomery 2003). Stevens grouped the native people into "tribes," though in the northwest they had been mostly organized loosely by families and fishing communities (*United States v. Washington* 1974:354–357). Stevens had translators who spoke native languages, but he negotiated the treaties in Chinook, a jargon developed for trade "with at most a few hundred words in common use, drawn from a mix of Indian languages, English and French" (Montgomery 2003:58). As federal courts later found, "Chinook jargon...was inadequate to express precisely the legal effects of the treaties, although the general meaning of treaty language could be explained" (*United States v. Washington* 1974:356). The treaties provided the Indians some government services, cash payments, and relatively small reservations of land, but the guarantee of the continued right to fish was most crucial to getting the Indians to sign. All of the treaties contained the following promise:

> The right of taking fish, at all usual and accustomed grounds and stations, is further secured to said Indians, in common with all citizens of the Territory....[Article III of the Treaty of Medicine Creek, Stat. 1133, cited in *Washington v. Washington State Commercial Passenger Fishing Vessel Association* 1978:674[1]]

Explaining the Treaty of Point No Point to tribes on the Olympic Peninsula, Stevens was quoted as saying,

> Are you not my children and also children of the Great Father?... This paper is such as a man would give to his children and I will tell you why. This paper gives you a home. Does not a father give his children a home? ...This paper secures your fish. Does not a father give food to his children? [*Washington v. Washington State Commercial Passenger Fishing Vessel Association* 1978:667]

Some commentators speculate that Stevens knew that northwest fisheries would radically decline in the decades ahead, given what was known at the time of the decline of salmon in Europe and New England (for example, see Montgomery 2003[2]). This seems questionable. In the 1850s, the decline of salmon in New England was not very far along. Many believed hatcheries would provide an adequate response, as was asserted in the northwest well into the 20th century. When the U.S. Supreme Court reviewed the Stevens treaties more than 100 years later, it concluded,

---

[1] Identical or nearly identical language was used in all other treaties negotiated by Stevens.

[2] "No matter how well or clearly the various treaties were translated into the Indian languages, there remained a simple underlying inequity. The Indians knew that there were plenty of salmon to share and had no reason to believe there might not be in the future. There had always been plenty in the past. The government Stevens represented knew of the decimation of salmon in England and along the Atlantic seaboard. Stevens not only orchestrated the negotiations but he also knew the game they were playing..." (Montgomery 2003:60)

when the treaties were negotiated, neither party realized or intended that their agreement would determine whether, and if so how, a resource that had always been thought inexhaustible would be allocated between the native Indians and the incoming settlers when it later became scarce. [*Washington v. Washington State Commercial Passenger Fishing Vessel Association* 1978:668, 669]

Salmon were, in fact, probably superabundant in the northwest when the treaties were negotiated, since the enormous decline in Indian populations would have dramatically decreased harvests. There may well have been "too many" spawning salmon, with overcompetition between individual fish for available habitat reducing the overall productivity of the runs, as today's theory of harvest management would suggest (see Chapter 8, pages 160–161; Taylor 1999).

In the years immediately preceding the Stevens treaties, Indian fishing in the northwest increased to support trade with whites (*United States v. Washington* 1974:351–352). Over the following decades, Indians continued to harvest the majority of fish in the region, as white settlers focused on logging, farming, and early industries. But new cannery technology and railroad connections made exporting salmon an economically viable business in the final decades of the 19th century. Indians were pushed aside as salmon gained the attention of white fishermen, and harvests grew to an industrial scale (Montgomery 2003). When the number of salmon began to decline noticeably because of these harvests and habitat destruction by whites, the state of Washington focused restrictions on Indians, setting a pattern for the next century. One of the first regulations the Washington Department of Fisheries enforced was a ban against nets in streams, which by the 1890s had become the Indians' primary method of fishing, after cannery traps displaced the Indians from river mouths and the Puget Sound shoreline (Montgomery 2003). Indian fishing in rivers was highly visible to the public, as were its effects on the dwindling number of spawners, making Indians—already subject to widespread prejudice—a convenient scapegoat. Later in the 20th century, fishing seasons and gear restrictions set by the Department of Fisheries would have eliminated even subsistence Indian fisheries. Many Indians defied these regulations, which led the state to escalate its public blame, even as the Department of Fisheries quadrupled the number of gill-net licenses it issued to whites and allowed a dramatic growth in recreational fishing (Montgomery 2003). In response, Indian tribes began to take their case to court in the 1960s, supported by the federal government.

The Boldt Decision: Establishing a Tribal Right to Half the Salmon Harvest

For well over a century, federal court opinions on Indian treaties have followed a "special" rule of interpretation, articulated as follows by the U.S. Supreme Court:

[I]t is the intention of the parties, and not solely that of the superior side, that must control any attempt to interpret the treaties. When Indians are involved, this Court has long given special meaning to this rule. It has held that the United States, as the party with the presumptively superior negotiating skills and superior knowledge of the language in which the treaty is recorded, has a responsibility to avoid taking advantage of the other side. "The treaty must therefore be construed, not according to the technical meaning of its words to learned lawyers, but in the sense in which they would naturally be understood by the Indians." [*Washington v. Washington State Commercial Passenger Fishing Vessel Association* 1978:675–576, cited from *Jones v. Meehan* 1899:11]

Under the Supremacy Clause of the Constitution (which makes federal treaties, along with the Constitution and duly enacted federal laws, collectively "the supreme law of the land"), Indian treaties are binding on all Americans, including state and local governments and private parties, "the laws of any State to the contrary notwithstanding" (quoted from Article VI of the United States Constitution). Congress can abrogate treaties, but "absent explicit statutory language" the Supreme Court has been "extremely reluctant" (*Washington v. Washington State Commercial Passenger Fishing Vessel Association* 1978:690) to find that Congress has done so. If Congress were to restrict the hunting and fishing rights of northwest tribes below levels protected by treaty, the United States would be obligated to compensate the tribes, based on past Supreme Court decisions (e.g., *Menominee Tribe v. United States* 1968).

The first interpretation of the Stevens treaties by the United States Supreme Court focused on the right of access that the treaties granted Indians to their traditional fishing locations, even when others owned the land or had exclusive state-granted licenses to fish there. Lower courts initially ruled that the treaties guaranteed Indians only the same rights as white citizens, which therefore could be superseded by state licenses and regulations. In 1905, the Supreme Court disagreed in *United States v. Winans*:

> [I]t was decided [in the lower court] that the Indians acquired no rights but what any inhabitant of the territory or state would have. Indeed, acquired no rights but such as they would have without the treaty. This is certainly an impotent outcome to negotiations and a convention which seemed to promise more, and give the word of the Nation for more....The right to resort to the fishing places in controversy was a part of larger rights possessed by the Indians, upon the exercise of which there was not a shadow of impediment, and which were not much less necessary to the existence of the Indians than the atmosphere they breathed....[T]he treaty was not a grant of rights to the Indians, but a grant of rights from them—a reservation of those rights not granted. [1905:380–382]

The Court found that the treaties gave Indians a "servitude," or property right, that burdened "every piece of land [where the Indians might fish] as though described therein." This gave Indians the right to occupy and make use of these lands despite "the contingency of future ownership." It was enforceable against subsequently established states, such as Washington, so states must respect treaty rights even though they were not party to the treaty. However, the Court suggested that the exercise of treaty fishing rights could be subject to state regulation—"language that proved to be the source of enduring controversy over the next 75 years," as law professor Michael Blumm later commented (see Blumm 2002).

With this seeming authorization, Washington State continued to discriminate against

Indian fisheries, supported by the state supreme court, as in the following 1916 opinion:

> The premise of Indian sovereignty we reject. The treaty is not to be interpreted in that light. At no time did our ancestors, in getting title to this continent, ever regard the aborigines as other than mere occupants, and incompetent occupants, of the soil. Any title that could come from them was always disdained....Only that title was esteemed which came from white men....These [treaty] arrangements were but the announcement of our benevolence, which, notwithstanding our frequent frailties, has been continuously displayed. Neither Rome nor sagacious Britain ever dealt more liberally with their subject races than we with these savage tribes, whom it was generally tempting and always easy to destroy and whom we have so often permitted to squander vast areas of fertile land before our eyes. [*State v. Towessnute* 1916, quoted in Blumm 2002:75]

In the 1940s and 1950s, federal courts issued a number of decisions requiring the states of Washington and Oregon not just to avoid discriminatory regulation of Indian fisheries, but to justify their regulation of Indian fishing as "indispensable" to conservation (*Tulee v. Washington* 1942, *Makah Tribe v. Schoettler* 1951, and *Maison v. Confederated Tribes of the Umatilla Reservation* 1963, as cited in Blumm 2002). In the 1960s, the U.S. Supreme Court at first seemed to restrict this standard just to license fees, but later modified its ruling, acknowledging that state regulations for conservation could actually serve as a form of allocation, "conserving" fish for catch by non-Indians (see *Puyallup Tribe v. Washington Game Department* 1968, 1973, 1977, as discussed in Blumm 2002). Consistent with this decision, in 1969 a federal district court in Oregon ruled, in *Sohappy v. Smith* (1969, also cited as *United States v. Oregon*) that Oregon could regulate Indian fishing only for the conservation of the resource and only in a manner that does not discriminate against the rights of treaty tribes. Protection of the tribal right to fish must be a "coequal" policy goal with conservation (*Sohappy v. Smith* 1969:902). "The state cannot so manage the fishery that little or no harvestable portion of the run remains to reach the upper portions of the stream where the historic Indian places are mostly located" (*Sohappy v. Smith* 1969:901). This case and the related U.S. Supreme Court decisions laid a considerable part of the legal foundation for *United States v. Washington*, the most important case for Indian tribes in the Puget Sound area.

In 1970, the federal government sued the state of Washington to clarify three key treaty issues: (1) whether treaty tribes are entitled to a specific allocation of salmon and steelhead *Oncorhynchus mykiss* harvested in western Washington; (2) if so, whether fish from hatcheries must be included in that allocation; and (3) whether the tribes have a right to the protection of habitat necessary for the continued production of harvestable salmon runs. Eighteen tribes ultimately joined *United States v. Washington* as plaintiffs.[3] The case was litigated in two phases, with phase I ad-

[3] Initially, the suit was brought on behalf of the Hoh, Makah, Muckleshoot, Nisqually, Puyallup, Quileute, and Skokomish tribes. Subsequently, those tribes and the following others intervened as plaintiffs on their own behalf: Duwamish, Jamestown Band of Clallam, Lower Elwha, Samish, Sauk-Suiattle, Snohomish, Snoqualmie, Tulalip, Upper Skagit River, and Yakama.

dressing the first issue and phase II intended to address the second and third. In 1974, Judge George Boldt made the initial district court decision in phase I. What became known in the Puget Sound area simply as "the Boldt decision"—one of the most controversial legal rulings in the history of the region (and a landmark decision for the rights of indigenous peoples internationally)—was affirmed 5 years later by the Supreme Court. Judge Boldt decided,

> By dictionary definition and as intended and used in the Indian treaties and in this decision, "in common with" means *sharing equally* the opportunity to take fish at "usual and accustomed grounds and stations"; therefore, non-treaty fishermen shall have the opportunity to take up to 50% of the harvestable number of fish that may be taken by all fishermen at usual and accustomed grounds and stations and treaty right fishermen shall have the opportunity to take up to the same percentage of harvestable fish....[emphasis in original; *United States v. Washington* 1974:343]

Prior to this ruling, all of the treaty tribes together had been catching only about 5% of the salmon and steelhead harvested in the region (figure from Cohen et al. 1986). Accordingly, opposition to the Boldt decision from non-Indian fishing interests was widespread and fierce. Private citizens sued in state court to block state regulations that Boldt ordered to implement his decision. In defiance of the federal courts, the Washington State Supreme Court ultimately upheld these suits, prohibiting the state Department of Fisheries from complying with Boldt's order. The state supreme court found both that the treaties did not give the tribes a right to a share of the fish harvest and that such a right would violate the equal protection clause of the Fourteenth Amendment, since it would not apply to non-Indian citizens (see *Puget Sound Gillnetters Association v. Moos* 1977 and *Fishing Vessel Association v. Tollefson* 1977). This led Judge Boldt, working with the local United States Attorney and other federal law enforcement agencies, to issue a series of orders giving Boldt direct authority to supervise state fisheries as necessary to preserve federally recognized tribal treaty fishing rights (*United States v. Washington* 1978). His action was upheld by the Ninth Circuit Court of Appeals, which commented, "Except for some desegregation cases..., the district court has faced the most concerted official and private efforts to frustrate a decree of a federal court witnessed in this century" (*United States v. Washington* 1978). Washington Attorney General Slade Gorton appealed this circuit court decision to the United States Supreme Court (which had earlier denied hearing the case, essentially affirming the decisions of lower courts; *United States v. Washington* 1975), seeking a final resolution of the issues raised by the state supreme court. In *Washington v. Washington State Commercial Passenger Fishing Vessel Association*, the United States Supreme Court quickly dispensed of the state supreme court's objection based on the Fourteenth Amendment:

> The simplest answer to this argument is that this Court has already held that these treaties confer enforceable special benefits on signatory Indian tribes, and has repeatedly held that the peculiar semisovereign and constitutionally recognized sta-

tus of Indians justifies special treatment on their behalf when rationally related to the Government's "unique obligation toward the Indians." [*Washington v. Washington State Commercial Passenger Fishing Vessel Association* 1978:673]

In regard to the tribal treaty right to an allocation of the fish harvest, the Supreme Court found,

> The division arrived at by the District Court is...consistent with our earlier decisions concerning Indian treaty rights to scarce natural resources....It bears repeating, however, that the 50% figure imposes a maximum but not a minimum allocation....[T]he central principle here must be that Indian treaty rights to a natural resource that once was thoroughly and exclusively exploited by the Indians secures so much as, but no more than, is necessary to provide the Indians with a livelihood—that is to say, a moderate living. [*Washington v. Washington State Commercial Passenger Fishing Vessel Association* 1978:685–686]

The Supreme Court did make some minor modifications to Judge Boldt's decision. Whereas Judge Boldt had excluded from the tribal share fish caught for ceremonial or subsistence needs and fish caught on tribal reservations, the Supreme Court ruled that all fish caught by Indians should be counted against their share of the harvest:

> Accordingly, any fish (1) taken in Washington waters or in United States waters off the coast of Washington, (2) taken from runs of fish that pass through the Indians' usual and accustomed fishing grounds, and (3) taken by either members of the Indian tribes that are parties to this litigation, on the one hand, or by non-Indian citizens of Washington, on the other hand, shall count against that party's respective share of the fish. [*Washington v. Washington State Commercial Passenger Fishing Vessel Association* 1978:689]

To implement this decision, the state and tribes have chosen not to follow a strict count of tribal and non-tribal harvests, but instead have annually negotiated a variety of details concerning where and when fish can be caught by tribal and non-tribal fishermen; these rules are intended to comply with the equal shares ordered by the court (P. Katzen, Kanji and Katzen, personal communication). Crucial to making these arrangements work, the courts have ordered that tribes be made "co-managers" of the fishery resource, requiring tribal consent on a variety of issues involving harvest regulations and hatchery operations. Individual tribes work with the state on issues affecting their "usual and accustomed" fishing grounds; collectively, the tribes work with the state through the Northwest Indian Fisheries Commission.

The Right to Habitat Protection: Waiting for Concrete Facts

Phase II of *United States v. Washington* did not proceed until after the United States Supreme Court's decision in phase I. By that time, Judge Boldt had retired and jurisdiction over the case had been transferred to Judge William Orrick. He had little difficulty ruling in 1980 that hatchery fish must be included in the tribal share of harvest:

> The record...establishes that the State has developed and promoted its artificial propagation program in order to replace the fish that were artificially lost....It is equally evident that hatchery fish represent an ever-increasing proportion of the total fish population in the case area....The inescapable conclusion is that if hatchery fish were to be excluded from the allocation, the Indians' treaty-secured right to an adequate supply of fish—the right for which they traded millions of acres of land and resources—would be placed in jeopardy. The tribes' share would steadily dwindle and the paramount purpose of the treaties would be subverted. [*United States v. Washington* 1980:198–199]

This decision was upheld on appeal (*United States v. Washington* 1982). The issue of a tribal right to habitat protection, however, has had a far more complicated history, which remains unresolved today.

The federal government and tribes did not initially allege any specific violation or seek any specific remedy with respect to treaty rights for the protection of salmon habitat. They sought approval of a standard requiring that future actions by the state, including its regulation of development and other actions taken by third parties, would result in "no significant deterioration" of salmon habitat (*United States v. Washington* 1980:207). Judge Orrick disagreed with that precise formulation of the standard, but he approved the general principle that the treaties "implicitly incorporated...[the] right to have fishery habitat protected from man-made despoliation" (*United States v. Washington* 1980:187). Orrick found that the tribes' proposed standard of "no significant deterioration" was derived from federal environmental legislation rather than the treaties, and so was inappropriate to the case. Instead, his order imposed the duty on the state (as well as the United States and third parties, including local governments and private individuals and businesses) "to refrain from degrading the fish habitat to an extent that would deprive the tribes of their moderate living needs" (*United States v. Washington* 1980:208). Orrick found that the fact that the tribes' harvest allocation was already set at 50% "creates the presumption that the tribes' moderate living needs exceed 50% and are not being fully satisfied under the treaties." Therefore,

> the State must...bear the burden...to demonstrate that any environmental degradation of the fish habitat proximately caused by the State's actions (including the authorization of third parties' activities) will not impair the tribes' ability to satisfy their moderate living needs. Naturally, the [tribal] plaintiffs must shoulder the initial burden of proving that the challenged action(s) will proximately cause the fish habitat to be degraded such that the rearing or production potential of the fish will be impaired or the size or quality of the run will be diminished. [*United States v. Washington* 1980:208]

This was a relatively light burden for the tribes and a heavy burden for the state, especially given the uncertainty of how "moderate living needs" should be defined.

This ruling was reviewed twice by the Ninth Circuit Court of Appeals, in 1982 by a panel of three judges and again in 1985 by an "en banc" panel of 11 judges. In its initial decision, the circuit court reversed Orrick's ruling, which it said would have established "a comprehensive environmental servitude with open-ended and unforeseeable consequences" (*United States v. Washington* 1982:1381). Instead, it ruled that the treaties required that "when considering projects that may have significant environmental impact, both the State and the Tribes must take reasonable steps commensurate with the respective resources and abilities of each to preserve and enhance the fishery" (*United States v. Washington* 1982:1375). The Supreme Court's decision in *Washington v. Washington State Commercial Passenger Fishing Vessel Association* "did not say that the treaty right guarantees the Indians that there will always be an 'adequate supply of fish'" (*United States v. Washington* 1982:1377). Since *Washington v. Washington State Commercial Passenger Fishing Vessel Association* set a maximum allocation of 50% for the tribes even if that amount did not meet the tribes' moderate living needs (1982:1377), the court argued that the Supreme Court's decision undermined Orrick's use of moderate living needs as a standard for a right to habitat protection (*United States v. Washington* 1982:1382). As two of the three judges on the 1982 panel said,

> The purpose of the Stevens Treaties was to settle any and all Indian claims to land title in the case area so that non-Indian settlers could develop their lands without conflict with the Indians. It would be ironic indeed if the fishing clause in the very treaties negotiated to *eliminate* property disputes between Indians and non-Indians became the source of continual litigation over the effect of the use of non-Indian property on Indian rights. To avoid this result, the environmental right must be tempered by a reasonableness requirement such as we have recognized. [Emphasis in original; *United States v. Washington* 1982:1389]

How this opinion related to the Supreme Court's *Winans* decision, which established an "environmental servitude" understood as a property right on all non-tribal lands, was not explained.

In an opinion officially concurring with his fellow two judges, Judge Stephen Reinhardt formulated the state's duty differently. He said the state must take "all reasonable measures... to preserve the share of fish to which the Indians are entitled":

> The fact that the treaty does not contain absolute protections should not obscure the important obligations that the treaty does impose....If it is inconceivable that the Indians would have agreed to be required to fish on the same terms as non-Indians, it is far more inconceivable that they would have allowed the State to permit the fishery to be destroyed altogether. [*United States v. Washington* 1982:1390–1391]

After further legal wrangling, this decision was appealed to the en banc panel of 11 judges from the circuit court, which issued a split decision in April 1985. The majority determined that the decisions of *both* Orrick and the earlier three-judge panel had been premature and

> contrary to the exercise of sound judicial discretion. The legal standards that will govern the State's precise obligations and duties under the treaty with respect to

> the myriad State actions that may affect the environment of the treaty area will depend for their definition and articulation upon concrete facts which underlie a dispute in a particular case. [*United States v. Washington* 1985:1357]

Seven of the 11 judges joined in the majority decision. Four of the seven, however, issued concurring opinions with different reasoning than that quoted above. Two of the three judges who issued the 1982 opinion were on the en banc panel (Judge Reinhardt was not); in joining the majority, they noted that they had not changed their position but believed it was "better to reach an opinion that is tolerable by a majority than...to adhere to one's preferred opinion" (*United States v. Washington* 1985:1360). Two other judges stated that, should a later decision affirming a right to habitat protection come to them, they would not necessarily find the state liable for treaty violations by third parties whose actions the state merely permitted or authorized (*United States v. Washington* 1985:1360–1362).

In dissent, two other judges agreed with Orrick's original decision, arguing, "A declaratory judgment need not resolve all the issues in controversy, as long as it resolves a significant disputed issue....Declaratory relief on the environmental issue would resolve a complex and long-lasting dispute over critical aspects of the parties' rights and responsibilities under the treaty" (*United States v. Washington* 1985:1364). Another judge agreed that a declaratory judgment was proper in the case, but chose not to express an opinion on what that judgment should be (*United States v. Washington* 1985:1368). Finally, another judge concluded that because the issues of hatchery fish and environmental protection were related (since hatchery fish serve in part as mitigation for environmental degradation), the en banc panel should never have accepted the appeal at all if it was not prepared to rule on the merits of both issues (*United States v. Washington* 1985:1370).

Culvert Repairs: The First "Concrete Case"

For nearly 16 years, no "concrete case" was filed to test the treaty right to habitat protection, while the tribes focused on implementing their co-management relationship and their participation in negotiating and implementing the Pacific Salmon Treaty. *United States v. Washington* remained open for sub-proceedings, which placed a variety of actions under court review. In January 2001, treaty tribes brought a sub-proceeding for a court order that would require the state of Washington to accelerate its program for identifying and repairing culverts that block passage of salmon under state roads. The tribes asserted that overall cutbacks in salmon harvests had decreased the total tribal catch to approximately its level before the Boldt decision and, therefore, well below their moderate living needs. They cited the state's own reports estimating that culverts owned by the Washington Department of Transportation blocked or obstructed "adult salmonid access to at least 249 linear stream miles, at least 407,464 square meters of productive salmon spawning habitat, and at least 1,619,839 square meters of productive salmonid rearing habitat," which the state reports estimated could produce "approximately 200,000 adult salmonids" if opened to passage (*United States v. Washington* 2001a:5). Based on current appropriations, the reports indicated that it would take 20 to 100 years for the state to remove all of these blockages. Additionally, the state's Department of Natural Resources and Department of Fish and Wildlife owned other culverts blocking fish passage, which both agencies were in the process of inventorying. The tribes asked the court to require that the state complete a comprehensive inventory of all its culvert blockages within 18 months and remove them within 5 years (*United States v. Washington* 2001a:6–7).

Prior to filing the lawsuit, the tribes had been negotiating with the state to accelerate the culvert repairs, but they sought more in these early negotiations than faster action on obstructions to fish passage. The tribes would not accept any settlement that did not include the state's formal recognition of a treaty right to habitat protection. The tribes considered culverts to offer a nearly ideal test case for this right. Opening passage to productive habitat is widely viewed by scientists as the simplest, quickest, and most reliable way to increase natural production of salmon in most cases. The state's own reports acknowledged responsibility for the problem and documented its extent, its consequences, and the actions necessary to fix it, thus settling many of the factual questions that might otherwise be raised in a habitat case. Once this case established a tribal right to habitat protection, the tribes planned to apply the right toward other causes of habitat degradation (M. Morisset, Morisset, Schlosser, Jozwiak and McGaw, personal communication). They saw such a right as potentially a far stronger tool than the Endangered Species Act to protect and restore salmon habitat, for reasons discussed in the introduction to this chapter (R. Anderson, University of Washington School of Law, and Morisset, personal communications).

Given the potential costs of recognizing such a right, the state of Washington was also unprepared to compromise on this point in negotiations. Notably, a treaty-based obligation to repair culverts would be a retroactive responsibility, rather than the prospective responsibility the tribes sought in 1980 to avoid future losses in productive habitat. If approved, this precedent could vastly expand the potential issues the tribes might raise in future litigation. Acknowledging that the tribes cited the state's own reports on culvert blockages, the state argued that it had substantially reduced the number of blockages on state roads since the time of the Boldt decision and therefore its culverts could not be the cause of the tribes' decreased harvests. As a practical matter, the state added, fixing the remaining blockages was not possible in 5 years. The work would cost hundreds of millions of dollars and the speed of repairs was limited by the "availability of qualified design and construction personnel, limited time periods for conducting instream work, and lengthy permitting time" (*United States v. Washington* 2001b:4). The estimates of lost salmon production in state reports assumed that production was limited only by the amount of available habitat, which the state said was not necessarily true—opening new habitat could potentially just redistribute existing population levels. More fundamentally, the state repeated arguments from the circuit court's initial ruling in 1982 on treaty rights to habitat protection, saying that the treaties only guaranteed that the tribes would receive a "fair share" of the available harvest, not that habitat would remain productive enough to provide them a moderate living from fishing (*United States v. Washington* 2001c). If there was any liability for lost production from the culvert blockages, the state argued that it belonged to the federal government, which had a trust responsibility to protect tribal treaty rights and yet had helped fund, or approved standards for, most of the problematic culverts. Additionally, the state argued that the tribes were prohibited from suing it under the Eleventh Amendment (*United States v. Washington* 2001d; see Chapter 6, pages 92–93).

The federal government has a complicated role in this lawsuit. Consistent with its historic role in the case and its trust responsibility to ensure fulfillment of treaty obligations, the federal government joined the tribes as a co-plaintiff against the state. The Eleventh Amendment offers no protection to the state if the United States seeks the same result from the lawsuit as the tribes (see *Arizona v. California* 1983 and *Mille Lacs Band of Chippewa Indians v. Minnesota* 1999). (The Eleventh Amendment may provide no protection to the state, regardless, since *United States v. Washington* today is a continuation of the earlier suit, in which the tribes had already been accepted as co-plaintiffs.) There is no guarantee, however, that the federal government and the tribes will ultimately seek the same result from the culvert case. In phase I of *United States v. Washington*, the tribes initially sought as large a share of the salmon harvest as necessary to meet their commercial and subsistence needs, while the federal government sought essentially the same result as the courts ultimately delivered—half the share of the harvest or what was necessary to meet tribal needs, whichever was less (*Washington v. Washington State Commercial Passenger Fishing Vessel Association* 1978:670). In the culvert case, the federal government has a stronger interest than it did in phase I to seek a different result than the tribes, since any treaty right to habitat protection would apply not just to the state but also to the federal government, as well as to local governments and private parties. However, even if the federal government would prefer to minimize treaty obligations for habitat protection, it is not wholly free to seek that result, since the tribes could sue it for allegedly breaching its trust responsibility.

Negotiations for a settlement ultimately proved fruitless and the case is now scheduled for trial in March 2007 (Morisset, personal communication). Whatever decision is reached will probably be appealed, first to the Ninth Circuit and potentially to the U.S. Supreme Court, meaning a final resolution to the case is still probably many years away. An early decision in favor of the tribes could, however, still be at least partially enforced prior to a final resolution if the tribes demonstrate that they would be irreparably harmed otherwise.

Tribal Water Rights and Other Potentially Relevant Cases: An Implied Right to Environmental Protection?

The tribes can cite a number of precedents supporting their argument for a treaty right to habitat protection. Perhaps the strongest precedents recognize tribal rights to sufficient water to fulfill the purposes of their treaties, including hunting and fishing rights as well as irrigated agriculture.[4] Judge Orrick's initial decision for the tribes in 1980 found that a right to habitat protection derived from the fishing clause in the Stevens treaties was "consonant" with this "implied-reservation-of-water doctrine," though he noted that the doctrine "reserves only that amount of water necessary to fulfill the purpose of the reservation, no more" (*United States v. Washington* 1980:204, 205; earlier case is *Cappaert v. United States* 1976:141). Three years later, the Ninth Circuit affirmed a district court decision in favor of the Klamath Tribes' water rights for on-reservation hunting and fishing, assigning the rights a priority date of "time immemorial" (*United States v. Adair* 1983:1411, 1414–1415[5]). Concerned this might impose a "wilderness servitude" against all changes since the treaty, the court tied the scope of the right to the Supreme Court's "moderate living" standard, as Orrick had done with the right to habitat protection. In a 2002 follow-up to this case, the federal district court in Oregon found that parties opposed to the amount of water the tribes claimed as their right must provide "persuasive evidence" that a lesser amount could meet this standard (*United States v. Adair* 1983:1278).

However, the initial Ninth Circuit decision that overruled Orrick in 1982 disagreed with transferring the water doctrine to habitat. This was largely because of its more fundamental conclusion that an environmental right was not necessary to fulfill the purpose of the treaties, given its view that the treaties guaranteed tribes "a fair share, as opposed to an adequate supply, of the fish" (*United States v. Washington* 1982:1384). As a practical matter, the court also noted that the scope of Orrick's environmental right included "all State or State-authorized activities affecting the environment, not just those involving appropriative consumption of water," which gave it "the potential to disrupt the existing state regulatory network much more severely than the implied-reservation-of-water doctrine has ever disrupted the system of prior appropriation of water in the Western states" (*United States v. Washington* 1982:1388).

Presumably with some of these same fears, the Washington State Supreme Court created a new category of "diminished" treaty rights in a 1993 case regarding the water rights of the Yakama Indian Nation. As evidence for the rights being diminished, the court cited "encroachment upon and significant damage to the Indians' treaty fishing rights" from an unspecified series of "congressional, executive, administrative and judicial acts" over much of the 20th century (*State Department of Ecology v. Yakama Reservation Irrigation District* 1993:1319–1323, as quoted in Blumm 2002:262). The tribe did not appeal, perhaps fearing that a hostile Supreme Court would affirm and give the case national implications, though no prior case law supported diminishing treaty rights without express authorization from Congress (Blumm 2002). Nevertheless, even recognizing diminished rights revolutionized the Bureau of Reclamation's operations on the Yakima River, leading lower courts to establish a duty of providing flows to "maintain all life stages" of salmon (Blumm 2002:263).

---

[4] The seminal case for this principle is *Winters v. United States* 1908.

[5] Affirming *United States v. Adair* 1979, as quoted in Blumm 2002:260.

In 2005, an en banc panel of the Ninth Circuit decided, on a 6–5 vote, that the Skokomish Indian Tribe could not sue Tacoma Public Utilities for damages caused by the city's 1930 diversion of the entire north fork of the Skokomish River out of the watershed and through Cushman Dam (*Skokomish Indian Tribe v. United States* 2005). The decision, which the Supreme Court denied to review on appeal (Suter 2006), turned on the surprising rationale that the treaty had not expressly provided for damages from third parties. It is not clear, however, whether the court would have decided against the tribe if it had sought compensation under a common law claim for damages to its property rights as established by the treaty—a fine distinction (*Skokomish Indian Tribe v. United States* 2005). Meanwhile, the Ninth Circuit later vacated part of its original decision, which found that the tribe did not possess water rights for fishing, after both the tribe and the United States requested reconsideration (Rodgers 2005).

Other cases have supported additional principles besides the implied reservation of water doctrine that are consistent with a treaty right to habitat protection. Courts have recognized treaty rights to habitat threatened by dam reservoirs[6] and timber sales,[7] as well as to water rights necessary to maintain cool water temperatures downstream[8] (which more closely parallels the relationship of fish habitat to land uses than do other water rights cases). Ultimately, law professor Michael Blumm argues that courts should, consistent with other principles of common law, recognize a principle of "no unreasonable interference" in the treaty right to fish harvests necessary for a moderate living.[9] This principle would require due consideration of the treaty right throughout the regulatory and permitting process; tribal participation could potentially be required in all major development decisions that could affect their treaty rights.

It will probably not be known definitively for a number of years what, if any, right to habitat protection tribes in the Puget Sound area will be granted. They may not win a right of "no unreasonable interference," but it seems probable that they will win a right sufficient to support at least some harvest, since a contrary decision would clearly thwart the purpose of the treaties' fishing clause. If habitat conditions in certain areas, such as the heavily urbanized Lake Washington watershed, are unlikely to be able to support harvestable levels of fish on a regular basis, affected tribes may be offered cash settlements (though arguably this would require congressional authorization; M. Blumm, Lewis and Clark Law School, personal communication). The tribes have a strong preference for a result that allows them to continue fishing (Morisset and Anderson, personal communications), but tribes whose "usual and

[6] For example, see *Confederated Tribes of the Umatilla Indian Reservation v. Callaway* 1973 or *Confederated Tribes of the Umatilla Indian Reservation v. Alexander* 1977, as cited in Blumm 2002: 254.

[7] See *Klamath Tribes v. United States* 1996, as cited in Blumm 2002:267.

[8] See *United States v. Anderson* 1982, as cited in Blumm 2002:259.

[9] The common law principles concern *profits a pendre*, the legal right to take and remove a resource from another's land (see Blumm 2002).

accustomed" fishing areas are most affected by the degraded habitat in these watersheds will have a greater incentive than others to accept cash instead of restored habitat, if the latter appears impractical or too expensive.

Tribal Treaty Rights and the Endangered Species Act

Because of the ESA's effects on harvest, hatcheries, and habitat, the act has a complex relationship to tribal treaty rights in Puget Sound. At least in the short term, the ESA potentially conflicts with treaty-backed goals of tribes by directly limiting harvest of listed species. There is also a potential conflict if the ESA restricts hatchery production to protect wild salmon, since that decreases the number of fish available for harvest, again at least in the short term. Though the ESA's protections for habitat can benefit the tribes, these protections are difficult to apply to non-federal lands, including nearly all of the lowland and nearshore habitats that are critical to Puget Sound salmon, as discussed in Chapters 7 and 8.

The National Marine Fisheries Service (NMFS) says it will apply the protections of the Endangered Species Act to improve conditions for listed salmon until "the abundance of fish is sufficient to satisfy treaty fishing rights and to fulfill the trust obligations of the United States" (USOFR 2000:42440). As discussed in Chapter 8, the 4(d) rule NMFS issued for Puget Sound Chinook salmon and other threatened salmon allows for some harvest of the species pursuant to approved resource management plans. In explaining the rule, NMFS defended allowing tribal harvest by noting that non-tribal mixed-stock fisheries in the ocean and parts of Puget Sound inevitably involve some incidental take of listed salmon. If tribes are prohibited from any take of listed salmon at their traditional harvest locations in estuaries and rivers, they would be held to a different standard of conservation than non-tribal fishermen, who already had caught substantial numbers of listed fish in the ocean. NMFS acknowledged that tribal harvest at terminal areas is "difficult to characterize…as 'incidental' take," but said prohibiting tribal harvest would be both discriminatory and unnecessary so long as resource management plans met the standard of not jeopardizing the survival and recovery of listed fish. NMFS did not establish more specific criteria than this standard for approving tribal resource management plans, saying that doing so would be inappropriate given the federal government's responsibility to treat the tribes as sovereign nations (USOFR 2000).

NMFS's approach on these issues has sought to comply with Secretarial Order 3206, on "American Indian Tribal Rights, Federal-Tribal Trust Responsibilities, and the Endangered Species Act," issued in 1997. The intent of the order was to "harmonize" federal responsibilities under tribal treaties and statutory law, recognizing "that Indian tribes are governmental sovereigns with inherent powers to make and enforce laws, administer justice, and manage and control their natural resources." The order required that whenever the Departments of Interior and Commerce consider actions under the ESA that might affect tribal interests they must "consult with, and seek the participation of, the affected Indian tribes to the maximum extent practicable."

Consistent with *Fishing Vessel* and other Supreme Court decisions on hunting and fishing rights in the 1960s and 1970s,[10] the departments must determine that all of the following criteria have been met before they restrict a tribal activity for taking a listed species:

1. The restriction is reasonable and necessary for the conservation of the species at issue;
2. The conservation purpose of the restriction cannot be achieved by reasonable regulation of non-Indian activities;
3. The measure is the least restrictive alternative available to achieve the required conservation purpose;
4. The restriction does not discriminate against Indian activities, either as stated or applied; and
5. Voluntary tribal measures are not adequate to achieve the necessary conservation purpose.

The order established no new legally enforceable tribal rights or federal responsibilities, but did help to clarify how the Departments of Commerce and Interior are to interpret those rights and responsibilities under existing law (Secretarial Order, section 2, Scope and limitations). Puget Sound tribes may ultimately argue that the way the ESA is being applied in the region violates the order, since restrictions on hatcheries and harvest in Washington waters have been more substantial than restrictions on habitat, as discussed in Chapter 8. However, the different degrees of restriction are arguably due more to the different ways the ESA applies to these activities than to any discretion NMFS has in enforcing the act. Tribes would probably not seriously consider suing to enforce ESA protections against habitat degradation until the culvert case is resolved, since their treaty rights for habitat protection may prove stronger than the ESA, particularly on non-federal lands.

Treaty Rights and Protecting Biodiversity in the Puget Sound Ecoregion

Just as state of Washington reports document lost salmon production due to state culvert blockages, watershed plans developed by local watershed groups under the Shared Strategy are documenting lost salmon production due to habitat problems throughout the Puget Sound area. Under the strategy, each plan is estimating the current ability of its watershed to support salmon production. The strategy asks that each plan compare this both to what would be required for recovery in that watershed and to the predicted improvement from actions the watershed group proposes to protect and improve habitat. If courts determine that the state must accelerate its culvert repair program to correct past violations of tribal treaty rights to habitat protection, watershed plans

[10] These were incorporated in the settlement of *United States v. Oregon* 1988. See "Questions and Answers—American Indian Tribal Rights, Federal-Tribal Trust Responsibilities and the Endangered Species Act" (http://library.findlaw.com/1999/Mar/18/128205.html), which accompanied Secretarial Order 3206.

under the strategy will provide an opportunity to apply those rights on a much more comprehensive basis across the Puget Sound region. Implementation of recovery plans under the Endangered Species Act is voluntary, but tribes may seek to make at least parts of watershed plans mandatory. If individual plans do not propose actions to achieve harvestable levels for populations of listed salmon in their watersheds (proposing less in heavily urbanized areas, for example), affected tribes may sue. Tribal treaty rights may thereby interact with the ESA to create stronger protections for salmon habitat than either could ensure alone.

In addition to the right to harvest salmon and steelhead, the Stevens treaties also protect tribal rights to harvest shellfish (except from "beds staked or cultivated by citizens") and the "privilege of hunting...on open and unclaimed lands." These clauses could potentially extend the significance of the treaties to aspects of the Puget Sound ecosystem not closely related to salmon. Courts have recognized a tribal right to harvest naturally occurring shellfish on the same basis as other fish—that is, half the harvest from a tribe's "usual and accustomed" locations, even where this involves crossing private property to access shellfish beds (see *United States v. Washington* 1998). If tribes win a right to habitat protection for salmon, these rights would probably apply to shellfish as well. The most important factor limiting shellfish harvest is typically contamination by bacteria that do not cause health problems for salmon. To increase shellfish harvest, tribes might seek large reductions in sources of pollution, including non-point sources that the ESA and the Clean Water Act generally have not addressed effectively (see discussion in Chapter 12). If tribes also seek protection of wildlife habitat for hunting, they would not be able to apply the same standard of protection, since the treaties provide for hunting only "on open and unclaimed lands" rather than "at all usual and accustomed" locations and describe this as a privilege rather than a right. Still, if game traditionally hunted by tribes has dwindled to a point where it can no longer be hunted at all, tribes may be able to win recognition of a treaty right to the protection of at least some wildlife habitat (Morisset, personal communication).

Potentially through all these avenues, tribal treaty rights to habitat protection are likely to become a critical part of the legal framework for protecting biodiversity in the Puget Sound ecoregion.

References

Arizona v. California, 460 U.S. 605 (1983).

Blumm, M. C. 2002. Sacrificing the salmon: a legal and policy history of the decline of Columbia basin salmon. BookWorld Publications, Lake Mary, Florida.

Boyd, R. 1990. Northwest coast, 1774–1874. Pages 135–148 *in* W. Suttles, editor. Handbook of North American Indians, volume 7: demographic history. Smithsonian Institution, Washington, D.C.

Cappaert v. United States, 426 U.S. 128 (1976).

Cohen, F. G., J. LaFrance, and V. L. Bowden. 1986. Treaties on trial: the continuing controversy over northwest Indian fishing rights. University of Washington Press, Seattle, 1986.

Confederated Tribes of the Umatilla Indian Reservation v. Alexander, 440 F.Supp. 553 (D. Or. 1977).
Confederated Tribes of the Umatilla Indian Reservation v. Callaway, No. 72-211, slip op. at 5-7 (D. Or. Aug 17, 1973).
Fishing Vessel Association v. Tollefson, 89 Wash. 2d 276, 571 P. 2d 1373 (1977).
Jones v. Meehan, 175 U.S. 1 (1899).
Klamath Tribes v. United States, No. 96-381-HA (D. Or. 1996).
Lackey, R. T., D. H. Lach, and S. L. Duncan, editors. 2006. Salmon 2100: the future of wild Pacific salmon. American Fisheries Society, Bethesda, Maryland.
Menominee Tribe v. United States, 391 U.S. 404 (1968).
Mille Lacs Band of Chippewa Indians v. Minnesota, 124 F.3d 904, 913 (8th Cir. 1997), affirmed 526 U.S. 172 (1999).
Montgomery, D. R. 2003. King of fish: the thousand year run of salmon. Westview Press, Boulder, Colorado.
NRC (National Research Council). 1996. Upstream: salmon and society in the Pacific Northwest. National Academy Press, Washington, D.C.
Puget Sound Gillnetters Association v. Moos, 88 Wash. 2d 677, 565 P. 2d 1151 (1977).
Rodgers, W.H. 2005. Judicial regrets and the case of the Cushman Dam. Environmental Law 35(3): 397-414. Lewis and Clark Law School. Portland, Oregon.
Skokomish Indian Tribe v. United States, 410 F.3d 506 (9th Cir. 2005).
Skokomish Indian Tribe v. United States, No. 05-434, U.S. Supreme Court, Petition for a Writ of Certiorari, Brief for the United States in Opposition. 2005.
Sohappy v. Smith, 302 F.Supp. 899 (D. Ore. 1969).
State Department of Ecology v. Yakama Reservation Irrigation District, 850 P.2d 1306 (Wash. 1993).
Suter, W.K. 2006. Letter to Mason Morisset, January 9, 2006, Office of the Clerk, Supreme Court of the United States. Washington, D.C.
Taylor, III, J. E. 1999. Making salmon: an environmental history of the northwest fisheries crisis. University of Washington Press, Seattle.
United States v. Adair, 478 F. Supp. 336 (D. Or. 1979).
United States v. Adair, 723 F.2d 1394 (9th Cir. 1983).
United States v. Anderson, 591 F.Supp. 1 (E.D. Wash. 1982), affirmed 736 F.2d 1358 (9th Cir. 1984).
United States v. Washington, 384 F.Supp. 312 (1974).
United States v. Washington, 423 U.S. 1086 (1975).
United States v. Washington, Phase II, 506 F.Supp.187 (1980).
United States v. Washington, 694 F.2d 1374 (9th Cir. 1982)
United States v. Washington, 759 F.2d 1353 (1985).
United States v. Washington, 157 F.3d 630 (9th Cir. 1998).
United States v. Washington, Civil No. C70-9213, Sub-Proceeding 01-01, Request for determination (W.D. Wash. 2001).
United States v. Washington, Civil No. C70-9213, Sub-Proceeding 01-01, State of Washington's answer and cross and counter requests for determination (W. D. Wash. 2001).
United States v. Washington, Civil No. C70-9213, Sub-Proceeding 01-01, Brief in support of Washington's motion for judgment on the pleadings, RE: law of the case (W. D. Wash. 2001).
United States v. Washington, Civil No. C70-9213, Sub-Proceeding 01-01, State's answer (W. D. Wash. 2001).
United States v. Winans, 198 U.S. 371 (1905).
USOFR (U.S. Office of the Federal Register). 2000. Endangered and threatened species; final rule governing take of 14 threatened salmon and steelhead evolutionarily significant units (ESUs), Federal Register 65:132(10 July 2000):42421–42481.

Washington v. Washington State Commercial Passenger Fishing Vessel Association, 443 U.S. 658 (1978).
Winters v. United States, 207 U.S. 564 (1908).

Chapter 14. Choosing an Alternative Future

> The social structures and institutions [of]...the Pacific Northwest have proved incapable of ensuring a long-term future for salmon, in large part because they do not operate at the right time and space scales. [NRC 1996:360]

The above statement, from the advisory body of the National Academy of Sciences, is now more than 10 years old. Despite much good work since then, it remains accurate today—all the more so when we look beyond salmon to include the rest of the Northwest's extraordinary natural heritage. Part II of this book describes *why* the statement is accurate. Part I proposes a way to meet the academy's challenge.

To elaborate on the academy's vague reference to "time and space scales," if we want to conserve our natural heritage, we must recognize the scales at which our ecosystems function and act accordingly. In the Puget Sound ecoregion, this primarily means treating Puget Sound itself as an ecosystem, extending from the crest of the Cascades to the heart of the Olympic Mountains. Watershed councils and the Shared Strategy for Puget Sound are a start toward this approach, but, unfortunately, a relatively feeble start. Neither has the authority to require elements of their plans, just as regional land-use planning bodies lacked enforcement authority prior to the Growth Management Act. Watershed councils and the Shared Strategy also have raised little money for implementation. They are no match for the forces of population growth and climate change over the next 50 to 100 years.

That is not their fault. These groups—and we—cannot counter such weaknesses just by working harder within our existing "social structures and institutions." Even where those institutions have been specifically designed to address environmental issues, they "do not operate at the right time and space scales." Part II offers many examples. The purpose of the Endangered Species Act (ESA) is to "conserve the ecosystems on which endangered and threatened species depend." Yet where most land is privately owned and regulated under state and local laws (which is to say, the great majority of the country, including the Puget Sound ecoregion), the ESA cannot address losses of habitat that accumulate over time and space even for currently listed species, let alone for the many additional species that deserve to be listed. The objective of the Clean Water Act is to "restore and maintain the chemical, physical, and biological integrity of the Nation's waters," yet it has no authority over land use, even though, over time, upstream land uses largely determine the integrity that is possible for receiving waters. The framework for Washington's land-use laws, the Growth Management Act (GMA), mandates that local governments "protect the functions and values of critical areas." Yet the GMA also mandates that local governments accommodate growth, while never acknowledging that the two mandates are impossible to reconcile across large parts of the landscape. The state's vesting laws undercut even existing growth management goals by favoring the desire of developers for certainty over the public's interest in sound land-use planning, to a degree not matched by any other state in the country. Washington water law never clarifies what "overriding considerations of the public interest" justify authorizing water withdrawals that conflict with stream flows "necessary...for preservation of wildlife, fish, scenic, aesthetic, and other environmental values." The Watershed Planning Act asserts that it "serves the state's vital interests" to place such decisions in the hands of local people, supposedly ensuring protection of both existing water rights and instream flows for fish. But in much of the state, water rights *already* conflict with instream flows needed for fish. Worse yet, across almost the entire Puget Sound ecoregion, the state has never even attempted to settle who actually *has* water rights or how much they total. In the few places where the state has defined flows needed for fish, they are scientifically suspect and legally junior to all water rights issued previously.

Over the past 40 years, we have enacted laws at the federal, state, and local levels to address specific environmental issues. Lawmakers have relied, at best, on the scientific knowledge available at the time and have made the political compromises necessary to get these laws adopted. Without question, these laws form a great legacy compared to what came before them. They have accomplished enormously valuable things. But taken together, they do not form a coherent program to conserve our natural heritage. Their weaknesses can seem forbiddingly complex, but I would argue they are also reassuringly simple. The complexity is why Part II of this book is more than three times as long as Part I. Analyzing the weaknesses of these laws and related programs is challenging. It requires detailed critiques and recommendations because implementation of any serious alternative ultimately involves such specificity. But articulating the fundamental arguments for an alternative, as I have tried to do in Part I, is much simpler, once one understands the most critical needs of an ecosystem.

I agree with Jack Ward Thomas, one of the architects of the Northwest Forest Plan, who wrote

> There is no final ecological truth. All knowledge is current approximation, and each addition to that knowledge is but a small, incremental step toward understanding. For not only are ecosystems more complex than we think—they are more complex than we *can* think. [Thomas 1992:15]

The details of any major ecosystem more than match the complexity of the legal and institutional issues that I have analyzed in this book. It may seem paradoxical, then, that I argue we should turn to the needs of the Puget Sound ecoregion to help simplify these issues. Our ecoregion is even more complex than the old-growth forest of Thomas' essay, since old growth is only one among its many major ecosystems. Yet if we step back to consider the most important places for how the ecoregion functions, they are obvious: floodplains, foothill forests, the Puget Sound shoreline, riparian areas, a few special places (e.g., the south sound prairies, the Snoqualmie Pass Wildlife Corridor, the forests along Hood Canal, and select refuge basins for salmon), and areas that are already well protected under the Northwest Forest Plan and other conservation plans. No major study has ever contradicted this list. Almost anyone with experience in the outdoors can understand it. If we focus on what these places need, we can build our conservation programs around those needs, rather than be driven by the institutional priorities of today's programs, which do not add up to conservation. In short, we should let "the land speak first," to quote the Central Puget Sound Growth Management Hearings Board.

The actions I advocate would match the "time and space scales" of the ecoregion's special places in two crucial ways. First, they would recognize the importance of these places across the entire ecoregion and prioritize protection and restoration accordingly. Second, they would create incentives and mechanisms for individual actions to support these priorities over time—through "environmental sin taxes," new approaches to mitigation, stormwater plans attuned to specific watersheds, compensation to landowners for ecological services, and other changes from our current approach.

The time scales of ecosystems are long. We would do well to emulate Native Americans, who still think in terms of many generations. It is fitting that their treaties, now more than a century and a half old, may provide the strongest legal basis for getting us to change our ways. Our choice truly is between "alternative futures," as the Willamette River study discussed in Chapter 2 phrased it. Staying on our current path, despite its complex regulatory structure, heated debates, and earnest efforts to save the environment, will continue our ecoregion's incremental decline, year after year. A different future is possible, but it requires that we change the scales of our laws and institutions to match those of our ecosystems. There is no other way to conserve our natural heritage, given the pressures of population growth and climate change.

Because we are a part of our ecosystems, we benefit from conserving them in a variety of ways. The economic benefits of my proposal alone would easily pay the added costs. Personally, though, I am more motivated by the spiritual benefits. These include keeping orcas, eagles, songbirds, and salmon a part of our lives, now and for future generations. They also include changes in our relationships with each other. Successful conservation requires that. As we work toward conserving this beautiful, unique, fragile yet resilient place that we share, I think we can meet Wallace Stegner's challenge to build "a society to match our scenery."

References

NRC (National Research Council). 1996. Upstream: salmon and society in the Pacific Northwest. National Academy Press, Washington, D.C.

Thomas, J. W. 1992. Wildlife in old growth forests. Forest Watch (Jan/Feb):15, Eugene, Oregon.

Index

A

B

D

F

G

H

P

Q

R

S

Y

Z